BRITISH THEATRE AND PERFORMANCE 1900–1950

Rebecc   or Lecturer in Drama at the University of the West
of Engl   dited books on early modern female communities
and 19   and published extensively on the plays of women
drama   argaret Cavendish, Agatha Christie, Daphne du
Maurie   ngelis. Currently she is preparing a monograph
on Bri   g the Second World War and a chapter on British
Drama

BRITISH THEATRE AND PERFORMANCE 1900–1950

Rebecca D'Monté

Series Editor: Patrick Lonergan

Bloomsbury Methuen Drama
An imprint of Bloomsbury Publishing Plc

B L O O M S B U R Y
LONDON • NEW DELHI • NEW YORK • SYDNEY

Bloomsbury Methuen Drama

An imprint of Bloomsbury Publishing Plc

Imprint previously known as Methuen Drama

50 Bedford Square	1385 Broadway
London	New York
WC1B 3DP	NY 10018
UK	USA

www.bloomsbury.com

**BLOOMSBURY, METHUEN DRAMA and the Diana logo are
trademarks of Bloomsbury Publishing Plc**

First published 2015

British Library Cataloguing-in-Publication Data
A catalogue record for this book is available from the British Library.

ISBN: HB: 978-1-4081-7492-0
PB: 978-1-4081-6565-2
ePDF: 978-1-4081-6603-1
ePub: 978-1-4081-6601-7

Library of Congress Cataloging-in-Publication Data
A catalog record for this book is available from the Library of Congress.

Typeset by Newgen Knowledge Works (P) Ltd., Chennai, India
Printed and bound in Great Britain

CONTENTS

Contents

ACKNOWLEDGEMENTS

Thanks are due to Martin Middeke, Peter Paul Schnierer and Aleks Sierz, whose book *The Methuen Drama Guide to Contemporary British Playwrights* recommended me to Mark Dudgeon, my ever-supportive and patient editor at Methuen Drama. Catherine Wood designed the appealing cover and Patrick Lonergan provided valuable feedback. I am grateful to Claire Cochrane, Penny Farfan and Steve Nicholson for responding to my request for contributory chapters and fulfilling their brief so well. Research leave generously offered by the University of the West of England aided the writing of the book, as did the support offered by UWE's library staff. I appreciate the help offered by Kristy Davis, the Collections Manager of The Raymond Mander and Joe Mitchenson Theatre Collection, Heather Romaine, Jill Sullivan and all at the University of Bristol Theatre Collection. Thanks must also be given to the staff at York City Archives, the Mitchell Library Glasgow, the Glasgow University Library Special Collections Department, The John Rylands Library at Manchester University, the Imperial War Museum and the V&A Theatre and Performance Library. Gary Farnell and Claire Warden were kind enough to answer my reference queries. I also owe a debt to Mike Davis, Dawn Fowler, Bill Greenslade, Ed Guy and Andrew Wyllie. The book is dedicated to my son, Sam Seal.

INTRODUCTION

The years 1900–50 are marked by dramatic and far-reaching events: two world wars, the rise of fascism and communism, the decline and fall of the British Empire, economic disaster, first-wave feminism and new cultural responses to the modern age. If we accept that theatre is part of 'the "cultural apparatus" of society', then it is inevitable that it would reflect the seismic changes taking place.[1] Surprisingly, therefore, there has been a tendency by critics to divide British theatre in the twentieth century into two halves: pre-Second World War drama and post-war drama (which by convention starts at 1956, with the appearance of the so-called working-class realism of John Osborne's *Look Back in Anger*). The former is considered conservative, commercial, and class-ridden, while the latter is radical and forward-thinking in subject matter and style. This categorisation, however, does a disservice to both ages. While it is true to say that early twentieth-century drama does refer back to the Victorian age, there is also a constant push towards a different type of stage that reflected the tumultuous socio-political changes taking place; indeed, almost everything that has been said about post-war drama was already in place during the first part of the century.

Contemporary commentators such as Beverley Baxter, W. A. Darlington, William MacQueen-Pope, Camillo Pellizzi, Ernest Reynolds and J. C. Trewin have been useful in helping to formulate a sense of how British theatre was viewed as it developed. However, their tendency was to concentrate on the commercial and professional theatre, especially that purveyed in London's West End, and little attention paid to the regions, the work of minorities, and theatre outside of the mainstream. There has also been a narrow focus on domestic comedy and drama. In contrast more recent critics have given a wider perspective to some of the epoch's most important themes: politics and ideology, gender and sexuality, class and race, family, work and identity. Different genres have also been taken into consideration – thrillers, revues, pageants, musicals and so on – to provide a richer and more complex picture. Chief among these larger studies are Christopher Innes's *Modern British Drama: 1890–1990* (1992), Jean Chothia's *English Drama of the Early Modern Period, 1890–1940* (1996), Richard Eyre and Nicholas Wright's *Changing Stages: A View of British Theatre in the 20th Century* (2000), Baz

Kershaw's *The Cambridge History of British Theatre. Volume 3 Since 1895* (2004), Mary Luckhurst's *A Companion to Modern British and Irish Drama 1880–2005* (2006) and Simon Shepherd's *The Cambridge Introduction to Modern British Theatre* (2009).

Each of these texts is commendable and adds much to our understanding of the theatre, especially at local, national and international levels, political drama and drama by women and the working classes. I continue this trend, as well as further considering the fluidity between the professional and non-professional, and the commercial and avant-garde. Moreover, while some works only have a perfunctory section on theatre between 1914–18 and 1939–45, it is my wish to explore these episodes in detail because, as S. Johanna Alberti has said, 'The war years can be read not as a discontinuity but as a continuation of an extended international tragedy.'[2] The residual impact of the Boer War marked the Edwardian era, which led into sudden preparations for the Great War. This caused not just the loss of a generation but brought about an instability in society, particularly when it became obvious that this was not 'the war to end all wars'. Rather than bringing about peace, the Armistice of 1918 sowed the seeds of the next war, which turned out to be 'five times more destructive of human life and incalculably more costly in material terms'.[3] Even after this, paranoia over the Cold War continued to shape global policy, and most importantly shock waves over the Holocaust and the atomic bomb even affected humanity's perception of itself. This book has therefore been structured around four uneven time periods: the Edwardian era, the First World War, the Interwar years, and the Second World War and after. I make no apology for this deliberate ploy to stress the way in which the first half of the twentieth century was dominated by war. It is also possible to argue that the material conditions of war such as blackouts, bombing campaigns, front-line warfare, brought about some of the most radical transformations to British theatre that would have ramifications for its future.

Social and technological changes – especially in terms of gender, sexuality, class and mass media – were impacted upon by war. The campaign for women's enfranchisement had been waged since the nineteenth century, but erupted into a more militant suffragette movement in the 1900s. While this undoubtedly had an effect, Nicoletta Gullace believes that 'Women's suffrage was forged in the crucible of war', and their work during it helped to validate 'feminists' long-standing arguments about the national and imperial value of female citizenship'.[4] Other critics, however, such as Dan Todman, find it 'hard to argue that wartime service led directly to enfranchisement for women'. Rather, he says, this was a result of short-term political calculations, including giving the vote to older women first in the belief that they would act as a bulwark against the extreme left politics coming out of Russia. Instead, Todman believes that the war had both positive and negative effects for women, such as increased confidence and awareness of other forms of lifestyle, while others 'placed increased emphasis on traditionally feminine behaviour as a reassurance against the shock of the war'.[5]

With some conviction, though, it can be stated that better political, legal and economic status for women caused them to become more visible in society, with an attendant simultaneous pressure to contain them within the home, or to categorise them as 'abnormal' when they rejected conventional behaviour. Significantly, also, the strengthening of capitalism during the first few decades of the twentieth century saw the female body commoditised and fetishised as commercialisation of the theatre grew apace and stronger links were made between, for example, fashion houses and the stage.

The policing of the nation's sexual morality was paramount during the war years, but ironically also became more difficult to sustain. Eventually stage censorship became anachronistic and, ultimately, futile. The representation of lesbianism and homosexuality, in particular, was in direct contrast – and therefore a threat – to the image of the unsullied 'Angel in the House' and the patriotic ideal of the all-conquering war hero.[6] This only serves, though, to highlight the push for a greater recognition of new sexual and gender roles.

Poor health of conscripts and despair at living conditions for returning soldiers encouraged education and welfare reform, and this was further advanced during the next war. Catastrophic decisions taken by those in power engendered a growing distrust of authority, especially among the working classes, who also resented the injustice and constraints of capitalism as well as class hierarchy; this, along with generational conflict, marked a rejection of unquestioning obligation and a move towards the rights of the individual. These tensions underpin the massive rise in political drama, also fuelled by world events such as the Wall Street Crash and Depression, Russian Revolution, Spanish Civil War and rise of fascism. The advent of cinema and radio provided a forum for this discontent, whether through the mass dissemination of news reports or the championing of the 'common man', as in the films of Charlie Chaplin.

Claire Warden has pointed out that 'There was a sense of rupture and change, affecting many different areas of life from politics and international relations to the economy and the societal structure'.[7] This fostered a greater artistic experimentation than ever before, with a rapid rise in new movements, styles and manifestos as various as Futurism, Dadaism, Expressionism and Modernism. Influences on the British stage came mainly from Europe, and included Henrik Ibsen, Anton Chekhov, Konstantin Stanislavski, Adolphe Appia, Vsevolod Meyerhold, Ernst Toller, Karel Čapek and Bertolt Brecht, although other world stages also exerted a force, such as Japanese Noh theatre and the American Federal Theater Project. All of this was driven by a realisation that there needed to be a break with the conventions of Victorian theatre, which had relied on the picture frame effect of a proscenium arch, the trappings of a 'realistic' box set, a hierarchically arranged audience and the vice-like control of the charismatic actor-manager.

Nevertheless, while there has been a surge of interest in the more radical elements of drama, it is important not to forget that much of the theatrical fare in the commercial theatre can be perceived of as 'middlebrow', and yet still worthy of attention. If the lowbrow revolved around music hall and melodrama, and the highbrow the avant-garde, the middlebrow focused on well-written but undemanding drama and comedy directed at the middle classes. In the 1950s Terence Rattigan unwittingly denigrated the woman who enjoyed his plays by labelling her 'Aunt Edna', while Kenneth Tynan saw the 'Loamshire play' with its middle-class country house setting as epigrammatic of British theatre's sterility.[8] However, it was a format that addressed the audience's concerns by reflecting contemporary society; it questioned the status quo, even if this was not ultimately challenged; and the community it represented functioned 'as an image of unity and totality against which to judge the dividedness of the modern world'.[9] Again, with relevance especially to women, middlebrow writing is 'about the "drama of the undramatic", the steadfast dailiness of a life that brings its own rewards, the intensity of the emotions and, above all, the importance of human relationships'.[10] Much of this was not possible to render within avant-garde theatre, and therefore equal consideration needs to be given to both modes.

Equally, it is important to note that the boundaries between the conventional and unconventional were perpetually in flux. As one of the most prolific theatre managers of the age, Basil Dean produced much middle-class drama, but he was also responsible for the Soviet-inspired pageant, *Salute the Red Army* (1943). During the 1992 revival of Enid Bagnold's *The Chalk Garden* (1956), Charles Spencer noted that when 'John Osborne's *Look Back in Anger* arrived at the Royal Court . . . elegant, well-made drawing-room plays like this were supposedly consigned to the dustbin of theatrical history. Yet it is Osborne's drama which now seems strident, sentimental and old-fashioned'.[11] Middlebrow drama has proved the saviour of repertory and amateur theatre, whereas high culture has become open to sponsorship, as can be witnessed by the growth in state subsidised theatre after the Second World War, the setting up of a National Theatre and the Arts Council. These, and many of the other examples I will describe, show the complexity of the theatre industry.

Another issue to be taken into account is that of national identity. From the turn of the century to the post-war era there were 'shifts in the internal balance of power whereby Britain increasingly became identified with England (and sometimes southern England at that), and the social, cultural and economic dominance of London and the home counties took on new dimensions'.[12] This image of England was deployed during political crises such as the two world wars, both as a shorthand form of propaganda and also as a means of bolstering the south as the power hub of the country. There was, though, resistance from the margins. While much was done to strengthen a sense of patriotic loyalty through pageantry, exhibitions and the celebration of history and culture, this was undermined by England's difficult imperialist relationship with Scotland, Ireland and to a lesser extent Wales. Seen in some quarters as the invading power, England was therefore the enemy, thus leading to a division of loyalties. Assumptions about national identity are equally challenged, a topic that continues to grow in relevance from the influx of people from the colonies after the Second World War to Nigel Farage's UK Independence Party (UKIP) in the twenty-first century, and from the Provisional Irish Republican Army's bombing campaign against England from the 1970s to contemporary debates for and against the devolution of Scotland.

In terms of the theatre, practitioners often rejected the term 'British' and saw their alliances lying with their particular locality. Even this, though, was fraught. Jen Harvie argues that

national identity can be oppressive when, for example, it is seen as homogeneous, superior, and/or unchanging and it acts to exclude or oppress minorities or perceived 'others' or to restrict cultural change. It can be enabling when it helps develop community identities. Often it is simultaneously, in different degrees, both oppressive and enabling.[13]

Thus, Irish drama came to the fore with the Abbey Theatre during the Edwardian era, and was part of the Celtic Revival movement. Yet while celebrating Irish culture, this also has the effect of pedalling a certain kind of

'Irishness' to its audiences that looked back to the past rather than forward to the future. Again, early twentieth-century Scottish theatre presented a form of 'Scottishness' but this became rapidly internationalised with the political drama of the 1920s and 1930s. Along with this it is interesting to ask why the objective of having a purely Irish or Scottish theatre should be treated as 'regionalism' rather than 'nationalism'. A similar case can be made for the regional theatre as well: if the centre of the theatre industry is splintered and redrawn in a way that moves it away from the metropolis, as happened during the Second World War, then it allows for an interrogation of what is meant by the 'regions' or the 'provinces'. Although such terms are used in this book for simplicity, perhaps now more than ever we need to rethink their applicability and draw away from viewing British theatre as applying to all parts of the United Kingdom in equal measure, and the convention of geographically situating theatre in relation to London.

As previously mentioned, a deliberate choice has been made to divide the book into approximately four time slots: 1900–14, 1914–18, 1918–39 and 1939–50. Although these are artificially contrived, this has been done to highlight the importance of conflict upon the first part of the twentieth century, a moment when Britain was either anticipating war, involved in war or recovering from war. Again, it has been a conscious decision to write about, not just canonical figures such as W. B. Yeats, George Bernard Shaw, J. B. Priestley, T. S. Eliot and Terence Rattigan, but also to cover those less well-known or regarded: Ivor Novello, Basil Dean, Joe Corrie, Miles Malleson, Esther McCracken, Una Marson and so on.

Chapter 1 engages with recent critical ideas about the destabilisation of history, suggesting that the Edwardian age was far less socially and politically secure than previously considered. There was a considerable desire to break away from the Victorian era, as evidenced through the rise of the Labour Party, women's militancy, problems with Ireland and industrial disturbances. This all showed itself in the theatre, which particularly charted the growing divide between the generations, eventually brought to a head by the First World War. Practitioners started to experiment with different modes of theatre, most notably with the Court Theatre's instigation of the repertory system and the suffragettes' use of political drama.

Chapter 2 tackles the function of theatre in wartime, considering how culture was pressed into service to proselytise for war by encouraging enlistment, demonising the enemy and celebrating British supremacy. Running alongside there was a concomitant concern with the dangers of warfare, arising out of first-hand experience and the growth of the pacifist movement. The ability of the state to control theatre through censorship begins to be put under pressure as different forms and locations of performance emerge: ad hoc revues, amateur theatre, productions at the front line, subscription clubs. By the end of the war the theatre industry had changed, as the reign of actor-managers was largely over, usurped by a new wave of single-minded businessmen determined to exploit its commercial opportunities, and the mass popular appeal of the cinema.

Chapter 3 follows on from Michael Woolf's view that in the aftermath of the First World War, and the ensuing events such as the rise of Fascism and the Depression, 'the theatre was both a means of escape from, and a means of engagement with, the political and economic realities of the time'.[14] Paradoxically, this was sometimes done through a rejection of realism and an embracement of dramatic techniques gleaned from around the world. One of the reasons for this was the sheer difficulty in coming to terms with the horrors of the war and the need to find a way of representing trauma; another was increased awareness of the possibilities of theatre as a tool, not just to reflect and critique, but to provide urgent social intervention.

Given the paucity of previous criticism on the subject, Chapter 4 covers theatre during the Second World War in some detail. Cultural value can be seen in the utilisation of popular genres and the English way of life to represent the country at a time of national crisis. Equally we can see that issues raised in the plays, as well as the material conditions led to an increased informality, and presaged the social, political and theatrical changes of the post-war period. By the 1950s a dehumanising and depersonalising sense of loss of identity had set in, instigated by insecurity over Britain's loss of global supremacy, disappointment over the failure to create a better society, and a lessened belief in authority. Anger surfaced, not just in kitchen-sink drama, but perhaps more productively through the civil rights movement which championed the interests of the dispossessed: women, homosexuals, people of colour. British theatre was poised on the cusp of a new era, but one that still had strong links to the past as well.

Essays by three expert contributors help to flesh out key issues in this book. During the first part of the twentieth-century theatre was not only opened up to amateurs, communities and schools, but the industry itself also became more professionalised. Skills were raised with the opening of a number of drama schools, and actors were better supported through the founding of the British Actors' Equity Association in 1930. This had already taken place for theatre producers, managers and owners in 1908 with the advent of The Society of West End Theatre Managers. Claire Cochrane's piece, '"Producing the Scene": The Evolution of the Director in British Theatre 1900–1950' suggests how the role of the director was also changing. At the beginning of the twentieth century, British theatre was broadly bourgeois; that is, designed overwhelmingly for the upper and middle classes, who responded to comfortable, well-made plays. Actor-managers such as George Alexander, Frank Benson and Gerald du Maurier who had all but dominated the theatre since the 1890s, were well aware of this, and responded accordingly. Cochrane traces how the omnipotence of the actor-manager gave way to a situation in which occupations were segregated – actor, director, producer, stage manager and theatre manager – giving more gravitas to each activity. This impacted upon all elements of production, from the pre-rehearsal process through to the use of the *mise en scéne* and the relationship with the audience. The new style of directors provided an intellectual or aesthetic approach to their work, previously missing when the main concern of managers had been to showcase their own talents. Again, in utilising smaller performance spaces, sometimes away from traditional centres of entertainment, they helped to widen the geographical spread of theatre across Britain. The implementation of European stagecraft and working practices, including the setting up of ensemble companies, also helped to move the theatre away from that of the nineteenth-century model.

Between the 1880s and the First World War British theatre was shaped to a certain degree by the plays of Henrik Ibsen's middle career: *Ghosts* (1881), *Rosmersholm* (1886), *Hedda Gabler* (1890), and most notably *A Doll's House* (1879). Penny Farfan analyses the effect of their queer and feminist dimensions on theatre workers in her contribution, '"Masculine Women and Effeminate Men": Gender and Sexuality on the Modernist Stage'. The point is made that the appearance of the New Woman in the 1890s – one who is economically independent, well-educated and politically aware – undermined society at a juncture when notions of masculinity and femininity were already in contention. Farfan claims figures such as Edy Craig, Christopher St John (Christabel Marshall) and Maud Allan as modernists who subvert gender and sexuality through their work and lifestyles: Craig and St John lived together in a ménage a trois with the artist Clare 'Tony' Atwood, and alongside Craig's mother, the actress Ellen Terry; the Canadian dancer, Allan achieved notoriety through her appearance in Oscar Wilde's play *Salomé* (1891) and in 1918 lost a court case about her purported lesbianism because of the resonances emanating from Wilde's 1895 own trial for sodomy and indecency. Farfan also considers the work of Nöel Coward, whose glittering career as actor, director and writer almost spans the period under investigation. Positing him as a modernist, Farfan demonstrates how Coward's plays not only reflect different ways of living, but also play a role in the creation of newly emerging gender and sexual identities.

Preserving morality was obviously of paramount concern to the state and plays that pushed at its boundaries were constantly monitored. Theatre censorship in this country fully came to fruition in 1737 with The Licensing Act that gave statutory powers to the Lord Chamberlain's Office to licence plays for the public stage. David Thomas, David Carlton, and Anne Etienne note that 'Censorship was clearly viewed by Home Office officials as an essential political tool to ensure that the theatre should be denied any opportunity for subjecting public figures to ridicule'.[15] Nowhere is censorship more evident than when the country was at war or during the preparations for it. Nevertheless, the rules were not always clear-cut. In 'Staging Hitler, Unstaging Hitler', Stephen J. Nicholson draws on the Lord Chamberlain's papers to show how depictions of the Fuhrer were muddled and dependent on the political mood, bringing about conflict between author and the censor and within the Lord Chamberlain's office itself. During the first part of the 1930s, the censor demanded that any negative depiction to the Nazis should be cut out or the play 'ruritanianised': that is, located in an unidentifiable foreign country.[16] After the invasion of Austria in May 1938 even that precaution was considered too dangerous, as confusion reigned over whether or not Germany should be treated as a potential ally or foe. Nicholson's research relates not just to the Second World War, but raises the wider issue of stage censorship and indeed propaganda. As I suggest in my Conclusion, there was a mounting compulsion for theatre practitioners to represent and critique all aspects of society, even that which had once been considered taboo, and ultimately this would strain to breaking point the relationship between state interference and artistic credibility.

In summary, this book is positioned as part of the continuing debate about the relationship between war and culture, the middlebrow and early twentieth-century British drama. It takes up recent developments in critical analysis, which have asserted the relevance of cultural studies, the uses of interdisciplinarity and the questioning of conventional oppositions; that is, private versus public, male versus female, middle class versus working class, middlebrow versus modernism, regional versus national and amateur versus professional. By investigating the role of the theatre between 1900 and 1950, it is possible to see it as a bridge between the Victorian age and the modern age, in terms of changes to the theatrical institution, as a means of underpinning or subverting the prevailing ideology, and as providing a lasting legacy in the way that we think about theatre today.

CHAPTER 1
THE EDWARDIAN THEATRE

Introduction

Queen Victoria's death just after the turn of the twentieth century in 1901 provoked widespread mourning. During her long reign she had presided over a remarkable process of industrial, scientific and cultural change which resulted in Britain becoming the largest trading nation in the world. As successor Edward VII continued to celebrate and strengthen British power through a series of exhibitions. This culminated sixty years after the Great Exhibition in the Festival of Empire, held at London's Crystal Palace in 1911. The solid Victorian values of diligence and thrift had led to an age of considerable material prosperity, where education was now available at a primary level to the whole population and there was an increased concern with humanitarianism and social welfare. It is not surprising, therefore, that in retrospect the period has been viewed with nostalgia, a world shattered by the brutality of the First World War.

This nostalgia did not reflect the true situation, though, as throughout the period there were simmering tensions that threatened the stable façade: militant demand for rights for women, clashes between the unions and management, and the vexed Irish question all brought into play key political issues to do with imperialism, nationalism and liberalism. The Fabian Society grew rapidly during this period. This was a socialist organisation founded in 1884 by George Bernard Shaw, and Beatrice and Sidney Webb, and went on to include many of the most influential thinkers of the time, such as Leonard and Virginia Woolf, H. G. Wells, Emmeline Pankhurst and – briefly – Bertrand Russell. The movement was named after the Roman politician Fabius the Delayer and endorsed egalitarianism through the gradual reform of injustice. The Labour Party grew out of socialist groups such as the Fabian Society and trade unions. Started in 1900 and led by Keir Hardie, it was created to support the working classes, and betokened a profound concern with the iniquitous situation where the vast majority of wealth was owned by one per cent of the population.[1] The Tories as well as the Liberal Government which came to power in 1906 saw these groups as a threat to the family and to the class hierarchy, but were unable to stop a series of devastating strikes taking place by coal, rail and port workers, among others. In the run-up to the outbreak of the Great War in 1914 there was serious talk of revolution or civil war. This pull between the old and new has occasioned Samuel Hynes to liken the Edwardian age to 'a narrow place made turbulent by the thrust and tumble of two powerful opposing tides'.[2]

In the Arts rapid changes in areas such as physics, psychology, technology and industry, led to the development of modernism. The work of James Joyce, Virginia Woolf, Pablo Picasso, Georges Braque, Arnold Schoenberg and others, redefined the nature of reality. The Manet and the Post-Impressionists Exhibition at the Grafton Gallery in London prompted Virginia Woolf to write 'On or about December 1910 human character changed'.[3] Sigmund Freud's psychoanalytic theories about the influence of childhood also began to filter through to Britain, provoking a considered debate about male and female sexuality.

The Edwardian theatre

During the Victorian era the rapid expansion of the population, economic migration, the growth of London as the largest city in the world, and the change from a basically agricultural and rural life to one that was industrial- and city-based had a concomitant effect on the theatre industry. Claire Cochrane notes its swift commercial development, especially in London, where

> there had developed a large number of play/musical comedy *producing* theatres in very close proximity in an example of what Max Weber called 'agglomeration.' Manufacturing firms, i.e. theatres, could cluster together to achieve economies of scale by concentrating production at one point – again benefiting from the pool of skilled services.[4]

Audiences were larger, more mobile, and increasingly middle class and female. Even the monarch gave her seal of approval, visiting the theatre over 800 times in her lifetime. The many new playhouses of the second half of the nineteenth century appealed to this new spectatorship, while also promulgating a vision of imperialist power through motifs from the Dominions. C. J. Phipps and Frank Matcham were two of the most important architects of civic buildings of the time; the first specialised in large auditoria and classical architecture; the latter redesigned interiors to improve stage sightlines which allowed the audience to see and be seen.[5] The classes were segregated, often with different entrances and bar areas, but allowing the less-well-off to 'appreciate' the display of wealth from a distance.

In London, theatre became part of 'the Season', a series of social events that those visiting the city from their country estates should be seen to attend. The advance of the dinner hour in polite society to 7 o'clock brought a change to theatre programmes. Instead of performances starting at 6.30 p.m. and a bill of fare continuing until midnight, new patrons came to theatre at 8 o'clock and were content to see a single play, or at most a play and a curtain-raiser. Matinees were introduced to cater for a more leisured and refined audience, with female audiences deliberately courted as a means to raise the tone. Tie-ins with fashion and beauty houses and other commercial enterprises enabled managers to maximise profits. As part of the leisure industry, the expansion of theatres had a concomitant effect on transport, hotels and restaurants, especially in tourist destinations like London's West End, with contemporary commentators such as George R. Sims observing the larger crowds swarming around the playhouses after dark.[6] This impacted upon stage works which, whether musical comedies or social dramas, began to focus more on recognisable, public spheres of work, politics and leisure.

Because of the rise of middle-class theatre, it has been suggested that the nineteenth century saw the theatre informally separate into two different kinds. The 'illegitimate' theatre consisted of music hall, burlesque, farce and melodrama, and was mainly for the working classes. Elsewhere the rowdy and sometimes violent audiences of the early nineteenth century were replaced by a more sophisticated clientele, and this new 'legitimate' theatre was almost entirely middle class in tone, setting and point of view. In London, these two types of theatre were demarcated by location: the working-class East End and the fashionable West End. However, the situation was more fluid than this with audiences attending both forms of theatre regardless of class. It is also important to note that, while the working classes were deemed to be in need of the morally edifying plays of the West End, transfers could also sometimes go in the opposite direction as well, as with the plays of Arthur Shirley and Benjamin Landeck.[7] Improved transport meant a greater ease of movement between geographical areas so that audiences could travel to a wider variety of theatres, although community theatre was still important. The Pavilion in the East End of London, for example, specialised in Yiddish

Theatre, as did the East London Palace.[8] Jewish playwrights including Alfred Sutro and Israel Zangwill also crossed over into the mainstream.

One of the most important changes in theatre in early twentieth century was its division into commercial and artistic companies, with 'theatre ownership and management' passing 'from limited liability partnerships to large publicly owned corporations'.[9] The former theatre was dominated by impresarios. Frank Curzon leased a number of London theatres, at one point having nine under his management. Alfred Butt, whose career as a theatre impresario lasted from 1904 to 1931, built an empire in the metropolis, which included the Palace, the Victoria Palace, the Adelphi, the Empire, the Gaiety and Theatre Royal, Drury Lane, as well as others across the country, such as the Alhambra Theatre in Glasgow. These powerful figures controlled all aspects of their theatres that were mainly run for financial rather than artistic reasons. This meant that difficult or challenging drama was eschewed for entertainment and spectacle, and long runs encouraged so as to maximise profits.

As Claire Cochrane points out in this book, actor-managers had held sway throughout the Victorian period, with material devised around their 'star' quality. This not only led to a limited repertoire and an attrition of other acting talent, but they also ensured the profitability of the theatre, increased its reputation and even toyed with new forms of drama. The system followed Victorian ideologies of economic practicality and patriarchy, and would continue until the 1920s. While there were several female theatre managers at this time, it was rare that they were actresses as well; Lena Ashwell is a notable exception, and Lillah McCarthy ran a series of theatres alongside her husband, Granville Barker.[10] The main male figures included Charles Wyndham who managed three London theatres: the eponymous Wyndham's, the Criterion and the New Theatre. George Alexander was lessee of St James's, which he ran with benevolent autocracy, specialising in the drawing room comedies of Oscar Wilde and Arthur Wing Pinero. Herbert Beerbohm Tree was an actor, director and manager of various West End theatres, most notably His Majesty's. His hallmark was lavish productions of Shakespeare, historical drama and the classics in which he tended to take the central role. Like Henry Irving, the pre-eminent Victorian actor-manager, his intention was to stir the audience's imagination through extravagant and quasi-realistic settings and costumes, even if this meant being historically inaccurate.

Tree took over from Irving as the main proponent of Shakespeare's work, a role eventually taken on by Lilian Baylis at the Old Vic. He built an international reputation for his Shakespeare productions, staging unusual plays such as *King John* and *Henry VIII*, and mounting an annual festival from 1905 to 1913. While his dramatic style quickly went out of fashion with the rise of playwrights such as George Bernard Shaw and Granville Barker, Tree also helped to promote the work of Ibsen, Maurice Maeterlinck and W. Somerset Maugham. He was also quick to see the possibilities of technology; his 1899 production of *King John* is the first-recorded film of a Shakespeare play and he went on to complete several others.

The other great actor-manager of the time was Gerald du Maurier. Well-connected, he was the son of George du Maurier, author of *Trilby* (1894) and brother of Sylvia Llewelyn Davies whose children inspired J. M. Barrie to write *Peter Pan* (1904). He took the dual role of George Darling and Captain Hook in this, as well as Ernest in Barrie's *The Admirable Crichton* (1902). As co-manager, with Curzon, of Wyndham's Theatre from 1910 to 1925 he held a position of power, enhanced by his considerable stage presence.

Fourteen new theatres were opened in London's West End between 1880 and 1900 and these, combined with the reconditioning of old buildings, provided greater comfort and ceremony. New names were introduced to match the increasing wealth and grading of middle class and lower-middle-class groupings: orchestra stalls, pit stalls and pit; dress circle and family circle; upper circle, amphitheatre and gallery. Foyers, saloons, smoking rooms and buffets were added to the front of house to make more of an all-round experience designed to replicate the home.

This verisimilitude helped audiences feel at ease in the theatre. It also educated them about correct social behaviour. This was popularised through the trend for drawing room comedies, also known as 'cup and saucer' plays, thereby reinforcing their sense of privilege and power. The box set allowed actors to play inside the scenery rather than in front of it, and the proscenium arch – now with an elaborate wide border – completed the full 'picture stage' frame; this fourth wall effect gave the audience the impression that they were watching a moving picture, while at the same time becoming part of it. Realistic scenery and props used to create replicas of drawing rooms that were furnished and designed by leading interior designers.

Paradoxically, technical advances both increased the sense of realism on stage and created the opposite as theatre managers vied with one another to provide the greatest spectacle. New machinery included pulleys capable of hauling actors up to the 'sky', trap doors, lifts, revolving stages and various smoke effects. Real horses were used for racing scenes in *Ben Hur* (1902) and *The Whip* (1909), the latter also including a dramatic train crash. In 1908 a tidal wave was recreated in a play of the same name.

Technological advances – the telephone, photography, cinema, radio – also had an impact on the connection between visual and oral modes of communication. Theatre buildings started to be fitted with electric lights after 1880, and once the front of house could be darkened, the relationship between audience and performer became more intimate. This meant that there was less of a focus on theatre as part of a social ritual where people went to see and be seen, and more on what was being presented on stage. Bruce McConachie argues that 'Many of the tensions in modern theatrical practice after 1900 can be traced to conflicts between the kinds of realities induced by photographic and audiophonic modes of communication.'[11] Photography suggested that objective reality only existed through the visual; the telephone and phonograph separated the voice from the body. We can see this with the emphasis placed upon the spoken word in plays by George Bernard Shaw and Granville Barker, for example, and the visual-driven modernistic theatre of Edward Gordon Craig. Moreover, the separation between the 'real' and the facsimile of the 'real', as with photography, led to an increased appetite for staging the body and for reinterpretations of reality, as well as a rise in celebrity.

Although acting was still on the whole considered an undesirable occupation, especially for women, the latter part of the nineteenth century and first decade of the twentieth century saw the gradual transformation of the acting profession, in terms of respectability, craft and actor training. George Bernard Shaw demanded a new form of acting in his preface to the second volume of *Plays Pleasant and Unpleasant* (1898). This rejected the bombastic and romantic gestural style of actors such as Charles Kean, William Macready, Irving and Ellen Terry, for one more suited to the new drama of the time. Because this was written to have a socially transformative effect, Shaw argued, acting needed to become more scientific, rational and enquiring.

Henry Irving became the first actor to be knighted in 1895, followed by Herbert Beerbohm Tree in 1909. Unionisation led to better conditions for actors and actresses in the ensuing decades, and professional training was given a boost with Tree's foundation of the Royal Academy of Dramatic Art (RADA) in 1904. Women were offered support and took an active role through initiatives such as the Theatrical Ladies Guild founded in 1891 and the Actresses' Franchise League (AFL, 1908). They also took on positions of authority, inspired by the suffrage movement that had increased numbers of women writing for the theatre. Elsie Fogerty founded Central School of Speech and Drama (CSSD) in 1906 and was instrumental in the field of voice training, Irene Vanbrugh was the first woman to sit on the administrative council of RADA, and women such as Athene Seyler, Sybil Thorndike, May Whitty and Judith Gick were members of various boards, helping to effect fundamental changes to the running of these places.[12]

Ibsen had a profound influence upon the development of drama in Britain country, although as Katherine Newey has acutely observed, his work quickly moved from being banned to becoming mainstream.[13] This fuelled an interest in social drama which dwelt on more problematic subject matter that reflected the realities of contemporary society, especially changes towards women. From the 1880s his plays were popularised by the theatre critic and reformer, William Archer, and socialist circles, such as that run by Eleanor Marx and her husband, Dr Aveling. Perhaps his most famous champion was George Bernard Shaw whose lecture *The Quintessence of Ibsenism* (1891) 'can be seen as the watershed between traditionalist and modern perspectives, with its call for a revolution in the nature and function of the dramatic experience'.[14] Because much of Ibsen's work was censored, private theatres and theatre companies were set up – frequently by women – in order to present his material. The actress Janet Achurch put on a production of *A Doll's House* in 1889, Elizabeth Robins and Marion Lea appeared in *Hedda Gabler* in 1891, and Florence Farr appeared in *Rosmersholm* at the Independent Theatre in the same year. Farr became Shaw's mistress and muse, and he much admired her New Woman lifestyle, but it is important to note that figures like Elizabeth Robins were less enamoured with Ibsen's politics than his ability to offer challenging female roles. Actress-producers were also inspired to write plays themselves, such as Robins's and Florence Bell's *Alan's Wife* (1893) and *Mrs Daintree's Daughter* (1894) written by Achurch.[15] Penny Farfan considers Ibsen's influence on the modernists in her chapter on pp. 213–22.

Popular genres

Melodrama

Literally meaning music with drama, melodrama has its roots in medieval mystery and morality plays and Italian commedia dell'arte. This developed into seventeenth-century tragi-comedy, a 'deformed hybrid' as David Mayer calls it.[16] Two centuries later this genre had an exaggerated plot, generally depicting a struggle between good and evil, and stereotyped characters. A gestural acting style reflected the central premise of melodrama: to express emotion. 'Autumn dramas' – collaborative melodramas created by Augustus Harris – were popular in the late nineteenth and early twentieth centuries. These were elaborate and technically advanced, but sized down for touring productions both in Britain and abroad.

On the one hand, the melodrama did more though than pander to the tastes of an unthinking mass audience. It exposed sites of tension arising from increased industrialisation and the shifting demography, with class, work, morality and sexuality as major themes. As a genre it grappled with the struggle between good and evil, order and disorder, and justice and injustice. Michael Booth sees the genre as 'anti-aristocrat, anti-employer, anti-landlord, anti-landowner and anti-wealth, often violently so'.[17]

On the other hand, however, it could also reinforce racial prejudices, imperialist propaganda and social anxieties. The villainy of the wicked upper-class gentleman or landlord gradually began to be replaced by xenophobic representations of corrupt Asians or 'barbaric' Africans who threatened the Christian way of life but were trounced by British heroism and moral supremacy. Again, Mayer notes the titles of a series of melodramas from the 1890s onwards written by Frederick and Walter Melville. These are '"backlash" pieces expressing many of the lower-middle and working-class fears of unruly New Women and a patriarchal society in consequent disarray . . . Walter's *The Worst Woman in London* (1899), *That Wretch of a Woman* (1901), *A Disgrace to Her Sex* (1904), *The Girl Who Wrecked His Home* (1907) and *The Shop-Soiled Girl* (1919), and Frederick's *In a Woman's Grip* (1901), *The Ugliest Woman on Earth* (1903), and *The Bad Girl of the Family* (1909)'.[18] Melodrama's reinforcement of the dichotomous view of women as Madonna/whore developed into a more complex engagement with women's changing role in society. While, as Sos Eltis has said, 'The discarded mistress, seduced maiden, and unmarried mother crop up again and again as the motivation behind untold acts of villainy and familial disruption', the appearance of the Ibsenite heroine, New Woman, and suffragette all problematised these archetypes'.[19]

Thus, melodrama, once the leading popular form of the Victorian age, started to decline as a genre during the first couple of decades of the twentieth century. Political drama took over the role of its representation of gender and class antagonism, and the moral imperatives of the earlier period became increasingly at odds with the more ambiguous social drama of the late Victorian and early Edwardian theatre.

Variety and music hall

As Victorian cities grew in size, more leisure time was available for the rising middle classes, and the working classes needed escape from the drudgery of industrial life. While eventually cinema would take over as the main form of entertainment for the working and lower middle classes, music hall started originally as a place where 'songs had been "the mouthpiece, the oracles of the people", where audiences had gone "not as spectators but as performers".[20] Its heyday was from the latter decade of the nineteenth century to about 1910, with its transformation into Variety bemoaned by many who disliked its over-capitalisation by big business. This, it was felt, led to the quashing of individuality and spontaneity and, with the appearance of foreign acts – especially those from America – the loss of an authentic and regional working-class voice. One offshoot of this was the necessity to find artists who could break through regional barriers to find national – and even international – fame. Harry Lauder was one such figure who anglicised his vocabulary, while using other Scottish elements to become acceptable to a wider audience. For example, the semiotic use of the kilt and other tartan trappings allowed him to 'negotiate images of Scottish identity that connected the present with the historic past through celebration of a shared culture'.[21] This larger-than-life Scottish persona proved popular throughout the world, and was successfully replicated by a number of other performers.

The London Hippodrome, opened by Frank Matcham in 1900, put on acts that were initially taken from the circus, but was also able to provide aquatic displays in its large water tank. These underwater spectacles could often be risqué, featuring young women in bathing costumes. Other venues in towns such as Birkenhead, Doncaster, Blackpool and Ipswich would bring together chorus lines and comedians, as well as specialty acts involving animals, acrobats, magicians and 'freak show' attractions. In 1898 the Australian-born Oswald Stoll and Sir [Horace] Edward Moss merged their businesses to form Moss Empires, and soon most towns or cities in Britain had an 'Empire' or a 'Coliseum' theatre. Here you could see the likes of Dan Leno, Marie Lloyd and Vesta Tilley, who became among the highest paid performers in the country. Their images were reproduced on photographs and postcards, as well as used to sell products, and their antics were a direct influence on the silent movie routines of comics such as Laurel and Hardy and Charlie Chaplin. Moss Empires was also instrumental in bringing to these shores some of the more avant-garde or experimental performers from around the globe, including the Spanish Ballets Russes, and the movement and light shows of American dancer Loïe Fuller.

Stoll Moss's major rival was Alfred Butt who was managing director of several regional and West End theatres, including the Theatre Royal, Drury Lane; his Variety Theatres Controlling Company Ltd started in 1910 and became Britain's second largest chain of music halls. From the 1890s music hall started to be gentrified and brought into line with the 'legitimate' theatre. Audiences were less likely to eat and drink while watching the shows and the repertoire became more standardised and polished. Musical theatre received legitimacy when the first Royal Command Performance was held in 1912 before King George V and Queen Mary.

Music hall has often been overlooked in traditional theatre histories because it is a form of popular entertainment associated with the working classes and the socially marginalised. There has been a divergence of opinion as to the function and influence of the genre. Some critics view it as essentially conservative in the way that it was seen to uphold dominant ideology. Laurence Senelick describes the Victorian acts that included the appeals to a flag-waving crowd by the political singer whose 'patriotic song was a panegyric to England couched in a vein of overblown chauvinism', with this unthinking jingoism becoming more prevalent in the period from the Boer War to the First World War.[22] Jacky Bratton also points to the genre's xenophobia. In works such as *In Darkie's Africa* (1893) the 'clowning is richly suggestive of the music-hall intervention in imperialist discourse: it burlesques triumphalist versions of the invasion of Africa, the heroic tales of explorers pitted against alligators and savages, and also the contradictory nineteenth-century visions of black races as noble and as savage'; songs such as 'Looking for a Coon Like Me' only helped to reinforce existing prejudices.[23]

In contrast, other critics like Gordon Williams position music hall as a form of opposition to the hegemony, especially in terms of addressing issues of nationhood, class or gender.[24] Acts could question the social hierarchy, expose tyrannical bosses or explore economic distress, as with Marie Lloyd's 'The Cock Linnet song'; also known as 'My Old Man Said Follow the Van', this humorous song was actually about a family forced to do a 'moonlight flit' to avoid paying the rent. Others emulated the 'Lion Comique', or young 'swell' who aspired to the good life, like George Leybourne's Champagne Charlie. Vesta Tilley's female-to-male cross-dressing act followed in the tradition of seventeenth-century 'breeches' roles, which allowed actresses not only to titillate the audience, but also to draw strength from an exchange of gender, enabling them to negotiate their way in a male world.

Moreover, as feminist film critic Mary Ann Doane attests, 'the transvestite wears clothes which signify a different sexuality, a sexuality which, for the woman, allows a mastery over the image and the very possibility of attaching the gaze to desire.'[25] In the process of a female parody of the male roles, Tilley moved up the social ladder (eventually becoming Lady de Frece), took direct control of her career and financial affairs, and established herself as one of the highest paid working women in Britain. Tilley's act parodied the prevailing male power structure through her satires on male authority roles – policemen, soldiers and aristocrats – and her songs poked fun at the rich; 'Burlington Bertie' and 'Following in Father's Footsteps' are two such examples. She signified the inequality of male dominance through her female presence, helping to lay a key foundation for a change in popular attitudes towards the emancipation of women in society. Yet she did not consciously challenge the prevailing patriarchal structures of society and her use of cross-dressing always signalled fact that woman's body underneath; her publicity material invariably showed a real photograph of her alongside her male impersonation and on stage there was the contrast between the physical appearance of a man and her own soprano voice. In this way she provided safe titillation for the audience and was therefore accepted by the theatrical institution and respectable society.

The wooing of the middle classes had started in the nineteenth century and continued into the next century, with Williams suggesting that the music hall was a production of capitalism, and attracted 'the bourgeoisie just as much as workers seeking respite from the ugly industrial grind.'[26] Operas were staged in the music halls and composers like Elgar were brought in to conduct their own work. Vulgar material was gradually reduced, and sentimental songs appealed to all classes, especially when performed by the likes of Gertie Gitana. However, even this was not enough to stop its slow decline as other amusements such as cinema, radio and television began to take over.

Pantomime

Pantomime first appeared on the London stage in the eighteenth century as part of an evening's entertainment. It had evolved from Classical theatre via Italian Commedia dell'arte, with the Greek word meaning 'an imitator of things'. Constantly reinventing itself to take in slapstick comedy, music, dance, acrobatics and theatrical illusion, it appealed to a wide-ranging audience to become a fixture of the Christmas season. This genre was popular during the Edwardian period but it often subsumed into others such as fairy plays, fantasy, musical and spectacle. Like music hall, cross-dressing was also a feature of pantomime, but with the exception of the principal boy, focusing mainly on female grotesques: the needy spinster, 'elderly widow and nagging wife'.[27] Dan Leno and Herbert Campbell were two of the most popular female impersonators in pantomime, and their success fuelled by Augustus Harris's lavish annual productions at the Theatre Royal, Drury Lane.

J. M. Barrie's *Peter Pan; or, The Boy Who Wouldn't Grow Up* incorporates cross-dressing and other pantomimic features. The character of Peter Pan originally appeared in a 1902 novel, *The Little White Bird* and was famously based on Barrie's relationship with the five sons of family friends, Sylvia and Arthur Llewelyn Davies. The first production starred Gerald du Maurier as Captain Hook and Nina Boucicault as Peter.

The tragedy of the story is that the central character remains a child while all other children grow up and take on the responsibility of adulthood. Wendy Darling provides solace as the mother figure, although her attraction towards Peter and the killing of the father figure, Captain Hook, have also been given a Freudian interpretation.[28] The parents and Hook represent the forces that crush spontaneity: Mr Darling's work takes him away from the house and children, and his inflexibility means that he is unable to fully participate in life. As the mother, Mrs Darling has the role of educating her children but this involves '*tidying up their minds just as if they were drawers*', a nod to the restrictions of Edwardian society.[29] This is highlighted by Hook's final words, 'Floreat Etona', the motto of the public school Eton College, a bastion of the Establishment. Peter Pan refuses to grow up 'Because I heard mother talking of what I was to be when I became a man'.[30] As his name implies, Peter Pan is linked to the Greek god of the wild, nature and the pagan, the opposite of social conformity. He may be narcissistic and impetuous, but he is also able to create a magic world with his mind. Peter's insistence that nature and imagination are more important than society and rationality is a rejection of the materialistic Edwardian age, and the audience are mischievously drawn into aligning themselves with this by a direct appeal: 'If you believe in fairies, clap your hands'![31]

The 'spectacular body' and musical comedy

Fascination with the 'spectacular body' – one that is meant to be looked at – manifested itself in a number of different ways. It could be both 'freakish', as with contortionists, strong men, and 'human oddities', or sexually titillating:

the chorus line and 'girlie' shows. The chorus line evolved out of variety and the music hall. The Manchester-based Tiller Girls were formed in 1890 by John Tiller. Tiller ensured that each chorus line was made up of women with the same measurements and their choreography was composed of precision movements, becoming famous for their high-kicking routines. It eschewed puritanical Victorian morality, with acres of flesh now on public display, and the regimentation of the body also provides us with a different interpretation brought forward by Futurists: this movement, launched by Filippo Tommaso Marinetti in 1909, spoke of a society ruled by machinery and technology, precision and automation.

This was most evident in a series of pieces based on the modern working woman taking her place 'within an emergent consumer culture, whose centre was the already theatricalised glamour of the purpose-built department store': *The Shop Girl* (1894), *The Girl Behind the Counter* (1906), *Our Miss Gibbs* (1909) and *This Way Madam* (1913) are cases in point. Peter Bailey argues that this was where 'older paternalist modes of authority combined with the newer patterns of industrial production, while the military ideal of well-drilled preparedness reflected the additional priorities of an imperial age'.[32] Scientific efficiency and economic usefulness are thus allied to more conventional erotic titillation, with use of the word 'girl' rendering safe this potentially disruptive figure.

Moreover, the stage settings sometimes replicated well-known shops, as when Swan & Edgar in London's Regent's Street appeared in facsimile at the Queen's Theatre next door for the production of *This Way Madam*, creating subliminal links between two forms of commodified space. In musical comedy's first flush of success, before the First World War, it represented a 'celebration of fashion, shopping and general excess', and was driven by the need for 'status and acceptability' within the theatre and by an awareness of women as consumers.[33]

George Edwardes's Gaiety Girls appeared in musical comedies at the Gaiety Theatre in the 1890s, bringing fame to women such as Ellaline Terriss, Lily Elsie and sisters Zena and Phyllis Dare. Celebration of the modern chorus girl was very much at the centre of musical comedy, as evidenced by a list of some of the most famous titles: *A Gaiety Girl* (1893), *The Geisha* (1896), *Floradora* (1899), *The Quaker Girl* (1910), *The Sunshine Girl* (1912) and *Maid of the Mountains* (1917).[34] The genre achieved its zenith of popularity between the decline of Gilbert and Sullivan's operettas in the 1890s and the rise of American musicals in the 1920s, and celebrated the more optimistic qualities of the period. Edwardes was quick to note a change in audience tastes and his provision of family-friendly entertainments gave him an almost unrivalled position in the commercial theatre. As well as the Gaiety, his London theatres included Daly's and the Adelphi, and he popularised the musical comedy format by touring his productions around Britain and abroad. The script, lyrics and libretto were generally written separately, with Edwardes skilled at choosing the right mix of people to work together. The genre had original scores rather than relying on existing tunes, scripts utilised light-hearted banter between the sexes that was flirtatious without being risqué, and uncomplicated plots gently mocked society or gambolled through romantic entanglements. This glamorous vision of the shop girl who ultimately escapes its confines through a profitable marriage is, as we shall see, at considerable odds with the more realistic portrait painted by women dramatists such as suffragist Cicely Hamilton.

An interesting variation on modern life was *The Arcadians* (1909). Written by Mark Ambient and Alexander M. Thompson, with music by Lionel Monckton and Howard Talbot, this musical comedy fused interest in classical times, already mined by Gilbert and Sullivan's *Iolanthe* (1882), with the new pursuit of aviation. Aghast by tales of corrupt London, the Arcadians crash land there to warn its denizens. Instead, they begin to be seduced by city's temptations, and while the play ends on a happy note, its social commentary is serious: a simple life is more preferable than that rooted in commercialism.

The irony of this was lost on Edwardes, who exploited his actresses' good reputations, leading to several of them entering into the peerage via advantageous marriages, or acquiring sponsorship deals with fashion and beauty houses.[35] Victorian and Edwardian actresses became acutely canny about controlling their own image, through advertising, autobiographical writings, and critical articles, and 'an actress's off-stage persona could become an entity in itself, not her "veridical" self but a persona that usefully complemented her on-stage repertoire'.[36] The cult of celebrity was fuelled through photography and film, because, as David Mayer makes clear, stage photography only took place from the 1890s as lighting techniques became more advanced; before this a 'simulacrum of the theatrical settings in which she [the actress] appeared at the theatre nearby' was set up in the photographer's studio.[37] A less salubrious side of this was the peddling of dressed and undressed photographs of artistes, often taken backstage to provide a frisson to the theatrical experience. In a similar vein, there was a fascination with the body of the female daredevil in figure-hugging outfits that mimicked nudity.[38]

Staging the empire

Ancient Rome, Greece, Egypt, Babylon and the Holy Land were popular settings on the Victorian stage, and continued to be so for the next era. This theatrical codification became a way to contrast contemporary urbanisation and industrialisation with an imagined golden age, to comment on national identity and the intrepid explorer/educator, and to titillate an audience with images of the exotic other. The literary 'worthiness' of the plays was emphasised through the *mise-en-scene*, which revelled in vivid colour, sumptuous settings and triumphal music.

Tree followed in the footsteps of Irving, both of whom were 'masters of the pictorial stage.'[39] Tree had already scored successes with plays such as *Julius Caesar* (1898), which was the opening show for his new theatre, Her Majesty's in the Haymarket, London. He went on to produce a string of classically inspired plays: *Paolo and Francesca, Herod* (both 1900), *Ulysses* (1902), *The Sin of David* (1904) and *Nero* (1906), all written by Stephen Phillips, the rising star of the Edwardian theatre, who had drunk himself to death by 1915. John Masefield, better known as a poet, wrote a series of plays on Classical or Biblical subjects, including *The Tragedy of Pompey the Great* (1910) and *Esther* (1921), as did Gordon Bottomley who became known for his verse drama.

Other forms of Classical Drama popular at the time were toga plays, a term for loosely related works and coined around 1895–6, eventually to be overtaken by the toga film, as with *Ben Hur* (1907). They focused on 'realistic spectacle' of Ancient Rome and tableaux vivant which depicted the Hellenic world, and drew on similar conventions to the 'sensation' melodrama. David Mayer suggests that 'By the final decades of the nineteenth century the concepts of Rome and the identities of Roman persons, objects and institutions had become inextricably linked to the nature and destiny of modern empires.'[40] The imperialist policy of Great Britain had been dented by the First and Second Boer Wars (1880, 1899–1902), therefore the subject matter of this kind of drama helped to bolster Britain's image of itself.

Both Biblical and Classical drama 'cleverly combined tropes about empire with titillating sexuality submerged in religious righteousness.'[41] The visual representation of the ancient world is similar to academic artists of the time such as Lawrence Alma-Tadema: a form of education, but one that had little to do with historical accuracy. Inevitably, the focus was the eroticised female body, alarmingly at odds with the militancy of the suffrage movement taking place at the same time. Penny Farfan also discusses the allure of exotic semi-nudity in relation to the dancer Maud Allan, on pp. 216–19.

George Bernard Shaw was one dramatist who used historical settings in a different way: as a comment on the contemporary situation. *Caesar and Cleopatra* (1906) may be set in Ancient Egypt but it is in fact about British Imperialism in Africa. *Saint Joan* (1924) is ostensibly about fifteenth-century France, but as Christopher Innes has pointed out, it 'reflects the contemporary struggle for Irish independence . . . Joan's martyrdom parallels the execution of Roger Casement, the Anglo-Irish patriot, while her canonization in 1920 – which was the overt inspiration for the play – also contains a modern political reference, La Pucelle having been the major propaganda symbol used by the French military during the First World War'.[42]

As well as classical settings, parts of the far-flung Empire were also mined for theatrical spectacle. John M. MacKenzie alerts us to the numerous plays and musical comedies set in India, reflecting Queen Victoria's 1877 inauguration as Empress of that country.[43] Other imperialist events, such as the Zulu Wars and the Anglo-Sudan War, were also represented, but it was the taste for exotic glamour that dominated. This was marked by the appearance of Gilbert and Sullivan's *The Mikado* (1885) and the popular musical comedies, *A Geisha Girl* and *A Chinese Honeymoon* (1901). The fashion continued with David Belasco's *The Darling of the Buds* (1902), one of the first important transfers from America's Broadway to London's West End. Herbert Beerbohm Tree restaged this with himself in the leading role. The *New York Times* describes the original production as 'a series of really splendid tableaus [sic], with long waits between them, of gorgeous costumes and gaily diversified crowds, of acrobats and tumblers, of choruses of Geisha girls from Geisha street, and all the rest'.[44]

The exotic spectacle functioned in a number of different ways. On a superficial level it was a way of flouting censorship and the desired and desiring body; scantily clad men and women supposedly became less concerning when positioned within a legitimate setting. This genre celebrated the civilizing effects of the white man's influence and superiority through bringing Christianity and the British way of life to all parts of the world, it showed off the trading links between this country and others, and created a sense of international unity by bonding the dominions to the motherland. Edward Said's seminal work on Orientalism has, of course, alerted us to the pejorative stereotyping explicit in Western imperialism, where 'Orientals' – drawn from a vast and unconnected area – were depicted as inscrutable, manipulative and sexually dangerous: the 'exotic other'.[45] Underpinning all of this, though, as MacKenzie has observed, the Orient 'had become a source of anxiety and strain, a place of complex trading relations and periodic warfare'.[46] On stage it could be controlled and rationalised, its mystery lying in glamorous costumes and picturesque settings, rather than the more dangerous reality.

A more direct way of staging the empire was through the use of pageants. These were a type of transient theatrical effect designed to consolidate hegemony. In Medieval times they were predominately a product of the church or the merchant classes: to cement power, promote trade guilds, celebrate civil pride and to provide a sense of community. At this time they moved from place to place on the back of pageant wagons – an early form of promenade theatre. Pageants were especially popular from the late Victorian period to the end of the Second World War. They were usually fixed to one spot, and designed to be educational (i.e. to provide a moral) or patriotic (to appeal to a sense of history). Countries around the world used fairs and exhibitions as a means to demonstrate their scientific, technological, artistic and colonial superiority. Examples include the Great Crystal Palace Exhibition (1851), the Paris Expositions (1855, 1889) and the St Louis World Fair (1904), with their imperialist, monarchist and trading objectives exploited through the production of commercial ephemera. Indeed, Ayako Yoshino sees pageants as instrumental in developing the tourist industry during the first decade of the twentieth century.[47]

Pageants can be seen in terms of what Baz Kershaw describes as 'spectacles of domination' or 'rituals of the powerful'; essentially, then, a conservative form.[48] As the British Empire grew, dozens of major exhibitions were organised in Britain, India and Australia as a means of deepening national pride, espousing the reach and power of its empire, and building trade links between the colonies. Bruce McConachie concludes that, 'As the "mother country", Great Britain displayed its noble traditions, royal munificence, ships and armaments, and, of course, its imperial leadership. A wide range of performances available to visitors from around the world – opening ceremonies, impressive parades, and royal receptions in addition to folk performances, costumed pageants, and music hall turns – cemented the interconnections made possible through the Empire'.[49]

One of the most spectacular was the 1911 Festival of Empire at the Empire Stadium (later Wembley Stadium), which took many years to plan. Subtitled 'An Historical Epic', it was designed to represent, as the souvenir book claimed, 'the gradual growth and development of the English nation, as seen in the history of this, the Empire City'. It was a huge undertaking, consisting of four parts, staged over three days by 15,000 volunteers, and ran for four months. It was organised by Frank Lascelles, who was known at the time as 'the man who staged the Empire' as he was also responsible for the Coronation Durbar in Delhi in 1911. Indeed this was one of many events held to celebrate the coronation of King and Emperor George V.

Lascelles directed scenes from British history, involving an ambitious series of tableaux performed before an audience of thousands; in hindsight it cannot help but call to mind the political rallies of Hitler and Mussolini. Taking place at Crystal Palace, sixty years after the Great Exhibition, the Festival of Empire opened with a 'Grand Opening Concert' on 12 May 1911. This consisted of an 'Imperial choir' of 4,500 voices, with music provided by the Queen's Hall Orchestra, the London Symphony Orchestra and the Festival of Empire Military Band. The concert included Elgar's arrangement of 'God Save the King' and his 'Land of Hope and Glory', as well as a 'Patriotic Chorus: For Empire and for King' by Percy E. Fletcher.

As with spectacle, construction of the 'exotic other' was all-important, but the pageant gave this an interesting twist. Originally it was mooted that the Festival of Empire would use 'blacked' up actors, leading to complaints from the Union of Students of Black Descent 'about the manner in which Africans were held up "to public ridicule"' and so the actor and producer André von Gyseghem persuaded the government to use real black Africans instead.[50] For many visitors this was their first encounter with the race and a way to test Rudyard Kipling's description of natives as 'Half-devil, half-child': Kipling's famous poem, 'The White Man's Burden' had been written in 1899 to celebrate the American take-over of the Philippines.

Pageants celebrating imperialism continued to be popular for several more decades, also acting as a means of deflecting away from current events. In 1924–5, a short while before the General Strike, the Great Empire Exhibition was held at Wembley, and MacKenzie describes the Glasgow exhibition as 'conceived in 1931 at the depth of the Slump as a conscious effort to provide employment and to advertise home-based depressed industries. Yet the exhibition remained imperial in appearance, in tone, and in name'.[51]

New theatrical forms

The latter decade of the nineteenth century was obsessed with the word 'new', evidenced by the appearance of societies and journals with titles such as 'The New Era', 'The New Dawn' and 'The New Age'. This term often occurred towards the end of a monarch's reign or the beginning of a new century: here the two events almost coincided. The appearance of the 'new drama' was part of this movement towards rejecting the past and seeking a different future.

The Victorian ideal of the theatre was that it should not only entertain, but also inform and teach morality through idealised views of the establishment. Plays were mainly about fashionable society, as in the works of Oscar Wilde, Henry Arthur Jones and Arthur Pinero. In contrast, continental theatre was more radical. In France, André Antoine started the Théâtre Libre (Free Theatre, 1887–94) which laid out the ideas of stage naturalism: new plays dealing with contemporary issues. Influenced by this, in Germany Otto Brahm set up the Freie Bühne (Free Stage, 1889), bringing the plays of Gerhart Hauptmann to public attention. Anton Chekhov's works struck a chord with the precepts of Konstantin Stanislavski and Vladimir Nemirovitch-Danchenko at the Moscow Art Theatre (MAT, 1897). Unlike British drama, Chekhov's plays had no clearly defined plots and little evident variation in dramatic intensity; it was the presentation of life as it is, dullness and all. In Belgium, Maeterlinck eschewed naturalism for symbolism, where the lack of action or conflict in favour of suggestion, became a precursor of absurdism. Finally, in Scandinavia the Swedish August Strindberg saw life as a psychological struggle, taken to the level of symbolic, elemental action, and the Norwegian Henrik Ibsen started by drawing motifs drawn from native folkloric traditions, before turning to social and political reform.

Moving on from surface realism, drama became more concerned with the study of human behaviour, in terms of psychology, heredity and social environment. Naturalism reached its zenith in the latter part of the nineteenth century. Its photographic realism drew on a host of theories, including Charles Darwin's evolutionism, William James's psychology, Auguste Comte's sociology and Hippolyte Taine's historical determinism. Emile Zola's work demonstrated his belief that human beings are affected by heredity and by the environment, an idea that underpins drama by Ibsen and Chekhov. Developments in acting technique led to a deeper understanding of, and engagement with, characterisation, such as that initiated by Stanislavski. Additionally, the ability to capture real-life people and events led to an interest in social issues and domestic lifestyles away from the moneyed world of the upper classes; this would impact upon the new drama of the period, particularly that in the regions. As McConachie claims, 'Where realist playwrights, directors and designers relied on photo-like stage effects for a variety of reasons . . . the naturalists believed that an accurate rendition of external realities was only the necessary starting point for an exploration of materialist causation.'[52]

Avant-garde theatre – the French term refers to the frontline of soldiers heading into battle, or advanced guard – also challenged theatre-goers with its rejection of logic. Designed as a riposte to bourgeois hypocrisy, the first wave started in the 1880s, followed by a later movement around 1910. McConachie argues that the movement's rise was 'partly to do with artists being cut free from traditional obligations of patronage and a new struggle for economic survival, plus a bourgeoisie unsure of its own artistic values'.[53] This kind of theatre espoused a creative ideology, disseminated through manifesto, and performances incorporated a variety of different forms: puppetry, mime, revue, songs and political skits, for example. European cities were more advanced than those in Britain, with Zurich's The Cabaret Voltaire and Krakow's The Green Balloon being two of the most well known.

Avant-garde movements spread across Europe and into Britain during the first three decades of the twentieth century, especially through the diaspora caused by war and politics. For example, technological developments, particularly in terms of warfare, transport and industry, had an effect on Italian Futurism: E. T. Marinetti's ideas were published in 1909, rejecting the art forms of the past for one that reflected the machine age. In turn, political upheaval, especially in Russia, led to the demand for art to be practised as a social force; hence Vsevolod Meyerhold's interest in constructivism. Anti-war fervour was disseminated through Dadaism, a movement which rejected rationality and logic for nonsense and intuition; Alfred Jarry's *Ubu Roi* (1896) was a precursor of Dadaism and Absurdism, with its representation of modern greed via its stylised acting and sets. All of this radicalism was a means to find new ways of expressing a deeper mode of existence.

British practitioners such as Edward Gordon Craig were also determined to move beyond surface realism to find a different and purer form of truth, but his extreme control of a production was even more autocratic than the actor-managers mentioned by Claire Cochrane in this book. Craig, son of Ellen Terry and brother to Edith Craig, was a *metteur-en-scène*. He rejected the romantic realism of Herbert Beerbohm Tree. Craig's work was at the other extreme. His minimalist sets and theoretical vision was influenced by Wagner's notion of *Gesamtkunstwerk*, an all-embracing art form, the lighting innovations of Swiss-born Adolphe Appia, and the work of Stanislavski. His non-representational settings were in direct opposition to the cluttered realism of the traditional Edwardian stage.

His notion of 'total theatre' refused to privilege the written word, instead concentrating on the symbiotic relationship between movement, sound, light and colour. Craig's radical works 'The Art of Theatre' (1905, expanded 1911), 'The Actor and the Über-Marionette' (1908), and 'A Note on Masks' (1910) explored his vision. He was a major influence not so much on his contemporaries, with the exception of W. B. Yeats, but on later designers and directors such as Peter Brook, Robert Wilson and Robert Lepage.[54] Perhaps his most profound statement was about the role of the actor: 'Do away with the actor and you do away with the means by which a debased stage-realism is produced and flourishes. No longer would there be a living figure to confuse us into connecting actuality and art'.[55] This rejection of the actor's body for marionettes was a concept that Samuel Beckett later reworked by severely limiting his actors' movements in plays such as *Endgame* (1957) *Happy Days* (1961) and *Not I* (1972).

W. B. Yeats was another innovator. He was awarded the Nobel Prize for Literature in 1923 as much for his theatre work as for his poetry. The former can be divided into three sections: the early plays such as *The Land of Heart's Desire* (1894) and *The King's Threshold* (1904), the middle period dominated by the Cuchulain Cycle (1904–39), and later works such as *The Dreaming of the Bones* (1931) and *Purgatory* (1938). Yeats' drama forms part of the early twentieth-century avant-garde tradition and he drew upon most of the key European movements of the time. Much influenced by Arthur Symons's *The Symbolist Movement in Literature* (1899) Yeats owed a debt to the use of colour and sound in the work of French and Belgium symbolists Stéphane Mallarmé, Paul Verlaine, Auguste Villiers and Maeterlinck.[56] He was also greatly excited by Craig's production of *Dido and Aeneas* in 1901 and intrigued by Craig's use of marionettes. Strong connections can also be found between *Calvary* (1921) and *The Words upon the Window-pane* (1930) and, respectively, Luigi Pirandello's *Lazarus* (1927) and *Six Characters in Search of an Author* (1921). Additionally, *The Death of Cuchulain* (1938), Yeats's last play, is described in terms of its anti-theatricality, showing how 'human experience was becoming automatised in a machine age', a key theme of modernism.[57]

Introduced to Japanese Noh theatre by Ezra Pound, Yeats was drawn to its 'otherness' and purity of form, fusing this with the 'internal unity and antirealism' of modernism.[58] This Japanese form of musical drama was highly codified and involved a chorus of voices set to music and movement. *Japonisme* was already a popular style at the turn of the century; this had developed out of seventeenth- and eighteenth-century orientalism, in turn created by colonisation, global trade links and new technologies. In this way, Yeats's dramatic works from *At the Hawk's Well* (1916) through to *The Death of Cuchulain* are centred around unifying the dancer and the dance, and he gradually became convinced that the

> conventional stage was inherently opposed to his poetic ideals. The artificial lighting and stage picture, and the physical barrier of the proscenium, as well as the large numbers of spectators required by any commercial theatre, effectively prevented attaining 'that state of perhaps real trance, in which the mind liberated from the pressure of the will is enfolded in symbols'.[59]

Ultimately, Craig and Yeats sought to free themselves from what they saw as the limitations of the stage; the former cut out the actor, the spoken word and eventually ceased performances altogether; the latter withdrew from 'the public stage . . . "to create for myself an unpopular theatre and an audience like a secret society"'.[60] Such dramatists and theatre practitioners were seeking a new way of representing reality by concentrating on what lies beneath the surface. One of the ways in which this was done was through the use of metatheatricality; that is, drawing attention to the play's artificial status to challenge the audience's construction of meaning. Another was to reach out to value systems that lay within the spiritual rather than the material world as a means to achieve transcendence. In this way, dramatists such as T. S. Eliot, Beckett and Pirandello would challenge the basic premise of theatrical representation. As the century wore on, past certainties are rejected, to be replaced by an awareness of fragmentation and disconnection; these modes were further strengthened by the impact of two world wars.

Censorship and the rise of the new theatres

Given the Edwardian era's social and political tensions, it is not surprising that new guidelines for the Lord Chamberlain were brought in during 1909. This demanded that 'Any plays that were indecent, "contained offensive personalities", invidiously represented either actual living persons or the recent dead, did violence "to the sentiment of religious reverence", or were calculated "to conduce to crime or vice . . . or to impair relations with any foreign power or to cause a breach of the peace" were not to be allowed'.[61] Thus, Shaw's women's rights play, *Press Cuttings* (1909), was denied a licence because of its less-than-favourable references to Arthur Balfour, H. H. Asquith, Alfred Milner and Herbert Kitchener.

Up until the beginning of the First World War, Parliament was constantly being challenged about the issue of censorship. There was a clash between the legacy of Victorian values and the new generation of playwrights from this Britain and abroad. In particular, Ibsen's exposure of middle-class hypocrisy and sexual inequality provoked a backlash against theatre censorship and demands for a more honest representation of society. In 1907 Granville Barker's play, *Waste*, was banned by the censor, leading notable figures like George Bernard Shaw to publicly protest against censorship, but its troubled history – it was eventually rewritten in 1927 and received its first public performance in 1936 – demonstrates the tight control of the establishment.

Nevertheless, the subject matter of the new drama kept the Lord Chamberlain's office busy during this period. This included a wide range of topics, from the Irish question to atheism, and from homosexuality to 'the House of Lords' traditional noblesse oblige.[62]

'Little theatres' sprang up where the subject matter and staging techniques could be more innovative away from the restrictive censorship codes of the Lord Chamberlain: independent theatres and clubs brought in membership fees rather than individually priced seat tickets, thus allowing these venues to hold 'private' performances. In this way avant-garde and advanced plays from this country and abroad could be put on without requiring a licence from the Lord Chamberlain's office.

One of the first of the new theatres was the Independent Theatre designed to 'search out plays that were "artistic," "interesting," and "literary".[63] This was founded by the Dutch-born impresario J. T. Grein in 1891, along with his wife Alice Augusta Greeven, Arthur Wing Pinero and Henry Arthur Jones, and did much to introduce European drama to London. They hosted German actors and directors, as well as organising trips abroad for various English companies, and put on the first English performances of Ibsen, Shaw and Hauptmann. In 1899 the Stage Society was set up to continue the work of the Independent Theatre. It put on Sunday performances of experimental plays and included some of the biggest names of the time: Granville Barker, Shaw, St John Hankin and Clifford Bax. Nevertheless theatre practitioners found it difficult to stage this experimental drama without prior training, nor did British playwrights find it easy to write work in a similar vein.

The Court Theatre – later the Royal Court – in London's Sloane Square would have far-reaching ramifications for the future of theatre in Britain. Started by Granville Barker and J. E. Vedrenne in 1904, it swiftly became London's most important radical theatre. Well-established by the start of the First World War, it helped William Archer in 1923 recall this as a period of 'almost miraculous renascence'.[64] These experiments would be difficult to achieve success, Barker pointed out, without public subsidy, and Stanislavski's state-sponsored Moscow Arts Theatre was held up as a useful model. This argument rumbled on in relation to the establishment of a national theatre, as discussed further in Chapter 4.

Influenced by the Independent Theatre, Archer's Stage Society and Fabianism, Barker's aim was to foster a 'modern national Drama' run on egalitarian lines that rejected commercial aims for artistic ones. This started a new form of theatrical organisation, called repertory: plays appeared in a rotating repertoire for a fixed period, not the unlimited runs utilised by the previous generation of actor-managers; there was ensemble playing by a permanent company, and the role of the writer and director became pre-eminent, as Claire Cochrane explains on pp. 199–200. To underline the social and moral seriousness of theatre, a series of different play-going rituals evolved, from eschewing matinée hats in the auditorium to applauding only at the end of the play rather than after each act.

Between 1904 and 1907 the Vedrenne-Barker season included works from Europe such as Hauptmann, Ibsen, Maeterlinck and Eugène Brieux. Established novelists and poets such as John Galsworthy, Thomas Hardy, Arnold Bennett and John Masefield, were also approached to write for the theatre. Barker also started the dramatic careers of Elizabeth Robins and Elizabeth Baker, although Shaw was by far and away the most performed dramatist there. Eventually the Court Theatre ran into financial trouble, leading to revivals of more commercially viable plays, but the venture had proved the necessity of a new type of theatre for a new generation of spectators.

Social drama

Drama that had hitherto remained largely aloof from actual involvement in the burning questions of contemporary society, now boldly took the lead as the mirror of the time. These plays rejected the moral certitudes of the Victorian period, with plots revolving around contemporary ethical dilemmas: in particular, intersections between sexuality, class and work formed the bedrock of the new drama. This attracted a younger, more socially and politically conscious audience, who thought that theatre should challenge rather than reinforce.

The demarcation between the old and new was frequently staged through generational conflict: the overthrow of patriarchal authority is key to such various plays as Stanley Houghton's *The Younger Generation* and *Hindle Wakes* (both 1912), Harold Brighouse's *Hobson's Choice* (1915), Galsworthy's *Justice* (1910) and Granville Barker's *Waste* and *The Voysey Inheritance* (1905). The oppression of the weak by the strong and their final triumph can also be seen to echo concerns about colonisation. The Boer Wars of 1880–1 and 1899–1902 were still fresh in the minds of the public and, even though the government attempted to shore up the Empire through its many spectacular exhibitions, there was a growing unease among the new dramatists about Britain's exploitation of its global power. This had also been stimulated by the country's introduction of concentration camps, which sowed the seeds of doubt about wisdom of the Establishment.

While the new drama may have challenged audiences in terms of subject matter – class, work, sexuality – this was not necessarily true in terms of technique. This was left to the avant-garde experimenters of the time. Playwrights such as Galsworthy and Granville Barker wrote what were essentially drawing room dramas; well-made plays with exposition, revelations and climactic curtains. Given the plethora of different artistic movements at this time, it is significant that realism remained the dominant form. This was a successful means by which to approach serious social themes of the day.

Shavian Realism was, in fact, another matter. Stuart E. Baker considers that Shaw wrote realist drama in terms of theme rather than technique. With characterisation Shaw 'accepts only a "realist morality", one which never asks "Is he good or bad?" but only "What are the effects of his actions"'. [65] This distinction allowed him to create characters from their own point of view, without judging them, helping the audience to make up their own minds about the moral dilemmas being presented to them. Shaw's problem plays and comedies were directly influenced by Ibsen and his own Fabianism. He rejected the aesthetic movement's 'Art for Art's sake', exhorting instead the promotion of political and intellectual ideas, especially via dialectical argument. Indeed, his creation of the 'artist-philosopher' was one that he presented as a serious figure of intent. These characters are generally shown in an exceedingly attractive light, apart from Eugene Marchbanks in *Candida* (1894), sometimes described as his favourite play.

Many of his plays had complicated stage histories. *Man and Superman: A Comedy and a Philosophy* was written in 1903, the 'Comedy' staged in 1905 and the 'Philosophy' in 1907. It was not until 1925 that the sections were brought together. This comedy of manners is witty, inventive and typical of Shaw's sophistry. It includes a long scene – known as Don Juan in Hell – based on a discussion of Shaw's theory of Creative Evolution. In Shaw's *Major Barbara* (1905) Andrew Undershaft is both an arms manufacturer and a considerate employer, highlighting the new drama's use of ambiguous characterisation. Shaw's historical plays are also technically unusual in that they show a move away from the past. *Caesar and Cleopatra* (written in 1898, with a first public performance in 1906) replicates the visual dazzle of Shakespearean productions by Herbert Beerbohm Tree and Henry Irving, but in an ironic way by mocking the audience's desire for spectacle and romance. Additionally it deliberately undercuts the classical heroism of the central characters by depicting their contemporaneous qualities. More importantly, at this time when Africa was being divided up among the colonising powers, Shaw's representation of Roman imperialism has a decidedly political edge to it. His technique of eliding history and contemporary situations also comes to the fore in his other Roman play, *Androcles and the Lion* (1913), where 'the persecution of the Christians clearly parallels the suffragette struggle for female equality'.[66]

Class

Many plays in the Edwardian era veered between outrage at social mobility and sympathy for the constraints of social hierarchy. During the Edwardian era, Michael R. Booth explains, West End comedies were 'conservative in the social and political sense, on the side of the established order against the parvenu, firm upholders of social distinction'.[67] This changed after the war, with more plays pushing for a more nuanced view of class, although not all social drama effectively managed this.

The then-popular St John Hankin was a key figure of the new drama but did not posit any real changes that could be made to society. In *The Return of the Prodigal* (1905) the rich and the poor are as idle as one another, but with the latter it is because of chronic unemployment. The ne'er do well son blackmails his father into providing him with an allowance or he will ruin his father's Parliamentary ambitions by going to live in a workhouse. His *The Cassilis Engagement* (1907), a retelling of T. W. Robertson's *Caste* (1867), mocks every class, but it is perhaps the commoner Ethel Borridge who is most severely castigated for trying to marry above her station.

Arthur Wing Pinero may have been sympathetic to the women's cause in *The Second Mrs Tanqueray* (1893), but he also held the view that it was difficult to write drama of any complexity about the 'English lower middle and lower classes' because of their 'reluctance to analyse, to generalise, to give vivid utterance to their thoughts and emotions'.[68] It is difficult to say with any certainty how far such views were common. Dramatic representations of the working classes tended to be of the comic servant variety, and plays derided attempts at social mobility. Music hall and the new drama were more comfortable with mocking or confronting class tensions head-on.

However, the new wave of playwrights were determined to put social issues under pressure. One such was W. Somerset Maugham who turned from novels to plays and was indebted to Ibsen and Oscar Wilde. His appeal to the emotions was different from Shaw's drama of ideas, but he was similarly concerned with critiquing contemporary society. Maugham's first piece, a one-act play, *Marriages are Made in Heaven* (1898) was rejected by London managers, but produced by Max Reinhardt's company in Germany four years later. Grein, who produced his plays at The Stage Society, a private theatre devoted to experimental work, saw his promise. By 1908 Maugham had four plays running at the same time in London's West End, the first time such a feat had been achieved. His theatrical career continued until 1933, when the failure of *Sheppey* caused him to stop writing for the stage.

Maugham's early plays are concerned with the restraints of society, particularly in relation to class hierarchy and sexual morality, and he uses comedy to undercut the audience's expectations. Two of his plays can be paralleled in this respect. *A Man of Honour* (1903) questions the word 'honour'. A gentleman marries the barmaid he has impregnated, but when she commits suicide, he risks social disgrace by refusing to take his own life. The eponymous *Smith* (1913) is a maid who marries her employer's brother. In their role as outsiders – she is working class and insignificant as intimated by her name; he has been living in the colonies – they are able to see high society for what it is: selfish, uncaring and insular.

In Galsworthy's first play, *The Silver Box* (1906), the rich thief who steals a prostitute's purse receives quite different treatment from a working-class man whom he drunkenly invites to take whatever he wants from his house. This theme is dealt with at greater length in *Justice*. William Falder, a junior office clerk, forges a cheque to help his mistress escape from the clutches of her drunkard husband. His lawyer's calls for justice go unheeded by the judge, and Falder is sentenced to three years penal servitude. The scene after this takes place in dumb show: the prisoner in solitary confinement moves 'like an animal pacing its cage'.[69] He loses his sense of identity and, driven insane, finally commits suicide by leaping from a window. The play influenced Winston Churchill – then Home Secretary – to improve prison conditions, but Galsworthy was only moderately gratified. His intention had been larger: to show how justice could never be fulfilled while society was blindly following rules and regulations to protect itself from 'the weak and diseased'.[70] By always 'dealing in types' Galsworthy was writing not about individuals but about large swathes of the population.[71]

J. M. Barrie's *The Admirable Crichton* is a subversive moral fable in which a peer's advanced theories about the artificiality of class divisions are diametrically opposed to his eponymous butler who believes them to be 'the natural outcome of a civilized society'.[72] The enforced removal from society, when the family are marooned on a desert island, persuades Crichton to revise his opinion when he assumes the role of leader – the 'Gov' – through his practical skills. This carnivalesque topsy-turveydom reaches its comic apogee when a relationship threatens between Crichton and Lady Mary. Given the date of the play, it is unsurprising that Barrie retreats from this dangerous outcome; the family are rescued and the status quo is re-established, with the butler retiring to avoid embarrassment to his employers. This debate about class also takes place in a later play by Barrie, *Dear Brutus*, written during the war in 1917. The female characters in particular take no pleasure in their elevated position in the social hierarchy, with Lady Caroline Laney most happy when she becomes the 'wife' of the butler Matey during a magical vision.

Shaw gives his own twist to the class issue in *Major Barbara*, viewed by anarchist Emma Goldman as 'one of the most revolutionary plays' of the period.[73] Shaw pinpoints what he sees as capitalism's more dangerous qualities, when military industrialists have been given the ability to gain control of society. Andrew Undershaft has both money and gunpowder and with these twin symbols of power can determine the course of history. The play shows the struggle for the 'salvation' of society between himself and his daughter, Barbara, who works for the Salvation Army. If poverty is, as Undershaft suggests, the root of all evil because it causes people to abandon their morals, then money must be seen as the root of all virtue. Because of this he pays his employees well, leaving Barbara to save those who are better off.

Pygmalion (1914) depicts the snobbery of Edwardian society by reworking the fairy tale of Cinderella. The casting of the forty-nine-year-old Mrs Patrick Campbell as the flower girl was less than ideal, but contemporary photographs suggest a charming appearance in the fashions of the day. The play's sharp edge was blunted by Herbert Beerbohm Tree's insistence on a sentimental ending as well as its later appearance as the musical *My Fair Lady* (1964). Shaw wanted his heroine to break free from male control at the end of the play, positioning her both as a New Woman and as a liberated subject, but this was rejected by his director and the bourgeois audiences of the time. However, it still remains a witty but savage satire on the pretensions and hypocrisy of the upper classes.

In *Pygmalion* Henry Higgins's transformation of Eliza exposes imperialist and patriarchal arrogance; based on the Greek myth of Galatea, it is the bourgeois male who 'breathes life' into the working-class female. Higgins's friend and confidante, Colonel Pickering, has already enacted this in colonial India by teaching its natives to speak English, and there is also here an obvious reference to Ireland's troubled relationship with England. Shaw depicts Higgins and Pickering as the 'ideologues and technocrats of the dominant culture, and Eliza's body and mind as that which has to be dominated and objectified'.[74] She is turned into a 'lady' by superficially aping her 'superiors' language, appearance and manners, but in the process loses her sense of self and class identity. Yet Eliza's language – 'done in', 'bloody' – is taken to be an eccentricity of high fashion rather than that of the streets, and her assumption of the role of Duchess is shown to be simply that: a performance made up of surface signifiers, exposing the performative qualities of high society, where superficiality has replaced substance.

Work and authority

Some of the social and personal consequences of the Industrial Revolution – poor working conditions resulting in poverty and illness, increased mechanisation leading to the dehumanisation, a competitive marketplace privileging profits – had already been depicted in a number of nineteenth-century works. This was continued by a new wave of dramatists who focused on those disenfranchised – spiritually or materially – by capitalism. John Galsworthy's *Strife* (1909) presages a series of strikes by dock, railway and mining workers between 1909–12, who were demanding fairer working conditions. Interestingly, Galsworthy does not side wholeheartedly with the workers, but gives a fair-handed representation of unrest at the Trenartha Tin Plate works: the miners are unable to provide food for their families, and the Board of Directors struggle to survive in a competitive market. The intransigence of both sides leads to the death of Mrs Roberts, the wife of one of the workmen's committee. Galsworthy calls for a greater sense of understanding between the two sides based on common humanity, but falls short of Shaw's polemical treatment of social issues.

Two plays by committed socialist Granville Barker – *The Voysey Inheritance* and *The Madras House* (1910) – revolve around the intersections between the work place and home life, not only demonstrating the capitalist incursion from one sphere to another, but also charting the slow disintegration of the family unit. In the former play, Edward Voysey learns that the respectable family business has been built on fraud passed down through the generations; it also becomes obvious that his mother and three brothers have colluded to keep the fraud secret so as to sustain their standard of living. Edward is presented with a moral dilemma: to reject his father's inheritance (both real and metaphorical), denounce the fraud and declare the firm bankrupt, or to continue to manipulate the finances until all the creditors are repaid; he eventually chooses this latter course of action. The 'House of Voysey' refers to both the commercial business and the family lineage, highlighted by the way in which the setting switches back and forth between the home and the work place. Each is cluttered with furniture, most obvious when the family is squeezed around the dining table. This reinforces Edward's entrapment in the family's corruption as well as its greedy materialism. Further, as Cary M. Mazer has observed, the play depicts the corruption inherent in the capitalist system, where 'all capital accumulation, investment and living off unearned income is theft' and this process continues across the whole of society.[75]

The Madras House also looks at public and private corruption. Philip Madras is brokering a deal with an American to rid himself of an inherited fashion house and start a career in politics. The name of the company highlights the exploitative side of Empire and capitalism, showing how trade and patriarchy flourish through the enslavement of others. His female workers – even those who are married – are forced to live on the company's premises, and his six unmarried female cousins are being used as drudges at home. Again, the American buyer, the significantly named Mr State, sees the new women's movement as nothing more than a marketing opportunity, highlighting the commodification of the female body at this time mentioned in my Introduction. This is visually depicted during the fashion show in the final Act of the play. There is a triple perspective, emphasising the inauthenticity and hypocrisy of consumerism. The shop has Moorish-looking furniture and trappings, but this is fake, the items having been '*designed and made in Tottenham Court Road*'.[76] The Parisian models are in fact cocottes and as they show off the clothes with blank faces and robotic movements, they are pawed over by the male buyers. Moreover, these figures are played by actresses who are displaying their own bodies in front of a paying theatre audience, as well as the fashions of the day. As Joel H. Kaplan and Sheila Stowell have observed, 'playhouses became second showrooms' with the actresses 'serving as living mannequins'.[77]

Once again staging is devised so as to show the web-like nature of capitalism: Granville Barker conducted 'rehearsals on a stage cloth marked out in one-foot squares for exact blocking, so that as one actor reported "every move was part of a pattern, so was every gesture, every speech"'.[78] In a reversal of the more usual prodigal son theme, Philip's long-absent father returns. He has rejected the decadence of the West, viewing the clothing industry as 'an industrial seraglio'.[79] However, his way of life is hardly better, having converted to Islam and become a polygamist. The lessons Philip learns about capitalism and gender helps him to renegotiate his relationship with his own wife.

A female perspective on the relationship between gender, capitalism and work is given by Elizabeth Baker, whose plays focus on the life of workers in respectable, but lowly paid positions of shop assistants, secretaries and clerks. In the symbolically titled *Chains* (1909) Charley Wilson wants to leave the drudgery of his clerical position to emigrate to Australia. Instead, he is forced to remain in his job when his wife falls pregnant. Linda Fitzsimmons notes that their lower-middle-class position 'is suggested to the audience through the detail of set and dialogue. The off-stage area and off-stage action are invoked to reinforce the claustrophobia forced on the family by their economic circumstance'.[80] Their poverty does not stop their dreams and ambition, but it does ensure that these can never come to fruition. The family's fortunes cannot increase given Charley's meagre wages, and social convention precludes his wife, Lily, from taking on a job herself. Every aspect of their life is controlled by economics, even to the point of the invasion of their domestic privacy because they are forced to take in a lodger to pay the rent. Ironically, it is this lodger, Tennant, who tempts Charley into fleeing his job, his wife and his country. Men take on work chosen for them by their fathers, for which there is fierce competition, and they are sacked so others can take their place at reduced wages. Altogether they are fodder for an uncaring and relentless labour market.

In contrast, Githa Sowerby's *Rutherford and Son* (1912) considers the world of work from the perspective of the employer. It was considered a triumphant exposé of capitalism until it was discovered that the author was female. Originally presented under the name K. G. Sowerby, the author had been keen to hide her gender from a male-dominated industry, as had other women of the time, but in fact as Maggie B. Gale has shown the first half of the twentieth century was extraordinarily fruitful for female dramatists, even when writing on hard-hitting subjects.[81] In the play, nothing matters so much to John Rutherford, seen as the embodiment of patriarchy, than the continuation of his company, 'Rutherford and Son'. However, he has alienated his two sons so that he is forced to consider someone outside the immediate family to continue the name. Mary, his daughter-in-law, offers her child, Tony, in return for his education and career; with this, she is aware that the values that she inculcates in her son will help to reshape the company. Gary Farnell sees Mary as a New Woman and Sowerby's work as a suffrage play in all but name. Although neither term is mentioned, female triumph over male patriarchy is at its core. Mary is as hard at driving a bargain as Rutherford, saying 'I've got something to sell that you want to buy', but it is her maternal love that drives her, not self-serving ambition.[82] Farnell argues, 'Mary carries the very logic of the "cash nexus" through to the point where there is a dialectical transvaluation of the value of cash payment itself in a *laissez-faire* political economy (of bodies pure and simple)'.[83] Thus Mary combines the 'softness' of the maternal woman with the 'hardness' of the business world.

Cicely Hamilton's social conscience can be evidenced by her suffrage plays, as discussed later in this chapter, but is also to the fore in *Diana of Dobson's* (1908). This predates Barker's *The Madras House*, with its exploration of the enforced live-in employer whose job and home is permanently at risk due to the vagaries of her (male) employer. Christine Dymkowski notes the play's topicality: 'the same night the play opened, the Amalgamated Union of Shop Assistants had organised a meeting at Queen's Hall to protest against the system'.[84] In contrast to Barker's work, which is predicated on the attractiveness and saleability of the female body, Hamilton depicts her draper's shop workers getting ready for bed at the end of the day by removing all those feminine items that are designed to make them appealing. This deliberately uneroticised performance was originally played out against the setting of a damp, comfortless dormitory, with five single beds and 'exactly one towel and one washstand for the five "young ladies"', reinforcing the contrast between appearance and reality caused by the pursuit of capitalism.[85] When Diana receives a small legacy, she decides to blow it on a taste of the high life. She is wooed by two men; one is her employer, the other is a fortune hunter who claims that he cannot live on £600 per year. When the latter discovers Diana's real identity as a member of the lower classes and previous shop assistant, the hypocrisy of Edwardian society is revealed. It is only when Diana becomes destitute that the fortune hunter realises he truly loves her. Although a 'romantic comedy' Hamilton had a serious message to impart: an *Era* critic noted that the play

> is produced quite apropos of the agitation against living in and of the cry for female suffrage. It voices very boldly the revolt of the modern woman against her subjugation, her craving for interest in life, her hatred of monotony, and her desire for a 'good time'.[86]

This was a dramatic difference from earlier plays by women, and showed the impact of the considerable socio-political upheavals taking place at this time.

Women and sexuality

As mentioned in the Introduction, the New Woman was a social phenomenon in the 1890s. Ibsen's *A Doll's House* was at the start of this trend and quickly taken up by playwrights of the day: as a figure of fun, an active threat and a political emblem. The suggestion that the pursuit of female desire was valid or that a woman could achieve autonomy from a man was profoundly controversial. Sydney Grundy's satire, *The New Woman* (1894), sees them as fraudulent; they are unable to be a man's intellectual equal, regardless of what they think, and for all their bluster, ultimately they want to marry and obey a man.

Nevertheless, there were more thoughtful considerations of a woman's changing place in society. Arthur Pinero's *The Notorious Mrs. Ebbsmith* (1895), Percy Fendall's *Mrs. Deering's Divorce* (1900), Henry Arthur Jones's *Mrs. Dane's Defence* (1900) and J. M. Barrie's *The Adored One* (1913), among many others, all opened up questions about sexual double standards as well as stimulating interest in the actresses' public and private lives. The fashion for depictions of the fallen woman throughout the Victorian age had gained in moral ambiguity from the 1890s up to the First World War, spurred by Ibsen's exploration of the sexual and political economy and Wilde's social comedies.

Paula, the heroine of Pinero's *The Second Mrs Tanqueray*, is married to a man who uses his knowledge of her past affairs to trap her into an elegant but dull world of convention.[87] The new actress playing the role, Mrs Patrick Campbell, enhanced interest in the character; her slim stylishness, theatrical collaboration (and later relationship) with Shaw would ensure that she remained a major Edwardian star. A strong and independent woman herself, she decried some of the roles she had to play. Of *The Notorious Mrs Ebbsmith* she said that the eponymous role 'and the first three acts of the play filled me with ecstacy . . . but the last act broke my heart. I knew that such an Agnes in life could not have drifted into the Bible-reading inertia of the woman she became in the last act'.[88]

Barker's first solo play, *The Marrying of Ann Leete* (1899) is set in the world of Georgian politics but is in fact an exposé of Victorian class and sexuality: the heroine comes to the slow realisation that marriage is a form of social, political and economic transaction between families in which her views are irrelevant. Ann rejects the aristocrats her father has lined up for her, choosing instead to propose to and marry the family gardener. This rebellious behaviour was shocking for the time in its denial of patriarchal authority, crossing of class boundaries and embracement of female desire. The theatre critic Michael Billington suggests that with this play 'Barker also invents a wholly new theatrical idiom: one that anticipates [Noël]Coward (born in 1899) and Pinter in its mixture of clipped, oblique statements with sudden blunt truths'.[89]

Shaw's *Mrs Warren's Profession* (1894) overturned every convention of the fallen woman motif, and there was considerable trouble trying to get this play licensed for public performance; this was not achieved until 1925. Mother and daughter are successful businesswomen, the former running a chain of brothels, the latter as an accountant. However, it is society that is castigated, not the mother's choice of profession. Shaw's 1902 preface to the play states: 'prostitution is caused, not by female depravity and male licentiousness, but simply by underpaying, undervaluing and overworking women so shamefully that the poorest of them are forced to resort to prostitution to keep body and soul together'.[90] Shaw's play *Getting Married* (1908) continued to provoke the censor by suggesting divorce was to be commended in certain situations. Granville Barker's *Waste* revolved around an affair between a man and a married woman who has an affair with a politician. Her death during an abortion similarly highlights the inequality between men and women. It is therefore not surprising that it was refused a licence by the Lord Chamberlain's office and had to be put on by the Stage Society as a private performance. Galsworthy's *The Fugitive* (1913) takes up a similar theme. A woman flees her husband, only to end up penniless. Her ladylike upbringing will not allow her to become a prostitute and her only resource is to commit suicide. Galsworthy wrote the play to show

how women were still not being suitably educated for the 'real' world and therefore unable to survive its difficulties.

Suffrage drama

It was one thing for a male dramatist to concern himself with the position of women in society, but it was left to female writers to take this one stage further and utilise theatre as a political tool. Suffragettes used visual iconography 'on a scale unprecedented in any Victorian pressure group' and the spectacle of mass demonstrations and rallies swiftly developed into theatrical activism.[91] Suffrage meetings and fund raisers would include performance items, such as songs, recitations, dances, tableaux and so on, to break the monotony. Spurred on to bigger and better things, plays were written specifically to suit the occasion, and large numbers of women began to view themselves as dramatists.[92] Starting with character sketches and monologues which contained some of the arguments for the vote, this progressed to one-act and full-length plays.

As one of the main proponents of suffrage drama so potently said, 'one play is worth a hundred speeches where propaganda is concerned'.[93] These tended to be structured like fables, which demonstrated how a woman (often working class) converted her husband or friends to the cause, or whose own political consciousness was 'awakened'. Popular plays in this category include Cicely Hamilton and Christopher St John's *How the Vote was Won* (1909), and Evelyn Glover's *A Chat with Mrs Chicky* (1912) and *Miss Appleyard's Awakening* (1913). Generally the first suffrage play is accepted as being Elizabeth Robins's *Votes for Women!* (1907), a homage to Ibsen's *The Master Builder* (1892).[94] She established a formula that other suffrage playwrights followed: a debate between those for and against the vote (anti-suffragists are unable to argue successfully against the suffragists' greater debating power); a conversion narrative (a female character changes her opinion and joins the suffragettes); and a reconciliation narrative (a male character agrees to support the cause).[95]

In Robins's drama, the suffragists are presented as attractive and feminine, and therefore demonstrably unlike the window-smashing harridans of the popular press. In a carefully constructed 'drawing room' conversation between Mrs Freddy and Vida Levering, Vida rationally and successfully argues her point that the suffragettes have created more awareness for their cause than the suffragists who are simply 'politely petitioning parliament'.[96]

Vida's behaviour and arguments help to convert the innocent Jean. In rejecting her former MP lover, George, she also rejects the role as a fallen woman for a more independent future, and blackmails him into presenting the suffrage cause to Parliament.

Persuaded that the vote would help improve women's economic and working conditions the Actresses' Franchise League (AFL) was set up in 1908 and was, Susan Carlson explains, 'the gravitational centre of the explosive phenomenon of suffrage theatre'.[97] This promoted women's productions on a larger scale and by the outbreak of the First World War it had 900 members across the country, with figures such as Lena Ashwell, Ellen Terry, Violet Vanbrugh and Lillie Langtry successful in using their fame, popularity and dramatic ability to promote suffrage. The first of AFL's purpose-made plays was performed at an exhibition at Prince's Skating Rink in Knightsbridge, 1908. This event and others like it did much to develop the public vision of the politically conscious woman.

An offshoot of the AFL was the Independent Women's Theatre Company, which briefly flourished before the First World War. This was organised by Inez Bensusan, an Australian-born actress and writer who was instrumental in promoting women's drama, as in her establishment of the Women's Theatre Company at the Coronet Theatre in 1913. The Women Writers' Suffrage League was similar to the AFL but not limited to those working within the theatre. Cicely Hamilton and Elizabeth Robins worked alongside figures such as Sarah Grand, Olive Schreiner, Marie Belloc Lowndes and Ivy Compton-Burnett to wield the pen as an instrument in the fight for the vote.

Another important initiative was the Pioneer Players, founded by Ellen Terry's daughter, Edith Craig, in 1911. This was designed not only to support the suffrage cause but also women working in all areas of dramatic production. Craig herself was a manger, director, producer and designer, as Claire Cochrane's chapter makes clear. In relation to this Katharine Cockin notes that 'Involvement in a diverse range of cultural activities in the women's suffrage movement seemed inevitable and lent itself to developing a feminist praxis which promised to challenge the competitive and individualistic ideologies of capitalism and the aesthetic'.[98] Many of the plays put on by the Pioneer Players were concerned with women's history and looked back to earlier female dramatists such as Hrotsvitha of Gandersheim, a tenth-century nun, and Aphra Behn, considered the first professional female writer in the seventeenth century.

Beyond their subject matter and political intent, suffrage drama could also be innovative in terms of location, genre and staging. Performances took place in private homes, commercial and independent theatres, and unconventional spaces such as parks, labour halls, streets and squares. Conventional genres were drawn upon to lure in audiences, but then subtly reworked. For example, Acts 1 and 3 of Elizabeth Robins's *Votes for Women!* are set in an upper class drawing room, similar to that of the well-made play. However, these frame a suffrage rally held in Trafalgar Square. Directed by Granville Barker at the Court Theatre the male and female speakers are staged so that they face the theatre audience, who merge into the crowd listening to the debate. The scene challenges the perception of separate spheres as women are not only seen as public speakers at rallies but also as performers on the stage.

Another form utilised was the pageant. For suffragettes this became a way to combine drama, social commentary and spectacle, as well as create a sense of commonality and group cohesion. They were also a natural consequence of the movement's large-scale demonstrations and rallies. Cicely Hamilton's *A Pageant of Great Women* (1909) was one of the most lavish, with dozens of performers in extravagant costumes: the pageant would go on to be presented in various cities with amateur actors drawn from the area. It appeared two months after William Gladstone had imposed forcible feeding for imprisoned suffragettes, and the main character – the generically named 'Woman' – demands freedom from Justice, while Prejudice, a man, argues against her. With a mixture of professional actresses and local activists, it presents a stream of positive images of women, including Sappho, Joan of Arc and Rosa Bonheur.

Metatheatrically, these are portrayed by some of the most famous actresses of the day who act out an allegorical trial to decide whether or not women deserve freedom. This, and similar ones like the 1911 Coronation Suffrage Pageant create a body of work that both reflect women's hidden history and highlight female creativity. In working together for a common cause, those involved with the suffrage movement – but particularly those working in the field of drama – were liberated in a highly public way. More subversively, as Penny Farfan has pointed out in this book and elsewhere, this production can also be viewed as a display of sexual dissidence: 'the decision of these performers to associate themselves, through performance, with the homosexual and/or cross-dressed historical figures that they chose to portray in the pageant suggests a deliberate use of performance to articulate and make visible a newly emerging lesbian identity within the larger context of a production serving the primary purpose of suffrage propaganda'.[99]

By 1914 suffrage drama became irrelevant in many respects as the political movement towards the vote was overtaken by world events. However, it had a profound effect on female participation in the theatre with more women than ever becoming involved in management, production, direction and writing.

Regional and repertory theatre

At the start of the twentieth century, provincial theatre was dominated by touring companies and divided into number 1, 2 or 3 venues depending on the quality of material put on at these 'receiving houses'. Productions were shown for a couple of nights before going back on the road to the next venue. To maximise profits, several companies toured different parts of Britain with the same popular plays. Some theatres specialised in the classic works or Shakespeare, such as Manchester's Queen's Theatre, and Frank Benson ensured that this playwright reached all parts of the country with his four Shakespearean companies.[100] More controversial or advanced plays included Pinero's *The Second Mrs. Tanqueray*, Shaw's *Caesar and Cleopatra* and Yeats's *The Countess Cathleen* (1911). All of this suggests that the provincial theatre was not as lacklustre as sometimes thought.

Regional theatre began to change during the Edwardian period. Many of those connected with Fabianism, socialism and/or the Labour Party created a theatre committed to social concerns which laid the foundation stone of the repertory movement. This would be based around resident companies who would rotate plays chosen from a specified repertoire, thus providing material that was more challenging as well as tailored to local audiences. After Granville Barker's experiments at the Court Theatre in London, he was of the belief that repertory would work better in the provinces: it would be easier to get subsidies there, cheaper theatre buildings were available and audiences more open to new ideas.

Barker was correct. Between 1904 and 1914, repertory theatres sprung up in many of the major cities of Britain, presaging the gradual movement away from the metropolis. This can be also connected to community, workers' and political theatre. Victorian philanthropy had already spawned an understanding of the importance of cultural activities such as debating societies, children's groups, cycling clubs and theatre groups, and it is notable that regional theatre did particularly well in cities that were pioneering in terms of such public educative ventures, as well as places where the suffrage movement was flourishing. Interestingly, Liverpool Repertory Theatre was started by local citizens rather than patrons and Barry Jackson's Birmingham Repertory grew out of the amateur Pilgrim Players, its manifesto being to 'serve an art instead of making that art serve a commercial purpose'.[101] Repertory theatre focused mainly on pieces from the Continent or contemporary work by British playwrights. As L. J. Collins notes, 'The Glasgow Citizen's Theatre in 1911 became the first British company to produce Chekhov' and in the same year Liverpool's Kelly's Theatre produced 'Galsworthy's *Strife* . . . a courageous choice considering there was serious unrest in the Liverpool docks'.[102] There was also an increasing interest in the idea of theatre as part of a specific community which fostered growth in regionalism, as with the Glasgow Repertory Theatre, which started 'to encourage the initiation and development of a purely Scottish Drama': as already discussed in the Introduction, the negotiation of regionalism/nationalism was a tricky one.[103] Two repertory companies stood out from the rest in terms of their impact.

The Abbey theatre and Irish drama

Up until the twentieth century Irish dramatists from Richard Sheridan and Dion Boucicault to Oscar Wilde had little choice other than to leave their homeland and pursue their career on the London stage. In 1904 W. B. Yeats and Lady Augusta Gregory set up the Abbey theatre in Dublin. Its celebration of Celtic roots, Irish culture and nationality ensured its authentic distinctiveness from British culture and acted as a riposte to Ireland's colonial status.[104] Ironically the Abbey was set up with English money gained through the imperialist tea trade. Annie Horniman who came from the unusual background of being a tea heiress gave financial backing to the Abbey having been inspired by the Barker-Vedrenne management of Court Theatre and the Irish Literary Theatre when it visited London in May 1903. The Abbey was also in the style of the free and independent theatres owned by Antoine, Brahm and Grein.

The Abbey's directors had to adhere to Horniman's regulations: these included higher ticket prices and no political plays. This latter was openly flouted by Yeats and Gregory, although their own autocratic rules led a number of actors to form their own company, *Cluithcheoiri na hEireann* (the Theatre of Ireland). While the Abbey theatre may have had its roots in the Irish Nationalist movement of the 1890s, a series of compromises had to be taken by those in charge. Lauren Arrington's recent research draws a picture of Yeats as a media-savvy and manipulative figurehead, who went to extraordinary lengths to protect his theatre.[105]

The Abbey Theatre has been described by Robert Welch as 'the conscience of modern Ireland' and was instrumental in the Celtic Revival movement, also known as the Celtic Twilight.[106] Its aim, in Yeats's words was to create a new type of Irish drama that would 'deal with passing issues until we have re-created the imaginative traditions of Ireland, and filled the popular imagination with saints and heroes'.[107] It arose out of the Irish National Theatre Society (INTS), designed to establish a specific Irish aesthetic, and William Fay's Irish National Dramatic Company. Maud Gonne's radical Inghinidhe na hÉireann was another organisation dedicated to Irish culture: these 'Daughters of Ireland' believed in an independent Ireland and equality for women, and formed their own cultural and political organisation when they were excluded from existing nationalist organisations.

All of these would act as a riposte to an increasing 'Anglicization' of the Irish people by rejecting music hall for the céilidh, drawing room settings for peasant kitchens, and genres unpopular in London like verse and one-act plays. The Abbey Theatre started as an independent, literary theatre and touting it as Ireland's national theatre was a ploy to change the political focus of the country from English colonisation to Home Rule. Playwrights utilised Irish history and mythology not only as a means to strengthen national identity, but also as a form of resistance to hegemonic control. Alice Milligan's *Last Feast of the Fianna* (1900) was the first play to completely draw on Irish sagas, shortly followed by Yeats's collaboration with George Moore, *Diarmuid and Grania* (1901).[108] Yeats's greatest dramatic work for over twenty-five years drew on the legend of the Irish warrior Cuchulainn: the story concerns a battle between father and son, which came to stand for the impossibility of bequeathing a national, civil society to the next generation. Cuchulain would become a figurehead for the Irish republicans who fought for liberation (1916–23) and a statue of him in Dublin commemorates the rebels executed during the 1916 Easter Rising.

When Frank Benson's Shakespearean Company staged *Diarmuid and Grania* it was hilariously obvious that the actors were unable to pronounce the Irish names of this famous Irish myth. To overcome the problem of Irish characters being represented by English actors, dramatic training and acting opportunities were provided by several groups. Gonne herself came to symbolise Ireland as the mother nation in Yeats and Gregory's *Cathleen ni Houlihan* (1902).[109] The play draws on the insurrection of 1798 'in order allegorically to asset the native heroism of the Irish, in keeping with a utopian formulation of nation-as-culture'.[110] Cathleen, the spirit of the nation, wanders the land recruiting men to fight for her, but while the play is rooted in the historical past it also reflects the present-day situation, with all of the actors – most notably Gonne – fervent activists for the nationalist cause; this helped to cement the position of the play as a powerful piece of patriotism.

While John Millington Synge had a brief stage career – his first works were written in 1902 and his sixth and last appeared posthumously in 1910 – he was very much at the heart of the Abbey's output. Like Yeats, Synge was influenced by French symbolism, and infused this with an awareness of Ireland's physical and cultural geography. This can typically be seen in Synge's first play, *Riders to the Sea*, published by Yeats in 1903 and performed the following year. This play did much to promote a specifically Irish style of poetic lyricism, where language can become so heightened that it has a transformative effect: shabby settings and shady characters become romanticised in a way that cuts across the reality. Thus, in *Riders to the Sea* Synge turns the ritualistic lamentations of women grieving for their men lost at sea into a mythic paeon to life and death. His *In the Shadow of the Glen* (1903) provoked violent controversy when it was felt that the liberated behaviour of a wife who leaves behind her loveless marriage to go away with a tramp was an affront to Irish womanhood and Catholic morality. There are echoes of *A Doll's House* in this – the heroine is named Nora – and the play was charged with being an 'Ibsenity' by its many detractors. In contrast to Yeats, even though Synge believed that theatre should represent the contemporary, the ordinary and the realistic, his *Deidre of the Sorrows* (1904) continues to mine the same vein of Irish folklore; this was first performed in 1910 with Yeats writing his own version in 1906.

Catholic nationalists were already less than enamoured with Synge's anti-Catholic sympathies. They also saw the INTS, under Yeats's dominance, giving too much credence to Anglo-Irish writers and directors. *The Playboy of the Western World* brought these simmering tensions to a head when it was first performed in 1907. Irish patriots blamed the playwright's protestant background for his negative presentation of Irish life. The theatre's management was also condemned for calling on the Royal Irish Constabulary, an Irish police force but one loyal to the crown, to quell the ensuing riots that lasted for a week. In this Rabelaisian play Christy Mahon bursts into a shebeen – a small tavern – to confess to his father's murder. His listeners see his behaviour as a strike against tyranny and refuse to hand him over to the 'peelers', the English police force. However, when the patricide is discovered not to have taken place, Christy's transformation from a timid peasant to a rebellious youth is shown to be a lie; he is not a playboy, a Christ-like figure or national hero. In doing this, 'Synge had exposed the Catholics' heroic image of themselves as a dangerous fraud'.[111] Moreover, the violence in the play alludes both to England's colonisation, represented by the patriarch Old Mahon, and the republican struggle which would become progressively bloody.

As well as the romantic and folkloric, Irish drama also provided naturalistic representations of the working classes. *The Playboy of the Western World* is in the style of peasant realism with its setting of a rural local pub, country dialect and references to the land and the simple pleasures of life. Synge continues in the mode of dramatists such as Padraic Colum, who worked for the Irish National Theatre Society and the Abbey Theatre. Colum's early plays depicting peasant life, *The Broken Soil* (1903, revised as *The Fiddler's House* in 1907) and *The Land* (1905), became part of a new realism in Irish drama. Born in a workhouse, Colum became a lifelong friend of James Joyce, but fell out of favour with Yeats over *The Playboy of the Western World* riots and has since been relegated the margins of Irish literature.

Shaw was the last major Irish playwright of the time to write the majority of his work for English audiences. However, he remained a champion of the Abbey Theatre in Dublin, and the only one of his full-length plays written wholly about Ireland, *John Bull's Other Island* (1904), directly influenced the finalising of the Anglo-Irish Treaty in 1921, after Lloyd George and Churchill saw a revival of it.[112] The stereotyped depiction of the Englishman and the Irishman was designed to uncover the absurdities of colonial policies, land possession and political corruption. Significantly, the play starts in a London Civil Engineers' office; on the walls 'hang a large map of South America' and a 'pictorial advertisement of a steamship company'.[113] This iconography of the Empire is embodied along racial stereotypes. Where Thomas Broadbent has plans to build a 'Garden City' in Rosscullen in the west of Ireland and is caught up in the romance of the place, his business partner, Larry Doyle, is in self-imposed exile from Ireland, seeing his homeland as one racked by poverty, ignorance and superstition. Brad Kent acknowledges that it is Shaw, 'a member of the Irish diaspora for twenty-eight years by the time he wrote the play in 1904, who possesses a willingness to acknowledge the changes occurring to the Irish peasantry, while the "rooted" Yeats presents an idealized and fixed image of this group'.[114] Ironically, then, while Yeats and others in the Celtic Revival where attempting to celebrate an authentic Irish identity, they were in effect creating one that was quite the opposite of their intention, further complicating the idea of nationhood.

The Manchester School

Yeats and Gregory fervently refuted all suggestions that the Abbey was a regional theatre, given that they were determined to redraw the lines of nationalism to privilege Ireland rather than England. In contrast, the Gaiety in Manchester has been described as the first important regional theatre of the period. Andrew Davies notes that 'Manchester's dynamism was founded upon the expanding textile industry, and the ferment which this provoked led to the creation of powerful political organisations – the Anti-Corn Law League was begun here, and the Chartists built up a formidable presence – and important cultural institutions like the Free Library (1852), the 1857 Art Exhibition, the Hallé Orchestra and the *Manchester Guardian*'.[115] It is not surprising, therefore, that Annie Horniman founded her new theatre here in 1907, wanting to change the West End of London's stranglehold on theatre, with its long runs and 'inner circle' of actor-managers; repertory was seen by her as the way forward.

During her travels abroad Horniman had already been impressed by subsidised theatres in Germany and by way in which theatre was treated as an integral part of daily life. She saw productions of Ibsen's work and, on her return to her home country, provided financial backing for Ibsenite actress Florence Farr's season of 'new drama' at the Avenue Theatre, London. It was a financial disaster, but Horniman shared in the ideals of the New Woman. She promoted the early careers of women, such as actress Sybil Thorndike, and dramatist Antonia Williams, whose play *The Street* (1913) had shockingly portrayed a middle-class woman forced into prostitution. This was in response to a common belief that critics were biased against women writers; indeed Gertrude Kingston at the Little Theatre went further by adopting a policy of withholding all authors' names so their gender was hidden.

The Gaiety built up a loyal following, mainly composed of local workers who, up until that time, had never visited the theatre before. Horniman's policy of allowing advance booking at 'popular' prices – an innovation at the time – was instrumental in this, as was the choice of plays which represented local life. Between 1907 and 1921, the Gaiety staged over 200 plays, of which more than 100 were new. Horniman was committed to the promotion of unknown, local playwrights who became known as the 'Manchester School'. Their plays were based on the specific detail of Lancashire life, setting and language, especially depicting the working classes. They also espoused a frank depiction of sexuality and social reality not usually seen on the London stage.

With Stanley Houghton's *Hindle Wakes*, London reviewers patronisingly commented on 'the novelty of "rough tongued Lancashire ways" for its audiences', but it is significant that nearly one hundred years later, the play was chosen to reopen Manchester's Royal Exchange in 1998 after the IRA bombings a couple of years earlier, a gesture of pride in the city's history.[116] Fanny is a mill worker who shocks her employer's son by going away with him for the weekend, but refuses to marry him.

Love you? Good heavens, of course not! Why on earth should I love you? You were just someone to have a bit of fun with. You were an amusement – a lark. I'm a woman, and you were my little fancy.[117]

Houghton's heroine is from the same mould as other New Women heroines such as George Moore's *Esther Waters* (1894) and H. G. Wells's *Ann Veronica* (1909), and a reversal of the 'fallen woman' theme so beloved by earlier writers. The title alludes to the need for the town – Hindle – to awaken to changes taking place in society, a major motif of the New Drama.

Other figures in the Manchester School included Allan Monkhouse who was a critic for the *Manchester Guardian* and had a long career in the literary world. His one-act plays – *The Choice* (1910), *Mary Broome* (1911) and *Nothing Like Leather* (1913) – deal with class, marriage and female emancipation. In *Mary Broome*, for example, the eponymous heroine is a housemaid who becomes pregnant by the son of her middle-class employer. Her pragmatic nature is contrasted with the dilettantism of the man she is forced to marry, and once she has overcome the tragedy of their baby's death, she leaves him to emigrate to Canada with a more suitable man. As with *Hindle Wakes*, the forthright treatment of sexuality and the rejection of conventional morality was a shock to some reviewers, but popular with the local audience who admired the advocacy of working-class common sense.

Harold Brighouse also wrote social problem dramas such as *The Price of Coal* (1911) and *Lonesome Like* (1911), although his most famous work, *Hobson's Choice*, was not produced by Horniman; it is also more conservative than others of the same ilk. Set in Salford during the 1880s, Brighouse's tale of a patriarchal shoe-shop owner, his ambitious daughter, and an impecunious cobbler, was rejected by London theatres which were prejudiced against regional drama, and only found success there after a premiere in New York. It shows a shift between the generations and the genders, turning the daughter, Maggie, into the most powerful figure in the play. In a reverse of the Pygmalion and Galatea myth, it is Maggie who says of Willie Mossop 'You're the man I've made you and I'm proud'.[118] However, making the play a costume drama rather than setting it in the present day lessens any contemporary commentary and places it firmly within Victorian values of thrift and hard work. Even Maggie's financial acumen and forthright nature is undercut when at the end of the play when her newly ambitious husband takes over the running of the business, once again perpetuating the patriarchal system.

Eventually the Gaiety Theatre ran into financial difficulties. It was only a small company with a comparatively small auditorium, therefore plays tended to run weekly rather than twice-weekly. Even though a season took place at the Coronet Theatre in Notting Hill, the company eventually disbanded in 1917, but not before helping to provide drama for working-class audiences and furthering the careers of figures such as Basil Dean who went on to set up the Liverpool Repertory Theatre in 1911, and inspiring Barry Jackson and John Drinkwater to open the Birmingham Repertory Theatre in 1913. Like Manchester, Birmingham was a city that was politically active, and had gained its wealth from industry and manufacturing, using this to provide utilities and services for its inhabitants. The difference was that the Birmingham Rep had its roots in amateur theatre, part of the industry that would flourish during and after the First World War.

Conclusion

The Edwardian era capitalised on the social, scientific and industrial advances of the previous century, retaining the belief that Britain was the most powerful country in the world. Exhibitions and pageants promoted the power of the monarchy and the trade links which underpinned the might of the Empire. Visual signs of prosperity could be seen in the growth of consumer goods and the wide range of leisure activities available to the socially mobile population. The view after 1914 that the Edwardian era represented the last halcyon years of England was at odds with tragedies such as the Boer Wars and the sinking of the Titanic in 1912, and did not reflect the fact that this was an increasingly politicised period for ordinary people. The fight for female enfranchisement had become steadily more militant, leading to clashes with the police, enforced prison feeding and even death. Unions grew stronger and a series of strikes threatened to bring the country to a standstill. Workers clashed with the establishment as they demanded better conditions and rates of pay. Above all, there was a growing debate about the need for a new political system, as evidenced by the foundation of the Labour Party and the Fabian Society.

The first fourteen years of the twentieth century turned the British theatre into a market-led industry, presided over by that remnant of the Victorian period, the actor-manager, but continental practices also impacted upon the rise of repertory theatre, as in Granville Barker's interest in an ensemble company, with its less formal play-going rituals. Genre, subject matter and dramatic technique were informed by Ibsen's social problem plays, Strindberg's psycho-dramas and Chekhov's naturalism, and wider artistic movements – abstraction, futurism, modernism – invigorated the theatrical renaissance taking place at this time.

The interest in more avant-garde or political theatre reflected 'minorities' such as the working classes who were increasingly demanding representation, and while this continued to happen in forms like the music hall and revues, it also pointed the way towards the workers' theatre of the interwar period. The move away from the metropolis had begun with regional theatres beginning in other cities across the country: Glasgow, Liverpool, Birmingham, Manchester, Bristol and Dublin all had their repertory theatres by the start of the First World War, and did much to break down the boundaries between professional and non-professional theatre. It was largely the work of women theatre managers like Annie Horniman that paved way to subsidised national theatres as we know them today, which combine classical and experimental drama, and helped to democratise the industry. This was also the period that women in the theatre engaged with their former role 'as troubling presence and speaking absence' with suffrage dramatists rewriting conventional history so as to include female voices.[119]

Technology had an undoubted effect on the development of theatre, both in positive ways and in ones that were more troubling. Short documentaries had started to be shown in vaudeville halls from 1896 onwards, and initially there was no awareness that film would grow into the mass cultural form of the twentieth century which would involve many playhouses being turned into cinemas. But it also led to a creative interplay between theatre and cinema as many plays were filmed for a mass audience, and actors moved between the two different media. The Victorian spectacle, aided and abetted by developments in scenography, electricity and machinery, continued during the Edwardian era, but ironically spawned a backlash in terms of a search for theatrical authenticity, as in Poel's Elizabethan Stage Society, and the 'total theatre' of Craig.

The outbreak of war in the Balkans in 1912 presaged an arms race with Germany, culminating in the tragedy of the Great War in which over two million were killed or wounded. Along with other forms of media, the theatre would struggle to find a language with which to convey society's manifestations of loss and despair. Ever-fearful of losing control of public opinion, the government would do all it could to promote the war message, but as we shall see, some of those in the theatrical world began to challenge the official view as the full horror of the conflict unfolded.

CHAPTER 2
FIRST WORLD WAR THEATRE

Introduction

When Britain declared war against Germany on 4 August 1914 and on Austria-Hungary on 10 August, it was meant to be the 'war to end all wars', with many commentators expecting it to be over by Christmas. The ensuing conflict brought about huge social and political changes for this country and across the world. It 'not only wreaked immediate devastation on lives, wealth, and established political power. It also sparked the Russian Revolution and civil war (1917–21), precipitated the decline of Western imperialism, and was an indirect cause of the rise of fascism and the worldwide economic Depression of the 1930s'.[1] For the most part, the divisions that had almost brought Britain to its knees in 1914 were healed as workers, suffragettes and political parties joined together in a common cause. Socialism and social reform began to be seen as anti-patriotic because it was deviating resources from the war effort, and pacifism was equally viewed in vitriolic terms.

Frank Field argues that while the continent was fully primed for war, it came as a shock to this country.[2] Some did not take it seriously, with George Bernard Shaw for one confidently stated that 'the right line to take about war was either to treat it neither as a calamity nor as glory, but simply as "an unbearable piece of damned nonsense"'.[3] However, it can equally be contested that Britain had been preparing for a major conflict long before the event actually occurred. Invasion literature had been common since the latter part of the nineteenth century, but this grew during the Edwardian period as Germany began to be considered more of a threat. These works were, as Paul Fussell says, 'designed to convey a *frisson* by persuading the middle-class audience that the Empire was being carved up by Continental powers as a result of democracy, sentimentality, and the deteriorating physique of the lower orders'.[4] Erskine Childers's *The Riddle of the Sands* (1903), William Le Queux's *The Invasion of 1910* (1906) and Guy du Maurier's melodrama *An Englishman's Home* (1909) all fit into this genre. The latter originally appeared anonymously, titled *A Patriot* and concerned the foreign invasion of a middle-class household, resulting in the father shooting a soldier and therefore to his own execution. It played to packed houses every night, and its message that Britain was unprepared for war, prompted a recruiting office for the Territorial Army to open in the theatre.

By the time that war broke out, the population was primed to defend its country: the remains of Victorian jingoism, the might of the British Empire, and a populist vision of war as noble and romantic meant that volunteerism was expected to be high. Indeed, at first the men of the country queued up to serve their country, and the belief prevailed that the country's healthy 'volunteerism demonstrated Britain's moral superiority over Germany'.[5] However, after much of the Regular Army had been decimated in the early years, conscription had to be introduced in 1916. Throughout Britain represented itself as 'drawn into a war not of its own making and was fighting for "Right"'.[6] It was the protector of countries less powerful than itself, like 'little Belgium' and of its own extensive colonies. At stake was the British way of life, which had to be preserved at all costs, and the image of itself as a world power. This was now being challenged by the strongest army in the world. It was therefore essential that the state drew its people together into a cohesive whole in order to fight this enemy, and culture was at the heart of this policy.

Theatre during the war

The stage had an essential part to play during the war. It underpinned the government's policies by engaging with everything 'from flag-waving to Hun-hating. It raised some millions for war funds. It stimulated patriotism and strengthened the faint-hearted. It cheered the armed forces on leave and the soldiers at the front. Above all, it kept the public in good spirits – a public upon whose morale the whole war effort depended'.[7] As Steve Nicholson's chapter in this book makes clear, propaganda and censorship were essential tools in this process, even if it would take the government a while to understand this.

When war was announced theatres were closed for a few weeks as the country prepared for mobilisation. A strange dichotomy occurred. On the one hand, far-sighted individuals believed that theatre was essential for the good of the country. As the Lord Mayor of Birmingham, Neville Chamberlain had once argued 'that the curing of the wounded was not merely an affair of drugs and dressing'; now as the first Director-General of the Ministry of

National Service he designated theatre as a restricted occupation, although employees still had to be available for essential work.[8] This mean that they were encouraged to register for National Service and theatre managers dissuaded from taking on younger male staff, but it did offer protection of a sort. On the other hand, and unlike other industries, the theatre was given no help by the government and struggled to keep going. Some arts theatres were forced to close down and several repertory theatres disappeared. The National Theatre movement was halted, and short runs were replaced by long ones that made experimentation more difficult. Performances used to be accompanied by an orchestra, but this tradition came to an end because of economic constraints and lack of manpower. There was a dramatic rise in theatre rents; paper rationing, limited advertising and rationing made theatre less appealing; travel restrictions and shortage of accommodation led to touring difficulties, causing audiences to fluctuate; enforced blackouts and curfews were imposed, meaning that theatres in large cities such as London had to shut early with sometimes only matinees being put on; and there was a chronic shortage of new plays because dramatists were in the services. In 1916 the government introduced an Entertainment Tax as a source of extra revenue, demanding a percentage of box office takings from theatres, music halls and cinemas, immediately squeezing the profit margin of venues. Concomitantly, theatres started to open on a Sunday in order to recoup their losses, leading to a storm of protest from those who felt that this was inappropriate. Salaries were also slashed and seat prices reduced until it was realised that people were prepared to pay well for their entertainment and that a new audience was opening up. Unsurprisingly, as Gordon Williams notes, 'It is indicative of the level of wartime exploitation that the deeply conservative acting profession became unionized by the end of 1918'.[9]

Anxious theatre managers provided a diet of inexpensive revivals and light entertainment to protect their revenues, and appeal to soldiers on leave and female workers. Evening dress was no longer *de rigueur* and it was quite acceptable for men and women to wear their service uniforms. This geographically mobile audience craved more stimulation than before, not just to counteract the drabness and trauma of trench warfare, but as a way of voicing their fears and concerns. Thus, while Walter W. Ellis's farce, *A Little Bit of Fluff* ran for 1,241 performances from 1915, this title was not representative of the vast majority of theatre at this time. Instead there was a remarkable diversity of productions on offer, which varied from exotic spectacle on the West End stage to ad hoc performances on the front line. By

1918 manager and playwright Herbert Farjeon could confidently state that theatre-going had 'become an integral part of national life'.[10]

Propaganda and censorship

Once it was obvious that the war would not be over by Christmas, there was an increase in state control so as to avoid total insurrection. Advertisements appeared in newspapers exhorting civilians to keep the troops cheerful by sending encouraging words to the front, and to not to think that they knew better than Field Marshall Douglas Haig who commanded the British Expeditionary Force from 1915 until the end of the war. Haig also issued his 'Backs to the Wall' Orders of the Day, threatening to shoot any soldier who disobeyed orders.[11]

At the start of the war the country had no propaganda agencies in place. The Liberal MP Charles Masterman took over responsibility for this, but it was not until 1918 that these were centralised under the auspices of the Ministry of Information. Philip Taylor has made the point that 'censorship and propaganda are Siamese twins, inseparable and inextricable'.[12] Both were carried out during the First World War in both overt and covert ways, functioning mainly through visual or aural forms (advertising, art, literature, film, song). The pre-eminence of Britain was stressed, Germanophobia whipped up and the populace warned against the dangers of anti-patriotic behaviour. However, if at the beginning of the war propaganda was important to get the country on board, boost enlistment and provide funds, by the end it was unclear as to whether it had actually worked. Most importantly, many felt that the realities of war had been deliberately misrepresented and it had all been a pointless tragedy. This was a view that would only grow during the next two decades.

As the war progressed, plays became more prone to being banned or censored, if there were 'inappropriate' comments about the war. Visual or linguistic references to Zeppelin raids, bombs, wounded soldiers and trench warfare, were more frequently removed after 1916 once the full horror of the war had become apparent: its reality had become too much to be replicated on stage. Also, as L. J. Collins observes, 'playwrights shied away from the more contentious problems created by the war; for example, what was to be done with the crippled and the maimed'? In fact, they were invariably 'treated as heroes rather than the victims of war', thereby upholding initial views of the conflict as a form of nobility or sacrifice.[13]

Even non-war plays were changed so as not to offend audiences, as with the 1915 revival of George du Maurier's *Trilby* in which the heroine triumphs over the evil Svengali.

Interestingly, given the stipulations of censorship, theatre managers' trepidation, and the government's need to keep up morale, some playwrights did manage to present various forms of violence, or mentioned the more disagreeable aspects of conflict. Women and children are threatened with or receive actual bodily harm; soldiers are humiliated and tortured, gassed and shell-shocked. Soldiers are terrified, prone to desertion, or view the Germans not as enemies but human beings like themselves. Attempts to contain and control were not always successful, and this was especially true of genres which were open to spontaneity, such as revues, or theatre in the services. Non-commercial or non-traditional venues afforded the best opportunities to question the war or expose the brutality of war. Ad hoc performances put on in smaller establishments got around the censor by adding last minute topical sketches that mocked political figures, the British Empire, the class system and other elements of society originally held in high esteem. This was theatre at its subversive best.

Popular genres

Revues

The musical revue started in Paris during the 1840s as a means to 'review' the events of the past year. As the genre developed, it differed from variety in that the sketches were linked together by a common theme. The impresario André Charlot popularised the form in this country when he brought it in 1912 to a London audience already attuned to music hall, variety and girlie shows: *The Bing Boys are Here* (1916) at London's Alhambra, and its spin-offs – *The Bing Girls are There* (1917) and *The Bing Boys on Broadway* (1918) – were exceedingly popular. The elastic, hybrid genre of the revue absorbed avant-garde influences from the Continent. It was also popularised American music, especially ragtime: 'The Cakewalk' became a dance craze in 1903 when it reached these shores in the first black revue, *In Dahomey*. Some of the biggest stars of the time – George Robey, Gertrude Lawrence, Noël Coward, Jack Buchanan – made their names in revues. In this way it crossed conventional boundaries of commercial/alternative stages, incorporating both the entertainingly inconsequential and the savagely critical; the latter was especially part of the *revues intimes*, held in small venues which fostered a close relationship between performer and audience.

The lack of footlights demarcating the stage space, artistes' use of the ad lib, and the free-wheeling between public information and personal gossip, resulted in a theatrically destabilising effect that helped erase the fourth wall tradition and the concept of stage verisimilitude. Moreover, the revue's episodic and fragmentary structure reflected the insecurity of the times, and the informal and intimate style enacted a break with past hierarchies. This 'theatre of disintegration', as Gordon Williams categorises it, was 'part of that fragmented modernist consciousness which found grisly expression in those fragments shipped endlessly back from France'.[14] When millions of men, under orders from 'rational' figures of authority, were mutilated and killed in the trenches, it was to be expected that there was a disjuncture between form and logic. The genre can also be seen as modernist, with its rejection of a conventional means of organising art for one that was more abstract and questioned 'truisms' about the nature of reality. Additionally, there are connections with Dadaism, a movement that possibly started in neutral Switzerland in 1916 at the Cabaret Voltaire, and born out of the horror of the First World War; reason was eschewed in favour of irrationality and the bourgeois rejected for the radical left. As we shall see the revues of this time would eventually lead to the more politically charged theatre of the 1920s and 1930s.

During the war, revues could be tub-thumpingly patriotic. Harry Lauder's popular Scottish turn was milked in a 1916 piece where he sang 'The Laddies who Fought and Won', followed by an appearance of a contingent of the Scots' Guards. However, the satirical origins of the revue were also highly prevalent, teetering at times towards a political radicalism that was sometimes missing elsewhere on the stage. Even in more traditional theatres such as the Hippodrome, a revue like *Flying Colours* (1916) gently pointed out the hypocrisy of the upper classes turning up at the Guildhall in their Rolls Royces to lecture the working classes on how to economise.

The dirty primitiveness of trench warfare was rarely represented except in all but the most comic kind of way. The revue sketch 'Bairnsfatherland' in *Flying Colours* (1916) was based on a cartoon strip for the *Bystander* by Captain Bruce Bairnsfather: these weekly 'Fragments from France' followed the adventures of Old Bill, a grumpy soldier sporting a balaclava and a walrus moustache, and his friends Bert and Alf. The audience, the reviewer observes, 'contained quite an unusual proportion of khaki' and they 'caught every point immediately'.[15] It was viewed as a 'lifelike scene from the trenches', flanked by attractive and 'normal' scenes representing a lavish fashion show, sunny Spain and a riding lesson. Bairnsfather also wrote *The Better 'Ole*, which got its title from a line by Old Bill. Turning to a moaning soldier as they sit in a trench under bombardment, he says, 'Well, if you know of a better ole go to it.' Staged by Charles B. Cochran in 1917, its fusion of cynicism, stoicism and dark humour encapsulated the zeitgeist. One of the audience members said 'The play was fully of the dirty, noisy scenes I knew well, and hate so heartily', but he – like other combatants – was unable to stay away, drawn by the recreation of a world he could never forget.[16]

Spectacles

The opposite of the *revues intimes* were the large-scale spectacles, also sometimes confusingly called revues. Technological innovations in lighting, engineering and mechanics had boosted Britain's place at the forefront of industry, and theatre managers vied with one another to take advantage of this. As mentioned in the previous chapter, London's Hippodrome had already become famous for its aquatic spectacles during the Edwardian period. Even under wartime conditions, this continued. Albert P. de Courville's specials were lavish in scale, and included a liner leaving the docks (*Joy-Land*, 1915), and an ice-skating championship (*Razzle-Dazzle*, 1916). Pantomimes also gave an excuse for utilising new stage effects to excite the audience, as in the use of mechanised figures and electric airships in Liverpool's *Red Riding Hood* (1917) and the Venetian setting and clever diving apparatus in the Palladium's *Cinderella* (1915).

This was the first war to be waged via a whole raft of new technology. In 1906 SS *Dreadnought* was built in this country and gave its name to a succession of big-gun battleships. Other advances included the use of tanks, aeroplanes and submarines, and therefore it is unsurprising that a different form of spectacle was enacted on stage. There had long been a tradition of theatrically rendering the dealings of the army and navy, especially during the Napoleonic and Crimean wars. By the Boer War this had declined but from 1914 this custom was drawn upon once more to display the nation's moral and martial supremacy. As the Navy was the most important means of protecting the country and indeed the Empire, it was inevitable that there would be a lot of plays written about this part of the services in this war. This showed a resolute refusal to bow to restrictions imposed because of the German offensive, and visual and aural symbols gave the impression of

British Theatre and Performance 1900–1950

an invincible nation that was powerful enough to stage such splendours at a time like this.

The regional theatres were as much involved in this as the West End. Gordon Williams quotes that the Newport Lyceum's production of *Beauty and the Beast* during the first Christmas of the war 'boomed a message of solidarity as allied troops "pass through the mist in scenes of battle, the wounded attended by boy Scouts and Red Cross nurses, and then in the blaze of day group themselves around Britannia as, with great guns pointed seaward, she guards the white cliffs of Old England"'.[17] *Tom, the Piper* (Princess, Glasgow, 1916) showed a German ship being blown up by a British Dreadnought and, in the last stages of the war – almost as a cry of victory – a replica of the HMS Queen Elizabeth, with guns blazing, appeared in Derby's *Dick Whittington* (1918). The Battle of Jutland was re-enacted in Frank Price's *Mother's Sailor Boy* (1916) and Seymour Hicks and Arthur Shirley's *Jolly Jack Tar* (1918) showed the Zeebrugge raid, when Britain attempted to block the Belgium port.

On Christmas Eve 1914 the first German bomb was dropped from an aeroplane near Dover Castle, and for the first time people in this country had to contend with a further mode of attack. Frequent Zeppelin raids augmented this, with a few even damaging theatres, including London's Strand and the Lyceum in 1915. Although the vast majority of civilian deaths resulted from air raid, this caused nowhere near the havoc that air raids did during the next war. Nevertheless people wanted to witness these remarkable occurrences with their own eyes and left the theatres to watch the skies; thus, the staging of a Zeppelin raid in Edgar Wallace's *The Enemy in our Midst* (1915) further added to a sense of theatre as spectacle.

Musicals

Musicals tended to fall into three categories at this time: the exotic, the romantic and the comic, although these often overlapped. Nijinsky's appearance on the 1913 London stage in *L'Apres Midi d'un Faune* had fed the appetite for the exotic, and Oriental influences can be seen in the subject matter of Harry M. Vernon and Harold Owen's *Mr Wu* (1913) and the costumes for Shaw's *Pygmalion*. Oscar Asche had previously staged *Kismet* (1911) and then took on *Mameena* (1914), based on H. Rider Haggard's novel about the Zulu wars, *A Child of the Storm* (1913). While *Mameena* was well received, the outbreak of war meant that it was not a financial success; the theatre suffered during those early, uncertain months. In contrast, Asche's next production was the smash hit of the First World War.

66

Opening at His Majesty's Theatre at the height of the hostilities in August 1916, Asche's reworking of *Ali Baba and the Forty Thieves* – *Chu Chin Chow* (1916) was undoubtedly a theatrical phenomenon, with 2,235 performances: this made it the longest running production in this country until Noël Coward's *Blithe Spirit* in 1941.[18] It was filmed several times, toured the provinces for decades, and revived in London during the next war. Audiences flocked to see it, including those who made the trip to London for the first time. Soldiers who had been used to the arid landscape of the battle fields of France feasted their eyes on the dazzling extravagance. The classical scholar, F. Hadland Davis suggested shortly after the production came to an end in 1921 that 'thousands of people have been attracted by "Chu Chin Chow" partly because that play was such a happy contrast to the life we lived during the war and the life we live now, when we are looking in vain for the fruits of victory'.[19] Some critics gave grudging admiration to Asche's spectacle: 'the really damnable thing about the play was its complete atrophy of drama . . . At least it made no pretence to be anything else than it was, namely, an honest shot at the negation of theatrical intellect and the apotheosis of show'.[20]

Asche took the lead role of Abu Hasan, leader of the forty thieves, who break into a rich merchant's palace in order to rob him, and is undone by the merchant's poor brother, Ali Baba. The plot was a minor element, though. *Chu Chin Chow* was a mixture of slapstick comedy, double entendres, catchy tunes penned by Frederic Norton and the 'realism' of live camels, donkeys and snakes. In other words, it was a revue with elements of music hall. Set scenes – The Palace of Kasim Baba, the Slave market of El Kabar, the Fashion Show of Mubabah – were enriched by elaborate settings and scantily clad men and women. Interestingly, later press photographs depict the actresses as if they were fashion plates, further emphasising the commodification of the female body mentioned in the last chapter.

Audiences, entranced by cinema, found that this 'Eastern Revue' emulated the celerity and exoticism of silent movies directed by the likes of D. W. Griffith and Cecil B. DeMille. As with other Classical and Biblical spectaculars, though, this was an inauthentic portrait of the East, with visual and linguistic references made to Cathay, Persia, Egypt, Java, India and China. However, such plays continued to enhance the notion of Britain as head of a vast Empire.

Asche also produced *The Maid of the Mountains*, an operetta romance set among the bandits, which ran for 1,352 performances in the West End, and revived successfully at several points over the next three decades. The songs were deliberately uplifting – 'Love Will find a Way', 'A Paradise for Two', 'My Life is Love' – reminding its audiences of better times ahead. Other popular shows were *Theodore & Co* (1916), *The Boy* and *Yes, Uncle!* (both 1917).

One of the biggest stars was French singer Alice Delysia, who had worked at the Moulin Rouge and Folies Bergère in Paris. In 1913 she was brought to England by Charles B. Cochran to appear in his revues and operettas during the war years. Her song from Cochran's first revue, *Odds and Ends* (1914) – 'We don't want to lose you but we think you should go' – was a major hit for obvious reasons. If the French-born Delysia was acceptable, there were complaints about what was seen as the anti-patriotic encroachment of the American musical comedy, also notable in the post-1945 period. However, Laurette Taylor won the hearts of British audiences in J. Hartley Manners's *Peg o' My Heart* (1914) as did Renée Kelly in *Daddy Long-Legs* (1916), an adaptation of Jean Webster's 1912 novel.

Variety

The last gasp of music hall in Britain was during the war years as the legitimate and illegitimate theatres became increasingly blurred. There was still the 'old style' music hall circuit, but there were also the variety palaces of London's West End, with their superior staging facilities. Gordon Williams describes these as providing 'a theatre of illusion in more senses than one, its cosiness of outlook reflecting that optimistic belief in an expanding industrial economy which, undeterred by war and recession, had continued blithely until 1914'.[21] Given its flexible format – 'turns' that could easily be swapped around or withdrawn – music hall was also suitable for entertainment during the war years, when insecurity of travel, accommodation and availability was at its height.

Harry Lauder, George Robey, Clara Butt, and many other entertainers 'did their bit' by working for charities to raise funds and to encourage others to enlist. Music hall impresario Fred Karno gave his name to a trench song, the first line of which was 'We are Fred Karno's army, we are the ragtime infantry'. The term came to be used by soldiers who were suffering from official disorganisation to mean anything chaotic. Karno also gave performance opportunities to film stars Charlie Chaplin, Stan Laurel and Will Hay, ironic given the demise of the music hall through the rise of cinema.

As in the earlier decade, the female form was used to bring in audiences, especially attractive to servicemen starved of the opposite sex. Inevitably, water shows were popular on the halls, as with Daphne's Diving Belles. William Fowell's *The Lovely Limit* included a bevy of swimming costumed beauties, as did the Ray Brothers' *Beauty Baths* (both 1915). Even though such performances could be patriotic – the latter chorus girls appeared on a facsimile of the HMS *Lion* – they also drew the attention of the censor. It was a fine line to preserve the morality of the troops and to ensure that they were kept entertained. Certainly, although the appearance of stage door Johnnies – men who courted actresses – in the vicinity of theatres was becoming something of a national scandal, material that would once have been considered *de trop* was now far more acceptable. Edward Knoblock suggests that mothers were now happy to laugh at off-colour jokes with their sons: 'What did anything matter so long as the dear boy was amused? They might very soon be informed officially that they were never to hear him laugh again.'[22] Thus music hall stars such as Marie Lloyd and George Robey – previously thought of as vulgar – started to appeal to a new audience.

Songs in the music halls helped to reinforce the point that the men and women of this country should sacrifice themselves to save a Britain that was worth salvaging: some of the most famous were Ivor Novello's 'Keep the Home Fires Burning', and others like 'It's a Long Way to Tipperary', 'Your King and Country Want You' (all 1914), 'All the Boys in Khaki get the Nice Girls' and 'Pack up Your Troubles' (both 1915). As Jay Winter points out, soldiers 'could (and did) put up with the awfulness of trench warfare in part because of their commitment to the world they had left behind, a world conjured up in vivid terms by popular entertainment'.[23]

The music hall can be seen as one of the most jingoistic genres of the period. John MacKenzie has noted that the Victorian music hall 'reflected the dominant imperial ethos of the day in topical and chauvinistic songs, royal fervour, and patriotic tableaux'.[24] During the Boer war John A. Hobson had written *The Psychology of Jingoism* (1901), a blistering attack on the state's use of propaganda in order to manipulate its people into believing this was a just and right war. As Williams explains, Hobson realised that if the music hall was entertainment for the masses, it could also be used to inculcate the official line. Williams summarises, 'since the halls presented ideas of national or imperial destiny, coupled with distrust of non-Britishers, the shift into war mode required only an addition of particularity'.[25] This can be borne out by the First World War, when the genre was utilised to show off Britain's power, and to extol audiences to remember that the fate of the colonies depended on this country winning the war.

Nevertheless, the oppositional argument can be proffered that the music hall continued its position as an 'illegitimate' form by presenting more subversive commentary. As with entertainment devised by the troops, variety acts could be cutting about those in authority. These include the extravagance of the higher classes in Michael Morton's *My Superior Officer* and Walter Ellis's *Too Late* (both 1916), and economic exploitation in Ellis's *Profiteer* (1917) and J. D. Beresford and Kenneth Richmond's *Howard and Son* (1918).[26] An oft-held belief by those at the front line was that those at home would not be able to understand the experiences they had been through, and there was also concern that the war was being trivialised in some quarters. For example, songs such as Vesta Tilley's 'I've got a Bit of a Blighty One' (1916), ticking off soldiers for pretending their wounds were bad enough to be sent home, is despondently mocked by Siegfried Sassoon's poem, 'Blighters':

I'd like to see a Tank come down the stalls,

Lurching to rag-time tunes, or 'Home sweet Home',

And there'd be no more jokes in Music-halls

To mock the riddled corpses round Bapaume.[27]

Patriotic plays

The Defence of the Realm Act (1914) made it an offence to directly oppose the war or in other ways cause alarm to the population. Demonstrating commitment to the cause was essential at every level of society, and the theatre was swept along by this jingoistic hysteria, especially in the first couple of months; this extended to refusing to put on works by 'enemy' playwrights. Gordon Williams states that: 'If hitherto the theatre had contributed little enough towards producing a juster society, it now played a conspicuous part in creating a warmongering one; and in the most direct way it turned many young men from civilians into soldiers.'[28] At times this could be subtle; at other times it was quite blatant. Even before men saw plays with propagandist subject matter, they had been met with enlistment placards at the entrances to theatres, and one theatre's safety curtain challenged its audience: 'The men of England are the safety curtain that shields our country from death and worse than death. Are you part of that khaki safety curtain? If not, why not'?[29] Significantly, Allan Monkhouse's discussion piece about whether or not to enlist was titled *Shamed Life* (1916); away from the frenzy of the war, his 1923 play was ironically titled *The Conquering Hero*. In this, the protagonist is torn between public duty and personal feeling as his mother protects him from the pressure of others. Cowardice, bravery and fear are all examined, and although the play ends with Claude agreeing to enlist, there is also a suggestion that he is yet another young man to be sacrificed to the war juggernaut.

Theatres across the country held recruitment meetings, with dignitaries making appearances to make speeches. Some variety artistes even made recruitment part of their acts, encouraging men to come up on stage and do their duty for their country. Actors themselves were fearful of being handed the 'white feather', a sign of cowardice, by a member of the audience, most of whom were in uniform; some theatre programmes went so far as to proclaim that 'Every Male Member of the Company has either actually served at the front, or has attested or is ineligible for Active Service'.[30]

Not joining up was seen as traitorous but also hinted at a lack of manhood as well; one of the most popular recruiting songs of the period was Clara Beck's 'I'll Make a Man of You'. Those who were unable to serve felt increasingly uncomfortable. Frank Pettingell, for example, penned a monologue called 'We Cannot All be Soldiers', justifying the numerous reasons why a man would not be able to serve his country.[31] By 1918 a large proportion of actors and actresses had been conscripted or were doing other forms of war work and there was a significant shortage of younger people working within the theatre.

Volunteer organisations such as the United Arts Force (UAF) were composed of members of the theatre world and put on plays and concerts to raise funds for the war. 'God Save the King' and 'Rule Britannia' were played at any and every opportunity, as were the national anthems of our allies. Tableaux were also utilised to show the political links between Britain, France and Russia, as in a 1914 show at the Middlesex Theatre.[32] Patriotic songs were inserted into musicals and revues, and even infiltrated the phenomenon of the day, *Chu Chin Chow*. Gordon Williams explains: 'As occasional intrusions, Baghdad's capture was celebrated by a party of Tommies entering an Arab street singing "Tipperary"; while on Armistice night, Lily Brayton as Britannia "released a peace dove into the auditorium, and robber chief Asche was transmogrified into John Bull"'.[33] Pantomimes played their part too; as convention demanded, contemporary songs like 'Take Me Back to Dear Old Blighty' were added, and there were numerous topical references to the war. So, in *Bo-Peep* at the Glasgow Coliseum in

1916, the villain is made to look like a German and the eponymous heroine says of Boy Blue:

He'll don khaki, and he'll face the foe.

For Britain's honour. He will strike a blow.[34]

Even those associated with the radical new drama of the Edwardian era produced work that contributed towards the war effort. Harley Granville Barker put on scenes from Thomas Hardy's epic Napoleonic drama, *The Dynasts* (1903–8), at the Kingsway Theatre in November 1914. This play was, Hardy himself tells us, 'staged mainly for patriotic and practical object[ive]s'.[35] British historical figures such as Wellington and Nelson in *The Dynasts*, and the eponymous *Drake* (1914) and *Disraeli* (1916) extolled past glories and a great nation that had to be preserved. At the beginning of the war the full horror of that cost had yet to be appreciated.

Early war drama stressed the importance of enlistment. At the start of the war, British forces were considerably lower than those on the continent, and while many responded immediately to posters demanding 'Britons: Lord Kitchener Wants You', heavy losses in battles like the Marne made it tragically obvious that thousands more needed to enlist if the country was not to lose the war in the first few months. J. E. McManus's *The Man Who Wouldn't* (1915) frames concerns about enlistment within a class debate. A middle-class solicitor says it is up to the working classes 'who haven't much to give up' to make the sacrifice for their country; his clerk suggests instead that it's 'the man who's lucky enough to have a successful career to look forward to . . . who ought to be first to enlist. He's got something to fight for'.[36] The solicitor changes his opinion after he dreams that his home has been invaded by the enemy.

That the whole country was expected to join forces to help the war effort is repeated in Mrs Horace Porter's *Patriotic Pence; or, The Home Fairy* (1917), further subtitled 'A Musical War Savings Play for Young People'. With lyrics written by George Bidder and music adapted from old English airs, the implication was that of the preservation of the past was needed to protect the future generation. Wives, mothers and girlfriends too were represented as cajoling their men folk to enlist, and deriding them when they refused, as in *The Sportsman*, *The Way to Win* and *The Call*, all of which were produced in 1915 at the height of fears about low enlistment.

Edward Knoblock's *A War Committee* (1915) depicts a group of aristocratic women more concerned with gossip than the war effort; Mrs

Arthur Hankey's *A House-Warming in War Time* (1917) pokes fun at the panic that ensues at a tea party when food is rationed; even though it does not mention the war Gertrude Jennings's 1919 play, *Waiting for the Bus*, is a satire on the selfish behaviour it had engendered.

Underlying all of these pro-war plays was a strong belief in authority; deference and conformity are qualities to be admired. Any character that disagreed with the government or refused to act in the common interest was shamed into falling back in line. Hoarders and profiteers are subjected to public ridicule. The soldier in Harold Holland's play, *True Values* (1918) lashes out at his sister and girlfriend for selfishly thinking about themselves rather than those fighting for the country, and it is obvious with whom the audience's sympathies should lie. Dreda Boyd's *John Feeney, Socialist* (1915) at the Glasgow Pavilion criticised those who concentrated on potential political ideology that could undermine the country. The fervent jingoism and blanket condemnation pacifism in Harold Owen's *Loyalty* (1917) was disliked by audiences and critics alike, but perhaps the most stinging of this type of play was Henry Arthur Jones's *The Pacifists* (1917). This was dedicated to 'the tribe of Wordsters, Pedants, Fanatics and Impossibilists who so rabidly pursued an ignoble peace that helped to provoke a disastrous war and are still seeking to bring about the tragedy of a delusive and abortive peace'.[37]

As well as denigrating those at home who were against the war, xenophobic representations of Germans were used to maintain hatred against the enemy, particularly focusing on the differences between the two countries and the superior morality of Britain. An early example, Lechmere Worrall and J. E. Harold-Terry's *The Man who Stayed at Home* (1914), contrasted the treachery of the Germans and the bravery of the British, but this was tame compared to later depictions of the enemy as brutal and sexually depraved. In Rudolf Besier and Sybil Spottiswoode's *Kultur at Home* (1916), a young Englishwoman is forced to leave her German husband when she realises how arrogant and militaristic he and his countrymen are; Count Otto threatens to burn down a nunnery and to torture and rape its inhabitants during Dorothy Mullord's *In the Hands of the Hun* (1915). This latter play came in for severe censorship, as did Myles Myddleton's *War, Red War* (1915) in which a German officer demands a baby's brains to be dashed out. As Steve Nicholson explores later on in this book, Britain had to provide a careful balance between rallying its populace and not overly antagonising of its foes. The heavy propaganda did not always go down well with critics and audiences. For example, a 1916 *Times* review of *Kultur at Home* suggested that 'there are playgoers for whom war plays exasperate, whose patriotism is not cheered but offended by a calculated appeal, who feel . . . that any actuality of the moment . . . is too heavy a burden for art to carry'.[38] More importantly, dramatists themselves used their work to warn about how propaganda incites chauvinism to the detriment of humanity; thus, E. Temple Thurstons's protagonist of *The Cost* (1914) correctly prophecies, 'Lies of the enemy's atrocities will be published in every paper to inflame our passions. We shall hear of all their brutalities, but none of our own. A month or two of that would kindle the beast in anyone'.[39]

Thrillers were formulaic, with the emphasis upon action rather than emotion, perhaps making them more palatable for wartime audiences. Further, the central figure of the gentlemanly, masculine hero upheld the notion that the country was indestructible because God was on its side. Sometimes this image was playfully deconstructed, as with the charming jewel thief, Raffles, who appeared in a series of books by E. W. Hornung, adapted for the stage in 1914.

The most common form of thriller, though, was that of the spy drama, with nearly hundred produced during the war. Initially this fed public hysteria about the threat of infiltration. L. J. Collins gives further reasons for the genre's popularity:

> the playwrights may have had little or no knowledge of fighting at the Front, and so any depiction of actual battle scenes was beyond their ken . . . the locale for a spy could be home-based and involve everyone . . . therefore appear[ing] more relevant and engaging to the home audience.[40]

Beyond this was the way in which spy thrillers could control and contain fears. It allowed dramatists to explore the clash between different ideologies, mainly democracy and fascism, and to consider such issues integral to war as patriotism, loyalty and treason. Because drama is liminal, the crime is able to be discovered, the perpetrator apprehended and punished, and the status quo restored, all within a few hours. Anxiety about traitors – the enemy within – was high, though not to the point of paranoia as in the next war. However, as a form of propaganda the spy thriller worked to allow the public to be on their mettle to root out insubordination, to cement national allegiance, and to demonise all enemies of the state. They were also a way of controlling the ever-pervasive terror of imminent death through lively re-enactment. More complexly, they can be seen to engage with a nexus of abstractions about truth, trust and duty, allowing audiences to shift or evade the moral ambiguities engendered by war.

This genre was a way of dealing with the political situation in a covert manner; plays could have a war theme, but not be set in or near a battlefield. Theatre critic W. A. Darlington stated that audiences suffered from a 'war-time neurosis . . . a resistance to realistic representation of the fear and suffering the population was enduring'.[41] Additionally, it can be suggested that there was no need to represent the war on stage when it was omnipresent. The spectacle of marching troops in the streets, the returning wounded at stations, and Zeppelin raids overhead, all gave rise to the view that the theatre of war was being enacted by the whole population on a daily basis. Thus the whole quality of the war had become performative, as Paul Fussell has astutely stated.[42]

Anti-war plays

Because of the propaganda machine and tightened censorship rules, anti-war messages were a rarity on the stage, at least until the next decade. An early piece was Thurston's aforementioned *The Cost*, which begins with Britain's ultimatum to Germany and proceeds to expose chauvinistic attitudes and ignorance about the real price being paid. In Marion Wentworth's *War Brides* one of the female characters revolts against being viewed as a 'breeding-machine' used to replenish the population in time for the next slaughter of war.[43] Unable to find a theatre backer brave enough to put this on in London, the play premiered in America in 1916 and was made into a film with the star Alla Nazimova.

For the new dramatists of the Edwardian period – John Galsworthy, Harley Granville Barker and J. M. Barrie – it was difficult to find the right language to deal with war in an adequate way, and they veered between 'doing their bit' and fulminating against the atrocities. John Galsworthy believed that the Edwardian England he loved was destroyed by the events of 1914–18. In *Defeat* (1917), a young German prostitute believes that the 'men who think themselves great and good' have succeeded in turning everyone into 'animals'.[44] Nevertheless he donated all the money he made at the time to the war effort, including *The Mob* which transferred from Manchester to London in March 1914: this portrayed a politician who runs counter to public opinion in decrying war, but is ruined because of these beliefs. J. M. Barrie's attempts to continue as before – *A Kiss for Cinderella* (1916) misguidedly puts topical comments about wartime conditions within a pantomime structure – ultimately proved fruitless. By 1917 he despondently stated that he had 'lost all sense I ever had of war being glorious. It is just unspeakably monstrous to me'.[45]

Many important writers, including Virginia and Leonard Woolf, Bertrand Russell, George Bernard Shaw and Rose Macaulay, were strongly anti-war, and the battle for and against pacifism became more sharply drawn as the government tried to assert the righteousness of war against a daily roll call of the dead and wounded.[46] On the stage, John Drinkwater's $X = 0$ (1917) tackled this subject, possibly escaping censorship because it was set in the Trojan War. This one-act blank verse drama has parallel scenes comparing the experiences of the Greeks and the Trojans, evidently meant to represent the British and Germans. The title refers to a moral paradox in which both sides cancel each other out. This is demonstrated when Pronax (Greek) kills Capys (Trojan) and Ilus (Trojan) kills Salvius (Greek). Moreover, Drinkwater infers that war involves not only the professional soldiers, here represented by Pronax and Ilus, but draws in and destroys the artist as well: Capys is a sculptor and Salvius a poet. Performed at the Birmingham Repertory Theatre, $X = 0$ provoked controversy. Drinkwater was embraced by the pacifists and conscientious objectors, but he was painted as someone who was acting against the interests of the country which may have had a detrimental effect on his subsequent career.

George Bernard Shaw's views on war changed according to historical events: he wrote his polemic *Common Sense about the War* in 1914 and became an anti-war protester, yet previously he had favoured military training and supported the Boer War, believing that it would provide a better system for the Afrikaners; he also wanted the defeat of the Central Powers in 1917. The First World War sharpened his satirical powers. His little-known work, *Augustus Does His Bit: A True-to-Life Farce* (1916) conveys the smugness and ineptitude of the military classes through the character of Lord Augustus Highcastle. *O'Flaherty V.C: A Recruiting Pamphlet* (1915) is an altogether more interesting proposal. It was not performed professionally until after the war had ended, although it received its unofficial première in 1917 in Belgium by the Royal Flying Corps. It had originally been commissioned to boost war recruitment from Ireland, but Shaw's almost treasonable take on this subject led to it being rejected by British officials. Irish recruitment was a deeply contentious issue. As mentioned in relation to the Abbey Theatre in the previous chapter, at this time Ireland was still undivided and counted as part of the United Kingdom, but many saw England as the enemy, not Germany. For the Northern Protestants the battle of the Somme, in which thousands of

Irishmen were killed or wounded, became a patriotic legend; for the South the 1916 Easter Rising made the complicity of Ireland in the war repugnant.

The eponymous O'Flaherty points this out to the obtuse British general, Sir Pearce:

It means different to me than what it would to you, sir. It means England and England's king to you. To me and the like of me, it means talking about the English just the way the English papers talk about the Boshes.

He goes on to refute the description of events as 'the greatest war ever fought', describing it instead as 'a big war; but that's not the same thing'.[47] Mary Luckhurst states that 'O'Flaherty's rejection of the term "great" underlines the ideological divide between the two: Britain's defeat would hardly be a matter of mourning to him. He may have been accorded a military honour, the Victoria Cross, for his "heroism" . . . but to the Irishman it is meaningless as a national symbol, and he is, at any rate, contemptuous of propagandistic discourses of comradeship, bravery and sacrifice.'[48]

Miles Malleson's 'D' Company (1915) and Black 'Ell (1916) also tested the boundaries of censorship, and copies of Malleson's work were seized by the War Office and Scotland Yard, an illustration of the state's regulation and control of public perceptions of the political situation. Malleson was one of only a minority of dramatists writing at this time about the war who had first-hand experience of the trenches; others waited until the 1920s and 1930s until writing of their experiences. He enlisted at the start, was invalided out a few months later, and became a confirmed pacifist. The one-act 'D' Company is uncrafted and honest. It was written towards the end of 1914 when Malleson was a territorial private stationed in Malta, but no knowledge as yet of the terrible loss of life still to come. It is set three months into the Great War when it is obvious that the soldiers 'are all very much English civilians under their khaki uniforms'.[49] Their ordinariness is stressed through the description of each soldier's previous life – coal delivery man, van-boy – and working-class banter. One man has enlisted because he was unemployed and his family gets money for him being in the army. In contrast, the Cambridge-educated Dennis Garside felt a duty towards his country. However, he is loath to kill anyone out of a sense of empathy:

I think if I aimed at a German officer, the obvious symbol of Prussian Militarism, I should be sure to miss him and hit a private who would probably be a Social Democrat with many an idea in common with

me, or a musician who has felt as I have over the passion of Wagner, or
a man who simply loathes fighting as much as I do, and has as many
friends behind him in his land as I in mine.

He advises aiming to miss, obviously not advice that the government would
share. The play ends with lights out after the soldiers have received letters
from home. Through the darkness comes 'howl after howl' of 'execration',
Malleson's dramatic expression of the horror of war.[50]

Black 'Ell was written after Malleson was invalided out of the army, and is again
a plea for a common humanity that was being ignored through warmongering.
Margery, a family friend, has absorbed the government's propaganda. She says
'it's terrific sport making shells' and mentions of a speaker that 'Dad used to
call him the biggest scoundrel unhung before the war – but it's wonderful how
it's brought all classes and people together'.[51] Pacifists are described as 'shirkers'
and beaten up for their views. Harold Gould returns from the front, having
been awarded a Distinguished Service Order (DSO) for killing six Germans
in battle: the paper describes him as 'Another Young Hero' (p. 43). Predating
Wilfred Owen's poem, 'Strange Meeting' and the bitter cynicism of 'Dulce et
Decorum est Pro Patria Mori', Malleson's fierce description of how Harold
killed a young German soldier conveys the reality underpinning the notion of
heroism. While the maid wishes 'black 'Ell' upon those who killed her young
man, it is evident that Harold is also in 'Ell and that both sides have made equal
sacrifices; understandably, this was a provocative claim at such a xenophobic
time (p. 54). Harold rejects his award, unable to understand how barbarism
can be celebrated. Malleson uses Harold as a mouthpiece to express his own
pacifist opinions about the bravery of the working classes and how they are
ignored until required to protect the country, that statesmen 'just sit at home
. . . and set us at each other', and he refuses to return to the trenches because 'I'm
going to stop at home and say it's all mad . . . I'm going to keep on saying it . . .
somebody's got to stop sometime . . . somebody's got to get sane again' (pp. 62,
64). Malleson evidently felt that no one was going to agree for the closing stage
directions are that Harold *'stands there, white, with clenched fists, and still the*
CURTAIN *comes quickly down and hides him'* (p. 64).

Theatre and the services

Entertainment for the troops was a hesitant process, initially pushed forward
by individuals such as Basil Dean and Lena Ashwell who were passionate

about its necessity. By the end of the war it had become much more organised and bureaucratic, and paved the way for developments from 1939 onwards. Commercial theatre managers feared that they would lose their 'khaki army' to camp theatres, but this did not happen. Soldiers visited the theatre on their way to and from the front, and the reproduction of the material shown there on the front line or in garrisons provided a healthy fluidity between the professional and amateur which would have a lasting effect on next three decades.

The theatre received little official recognition during the war, and sometimes lack of support as well, particularly at the beginning. In some quarters, as J. G. Fuller observes of concert parties, there was disapproval of 'such "luxuries" as out of keeping with a serious national effort; others maintained that, "such trifles made the men "soft" and unfitted them for hard trench warfare conditions".[52] However, it became increasingly obvious that troops had to be kept entertained, both at home and abroad. This was not just to boost morale or relieve the tedium of training or life in the trenches, but also to prevent drunkenness, sexual licentiousness and disorderly behaviour as well.

The first concert party to visit the front – headed by Seymour Hicks and his wife Ellaline Terriss – was left to their own devices, but gradually several external organisations were set up to provide distractions for the troops, including the Soldiers' Entertainment Fund. This consisted of professional and amateur performers, demonstrating how the conditions of war made possible such flouting of boundaries. More significantly, an Entertainments Department was set up by the armed services in 1916, with the assistance of Basil Dean. Dean had joined Annie Horniman's Gaiety Theatre as an actor, but then started working as a producer at Liverpool Repertory Theatre before moving to London. His war service as Captain in the Cheshire Regiment led to him becoming director of the Navy and Army Canteen Board, where he took charge of fifteen garrison theatres and several touring companies.[53] Between 1917 and 1918 Dean became head of War Office theatres, all of which would stand him in good stead for the next war when he ran the Entertainments National Service Association (ENSA), to be discussed later on in this book.

While the army initially took control of troop entertainment, Lena Ashwell was the figure who extended this on an unprecedented scale. As mentioned in Chapter 1, Ashwell managed the Kingsway and Savoy Theatres and was a founding member of the Actresses' Franchise League. Immediately war was declared, Ashwell like other suffragettes turned her energies to the war effort, starting the Women's Emergency Corps (WEC) with Decima and Eva Moore, and Eva Haverfield. She saw the positive qualities of entertainment for soldiers, and her stated aim was to provide as many camp theatres as possible. Receiving no interest from the government, she almost gave up hope until receiving a royal request from Her Highness Princess Helena Victoria, Chairman of the YMCA's Women's Auxiliary Committee, to organise a concert party to Le Havre. By February 1915 Ashwell's first self-funded concert party was touring France.[54] This became the Women's Theatre Camps Entertainment group, a repository to bring together the skills of female writers, actors and directors; fully aware of the political situation on female employment in the theatre industry, Ashwell also established the Three Arts Club Emergency Relief Fund. The group toured military bases throughout the country, and the Lena Ashwell Players performed for allied soldiers abroad; for this she was awarded the Order of the British Empire (OBE). By the end of the war repertory companies were established at several French towns and cities, including Étaples, Rouen, Le Havre and Paris.

The belief that troops only wanted 'pieces with pretty music, charming scenes and nothing at all to stir unworthy passions' showed a profound lack of awareness of the current situation, an outmoded morality, and an underlying fear of theatre's ability to disturb.[55] Lena Ashwell and others saw that soldiers were more than ready to embrace a wider range of genres and styles: new writing, Greek drama, Shakespeare, Sheridan and Shaw were all popular. Cicely Hamilton worked with Ashwell's company and with members of the Women's Auxiliary Army Corps (WAACs) at Abbeville to bring theatre to the trenches. It was here on the front line that her nativity play, *The Child in Flanders* (1917), was first performed. This one-act piece rewrites the masculine genres of trench drama and the religious play through her domestication of the nativity scene. Three soldiers from England, Australia and India seek refuge on the road to Arras. Their meeting with a French man and woman and their newborn baby transforms their lives in ways that are both sentimental and affecting. Gertrude Jennings was another stalwart of suffrage theatre, and she appeared in her own one-act plays across France. Acting in a war zone was challenging; often this was done outside, with limited props and costumes, or in a military hospital amid the wounded and dying. Productions could be halted at any moment, and danger was omnipresent.

Patients in military hospitals were visited by entertainers or, if they were well enough, taken on trips to the theatre and music hall, or to hotels where stars of the day performed for free. Neville Chamberlain believed that the soldiers 'needed to be given the opportunity to forget the experienced hardships, injuries and traumas of combat'; a cynic would suggest that this was of prime importance to a government who had to constantly replenish the front line.[56]

Theatre was even provided for foreign troops and Prisoners of War (POWs). L. J. Collins notes that this 'was employed as a means of relieving the tedium of incarceration. To the authorities, on the other hand, attendance at the theatre was seen as a "privilege" and was used as a means of maintaining control'.[57] If POWs were insubordinate or did not carry out their duties, access to entertainment was restricted or removed, but the activity of providing leisure pursuits was relayed to the media and public alike as symbolic of this country's 'civilised' behaviour. Like British troops, POWs also organised their own productions, which included a range of world drama, as well as the usual concert parties. Camps were often ideal places for honing theatrical skills, sometimes having proper stages and auditoria, backstage facilities and extended periods of leisure time. If theatre professionals were interred, then their knowledge and experience could be drawn upon to provide highly proficient productions. Once the Americans entered the war in 1917 the theatre was part of the means by which to cement relations between the two allies. On Sundays 'at the Palace Theatre in the West End, "a great entertainment would be given, to which American and British troops should be admitted free- and fraternize"', and US troops were entertained by some of the biggest stars of the time.[58]

Both at home and abroad troops provided their own entertainment, either rehearsed and with the blessing of officials, or by putting on impromptu performances. Their use of song, slapstick and satire all spoke of a life back home while also helping them to cope with their present-day situation. Gordon Williams has suggested the following: 'That soldiers were supposed not to like them [war plays] merely concealed unease that to represent war on a legitimate stage dominated by naturalistic convention risked jeopardizing official policy and public morale.'[59] Certainly the oft-repeated view that soldiers wanted to be diverted from what they had just left or were just about to head towards is undermined by the amount of theatrical activity taking place on the frontline and the number of plays written about the war as it was taking place: Heinz Kosok counts at least sixty plays with a war theme written between 1914 and 1918.[60] Indeed, Mary Luckhurst argues that 'Theatre was a major preoccupation with British soldiers in particular,

81

many looking to the intensity of performance as a way of making sense of their own identities as combatants in the theatre of war.'[61]

There are a number of reasons for this. The most deep-rooted, Paul Fussell perceptively observes, was that the theatre of/and war had profound psychological implications: "'Our own death is indeed unimaginable", Freud said in 1915, "and whenever we make the attempt to imagine it we can perceive that we really survive as spectators". It is thus the very hazard of military situations that turn them theatrical'.[62] Trauma at the events of which a soldier was forced to be part had turned him into an actor, which had the effect of splitting his identity in two.

Other reasons are more straightforward. The army, made up for the most part of civilians, and the working classes at that, brought an interest in popular entertainment with them 'which reminded soldiers that they were in uniform only "in parentheses", as it were'.[63] Populist genres were utilised, such as music hall, revues, comedy and pantomime, invoking nostalgia for familiar entertainments. Songs and sketches could help soldiers maintain a public, brave face if the horror of war could be presented in a comic light. Moreover, the difficulty of putting distressing experiences into words could be circumvented through visual imagery. These reminders of normality were particularly poignant given that many of the performances were given on the front line, within sight, sound and smell of shell fire and imminent danger of death; the juxtaposition of these two Theatres of War was encapsulated by Edmund Blunden in his 1928 poem 'The Concert Party: Busseboom':

To this new concert, white we stood;

Cold certainty held our breath;

While men in tunnels below Larch Wood

Were kicking men to death.[64]

J. G. Fuller notes that 'In the British army, private soldiers were painfully aware of their own vulnerability before authority'; equally, the officer ranks were fearful of indiscipline, desertion and even mutiny.[65] Unswerving loyalty, regardless of the personal consequences, was demanded and refusal to follow orders, however irrational or imprudent, was met with swift punishment and even execution. Theatre became one means of exerting an agency over such powerlessness, both in terms of the blind devotion to war and entrenched class hierarchies. In other words, such ephemeral performances – often not even transcribed or collated – can be seen in Gramscian terms as resistance to the hegemony. This public display of grievances helped to create camaraderie between soldiers via black humour and a common shared experience, also evidenced in *The Wipers Times*, an unofficial magazine of the trenches.

Given the large proportion of working-class soldiers in the trenches, it was inevitable that old class hostilities also surfaced, with privates sending up the senior ranks to the evident enjoyment of their comrades in the audience. More subversively, sketches were often openly critical of the ruling classes and governmental policy, the very nature of these types of performances allowing them to evade censorship. This can also be evinced in popular songs of the time. One well-known recruiting tune, 'Come, My Lad, and be a Soldier', was rewritten to include the cynical lines:

I don't want a bayonet in my stomach,

Nor my eye lids shot away,

For I am quite happy

With my mammy and my pappy –

So I wouldn't be a soldier any day.[66]

Performances contained not just black humour and satire, but risqué material as well, which became a way of channelling sexual urges. Men dressing up as women were a common part of the entertainment and first-hand accounts describe the lustful fancies they provoked, easily possible given that generally no attempt was made to caricature the gender reversal.[67] The idealisation of women – as glamorous and romantic – would certainly cause social unease when the soldiers returned home to find their womenfolk more set upon independence than falling back into pre-war roles. More interestingly, a concert party made up of soldiers openly called itself 'The Queerios', with a similar situation also occurring during the next war, as I mention on p. 158. There are also contemporary news reports of men masquerading as women outside of the theatrical arena. Their 'entrapment gives some indication of the anxiety about transgressive male sex/gender identity and behavior which the pressures of war might exert on secure notions of masculinist and patriarchal culture.'[68] The slippage between homosociality and homosexuality had already been presented for public view in the 1895 trials of Oscar Wilde, with Penny Farfan making the connection between this and the reception of female performers on pp. 216–19. Here we see how the fragility of gender and sexual roles was heightened by war. Non-enlisters were depicted as effeminate, those who were scared were 'soft', and deserters were not real men. There was strong evidence that both men and women fetishistically viewed uniforms, and large numbers of soldiers together without socially acceptable means of sexual release were perturbing to the authorities.

David A. Boxell astutely argues that 'The theatrical stage was the site where the pleasures and anxieties of same-sex relations could be made manifest, embodied and enacted as public spectacle for the gaze of those experiencing the crisis of male-male relations'.[69] The site and sight of the anachronistically named 'concert party' gave a carnivalesque quality to the proceedings, allowing for an overthrowing of social conventions: privates could mock officers, and men could play women. The paradox was that the ultimate homosocial activity that reinscribes manliness – war – could also bring about a rupture in notions of masculinity and femininity, heterosexuality and homosexuality. Boy actors in the theatre had long been associated with erotic desire, and men masquerading as women off-stage were perceived of as criminally deviant. Thus, as Boxell states, 'cross-dressing did not necessarily guarantee itself as a signifying practice of homosexuality; but certainly, by the time of the Great War, it could not be divorced from connotations of sexual perversity and aberrant desires'.[70]

Women and war

In his book, *A War Imagined*, Samuel Hynes observes the way in which a war is automatically drawn along gender lines, noting that 'A nation at war *is* a male nation', and that 'War – any war – is for women an inevitably diminishing experience. There is nothing like a war for demonstrating to women their inferior status'.[71] This statement achieves greater complexity when considering the First World War, given the inroads women had been attempting to make towards political visibility up until the start of the war. Although campaigning for the vote was for some women an end in itself, for others – as explained in the previous chapter – it was part of a wider goal involving the transformation of women's lives, and indeed the whole of society.

When the war started, some suffragettes became committed pacifists, joining a No-Conscription Fellowship in December 1914; others put their energies into the war effort. Emmeline and Christabel Pankhurst, for example, changed the slogan of the Women's Social and Political Union from 'Votes for Women' to 'For King, For Country, For Freedom', and the name of their newspaper from *The Suffragette* to *The Britannia*.

However, the suffrage movement did not end in 1914 and, as my Introduction intimated, the war brought the notion of the female citizen to the fore. In 1918 the Qualification of Women Act gave the vote to some women over thirty (superseded by the 1928 Equal Franchise Act), in 1919 the Sex Disqualification Removal Act opened up the professions for women, and Oxford University degrees were conferred on women a year later. Krisztina Robert argues that the war disrupted 'the spatial organisation of gendered work in prewar Britain . . . generating new, conflicting discourses of "home" and "front"', a process that would only increase during the Second World War, as Chapter 4 will further elucidate.[72]

As men recruited and were then conscripted, women moved into roles they had once inhabited, including as theatre managers, stage managers, directors and producers. It was women's participation in the war effort that helped to bring about their enfranchisement, and theatre in the 1920s and 1930s saw an increased concern with changing gender roles. During the first decade of the century, Cicely Hamilton, Lena Ashwell, Elizabeth Robins and others, had expressed their suffragette sympathies through dramatic means; as mentioned in the last chapter the Actresses' Franchise League was set up for this purpose. A number of women also had the opportunity to manage theatres, including Gladys Cooper who ran the Playhouse Theatre with Frank Curzon from 1917 to 1927, and then on her own until 1933.

Staging social change

The theatres' perceived lax morals had long been a concern, but this was heightened by the war and a need to ensure that the 'khaki army' was kept sexually and morally 'pure'. Nevertheless, while stage references to the war were stringently policed, by contrast there were higher levels of sexual content, innuendo, and nudity than ever before. This was due to a number of reasons: the need to keep audiences entertained, commercialisation of theatre which led to increased competition, and the influence of cinema, where films such as D. W. Griffiths's *Intolerance* (1916) and J. Gordon Edward's *Cleopatra* (1917) were testing the boundaries of acceptability. On stage, Clive Barker charts 'A riot of bedroom and pyjama plays includ[ing] *Please Get Married, A Sleepless Night, The Parlour, Bedroom and Bath, Up in Mabel's Room, The Dancer.*'[73] As we have seen with the music hall, double entendres and smutty jokes that might not have past muster before the war, especially in mixed company – were now to a certain degree forgivable in the drama of the time; soldiers fighting for their country needed a comic and sexual release and women working away from home and in conventionally male occupations became more used to such language.

All-female productions took place on occasion because of the lack of actors, only serving to fan the winds of change. These raised the profile of the female sex; as with Fred Karno's *All Women* (1915), which showed women in a series of gender subversion roles 'as munition workers, policemen, dustmen, carpenters, gardeners, &c'.[74] The depiction was not always flattering. A number of variety acts gave women overly masculine qualities contrasting with their more effeminate men folk; a case in point is Denton Spencer's *Ruling the Roost* which has a man's independent wife embarrass him by dressing 'in knickerbockers and Norfolk jacket', and in Israel Zangwill's *Too Much Money* (1918) the point was made that 'Man being so thoughtless as to make war, has left his place open to woman, and she has occupied it'.[75] H. F. Maltby's all-female farce, *Petticoats* (1917) similarly showed women taking control while the men were away. In pantomime, Gordon Williams reflects that the 'preference for the new woman as principal boy registers not only a shift away from Victorian taste but the different meaning which the war had attached to the role. As women increasingly took over jobs traditionally assigned to men, along with a more masculine style of dress to facilitate the work, the principal boy might reasonably symbolize that social reality'.[76]

Fears about female transgression were tempered by more conventional displays of the female body. As previously mentioned, aquatic spectacles, made possible by large water tanks under the stage, were already popular before the war. These shows, with their suggestive costumes and energetic gymnastics, frequently ran foul of the censor. However, it was the revue, *Odds and Ends*, which tested the boundaries of acceptability. This opened with a seductively sounding sketch titled 'My Lady's Undress'. In this the French actress Alice Delysia undressed behind a screen, displaying her upper thighs to the audience, until the stage was plunged into darkness. Once the censor visited, changes were made, but theatre managers continued to find new ways to attract servicemen on leave.

Such performances were grist to the mill for stage reformers; for example, in 1916 Arthur Winnington-Ingram, the Bishop of London, fulminated against 'lecherous and ... slimy plays', claiming that 'a tremendous percentage of [venereal] disease had been traced to certain music halls in London'.[77]

Another problem was the threat to the reputation of women who often left home for the first time to work for the war effort, or who found themselves living near an army camp. The Archbishop of York chaired the Committee on Illegitimate Births and, while the reality might not have been severe, the perception of it was a cause for concern. The subject had to be treated delicately in order to avoid censorship.

The social problem play was pushed to one side during the war years, but there were still a few notable exceptions. The ban on Ibsen's *Ghosts* was finally lifted in 1914, suggesting that society had progressed enough to finally be able to deal with the more difficult subject matter of the New Drama. *Era*'s theatre critic described it as leaving 'a more fervent desire to strike, in however a tiny way towards progress and enlightenment'.[78] Eugène Brieux's 1901 work *Les Avariés* was banned by the censor but reappeared as *Damaged Goods* in a theatre club especially created for its British premiere in 1917. The play was about a man who infects his pregnant wife and therefore son with syphilis. Interest in this reworking of Ibsen's theme surprisingly occurred during a time when the moral and physical fitness of the troops was important, and perhaps indicated a seismic shift in the depiction of sexuality on stage.

Again, the impact of the New Woman continued during this period, enhanced by the war and the continued push for enfranchisement. In Hubert Henry Davies's *Outcast* (1914) Ethel Levey rejects Gerald du Maurier's offer of marriage, choosing instead to be his mistress. Its popularity was ensured by being filmed several times over the next couple of decades, a further example of the symbiotic relationship between the theatre and the cinema. Again, the representation of the independent woman was not always flattering, however. In H. V. Esmond's play *The Law Divine* (1916) the wife is working so hard on her war committees that she neglects her husband, and it takes an air raid to bring her to her senses.

The Edwardian concern with class mobility and 'unsuitable' marriages also continued, as with Alfred Sutro's *The Marriage . . . Will Not Take Place* (1917). This explores a baronet's son potential entrapment into marriage by a musical actress; although she does not turn out to be the anticipated gold-digger, the piece taps into concerns about the fragility of class boundaries. As women pushed for legal rights during the suffrage movement and now were ever-omnipresent in the world of work, the fear was of even further social instability. This would continue during the interwar period with the appearance of the sexually liberated 'flapper' and the financially secure career woman.

Relationships between men and women often revolved around ethical ambiguities thrown up by the war. Thus a number of works focused on wives remarrying because they believed their husband had been killed; given the confusion in accounting for the missing and dead, this was inevitably of major concern, and featured the neurological impact of war such as shell shock and memory loss; self-sacrifice was also a key component, although this tended to be on the part of the woman rather than the man. This theme would become even more pronounced during the 1920s, as I will discuss in the next chapter.

Given the large numbers of working-class men who went to war, it is significant that several plays written at this time presented events from their perspective, stressing their loyalty and courage. At times representation of the working classes still centred on stereotypes, even with Annie Horniman's championing of dramatists such as Allan Monkhouse, Stanley Houghton and Harold Brighouse at the Gaiety Theatre, Manchester. There are some notable exceptions. Miles Malleson's work gave a considered study of the working-class soldier in the aforementioned 'D' Company and Black 'Ell; in 1938 he would go on to write about the Tolpuddle Martyrs in Six Men of Dorset. J. E. Harold Terry's General Post (1917) was part of a determined attempt to present the working-class experience during the war, even if this was portrayed in comic fashion. In this play Sir Dennys Broughton is against his daughter marrying Mr Smith, his tailor. The situation changes when Broughton and his son Alec join the army in lowly positions while Smith's bravery moves him rapidly through the military ranks. As Brigadier General, Smith is now considered a worthy addition to the family although snobbery against other working-class characters still prevails.

The start of the Russian Revolution in 1917 led to additional apprehension about the working classes getting beyond their 'natural station' in life, and most playwrights continued to privilege the upper and middle classes, and show approval for sharply demarcated class divisions. But it was obvious that those at the bottom of the social hierarchy were not necessarily going to toe the line, and when a character in Harold Owen's Loyalty makes the comment that 'The common people never have ruled . . . and never can' it was shouted down by audiences in the gallery.[79]

Shakespeare and war

If some productions looked to the future, particularly in terms of the depiction of women and class, others retreated to the past. Costume drama of the time presented a hagiographic view of the historical figures of 'this green and pleasant land', and it is no coincidence that William's Blake's poem 'Jerusalem', from whence this quote comes, was set to music by Sir Hubert Parry in 1916. As England's foremost cultural icon, it was obvious that Shakespeare would also be co-opted for the war cause. John Drinkwater, who had travelled to the Front with Lena Ashwell's Concert Party and was greatly influenced by William Morris and the Aesthetic Movement, asserted three days after the outbreak of war that the government should 'send companies [of actors] into the villages to play Shakespeare and the work of our other great and fine dramatists, and in less than a generation the people will require decent conditions . . . When we have passed through this present calamity, social reorganization will inevitably begin on a scale hitherto unknown'.[80] Belief in this moral and educative force of poetry and drama would become a driving force and instigator for change during and after the next war.

At the moment, though, this idealistic notion of Shakespeare as leading the way for 'social reorganisation' was lost in favour of his more obvious uses. Mary Packington's *Shakespeare for Merrie England* (1915) repackaged the dramatist's work to present a pro-war message. A German professor claims Shakespeare as a fellow countryman, but in a dream he has the dramatist's heroines chide him for his ridiculous viewpoint; it ends with Titania placing an ass's head on his shoulders. Specially written series such as *Shakespeare's War Cry*, by Frank Benson, were forthcoming, as were performances of plays chosen for their topical and pertinent observations about the nature of war and warfare. The line in G. R. Foss's 1917 production of *King John*, 'This England never did nor never shall/Lie at the proud foot of a conqueror', was noisily approved of by the audience and placed over the proscenium arch for the duration of the war. Henry V's patriotic speech at Harfleur also appealed:

Once more unto the breach, dear friends, once more

Or close the wall up with our English dead.

Obviously, the reception of this could differ, depending on whether it was performed before new recruits ready to do their duty, or battle-weary combatants.[81] Shakespeare also represented English literary traditionalism. He was 'increasingly perceived as high culture's answer to the threats of the new disorder [and] became a secure foundation against

European radicalism in the arts and an opportunity to recapture some pre-war certitude'.[82] The pseudo-historical realism in the style of Herbert Beerbohm Tree proved difficult to dislodge: while lengthy scene changes held up the action, audiences were dazzled by the spectacle of large casts and extravagant costumes.

Yet there was an attempt to redraw Shakespeare along more radical lines. In contrast to the previous generation's elaborate Shakespearean productions, often with a heavily edited text, the new directors took a different direction. Granville Barker espoused a symbolic simplicity for Shakespeare plays. Christopher McCullough shows how his productions of *The Winter's Tale*, *Twelfth Night* (both 1912) and *A Midsummer Night's Dream* (1914) draw on the visual arts movements of *art nouveau*, orientalism and Post-Impressionism. It is these changes in scenography, as well as the delivery and understanding of the text (fast-paced and involving 'the modernist concept of interior character'), that marks Granville Barker out as radically moving forward the style of Shakespearean productions.[83]

William Poel and Ben Greet pushed for a return to the minimalism of Elizabethan productions (although still played on a box set).[84] Greet started the Elizabethan Stage Society in 1895, and toured to great success, especially in America. During the war he was director of the Old Vic, making his pared-back Shakespeare productions a major success with audiences.

The other important figure to revivify Shakespeare at this time was Lilian Baylis. Her early life was influenced by the suffrage movement, which helps to place her in context of women such as Cicely Hamilton, and her aunt, Emma Cons, who represented radically different ways of living to a woman born during the Victorian era. In 1912 Baylis became manager of the Royal Victoria Hall (later called the Old Vic), thus laying the foundations of the Royal National Theatre, the English National Opera Company, and the Royal Ballet. The Old Vic became known as the joint home of Shakespeare and opera, and while Baylis's heart lay with the latter, she realised the importance of commerciality, and so ended up inadvertently championing the centrality of Shakespeare in the British theatre.

Between 1914 and 1923 the Old Vic presented Shakespeare's complete repertoire to honour the 300th anniversary of the First Folio. It started with *The Taming of the Shrew*, with the lead roles going to William Stack and Hutin Britton. The cycle was mainly directed by Robert Atkins and Ben Greet, but while they were influenced by the pared-down staging of William Poel, their productions lacked the flair of Granville Barker's seasons at London's Savoy Theatre between 1912 and 1914. On 23 April 1916, Shakespeare's

Tercentenary was celebrated at Stratford-upon-Avon: Coppèlia Kahn critically describes the memorial book produced to commemorate this as a 'cultural performance' designed to reinscribe communal identity and the might of the British Empire. [85] This was followed in May by an all-afternoon Shakespeare Pageant at Drury Lane, with many of the most popular actors of the day, including Ellen Terry as Portia, Charles Hawtrey as Falstaff and Mary Anderson as Hermoine. Other felicities continued at the Front and in POW camps. Ironically, the commemoration of Shakespeare's death had to be called off in Ireland due to the Easter 1916 Rising, which began on 24 April, showing the huge disparity between the history of the English and Irish, and it also took place just a few weeks before one of the bloodiest battles of the whole war: the Somme. J. G. Fuller describes this conflict as 'a watershed, when earlier idealism gave way to stoical endurance'.[86] Indeed, the work of Shakespeare, especially his history plays, may have chimed with contemporary audiences, but it could be argued that they also had the effect of distancing the actual realities of the war currently being fought. The horror of this still remained to be tackled in any great depth.

Conclusion

By 1918 Europe was an entirely different place from that before the war. In Russia Tsar Nicholas II had been killed and the Soviet Union established under the leadership of Vladimir Lenin. The Armistice had stripped Germany of its territories and Kaiser Wilhelm II had abdicated and gone into exile. The Austro-Hungarian Empire no longer existed and America was starting to become a dominant player in terms of global power. Britain had also undergone radical changes. While its Empire still remained more or less intact, the following decades would see this gradually being dismantled. More importantly, the concept of colonialisation itself was under attack. E. H. Carr highlights this when he describes the First World War being the end of a 'golden age of continuously expanding territories and markets, of a world policed by the self-assured and not too onerous British hegemony . . . and that what was right could not be morally wrong'.[87]

The shock felt by the British public was huge. As Trudi Tate says, 'The pinnacle of industrialization was not, as had been hoped at, say, the time of Great Exhibition (1851), peace, prosperity and progress, but the end of civilization, the death and mutilation of immense numbers of people, and the destruction of vast areas of landscape.'[88] Nevertheless, the war instigated rapid changes in this country. Social reform was brought to the fore and Britain's gender and class system put under increasing scrutiny as men and women who had fought for their country wanted their loyalty to be rewarded by better living and working conditions and a greater political voice. At its start most of the population only had a partial vote; at its end, all men had received the vote and some women, with full enfranchisement for women being achieved a decade later. Again, everyone was covered by National Insurance after 1920, leading to greater welfare for all parts of the population; the raising of the school age to fourteen and better training schemes meant more opportunities for social advancement as well. Authority, too, had been challenged. There had been mounting displeasure and indeed abhorrence at the behaviour of leaders such as Sir John French whom many believed had exacerbated the number of deaths and wounded through their military campaigns.

Views of the war shifted as time went on. At the beginning the emphasis was upon ensuring that enthusiasm and enlistment was kept high. As the horrors of the battlefield became apparent the tone shifted to negative representations of the enemy, but throughout there was an awareness of how war changed people's behaviour. This took a number of forms, ranging from satires about petty-mindedness and self-serving greed to doom-laden warnings about the destruction of humanity.

Popular culture had been transformed into the mass entertainment of cinema and radio, leading to the waning of some parts of the theatrical establishment such as variety and the redevelopment of theatres as movie palaces. On the surface, the theatre continued with Edwardian traditions, particularly in London: it was still part of the social calendar, with its adhesion to first-nighters and the formality of evening dress. Entertainment Tax brought in by the government led to a disproportionate rise in the cost of cheaper theatre tickets. The domination by actor-managers was no longer as strong, and London's theatres had effectively been bought up by a small group of speculators who ran them for profit. Ownership or lesseeship of playhouses thus moved from the hands of creative artists to business interests that profited from sub-leasing theatres to short-term producing managements.[89]

However, a regeneration was beginning. This was signalled by a gradual move away from the dominance of the metropolis to regional theatres due to the work of Annie Horniman and Barry Jackson, among others. Elsewhere, small club theatres began pushing the boundaries of censorship in ways that had not been seen before.

Even before the signing of the Armistice on 5 November 1918, there was an awareness of the sharp division between the pre-war world and the loss of innocence brought about by events at Passchendaele, Ypres, the Somme and the like. Theatre during next two decades would be concerned with the contradictory process of understanding, accepting, criticising and memorialising war, and a growing awareness of the next cataclysmic event. As the editor of the *Era* pointed out in January 1919, 'The real war play will come after the war'.[90] This is just what the next chapter will chart.

CHAPTER 3
INTERWAR THEATRE

Introduction

While David Lloyd George called a general election in the immediate shadow of the Armistice in 1918 and his Liberal Party was returned to power on a ticket of reconstruction and 'a land fit for heroes', the ensuing financial collapse led to increasingly vocalised dissent and an awareness that the war had opened up fissures in society that could not easily be bridged. The first Labour Party, under the leadership of Ramsay MacDonald came to power in 1924 but, without a majority, had difficulty in putting through any socialist legislation and only lasted nine months. It was left to Stanley Baldwin and the Conservative Party to deal with the General Strike of 1926. This lasted for nine days in May, bringing the country almost to a standstill, and making the upper echelons of society all too aware of their precarious position. Coal supplies had been depleted by domestic use during the war and when mine owners demanded a reduction in wages and longer working hours, the Trades Union Congress (TUC) called for a national strike.

The Wall Street crash three years later prompted many to consider that capitalism had had its day, whereas Communism seemed to be going from strength to strength in Soviet Russia: indeed the General Election of 1935 saw the first Communist MP – Walton Newbold – return to Parliament. It was felt by many socialists that the Labour Party was not doing enough to deal with the developing social and political tensions, with the industrial areas of the Rhondda Valley and Tyne and Wear particularly known for having strong Communist tendencies. A crisis was reached in 1931 when there was a lack of confidence in Ramsay MacDonald's government. MacDonald formed a multi-party National Government with the Conservatives. Because of this, the Labour vote fell sharply, and Conservatives, led by Stanley Baldwin, won a huge majority in the general election (although the prime minister of the austere National Government was still MacDonald).

One of those disgruntled with the Labour Party was Oswald Mosley, a former Labour MP. He went on to form the New Party which merged with the British Union of Fascists in 1932. His followers were the Blackshirts, who took their name from the uniforms they wore and the Italian paramilitary squads formed by disgruntled soldiers after the end of the First World War. They took part in various disruptive and violent activities throughout the country. The most famous of these was the Battle of Cable Street in October 1936, when Mosley led his supporters through the East End of London, where there was a large Jewish population. The ensuing clash with the Metropolitan Police triggered the 1936 Public Order Act and the decline of Mosley's party. However, the rise of fascism in countries such as Germany, Spain and Italy sparked apprehension that another war was imminent. Adolf Hitler's ascendancy to Chancellor of Germany in 1933 marked the growth of Nazism. His totalitarianism enshrined punitive anti-semitic laws, and an aggressive territorial approach led to Austria and Czechoslovakia being seized in 1938 and 1939 respectively.

The appeasement policy of Neville Chamberlain, who became Prime Minister in 1937, was deeply controversial. Some praised his attempts to keep Britain out of another war; others argued that it allowed Hitler to become too powerful. Noël Coward lambasted this with his song 'Don't Let's Be Beastly to the Germans' (1943):

Let's be meek to them –
And turn the other cheek to them
And try to bring out their latent sense of fun . . .
But don't let's be beastly to the Hun.[1]

By 1922 Britain ruled over one-fifth of the world's population. However, even though a series of Empire exhibitions took place during the 1920s and 1930s, many remained discomforted about the role of the British Empire. This was not helped by the belief in some quarters that the First World War had been an imperialist war. The Treaty of Versailles in 1919 had boosted Britain's global power, but events such as the Jallianwala Bagh massacre (also known as the Amritsar massacre), which took place in the same year, dented faith in the notion of colonisation. Other countries struggling for independence included Egypt and Iraq. The Anglo-Irish war and ensuing creation of the Irish Free State in 1921 brought these issues closer to home.

The country was further rocked by the abdication crisis in 1936, when King George V removed himself from the throne in order to marry an American divorcee, Mrs Wallis Simpson. While the monarchy continued to be supported by the majority of the population after the ascendance of George VI, the period was also marked by considerable class conflict.

Even given the Depression, however, the interwar years brought increasing prosperity to parts of the country. Various governments enacted a policy of slum clearance. Four million new houses were built between the wars and there were considerable medical and education gains, especially for those in the south of England. There were also improvements to the lives of the working classes, with the growth of trade unions, and to the role of women, as discussed in the last chapter.

Interwar entertainment

Other changes included a growth in mass media, especially radio and cinema. The British Broadcasting Company (BBC) was founded in 1922 under the directorship of Sir John Reith, who wanted to raise the educational, cultural and moral standards of the listeners. Although the all-talking cinema had threatened to eclipse the theatre, ironically, some stage stars were invited to provide a show to open cinemas, as with Gracie Fields and George Formby at the Gaumont State Cinema, Kilburn, in 1937, also recorded for radio broadcast: this was not as strange as it might sound, given that the new 'movie palaces' were frequently built as multi-functional ciné variety theatres, or known as cinema theatres, and indeed many interwar cinemas had stages used for live performances.[2]

The theatre industry fought back in a number of ways. Several new venues were built. In London alone, four theatres appeared in 1930 (Prince Edward, Cambridge, Phoenix, Whitehall); the Adelphi was rebuilt, and the following year a further three were established (Sadler's Wells, Westminster and the Saville). Ernest Reynolds noted that playhouses tended to be built in the style of the previous century, with exceptions being places such as the Birmingham Repertory Theatre which was championing a new type of drama.[3] It also made good use theatrical extravagance: *Late Night Final* (1931) had five stages used simultaneously, and Coward's *Cavalcade* (1931) reached a new apotheosis when it employed 'six hydraulic lifts, a cast of something over four hundred, a locomotive, a troopship, fog, and several other aids to high living'.[4] *Cavalcade* also exploited some of the theatre's key features: immediacy, interaction between performer and spectator, and communality. Again, much was made of exotic locales as in the Tyrol setting in Dodie Smith's *Autumn Crocus* and *Waltzes from Vienna*, originally by A.

M. Willner, Ernst Marischka and Heinz Reichert (both 1931), while new genres appeared to populist acclaim: Agatha Christie and Edgar Wallace turned to the stage with their murder mysteries, for example.

The cinema also provided a new means of disseminating drama to a wider audience. Actors reproduced their stage performance for film audiences or adaptations were created on celluloid. Some augmented their income by working on films during the day while continuing to appear on stage in the evenings. Not all were as adept at both styles of media, but wildly popular figures such as Ivor Novello and John Gielgud moved between the two with aplomb. Film was also a way of bringing to the masses different locations and voices, from *Hobson's Choice* (1920) and *Love on the Dole* (1941) to *The Vortex* (1924) and *Dear Octopus* (1938), although to be fair, as Stephen Shafer's researches show, by the end of the 1930s 'fewer than one in five films was taken from stage plays'.[5]

The radio was also another vehicle for drama and by 1930 there were more plays on the radio than in London's West End. Claire Cochrane notes that the first drama transmission from the BBC was in 1922: a scene from *Julius Caesar*.[6] Shakespeare was a popular choice for radio drama, but gradually playwrights started writing specifically for the medium. The first production was Richard Hughes's *Comedy of Danger* (1924) and later radio would draw such luminaries as W. H. Auden and Louis MacNeice. As radio drama became more familiar the BBC Drama Repertory Company – known colloquially as 'the Rep' – was set up in the 1930s to bring together a group of skilled radio actors, which became even more prominent during the Second World War.

Broadcasting from urban areas was scanty and so regional and amateur stations were used to supply more material. This led to drama specifically positioned for local audiences. Adrienne Scullion argues that Scottish broadcasters 'tended to look to what was immediate and to use the cultural products and reference points of their own world view'.[7] However, representation of the working classes was severely hampered by the belief of Reith that Received Pronunciation was necessary on radio and television.

'Little', amateur and regional theatres

An abundance of riches was available to the interwar theatre-goer who stepped away from the larger, more established venues. In London plays were put on at small club theatres such as the Everyman, the Gate and the Embassy, or 'at subscription club theatre groups which hired or ran venues such as The Savoy and The Kingsway. Although there were exceptions . . . many of the dramatic successes on the West End stage started life in these "other theatres".[8] Other places included Theodore Komisarjevsky's conversion of a cinema in Barnes and Ashley Dukes's Mercury Theatre, which put on the first London production of T. S. Eliot's *Murder in the Cathedral* (1935) and became a venue for the Ballet Rambert (Marie Rambert was Dukes's wife). Outside the capital there were venues such as J. B. Fagan's Oxford Playhouse and Terence Gray and Harold Ridge's Cambridge Festival Theatre, founded respectively in 1923 and 1926; both of these started the connection between universities and drama, although this would not come to fruition until after the next war.

There were also the small theatre societies, set up to allow for Sunday performances, and also, as previously mentioned, to evade the Lord Chamberlain's stringent censorship laws. By remaining outside of the West End, producers had to worry less about building regulations (as several were in ramshackle structures) or commercial viability. Several of these societies had a reasonably large and loyal subscription base, drawn from the surrounding area, so that they were in effect community-driven. This early form of fringe theatre included the Phoenix Society, the Three Hundred Club and the Play Actors, set up in opposition to the more conservative West End. The most important of these was the Incorporated Stage Society, which premiered R. C. Sherriff's *Journey's End* in 1928 after all West End managers had turned it down.

All these places were small and run on a shoestring, so staging effects were limited, but this also had the effect of creating a strong relationship between performer and audience. Norman Marshall, who took over Peter Godfrey's ownership of The Gate Theatre in 1934, likened the effect to radio or cinema. He explains that the actor 'could get over to the audience subtle variations of tone usually only possible in a broadcasting studio' and the 'lack of proscenium arch, footlights and orchestra pit made a direct connection even more possible'.[9] This intimacy, of course, presages the effect created by theatre in the round, which would become a popular style of theatre space style in the decades after the war. The tiny backstage space meant that the actors' dressing rooms were only a few feet away from the audience, so once again 'the actor was "in" the show', even when not on stage; at times the cast even had to change their costumes onstage.[10]

The Little Theatres also shifted attention from theatre-going as part of the social calendar to one which focused more on the production itself –

which varied from well-known British and European classics to new, radical works – to the possibilities of staging. At the Oxford Playhouse Fagan's 'short rehearsal period . . . produced acting which, though "rough and unpolished . . . strove to develop the style and mood of the play, and to reproduce the author's characterisation as exactly and vividly as possible".[11] Again, Gray's Cambridge Festival Theatre destroyed theatrical illusion by doing away with the proscenium arch and using the auditorium as part of the playing space. The next logical step was to remove the wings and scenery on stage, so the audience could view the mechanics of theatre, with the actors waiting to make their entrance, and the crew working backstage. In later years, this style would become popular, but by the start of the Second World War these little theatres were struggling, as were the Sunday societies. The Everyman and the Regent were turned into cinemas, the Leeds Civic Playhouse and the Cambridge Festival Theatre closed in the early 1930s, and the Oxford Playhouse dwindled into a nondescript repertory theatre.

It is clear that there has always been a division made between professional and amateur theatre, with the latter seen in more pejorative terms. Nevertheless, as the research of Raphael Samuel, Colin Chambers, Peter Billingham, Claire Cochrane and others has shown, the boundary between the two is fluid.[12] Actors and directors moved freely between the two, which helped to reinvigorate both forms of theatre. The interwar years have been considered the golden age of amateur theatre, and spanned across the classes. Over 700 local amateur groups were affiliated to British Drama League in 1920s and these varied from community groups looking for a means of entertainment to those who had a radical agenda. Small festivals also sprang up at places such as Angmering-on-Sea in Sussex, and Ellen Terry's house, Smallhythe in Kent, where, as Peter Billingham has explained 'it was quite common for professional actors and directors to be invited to "guest" at [amateur] festivals.'[13] University societies such as the Cambridge University Amateur Dramatic Club (CUADC) and the Oxford University Dramatic Society (OUDS) also became more influential, particularly in terms of their focus on the intellectual and aesthetic challenges of the stage.

The British Actors' Equity Association (1930) helped to change views about the profession, although Patricia Dellar, who was heavily involved with theatre in Hull claimed that Equity 'made it very difficult for professional companies to introduce local talent into their productions, even on a non-payment basis'.[14] Nevertheless, community and regional theatre, which often also included non-professional workers, was one way of addressing a local audience and providing a voice to those who might have felt dispossessed by the industry.[15] Cochrane asserts that 'Just as in Wales, the play competitions held as part of the eisteddfodau could draw audiences running into thousands, so in Scotland local drama groups were followed as keenly as football teams.'[16] 'Kailyard' literature – a term relating to the kitchen garden – was a strain of popular writing that presented a sentimentalised and apolitical view of rural life, and had much in common with the Celtic Revival in the way that it looked to the past. In comparison, drama of the Scottish Literary Renaissance of the interwar years had strong links with the modernist movement and focused more on contemporary depictions of the city and the workplace. The pioneering Glasgow Repertory Theatre may have folded at the start of the war, but it gave rise to companies such as the Scottish National Players (1921–47) and the Scottish Community Drama Association (SCDA); the latter founded in 1926 provided a network of amateur companies across the country. Early twentieth-century plays tended to deal in Scottish stereotypes. Exceptions included George Blake's *Clyde-Built* (1922), which charted the changes taking place to the shipbuilding industry, which was at the heart of the area's civic identity. Plays like these were absolutely rooted in the region, but Adrienne Scullion asserts that theatre companies – such as Glasgow Workers' Theatre – became increasingly politicised: 'theirs was not really a commitment to local representations, to "Scottish" culture *per se*, but to the development of an internationalist workers' culture.'[17]

A host of Scottish dramatists, including Robert McLellan, Joe Corrie and James Bridie (a pseudonym for Osborne Mavor) played their part in this resurgence of literature, drawing on local issues, dialects and characteristics. Like Harry Lauder, the playwright Graham Moffat chose not to produce the Scottish language, but 'Scots-accented English with a few Scots words dropped in for local colour'. This was done to make his plays more accessible to a wider audience, but as Ian Brown's research has shown, Moffat subconsciously used more Scottish words than he realised, suggesting 'someone conflicted – at the very least – about his use of language.'[18]

This was also true in Wales, where there was a complex negotiation between the usage of the Welsh or English language, and between regional and national identity. Sanders Lewis's *Blodeuwedd* (1923–5) is considered the quintessential Welsh language play, but he also wrote radio plays in English as well.[19] Thomas Scott-Ellis, 8th Baron Howard de Walden, was an English aristocrat who, after inheriting estates in Wales, learnt the language and championed the foundation of a national theatre of Wales, although this did not come to fruition until the twenty-first century, with the appearance of Theatre Genedlaethol Cymru and National Theatre Wales. De Walden's bi-lingual Welsh National Playhouse in Llangollen, north-east Wales, also foundered when not enough native speakers attended, lasting only from 1933 to 1939.

The Swansea Stage Society (originally the Swansea Amateur Players Society) put on plays such as *Land of My Fathers: A Play of the Distressed Area* (1938), by the ex-miner and political activist, Jack Jones. Jones also adapted *Rhondda Roundabout* (1934) from his novel of the same name, which looks at the impact of the failed General Strike and Depression on inhabitants of the Welsh valleys. Both plays had successful London productions, suggesting that theatre managers and audiences were sometimes more open to amateur works and regional subjects than previously thought. This is also true of Emlyn Williams, who was both a dramatist and an actor. The backdrop of his commercially successful *The Corn is Green* (1938) is often forgotten. This is of a poverty-stricken mining village in the nineteenth-century, where the schoolmistress, Miss Moffat, attempts to educate the workers into a better life. This puts her in opposition to the local Squire, who is fearful of losing his paternalistic control. Miss Moffat stands up to him, saying that 'there is a considerable amount of dirt, ignorance, misery and discontent abroad in this world, and . . . a good deal of it is due to people like you'.[20] The notion of colonialism is raised but not fully worked out: the Squire is from England, but then so is the schoolmistress, suggesting both tyranny and salvation.

After 1910, when Annie Horniman withdrew her subsidy from the Abbey Theatre in Dublin, Yeats had less to do with its day-to-day running. Instead he started to incorporate movement into his work, influenced by the work of Ezra Pound and Japanese Noh drama. His *Four Plays for Dancers* (published 1921) – *At the Hawk's Well*, *The Only Jealousy of Emer*, *The Dreaming Of The Bones* and *Calvary* – can be seen as a rejection of the naturalistic plays of contemporaries such as George Bernard Shaw, and were performed for more elite audiences in private drawing rooms or independent theatre clubs. By the mid-1920s, when the Abbey had become the National Theatre of the Irish Free State, Yeats's style had changed again. Works such as *The Words Upon the Window Pane*, *The Herne's Egg* (pub. 1938, first performed 1950) and *Purgatory* are 'the triumph of the everyday over the heroic, the material over the spiritual', thus pointing towards the 'absurdist visions of another Irish playwright, Samuel Beckett'.[21]

Sean O'Casey wrote plays for the working classes and his professed desire was to shock audiences out of their complacent attitudes towards politics, society and religion. His Dublin Trilogy (*The Shadow of the Gunman*, 1923; *Juno and the Paycock*, 1924; *The Plough and the Stars*, 1926) focused on the deception of those who lived in the Dublin tenements by the Easter Rising. This was meant to improve the lot of the working classes but in fact simply consolidated the power of the Irish Catholic bourgeoisie. The epigram to each play is taken from the work of Patrick Pearse, an Irish national hero who was executed during the Easter Rebellion. Colbert Kearney sees the connecting theme as that of blood sacrifice: 'the shedding of blood in battle is redemptive and essential for the manhood of a nation; blood spilt in battle is like wine poured in sacrifice to God; Ireland should welcome war in order to experience the exhilaration of heroism; Ireland will never accept British rule as long as it is inspired by the miraculous power associated with the sacrifices of previous generations'.[22]

In *Juno and the Paycock* poverty and the Irish Civil War threaten to split apart the Boyle family whose hopes are raised and dashed by the possibility of an inheritance. Juno, the mother, is the only one that works, husband 'Captain' Jack is a retired seaman who spends his days in the pub, son Johnny has lost an arm fighting for the Irish Republican Army (IRA), and daughter Mary is on strike. Nationalist idealism is contrasted with the reality of warfare, expressed by Juno's blistering outburst: 'What were the pains I suffered Johnny, bringin' you into the world to carry you to your cradle, to the pains I suffer now bringing you out o' the world to carry you to your grave'.[23] The central conceit is that of betrayal. Jack has given up on life. Mary rejects her trade unionist lover and her political principles for the promise of a more comfortable life with a schoolteacher. He, in turn, lies about the potential inheritance and leaves her pregnant. Johnny betrays his friend, Robbie Tancred, and they are both mutilated and killed in revenge. The play was based on O'Casey's 'firsthand experience of urban warfare, seen from a civilian's viewpoint, with some knowledge of military matters [. . .] as a member of the Irish Citizen Army'.[24] It attests to the human cost of imperialism and liberation, and underlines how the zealous ideology leads to loss whatever the political persuasion.

Many of O'Casey's plays were controversial, most notably *The Plough and the Stars* which caused a riot during its first run at the Abbey Theatre, led by the mothers and widows of the 1916 Easter Rising. As with Synge's earlier *The Playboy of the Western World*, it was the besmirching of Irish womanhood that caused moral outrage. Critics dwelt on a scene in which the prostitute Rosie Redmond's seduction of a client is intermingled with a call to arms by a character based on Pádraic Pearse, a martyr of the Easter Rising. The play is both intimate (the events are viewed through the eyes of ordinary characters in the Dublin tenements) and epic (about the political struggle to forge a new nation). The first two Acts are set in November 1915, when the rebels are looking forward to the liberation of Ireland by its citizens. The last two Acts are set in Easter 1916 as the suppression of the rebels is taking place. Jean Chothia notes that 'O'Casey's location of his Dublin plays among the city's tenement dwellers in the context of actual and very recent political events, the independence war, the civil war, and then the Rising, broke new ground, even in a period notable for plays engaged with historical reality'.[25]

The jab at the intransigence of all political sides also did not go down well. Synge was a Socialist and former member of the Irish Citizens Army, who believed that workers' issues were being undercut by the drive towards nationalism. The title of the play gets its name from the flag of the Citizen Army, but O'Casey's own views are put into the mouth of the Covey: 'it's a flag that should only be used when we're buildin' th' barricades to fight for a Workers' Republic!'[26] The fight against the imperialist English is implicitly linked to the war taking place across the Atlantic. Both are seen as ultimately futile, leading to greater losses. As the curtain falls at the end of the play, soldiers can be heard singing 'Keep the Home Fires Burning', the popular wartime song by Ivor Novello which reminded those in the trenches of their life back in Blighty. Here it is ironically sung against the backdrop of fires burning as the Irish rebellion is crushed, while earlier in the play we hear 'It's a Long Way to Tipperary' as the Irish soldiers head off to the Front, reminding audiences of the numbers killed when fighting alongside their (English) enemy. The style of the play is naturalistic, but the structure in non-linear, plot lines are thematic rather than narrative-driven, and there is an awareness of the slippage between language and meaning later utilised by Absurdist writers.

By the end of the 1920s, the Abbey Theatre had lost its experimental roots and dwindled into rusticism, even given Yeats's foray into different theatrical forms. Its place was taken over by the Gate Theatre Company in Dublin, established by the Irish actors, Micheál MacLiammoir and Hilton Edwards. While MacLiammoir was also drawn to Celticism, he increased the repertoire with modern writing, especially that drawn from Europe and America.

Experiments in drama

Bruce McConachie charts a change that took place on the avant-garde scene: 'the worldwide economic depression of the 1930s turned many citizens towards their own nations and away from the international scene. Most of the avant-gardists were utopians of one stripe or another, but Stalinism, Nazism and fascism had already deadened most international utopian hopes in Europe by the outbreak of World War II in 1939'.[27] Ernst Toller was a key figure for British avant-garde theatre. The German-born Toller wrote political dramas in an Expressionistic style, including *The Machine Wreckers*, directed in 1923 by Nugent Monck for the Stage Society, and the anti-Nazi *Pastor Hall*, translated by Stephen Spender and W. H. Auden in 1939. Theodore Komisarjevsky, the Russian émigré who went on to marry Peggy Ashcroft, was a key figure in bringing across the ideas of Stanislavsky and Meyerhold. He directed many experimental productions in the 1920s and 1930s, including *The Three Sisters* (1926) with John Gielgud and *Le Cocu Magnifique* (1932) with George Devine. Again, Michel Saint-Denis established the London Theatre Studio in 1935. Here professional actors and students were brought together to undergo extensive physical and emotional training in the style of Saint-Denis's uncle, Jacques Copeau.

There are contentious views on the difference between modernism and the avant-garde, with some critics suggesting that the former is aesthetic, literary focused and English and the latter experimental, political and European. Nevertheless, it is fruitful to consider the similarities between a poetic-based theatre and a political-based theatre. Both movements used the manifesto as a way to express their beliefs, whether this was Auden's view that 'ideally there would be no spectators. In practice every member of the audience should feel like an understudy', or Theatre Workshop's claim that theatre should be forged 'in the clash and turmoil of the battles between the oppressors and the oppressed'.[28] Plays are mainly anti-realistic, relying instead on symbolism or vivid imagery, non-linear or logical plot, structure and character, contemporaneous themes, meta-theatricality and intertextuality.

Poetic drama

The Group Theatre was less concerned with political drama than an avant-garde venture dedicated to 'total theatre': that is, bringing together music, dance, poetry and drama to involve the audience in the action. It was founded in 1932 by Robert Medley and his partner, Rupert Doone. Doone had worked with the Ballets Russes and his use of choral chanting, masks, mime and tableau led to exaggerated spectacles that were a far cry from those to be found on the West End stage. It was, however, a short-lived experiment and closed on the advent of war in 1939, reinventing itself as the Group Theatre Ltd. in the early 1950s.

Within this short span, however, collaborations were forged with some of the key writers of the 1930s – Auden, Isherwood, Eliot, MacNeice and Spender – who all wanted a return to 'serious' drama and attempted this through their experiments with verse drama. This was a bold move for, as Christopher Innes reminds us, 'Even before naturalism established a new criteria of authenticity, verse had been relegated to historical pageants: a dressed-up speech for costume plays.'[29] Far from elitism, Eliot was concerned that his drama cut across class barriers and directly connected with all audiences. Nevertheless, it is interesting that London's Unity Theatre, who shared their facilities with the Group Theatre, believed that their work was entirely out of touch with the working classes.[30] Certainly, though, the plays of Auden can be viewed as political in subject matter and in style.

Robin Grove has observed how verse drama's use of subtitles – Auden's *Paid on Both Sides* (1930) is a 'Charade'; Eliot's *Sweeney Agonistes* (1933) is 'Fragments of an Aristophanic Melodrama' – 'point to an inter-war theatre of evacuation or displacement of settled modes'.[31] This also fits into a modernist frame of reference, where language is slippery, playful and self-reflexive. Eliot's first play, started during the 1920s, was never completed and consists of two scenes eventually performed as a one-act verse drama: *Fragment of a Prologue* (1926) and *Fragment of an Agon* (1927), eventually published and performed together in 1932 as *Sweeney Agonistes*. It contains the rhythms of music hall, jazz music and the common parlance of the streets; its ritual form demanded a greater level of participation from the audience than more conventional work. The character of Sweeney had already appeared in several of Eliot's poems, representing the debasement of man: raw, sensual and secular. The play develops this by suggesting that Sweeney is aware of his potential. There is comedy and tragedy in the human condition, pre-empting the work of Samuel Beckett and other Absurdists, and Doone's use of a series of blackouts was designed to destabilise the audience and emphasise the lack of certainties in a fragmented post-war world.

Eliot's career in the theatre began properly in 1933, when E. Martin Browne, an influential figure involved in the revival of religious and poetic drama during this period, asked him to write a pageant to raise money for North London churches. *The Rock* was the result, duly staged in 1934. *Murder in the Cathedral* followed a year later. Directed again by Browne, this was a site-specific piece to be performed to a Christian audience in Canterbury Cathedral. Its success at the Canterbury Festival and again in the West End influenced Eliot into writing the poetic drama favoured by Browne. Eliot's mixture of poeticism and Christianity, which he continued in *The Cocktail Party* (1949) and *The Confidential Clerk* (1953) was an attempt to explain the disconnect between two worlds: the material and the (more real) spiritual. However, John Worthen points to Eliot's inability to move beyond verse in his plays, or to be able to create realistic conversations, which make them stilted and artificial. He quotes Virginia Woolf, who on seeing *The Family Reunion* in 1939, remarked: 'not a dramatist. A monologist'.[32]

W. H. Auden's engagement with the theatre was as radical as that with poetry. Between 1928 and 1929 he had lived in Berlin and witnessed Hitler's rise to power. Like Unity he believed in a theatre of commitment, one that would find a new dramatic language to express his left-wing political beliefs. *The Dance of Death* (1935), a one-act Masque, ostensibly harks back to the Greek use of the chorus, but commentators have also made a connection with contemporary Marxist productions. Arthur Koestler pointed out that Auden would have been familiar with these from his visit to Berlin in 1928: 'the highest form of music was the choral song because it represented the collective, as opposed to the individualistic approach'. Similarly, 'Since individual characters could not be banished altogether from the stage, they had to be stylised, typified, depersonalised'.[33]

Thence followed three plays in collaboration with Christopher Isherwood. The first of these, *The Dog Beneath the Skin* (1934–6; sometimes abbreviated as *Dogskin*), was a Marxist interpretation of Gilbert and Sullivan. Several versions exist with different endings and there is a similar structure to that of a Brecht play, with a Chorus-narrator and stand-alone scenes. The hero is Alan Norman, whose name indicates his ordinariness. He embarks on a quest across Europe, which mimics the St George and the Dragon legend, to find the heir of Honeypot Hall, Sir Francis Crewe. The aristocrat who is disguised as Norman's companion, a large dog, manages to gain a shockingly new perspective on bourgeois society. The injustice and cruelty of the state is exposed, leading him to question a world he had previously accepted without thinking. The play is a parable of different forms of governance and political ideology: European countries are non-democratic, having monarchies and fascist dictators, but England too is threatened by figures such as the vicar and general who rule over their 'brigade' of boys 'with discipline of iron' in order 'To train the tender plant of Youth/And guard the moral order'.[34] The play had to undergo several cuts for its attack on Germany, which was typical of the time, as Steve Nicholson explores in his chapter in this book.[35]

Auden and Isherwood's play, *The Ascent of F6* also tackled Fascist ideology. Written in 1936 and performed a year later, this followed Michael Ransom, a white man who is pressured by the press and his MP brother to reach the top of F6, the world's highest unconquered mountain. Situated on the borders of a British colony and that of another colony, owned by the fictional nation Ostnia, a perilous race begins between climbers from both countries. In his efforts to reach the summit (the play's original name), Ransom is consumed by personal ambition and patriotic fervour, which ultimately leads to his death and those of his fellow climbers. The play was based on the life of D. H. Lawrence, explorers such as T. E. Lawrence, George Mallory and Robert Scott, as well as Auden's own issues with becoming a public figure. The style deliberately parodies the adventure stories of authors such as John Buchan and Henry McNeile, mocking the British Empire, imperialism and nationalistic pride. *On the Frontier*, significantly published in 1938, does something similar: an outbreak of war between Ostnia and another fictional country, Westland, leads to an unthinking jingoism.

Political theatre

During the 1920s socialist co-ops had 'sponsored hundreds of drama classes and theatrical troupes', but theatre was primarily seen 'as an arena for education and improvement'.[36] The Independent Labour Party Arts Guild, led by Miles Malleson, evolved from social events held to raise funds and bring people together from the same political persuasion.[37] These nascent forms of political theatre were taken a stage further by national and international tensions and ideologies: between workers and bosses, capitalism and communism, and fascism and democracy. During the 1920s there was growing disillusionment with the government's promised better life for returning soldiers and the high levels of unemployment, which lasted until the early part of the Second World War. Strikes continued to break out across the country, focusing on workers' rights and conditions. Once-strong industries struggled and there was rising unemployment.

Against this background it is understandable that political theatre proliferated. Within a few years Colin Chambers notes that 'Groups sprang up around Britain, mainly in big cities with high unemployment, and took names like Sunderland Red Magnets, Dundee Red Front Troupe, Southampton Red Dawn or Salford Red Megaphones'.[38] This counter-culture was anti-establishment not just in terms of its subject matter, but in other ways as well. 'Popular' prices were common, evening dress no longer required, and plays were by and about the working classes. Fourth wall naturalism was rejected in favour of unusual locations and staging. This consisted of short sketches, often with music, song, dance and broad comedy, with simple emblematic props and costumes (e.g. management wore bowler hats and workers wore flat caps). Docudrama, socialist realism and agitational propaganda were all popular forms.

The Workers' Theatre Movement (WTM) was inspired by the Russian Revolution. It started as a Council for Proletarian Art in 1924 and took on its new name two years later before being taken over by Tom Thomas's Hackney People's Players. The Hackney branch of WTM called itself Red Radio, and the titles of early productions show the political credentials: *Malice in Plunderland*, *Strike Up* (both 1929), and *Their Theatre and Ours* (1933). Theatre was to be taken to the masses, and performed for free on 'open platform' stages (backs of lorries, streets, parks, factories, etc.). Like the earlier suffrage theatre groups, performances raised funds for the cause – usually for striking workers – and revolved around specific issues; in this case, these were anti-bourgeoisie, anti-capitalist and anti-imperialist. Early productions drew on the work of European dramatists; Ernst Toller's *Masses and Man* (1921) and *The Machine Wreckers*, and Karel Čapek's *RUR (Rossum's Universal Robots)* (1920) among them. There was also homegrown talent, including Joe Corrie's *In Time o' Strife* (1926), about the mining strikes in 1926, and Tom Thomas's adaptation of Robert Tressell's Marxist book, *The Ragged Trousered Philanthropists* (1927).

Unity Theatre brought together amateur and professional theatre workers who had been politicised by the growing anti-fascist movement, and had strong connections with the Left Book Club and the *Left Review*; throughout its history it was watched with suspicion by the Government as several of its members were affiliated to the Communist Party. Originally formed from two Hackney organisations – Red Radio and the Rebel Players it spawned a number of other companies around the country; the most significant of these were in Liverpool, Merseyside, Manchester and Glasgow. The mission was 'To foster and further the art of drama in accordance with the principle that true art, by effectively presenting and truthfully interpreting life as experienced by the majority of the people, can move the people to work for the betterment of society.'[39] Clifford Odets's *Waiting for Lefty* (1935) was a seminal work for the company. This American play used a proposed strike by taxi drivers as a way of critiquing the continuance of capitalism during the Depression. The struggle between workers and management had an easy appeal for the working classes. The bare setting emphasised its universality, and by planting cast members in the auditorium, the audience were drawn into the action: the performance invariably ended with the spectators imitating the actors' call for a strike. Realistic scenes were interspersed with agitprop where characters delivered their personal testimony. Colin Chambers argues that 'The intercutting scenes, which were innovative then and showed the influence of the newly-emerging cinema, add up to a picture of a society in crisis in which everyone is affected and no one can be neutral – a common theme of plays in the 1930s.'[40]

Unity drew upon British working-class forms, especially variety and music hall, as well as Living Newspapers, a documentary style in which topical events were utilised for political effect. First used in Russia by the Blue Blouse groups (1923–8) – who got their name from the colour of the workers' shirts – this use of agitprop was a deliberate attempt by a theatre group to align itself with Soviet Russia. It was also taken up by Erwin Piscator and Brecht in 1920s Germany, and the American Federal Theatre Project (1935–9), with which Odets was involved. One of Unity's most typical pieces was *Living Newspaper 1: Busmen* (1938), based on a bus strike the previous year when thousands of drivers had protested against their working conditions. The play fuses factual evidence, voiceovers, political commentary and social realism. Central is the dehumanisation of workers through being treated like machines, a key concept of modernism.

Another dramatic technique was the use of mass declamation, as in Jack Lindsay's *Who are the English?* (1936). The Australian author was a prolific author and critic, whose Marxist views led him to believe that capitalism had forged a chasm between art and the masses: by fusing different genres – poetry, music, dance, pageants – the working classes could reclaim ownership of culture. *Who are the English?* provides an alternative history of the country by focusing on rebellions such as the Peasants' Revolt, the Levellers, Luddites, Chartists and strikers of 1926. A large chorus, dressed in workers' overalls and red masks, uses stylised movement and recitation to provide a collective response to the orthodox definition of Englishness.

Elsewhere, in Manchester Ewan MacColl's Red Megaphones (1931) underwent several manifestations once he had joined forces with his future wife, Joan Littlewood: thence followed Theatre of Action (1934), Theatre Union (1936) and Theatre Workshop (1945). These companies were both local and international. Red Megaphones put on plays about the ailing cotton industry around Lancashire and Cheshire, thereby guaranteeing an interested audience who recognised both the support of their political concerns and the depiction of their situation. This was furthered through

MacColl's use of dialect as a way of presenting an authentic working-class language. However, they were also sent scripts from exiled theatre groups in Europe and America, suggesting that Britain was fast becoming a place where radical theatre could be performed (within reason) outside of censorship laws.

Actors were taken through a long training process, and staging techniques were taken from Piscator and Brecht as well as Yevgeny Vakhtangov and Vsevolod Meyerhold. This Continental influence is evident in *John Bullion* (1934), which Littlewood presented as a short 'constructivist ballet with words'. This creates a sense of solidarity between the working classes across the world; at the end '"the INTERNATIONALE flowers into several languages. Workers march onto the stage from all sides", while the Capitalists "collapse like deflated balloons in a heap"'.[41]

The rise of commercial theatre

As Claire Cochrane makes clear, by the end of the First World War, artistic control now passed to 'producers'; these became new kind of stars by virtue of putting their own recognisable stamp on a production. Basil Dean was the most important during the interwar years. He started as an actor and worked with the Gaiety Theatre, Manchester. Thereafter, he became the first director of the Liverpool Repertory Theatre and founded his own production company ReandeaN in 1919 with Alec Rea. He was also responsible for setting up the Entertainments National Service Association (ENSA), discussed in the next chapter. Dean moved fluently between the stage and the cinema, which invariably affected his directing style. In 1929, with Reginald Baker, he founded Associated Talking Pictures Ltd which later became the Ealing Studios. While Dean's reputation rests on works with popular appeal, such as the stage and film versions of Margaret Kennedy's 1924 novel *The Constant Nymph* (1926 and 1933 respectively), and Gracie Fields' film *Sing as We Go* (1934), he was also responsible for some cutting edge work as well. As I explore later on, this meant that some of his material was comparatively radical, further complicating the boundaries between commercial and non-commercial.

On the whole, though, many interwar theatre commentators were dismayed about the lack of innovative material on offer. Camillo Pellizzi complained about the musicals, variety and revues on offer, and the emphasis upon 'a type of spectacle which has a fundamental lack of *seriousness*'.[42] J.

C. Trewin backed this up by saying that society was now only concerned with 'the gay froth of existence'.[43] William Poel believed that it was the stranglehold of businessmen within the industry that had destroyed its freshness, arguing that the only plays being produced were ones 'likely to appeal to the undiscriminating in all parts of the English-speaking world'.[44]

Farces and musicals

Two genres in particular fell into the category of undemanding 'froth': farce and the musical, although they could both include subversive or innovative elements. Three West End theatres specialised in comedy, with a favourite comic at each: Charles Wyndham, actor-manager at his eponymously named theatre, Cyril Maude at the Haymarket, and Charles Hawtrey at the Comedy. However, the most successful of all was an almost continuous run of ten farces at the Aldwych from 1923 to 1933; these were penned by Ben Travers, who had seen service as a pilot during the First World War.

The Aldwych farces looked back to Greek and Roman satyr plays, designed to mock those who are pompous or tyrannical, as well as emulating the silent cinema antics of Harold Lloyd, Charlie Chaplin and Buster Keaton. At the centre is the 'little man' set against the figure of authority who is eventually unmasked or humiliated. Travers utilised the comic talents of his co-stars: Robertson Hare played the butt of the joke, the lower-middle-class man who always loses his money and his trousers, Tom Walls appeared as a cunning member of the middle classes, and Ralph Lynn took on the role of the monocled Edwardian man-about-town, a reworking of the Lion Comique and known as a 'knut'.[45] These well-known 'types' celebrated British eccentricity at a time when national identity was pre-eminent. Clive Barker also notes that how these farces mark a shift in class from the 1920s to the 1930s: the earlier ones focus on the bourgeoisie, whereas the ones in the 1930s centre more on Robinson Hare's wage slave.[46] This shows an awareness of the impact of the Depression and the victimisation felt by the common man.

Travers's bedroom antics can be seen as innocent enough to evade censorship, but in fact they were deliberately staged so as to draw out the maximum of titillation. Actresses such as Winifred Shotter are frequently seen in a state of undress and situations revolve around people being found in increasingly compromising situations. Yet far from being a cynical way of making money for the theatre, farce allows Travers to mock social hypocrisy about marriage, sexuality, class and money: *A Cuckoo in the Nest* (1925) is a commentary on the current divorce laws, and the characters in *Plunder* (1928) are all fraudulent in one form or another, the traditional country house location mocking the rectitude of its inhabitants. Nevertheless, Travers could also confirm the status quo, especially apparent in his xenophobic representations of foreigners as with the Prussian Putz in *Rookery Nook* (1926).

The interwar years were one of the high points of the musical in this country, which took many forms. These could be excuses to reprise popular variety acts. *Somewhere in England* (1939) included Will Hay's well-known comic antics as a school master. The thin plot of *Seeing Stars* (1935) was designed to show off the talents of Leslie Henson, Richard Hearne, Fred Emney and Florence Desmond, who appeared alongside the variety act of the Four Crotchets and Kay Foster. Others created roles that would once have existed on the music hall stage: Lupino Lane originated the role of the Cockney tout, Bill Snibson, in *Twenty to One* (1935), followed by *Me and My Girl* (1937) with its dance craze, the Lambeth Walk.

Theatre managers continued to offer spectacles, hoping to repeat the sensational success of *Chu Chin Chow*. James Elroy Flecker's *Hassan* was composed before the War, but not produced by Basil Dean in 1922, after Flecker's death. Its writer saw the play as uncommercial and unstageable, but Dean's intervention led interwar audiences and critics alike to respond positively to its visual splendour.

Like Asche's *Chu Chin Chow* and *Kismet*, it was based on *The Arabian Nights*, a source of inspiration for Orientalists. Set in Iraq and based on Middle-Eastern legend, *Hassan* had music by Delius and ballets by the Russian choreographer, Michel Fokine. Indeed, the producer deliberately referenced Fokine's earlier work for the Ballets Russes, sparking yet another rage for all things Oriental.[47]

Nevertheless, *Hassan* can be seen as providing a complex – and troubling – representation of the East, reflecting Flecker's own ambiguous relationship with it; for him, it was at once excitingly vibrant and uncompromisingly violent. This is represented in the play with the contrast drawn between its beautiful settings and lyrical language, and the almost sado-masochistic treatment of characters, especially women. The simple Hassan saves the life of the Caliph, the Muslim leader, and moves into the palace. Here he is overawed by its sumptuousness, but at the same time he witnesses the trial of Rafi, who tried to kill the Caliph as revenge for the mistreatment of his people and the kidnapping of his lover Pervaneh. In scenes of graphic violence, both are tortured and then executed, returning as ghosts to haunt the palace. Dismayed, Hassan and his poet friend Ishak escape and take the road to Samarkand, already evoked by Flecker in his poem 'The Golden Road to Samarkand'.

For a post-war audience this was a resonant ending; Hassan and Ishak leave behind past traumas for a more optimistic future, but as Claire Warden's researches have shown, 'the rugged landscape painted behind them was dwarfed by the enormous sky that seemed to suggest both a sense of loss and emptiness'. Thus this Eastern spectacle was changed from Fletcher's original vision of 'an *Arabian Nights* farce', to one with darker overtones as war approached and his own sense of mortality beckoned.[48] Moreover, Rafi's challenge to the Caliph's power on the grounds of injustice and corruption foreshadows a debate about authority and power in the Western world that would be echoed in the growth of political drama during the 1920s and 1930s.

American imports also made their first substantial appearance at this time; notably Jerome Kern's *Show Boat* in 1927 and Cole Porter's *Anything Goes* in 1935. Other musicals were based on classical music or the lives of composers, as with *Lilac Time* (1922), revived seven times in the 1920s and 1930s; this featured the music of Franz Schubert. *Paganini*, with music by Franz Lehar, premiered in Vienna in 1925 and was a popular hit of London's West End twelve years later. These latter works featured exotic settings and sometimes spectacular staging, also utilised in the much-parodied 'Ruritanian' musicals mentioned earlier. These were set in fictional countries in Eastern Europe, allowing the writer and designer to pander to the fashion for romantic exoticism, also prominent on the silver screen.

Chief among the proponents of this genre was the matinée idol, Ivor Novello. Noted as much for his famous profile as for his appearances on stage and celluloid, Novello's career spanned from the First World War to the 1950s and, as well as being an actor, he was also a composer and director. Novello was a popular figure with the working classes; his upper class appearance and demeanour was a construct as his grandfather was a Welsh miner. His musicals have been lampooned for their overuse of the royalty of imaginary foreign countries, although Novello himself was not above parodying his own work, as with his last musical, *Gay's the Word* (1951), whose title may well have been a reference to his own homosexuality.

His musicals for the Theatre Royal, Drury Lane, were light in tone, although not without their social and political commentary. One of two 'patent houses' allowed by Charles II to stage 'serious' drama during the Restoration, Drury Lane was in danger of closing down in the 1930s due to dwindling audiences. Novello was twice called upon to save 'the Lane', coming up with the extravaganza, *Glamorous Night* (1935), and later *The Dancing Years* (1939). Both works explore the tension between love and duty. The former was based on a real event; the King of Rumania gave up his throne to marry Romany actress Mme Lupesco, foreshadowing Edward VII's abdication to marry divorcée, Wallis Simpson, a year later. At first glance *Glamorous Night* appears consistent with the formulaic plot and staging of the musical. It is a visual and aural delight. Set in a foreign locale, there are stirring, romantic tunes, numerous scene changes, spectacular set pieces and a large cast complete with exotically attired gypsies. However, it also made several significant changes to the genre. It starts in a suburban street, rather than a palace, and it ends unhappily when the hero does not get the girl, who marries someone else to save the kingdom. Interestingly, the hero of the piece is the inventor of a television system who ends up watching the marriage of his beloved to the King of Krasnia. It is also technologically advanced, using Drury Lane's hydraulic lifts, and it replicated Victorian spectacle when a ship had to explode and sink onstage. Also notable is the fact that Novello used a woman director, Leontine Sagan, and showcased the black singer, Elisabeth Welch, who had found only limited work in her native America before joining Josephine Baker in Paris cabaret.

Thrillers and horror

The thriller was one of the major genres of the interwar period, sparked by Gerald du Maurier's stage recreation of Captain Hugh 'Bulldog' Drummond in 1921. Based on the books by Sapper (pseudonym of Herman Cyril McNeile), this staunch British character uses the skills acquired as an officer during the war to set himself up as a private detective. Drummond and his crowd are all 'returning soldiers', whose sense of masculinity and morality has been affected by the war. John Stokes argues that 'violence would now hold centre-stage as a release for the frustrations of a wounded officer class fighting hard to claim its place in a modern world, a claim bolstered by imperialist racism (in the form of Asian servants as well as foreign villains) and comic Cockney by-play from what remained of the other ranks'.[49]

The thriller/murder mystery revolves around a number of key paradoxes for the post-war generation. The first is that of presence/absence: the dead body is both represented onstage, but also signifies loss. The second is the need for justice in a world seemingly incapable of providing that. The third concerns the polarities of heroism: if both sides are nobly fighting for their country, how can they both be in the right, and indeed where do the authorities who used soldiers as cannon fodder fit into this picture?

Moreover, while figures such as Captain Drummond entertain audiences with their thrilling adventures, Stokes observes that they also enact 'the post-war idea of the murderer as Everyman'.[50] This dark theme can be seen in other plays, where no-one is what they seem, even if the work is ostensibly a comedy. Agatha Christie's gradual unmasking of the killer among a group of ordinary people in plays such as *Black Coffee* (1931), *Ten Little Niggers* (1943) and *The Mousetrap* (1952) is a working out of her personal nightmare – the gunman who can transform himself into anyone he likes, even family members or friends – but also a statement about the insecurity of a country repeatedly ravaged by war. Similarly, in J. B. Priestley's popular *Dangerous Corner* (1932), the victim turns out to be a drug addict and rapist, while the innocent ingénue is actually the murderer, highlighting the continued concern about the enemy within.

The British theatre was used to horror, from the violence of Elizabethan and Jacobean drama to Gothic and melodrama. A new form appeared in this country when Le Théâtre du Grand-Guignol, based in a tiny Montmartre chapel, toured this country in 1908. The name has been translated as The Theatre of the Big Puppet, and links a well-known puppet character – Guignol – with the commedia dell'arte-influenced Punch and Judy. It had in part been inspired by Emile Zola's scientific naturalism and focused on the gritty life of the social underclass. José Levy, a Francophile impresario born in Portsmouth, developed the genre with his *Seven Blind Men* at the Palladium in 1912, later revived in 1921. When he found a permanent London base in 1920, he chose the Little Theatre. Sandwiched between the Strand and the Embankment, this had a 'marginal' place in the capital's theatre land, being close enough to the West End to draw audiences, and yet slightly off the beaten track. It also had an established air of rebellion, being originally set up in 1910 by Gertrude Kingston as a place to stage suffrage drama; the Pioneer Players and the Abbey Theatre's Irish Players also performed here.

Nevertheless, Levy was careful not to be too unorthodox. As well as importing existing French plays, he also called for new one-act plays 'without the sugar coating, or saccharine centre of the so-called "popular" play'.[51] This had the effect of appealing to established figures and emerging writers such as H. F. Maltby, Edgar Wallace and Noël Coward, although Joseph Conrad's submission, *Laughing Anne*, was rejected.[52] Levy recruited a specific company of actors and the involvement of figures such as Sybil Thorndike, her brother Russell, and her husband, Lewis Casson, also helped to give the plays an air of respectability, as well as attracting other actors and writers.

Tellingly, the genre's highpoint in this country was between 1920 and 1922. The very 'self-referencing', 'joking' and 'playfulness' of theatre of horror as mentioned by Richard J. Hand and Michael Wilson, allowed death to be treated as a form of 'entertainment', while also playing on audience fears about the national and international political situation.[53] Moreover, the frequent portrayal of physical and mental incapacity also referenced the ravages of war experienced since 1914. Christopher Holland's *The Old Women* (1921) is set in a lunatic asylum, ending with the torture of one of the inmates. The eponymous *Seven Blind Men* are locked into their workshop by their manager, leading to panic-induced death when they imagine the place to be engulfed by fire. In *The Nutcracker Suite* (1922) a couple are crushed under a moving ceiling, represented by the descending curtain at the end of the play; the woman becomes hysterical, but the man believes that 'One must be able to meet death with one's eyes open'.[54] Maltby's *The Person Unknown* (1921) makes the referencing of war explicit. In this short play, a man traps in a room a music hall singer who had once encouraged him and others to recruit. Wounded in the face, the soldier resembles the gruesome paintings of Henry Tonks: 'I ain't got much face left – not the lower part anyway . . . Men want to spew when they see me.'[55] When he takes off his bandages to demand the good luck kiss she promised, the singer dies of fear.

Dramatising the first world war

While literary works about the war were produced as it unfolded, it was in the following two decades that there was a tumult of work attempting to understand, explain and come to terms with what had happened. These included poetry collections: Siegfried Sassoon's *Counter-attack* (1919), Wilfred Owen's *Poems* (1920); memoirs based on personal experiences: Enid Bagnold's *A Diary without Dates* (1918); Robert Graves, *Goodbye to All That* (1929); Sassoon's *Memoirs of an Infantry Officer* (1931), Vera Brittain's *Testament of Youth* (1933); and novels, from the successful thrillers of John Buchan to modernist experiments such as Virginia Woolf's *Jacob's Room* (1922). Elsewhere, modernism also shaped responses and representations of the First World War. The art of Paul Nash and Vorticist Wyndham Lewis, for example, did not just illustrate the battlefields of France, but expressed the pain and despair through their jagged abstractions and limited colour palette, as did atonal music by musicians such as Arthur Schoenberg.

Some commentators thought that the theatre would not be able to adequately respond to the events of 1914–18, nor should it try to do so. The views of St John Ervine, the right-wing critic and dramatist, chimed with others about the stagnation of British drama:

> We are an exhausted people, sick from a great effusion of blood, and we will not create a great drama or a great anything else until we have recovered our health.[56]

Ervine's contention that the population was only able to cope with light entertainment has been a view that has persisted, even though the evidence does not bear this out. While commercial theatre managers were wary of alienating audiences, a veritable tidal wave of war plays appeared in the 1920s and early 1930s. Interestingly the vast majority deal with the sickness of the nation that Ervine mentions: subjects cover the terrible conditions of trench warfare and the futility of the loss of a generation, and express anger towards those who were in charge. Beyond this there was an interrogation of the meaning of words such as duty, loyalty and heroism, as well as questions about the point of it all. Some dramatists were quite blatant in this. Maugham's *The Unknown* (1920) caused outrage when a vicar tells a grieving mother that 'World War I was due to the loving kindness of God, who wished to purify the nation by suffering'. The mother's blasphemous response is '"Who is going to forgive God"'?[57]

War plays

As the last chapter demonstrated, first-hand experience of the battle field was charted as the war unfolded by dramatists such as Miles Malleson and Allan Monkhouse. The latter's *Night Watches* (1916) is set in a military hospital and bravely depicts the psychological trauma inflicted on its combatants. Three unnamed soldiers – as symbolic, perhaps, as the figure buried beneath the Cenotaph in Whitehall – begin to realise that they themselves could potentially be able to find a cure for their suffering, in contrast to the medical establishment who have no understanding of their condition. Oddly, Monkhouse wrote this one-act play as a comedy, perhaps to temper the seriousness of the subject matter. In the ensuing two decades, works that retrospectively dealt with trench warfare, almost as a cathartic process, included Harry Wall's *Havoc* (1923), Hubert Griffiths's *Tunnel Trench* and J. R. Ackerley's *Prisoners of War* (both 1925), R. C. Sherriff's *Journey's End*, W. S. Atkinson's '*Glory Hole*' (1932) and Lawrence du Gard Peach's *Shells* (1937).

However, perhaps the most quintessential First World War play is Sherriff's *Journey's End*, a position further cemented by recent revivals, including that by David Grindley in 2004 and 2011. Sherriff's play was originally written for his rowing club's amateur dramatic company, achieving success more widely because it was seen to express authenticity about the soldier's war. It contains, as Samuel Hynes reminds us, various aspects of the myths created through the retelling of the First World War as a 'great *imaginative* event': the stock characters ('brave, hard-drinking commander . . . the lower-class New Army officer'), the stage action ('the raid that fails, the death scene') and the set speeches ('Don't you think I care?', 'I drink to forget').[58]

Sherriff's play is set in a dugout at St Quentin in the three days leading up to Operation Michael (*Der Kaiserschlacht*). The tragic irony is that the soldiers are awaiting the start of the most intensive German offensive of the war, a mission in which they are almost certain to die, and that this took place in May 1918, only a few months before the war ended. Recent productions have emphasised the claustrophobic conditions of trenches, which Sherriff was at pains to depict, as well as the frustration and boredom of confinement. The use of the dark and the silence add to the sense of terror, as does the slow pace which suddenly speeds towards an inexorable inevitability in the last section of the play. The single set adds to the lack of relief and tedium for both the characters and audience, and also gives a sense of acute compliance: the audience becomes aware that these young men are cannon fodder, waiting to be killed when the signal is given, and having no control over their fate. Trudi Tate describes this as contributing to a new form of war trauma, as the 'trenches forced soldiers into extremes of passivity – in effect, waiting to be shelled – at the same time as the war demanded immense courage, resourcefulness and action. Threatened constantly with death or mutilation, frequently witnessing the grotesque deaths of their friends and companions, men often felt at the mercy of immense machines that always seemed to be winning'.[59]

One of the most disturbing elements of the play is the effects of war on men and the exposure of heroism. The eighteen-year-old Lieutenant Raleigh, new to the battlefield and full of innocent idealism, is contrasted with his boyhood hero, Captain Stanhope, whose three years at the front have turned him into a hard-drinking cynic. Death can only be coped with through losing oneself in nostalgic reminiscences about the past or immersion in present-day rituals: excessive drinking, grievances about the food, writing and receiving letters. It is only when death is upon them that heroism emerges, but this is difficult and certainly not inevitable or innate: Second-Lieutenant Hibbert's physical and emotional breakdown in the face of death is shocking for an audience at the time, both for those who have experienced this first-hand and also for those who have accepted myths about the valour involved in warfare. The play emphasises other unpalatable truths about war: the loss of youth (it is stated that the best soldiers to have are young men straight from school); the propaganda which leaves those back home with no understanding about what is happening abroad; the randomness of military decisions and dangers of duty; the realisation that the enemy is also human.

It is significant however that, although *Journey's End* is a moving rendition of the trench experience, it is also essentially unchallenging, which may explain its success with audiences and critics. Certainly Sherriff's choice of realism in terms of language, staging and characterisation separates it from some of the more radical representations of war. While the play deals with the tragedy of trench warfare, the focus is squarely upon British decency rather than outright condemnation of the war. Even the cynicism of Stanhope is shown to be a façade at the end when he tends to the dying new recruit and leads his men into battle. Yet the final sense is that of pointless loss as Stanhope exits the trench to his probable death: '*The whine of a shell rises to a shriek and bursts on the dugout roof. The shock stabs out the candle-flame . . . Very faintly there comes the dull rattle of machine-guns and the fevered spatter of rifle fire.*'[60]

Muriel Box's *Angels of War* provides a female perspective. This is a realistic portrayal of the work done by women on the front line, namely those members of the Queen Mary's Army Auxiliary Corps who are mainly ambulance drivers. Published in 1935, this play did not receive a professional production until 1981, by the feminist theatre company, Mrs Worthington's Daughters, a group dedicated to reviving forgotten plays by women; interestingly though it was also performed by the amateur Brunton Gibb Players in Sydney in 1937. A local reporter damningly compared it with *Journey's End*, saying 'It's not a lady-like play, but it teaches its lesson.'[61] Along with M. E. Atkinson's *The Chimney Corner* (1934), which was about resistance workers in Belgium, *Angels of War* is one of the very few plays by a woman, which was written about the war itself, rather than its aftermath.[62] This was even more unusual, given that Box had no personal knowledge of the war zone, being only nine at its start. Like many of her male counterparts, Box rejects the romanticised view of war as a noble endeavour. For example, when a visitor remarks to the ambulance drivers that she is 'with you in spirit, the spirit which has built our glorious Empire and inspired our men to sacrifice their lives for its protection', these words are contrasted with scenes that show how war is boring, messy and dangerous.[63]

Other plays struggled to find a stage language as a means to convey the horror of war, with Mary Luckhurst observing that 'the real reluctance, or difficulty, of dramatizing 1914–18 lies in the sheer scale of the trauma and outright losses that British theatre, and everything else, suffered in that bloody and seminal chaos'.[64] As with the Grand Guignol, setting, lighting and sound effects became important dramatic tools. Many plays convey the claustrophobic effect of the trenches, but D. E. Hickey's *Over the Top* (1934) goes further by being situated in a tank. Throughout the third act of Griffiths's *Tunnel Trench* the terrible sound of digging can be heard as Germans burrow their way underneath to plant mines. A character's breakdown is heightened by the scenery in Ackerley's *Prisoners of War*, where the sun has a '*burning, eye-wearying brilliance*' and '*the snow seems more white, the rocks more black, and the glaciers more green than is natural*'.[65]

More significantly, playwrights shrank from the dominant British genre of realism, turning more to European models and allegorical forms, as with C. K. Munro's *The Rumour* (1922), Hans Chlumberg's *Miracle at Verdun* (1932) and Priestley's *Johnson over Jordan* (1939). While Sean O'Casey's Dublin plays are naturalistic, later plays such as *The Silver Tassie* (1928), *Within the Gates* (1934) and *The Star Turns Red* (1940) are highly stylised, drawing in particular on Expressionism. Claire Warden argues that 'In this post-First World War era with its ongoing political threats, material inadequacies and fractures in the very structure of society, the Expressionist form (somewhat peculiarly given its level of abstraction) directly reflected the everyday lived experience.'[66]

The Silver Tassie was rejected by the Abbey Theatre, and its failure there in 1935 led eventually to the dramatist's self-imposed exile. The play also had no success in London, where it left audiences puzzled. Three of the acts are in a heightened realism, typical of O'Casey, but Act 2 is set during war and highly influenced by German expressionist drama. There is a symbolic set, designed by Augustus John for the London production, chanted choruses, rhythmic movement and gestures, a non-specific 'war zone', and a more elaborately formal style of writing. All of this was designed to universalise its subject and became the style O'Casey adopted for his later plays. The language achieves a minimalist poetic beauty which at once looks back to Greek Tragedy and Shakespeare and forward to Beckett and Sarah Kane:

2nd SOLDIER	Lifting shells.
3rd SOLDIER	Carrying shells.
4th SOLDIER	Piling shells.
1st SOLDIER	In the falling, pissing rine and whistling wind.
2nd SOLDIER	The whistling wind and falling, drenching rain.
3rd SOLDIER	The God-dam rain and blasted whistling wind.
1st SOLDIER	And the shirkers sife at home coil'd up at ease.[67]

Anti-war plays

Some of the dramatists writing front-line plays were content to present a snapshot view of the trenches, with little or no reflection on the notion of war, let alone providing an anti-war message. This was surprising, given the groundswell of public opinion towards pacifism. Peace societies sprang up at national and international levels after the outbreak of the First World War and continued during the next two decades; these included the Fellowship of Reconciliation, the Women's International League for Peace and Freedom and, of course, the League of Nations Union. Some writers were active in the pacifist movement and their writing made overt the moral ambiguities of war, with its causes being ascribed to male aggression, technological advances and/or capitalist greed. Vera Brittain, Winifred Holtby and Storm Jameson also linked feminism and pacifism, and most eloquently Virginia Woolf's polemic *Three Guineas* (1938) 'sets out to demonstrate the existence of a causal link between war, fascist ideology and the psychological and institutional make-up of patriarchal society'.[68] More simplistically, the heroine of Olive Popplewell's play *The Pacifist* (1934) sets herself up against her fiancé to give a rousing speech opposing war, and Elizabeth Rye's *The Three-Fold Path* (1935) stages moments from women's history, ending with the view that 'if women had more power there wouldn't be so many wars'.[69] In contrast Despair is represented as female in Ida Gandy's allegorical *In the House of Despair* (1937), and destroys all attempts at peace by allowing the tools of war to be built. The inherent violence of human nature is brought out in Cicely Hamilton's *The Old Adam* (1924) and *Peace in Our Time* (1934), written by Box, this time with her husband, Sydney. As the world moved further towards another war in the 1930s, fears about new forms of destruction took hold, as evidenced by Cicely Louise Evans's *Antic Disposition* (1935), which focuses on the use of germ warfare and Clemence Dane's *Shivering Shocks* (both 1935), in which a new explosive is discovered to 'crumple the armies of the earth like a gardener spraying green fly'.[70]

Two of the most experimental anti-war plays were Velona Pilcher's *The Searcher* (1929) and Vernon Lee's [Violet Paget] *Satan the Waster* (1920). The American Pilcher co-founded the Gate Theatre Studio in London with Peter Godfrey in 1927. This was a subscription club – and therefore able to evade censorship laws – which specialised in new writing, especially that influenced by European modernism. Ironically, Pilcher's own play was considered too expressionistic and was finally performed at the Grafton Theatre, another of London's 'little' theatres, in 1930. Inspired by her war experiences in 1918, the satire is set in an evacuation hospital close to the Front as doctors and nurses 'celebrate' as thousands of wounded soldiers flood in on a daily basis. Incorporating music by Edmund Rubbra, official documents and instruction manuals, verse and repetition, the play is both uncompromisingly non-realistic and an accurate representative of the war experience. The female 'Searcher' of the title is both looking for lost men and for Truth, and as Steve Nicholson explains, 'the audience is invited to watch the action not objectively but through the distorted and "tortured vision" of a woman driven insane by the horrors of war'.[71]

Vernon Lee wrote her anti-war play, *The Ballet of the Nations* at the time of the sinking of the RMS Lusitania in 1915. This was reworked as a 'Philosophic Trilogy with Notes and Introduction', and designed to be read aloud as prose. For Lee the war was 'like some ghastly "Grand Guignol" performance. It could, as it seemed to me, have been planned by the legendary Power of Evil'.[72] Because of this Lee creates a hybrid work that draws on the emblematic figures of Medieval masques, including here Sleepy Virtues and Human Passions, presided over by Death, and staged by Satan for Clio, the Muse of History. Satan's prologue frames the central philosophical and religious debates thrown up by war about the nature of evil, the possibility of progress, and the inevitability of individual sacrifice. It starts in Hell and moves to 'No place, Nowhere' and the ensuing ballet becomes 'the vastest and most new-fashioned spectacle of Slaughter and Ruin I have so far had the honour of putting on to the World's Stage'.[73] Published with a lengthy Introduction and 190 pages of Notes, it was immediately attacked by critics who were baffled by its unusual staging and format, but it also garnered praise from Edith Wharton and George Bernard Shaw, the latter of whom admired Lee's intellect and commitment to aesthetics.

Shaw himself was so disturbed by the tragedy of war that nearly every play he wrote afterwards was about how to avoid it through the best means of governance. *Heartbreak House* (1919), *The Apple Cart* (1928) and *Geneva* (1938) are cases in point. Shaw started writing the first of these in 1913; it was completed during the war at the same time as the Battle of Verdun and the first Zeppelin raids, and performed in New York a year before it appeared in London in 1921. The play is set during a dinner party held at the home of Captain Shotover and his daughter Hesione Hushabye. Shotover is angered by the political apathy of intellectuals which has led to the country's blindly walking into war. He is perfecting a death ray to blow up all profiteers, such as the industrialist Boss Mangan, whom his daughter is about to marry: this character was based on Lord Devonport, Food Minister during the war, whom Shaw despised. The play ends with the death of Mangan, who is killed in an air-raid – one of the first stage representations of such an event – as he hides in the gravel pit where Shotover has stored dynamite.

Shaw's treatment of an insular and self-indulgent upper class family on the eve of war is that of a fable about contemporary England and Englishness. Ruled by capitalists, the socialist Shaw depicts society on point of destruction, dramatically rendered through a series of complex references. The play is an allegorical interpretation of Wagner's Rhinegold; Shaw saw the Ring of the Nibelungs as a socialist parable. The subtitle, 'A Fantasia in the Russian Manner on English Themes' draws attention to Chekhov's naturalistic influence; as with *The Cherry Orchard*, the turpitude of Shaw's characters and their gathering at a country house is symbolic of an aristocracy sleep-walking its way to disaster.

The play also makes direct reference to Shakespeare, in particular *King Lear* and *The Tempest*. Captain Shotover is Lear, and the title is taken from his words 'Break, Heart, I prithee break'. Shotover's two offspring – Hesione and Ariadne – and his third 'unofficial' one – Ellie – represent the father-daughter relationship in *King Lear*, but the differences show up the damaged morality; there is no one Edmund figure but rather several male dalliances to demonstrate the corruption of society. Additionally, Hector Hushabye replaces Albany's moral fortitude with a superficial charisma that hides his amorality.

Shotover is not just Lear, but Prospero as well, conducting proceedings with an autocratic recklessness; Ariel is the flute-playing Randall Utterword, described as perhaps the laziest man in the country; and the pit outside the house that holds dynamite is like the cave of Caliban, itself associated with the dark powers of Sycorax. Nothing is real in the play, especially not the hold over the Empire, mentioned via Shotover's navigation of the world, marriage to his West Indian wife, and Ariadne's life overseas with her husband. Even the heartbreak of the title is unreal. Rather than a sudden shock, Shaw is really referring to what he called a chronic complaint; that is, the despair he felt over the short-sighted intelligentsia and the governing classes who do not govern, but instead leave it to 'Captains of industry' like Mangan, who are unfit for public service. Ellie's excitement at the bombs that fall at its end echo these events as well as representing a country trembling on the edge of destruction and transformation. A comically savage play, this has a strong anti-war message about how apathy allows capitalistic forces to be unleashed, leading to unimagined violence.

Staging loss

Clive Barker sees the rise during the interwar period of Grand Guignol, crime dramas, thrillers and 'illusory portrayals of Death', as a way to deal 'the pains of absence created by the mass slaughter of war'.[74] He also notes how dramatists of the two decades following the war used time slips as a means of dealing with very recent history, where memory and myth, dream and reality, had become complexly interwoven. One of the best examples of this is J. B. Priestley's *Time and the Conways* (1937), which moves between 1919 and 1938, presciently showing how the seeds of the probable coming war had been sown at the end of the previous one, through class arrogance and complacency. Here he drew on the thriller genre in which 'we have witnessed what we then are unsure has actually happened'.[75] There was also an awareness of J. W. Dunne's *Experiment with Time* (1927), with the idea that the past, present and future co-exist, also taken up in Virginia Woolf's modernist novels of the 1920s. Again, Priestley became interested in the work of Russian mystic P. D. Ouspensky, whose views on eternal recurrence were reproduced in *I Have Been Here Before* (1937). Playing with time is utilised by Priestley and others such as Clemence Dane for two reasons: the first is that the distancing effect gives an impression that there has been enough time to assimilate, understand, or even control the effects of the war, even if barely any time had passed at all; the second is to provide a means by which the past can comment on the present, or *vice versa*. It becomes apparent, though, that not all playwrights knew how to react towards the recent seismic events – whether of the war, or of alterations in society.

Time and the Conways starts and ends in the 'present moment' (just after the end of the First World War) and the middle Act 'jumps forward' in time to the future (1937, the real present moment for the audience). 'Because of the reversal of time', Maggie B. Gale observes, 'what we witness is both a vision of the Conways' future and a time contemporary to the audience'.[76] In this way Priestley explicitly explores how the war has impacted upon one family, and implicitly suggests that this is a microcosm of the whole of society. Mrs Conway and her family gather at the beginning of the play to celebrate the end of the war. They abound with optimism for their future and that of the world. However, while 1919 and 1937 look exactly the same – and indeed the stage directions state that '*for a moment we think nothing has happened*' – in fact it is the people themselves who are now different, both in terms of life events and in terms of more profound changes.[77] Christopher Innes notes Priestley's deliberately psychological staging. The play opens with 'a dark and empty stage, cut off from the light and music of human activity that filters through from beyond a curtained archway; and this metaphorical ante-chamber of consciousness forms the basis for the focal tableau that bridges each Act'.[78] The vibrant Carol will die, Hazel's marriage to a wealthy man is unhappy, Robin and Joan are estranged, Kay's literary success remains elusive, and Madge is disillusioned with socialism. Returning the audience to 1919 in the final Act makes poignant the withered dreams, and points out the disparity between pre- and post-war Britain.

J. M. Barrie also plays with the idea of time, although this cannot be seen as a response to the war as he was already doing this before 1914: the eponymous *Peter Pan* and his Lost Children refuse to grow up and the heroine of *Quality Street* (1902) disguises herself as a younger woman by travelling back ten years. In *Dear Brutus* (1917) characters get a second chance at life when they visit a magical forest. The idea of redemption continues in another of his popular plays, *Mary Rose* (1920), which concerns a woman who disappears for twenty-one years, only to find that when she returns unchanged the rest of the world has moved on. Although touching on many philosophical and social ideas, Barrie's plays are the antithesis of political drama; they mainly take place in fantastical or dream-like locations that represent society at one remove, without fully challenging the assumptions being set up by the establishment. His characters see the past rather than the future as the answer to their predicament, but more than that, the change in society is supposed to come from the individual rather than the wider political structures; this view is enhanced by Barrie's Shakespearean and mythical references which have the effect of removing his situations from their immediate historical contexts.

The unsurprising surge in spiritualism during the 1920s and 1930s led to the depiction of a number of stage ghosts across a range of genres and styles. Barrie's short play, *The Well-Remembered Voice* (1918), depicted a father being reunited with his dead soldier son at a séance, a poignant reminder for the audience of what had been lost over the last four years. The popular *Ghost Train* (1925) by Arnold Ridley brings together a range of characters stranded in a remote railway station where they are warned that death will come to anyone who hears an approaching train. Noël Coward's plays also include several ghosts, from the disembodied figures at the end of *Cavalcade* who mourn the past and the present to the strident *Post Mortem* (1930), experimental *Shadow Play* (1936) and comic *Blithe Spirit* (1941). All of these plays underpinned the era's desperate need to make sense of the unfolding tragedy and compensate for the loss of what would amount to a generation.

Germany's theatre also had a leitmotif of the dead returning during the 1930s, but to a quite different end. These focused on avenging resurrection. Gerwin Strobl notes that 'Armies of ghosts appeared in Germany between 1933 and 1935. Faces whitened under their steel helmets, the fallen of the Great War marched in battalion strength across the arenas and open-air stages of the new Reich'.[79] A different response was that by Hans Chlumberg in *Miracle at Verdun*, based around the Battle of Verdun. This was the longest and bloodiest of the war with no real military outcomes; it is estimated that 2 million soldiers took part, of which half were killed. Set in August 1939, twenty-five years after outbreak of the First World War, its opening scene cynically depicts a crowd of xenophobic tourists who are visiting the Petit Cimitiere in Argonne, where heavy fighting took place especially between 1916 and 1917. They show contempt for the dead, pulling out their guide books, taking photos and eating their picnics. A messenger wakes up the soldiers of Verdun in a scene reminiscent of Stanley Spencer's resurrection paintings, but the jubilation of the living turns to anger, especially when the dead ask questions of the countries' leaders, and predict another war. Stylistically it is similar to *The Silver Tassie*'s fusion of naturalism and expressionism, but its set tableaux and static action is miles away from O'Casey's work.

Thematically *Miracle at Verdun* relates to Noël Coward's *Post Mortem*, an out-of-character vitriolic attack on those who had condemned a generation to death. Written after he had been acting in *Journey's End* for a few nights, it was performed in POW camps, but only received its first professional production in 1992. It was originally banned for its contemptuous view of all those who keep the war-making machine in business: editors who peddle patriotic myths about heroism, mothers who readily give up their sons, and old officers who wish they were back on the battlefield. The play begins in a dug-out in 1917, where John Cavan is mortally wounded. His ghost returns in the last act to exhort family and friends to face the reality of war. At first he is welcomed back, but this changes as his 'truth' is at vagaries with their own 'truth'. Perry speaks for the author when he says:

> Everyone will write war books and war plays and everyone will read them, and see them and be vicariously thrilled by them, until one day someone will go too far and say something that's really true and be flung into prison for blasphemy, immorality, lèse majesty, contempt of court, and atheism.[80]

Coward himself did not press for a production during his lifetime. As Mary Luckhurst argues, 'This is perhaps not surprisingly for a man acutely conscious of his public image and whose celebrity was based on a certain kind of Englishness that depended on just the sort of stereotypes he describes above.'[81]

The return of the soldier

Even as the war was underway, the process of 'memoralising and remembrance that seeks to validate the sacrifices of the Great War' started up, but this stood in stark contrast to what Claire Tylee reminds us of being two of the main narratives about the First World: '"The Somme Myth" as Paul Fussell calls it, the other is what [Robert] Wohl identified as "The Lost Generation Myth" . . . Both myths deal with the loss of English manhood.'[82] Many male dramatists of the interwar period deal with these ideas in one form or another.

The male population of several communities had nearly been wiped out – the so-called Pals regiments – and those that had returned were often suffering from shell shock, neurasthenia and depression, as well as horrendous injuries to the body. These men – and the 'surplus' women who no longer had the opportunity to marry – became a reminder of the 'lost generation', 'an emotional and psychological reality which made a lifelong impact on its surviving members'.[83]

The representation of the physical and psychological effect on the returning soldier and his community is charted in terms of realism in plays such as Somerset Maugham's *The Sacred Flame* (1928) and *For Services Rendered* (1932). Both plays have a man physically and mentally scarred by war. Reaction to the latter work and *Sheppey* a year later caused Maugham to give up writing for the stage. Maugham's comic touch had gone and his plays had become increasingly critical and vituperative. In particular, audiences could not stomach the savage exposé of the effects of war in *For Services Rendered*. Sydney Ardsley has returned from war to find his family still accepting the heroic myths peddled about the war. Like O'Casey's returning soldier in *The Silver Tassie*, Sydney has been blinded, a metaphor for the inability of his father and others to see the real state of England. Because of his enforced sedentary lifestyle Sydney feels emasculated, further reinforced by his new activity of knitting. He slowly spirals into depression and isolation, aware of the wasted lives around him. His friend who was awarded the DSO for wartime bravery had not returned to a 'home fit for heroes' and commits suicide to avoid shame of bankruptcy. Eva, his sister, is no longer able to find a man to marry and is devoting her life to looking after him. The chilling final curtain ends with Eva singing the national anthem '*in a thin cracked voice*'.[84]

Journey's End was brought to the West End by Maurice Browne, a producer who had founded the Chicago Little Theatre and oversaw the beginnings of a drama programme at Dartington Hall. He also invited Robert Graves to write a war play, which would become *But It Still Goes On* (1930). In Graves's *Good-bye to All That*, he remarks that on being wounded and sent home in 1916, 'England looked strange to us returned soldiers. We could not understand the war-madness that ran wild everywhere . . . The civilians talked a foreign language; and it was newspaper language.'[85] His work was in direct contrast to the typical stylised war narrative of the time, being more of a fragmentary and rambling 'meta-memoir'.[86]

Equally, *But It Still Goes On* was quite different from Sherriff's claustrophobic trench setting and worthy speeches about the conflict between patriotic loyalty and the dangers of life at the Front. Instead, Graves presented Browne with a farce set in London, which satirises English morality and at time seems almost Ortonesque in its surreal juxtaposition, and brusque treatment, of sexuality and death. A nihilistic tone hangs over the whole play, encapsulated by an early comment by Dick, a poet who had been in the war. He stops the globe he has been spinning to remark that the whole world 'still goes on like – like the watch in the pocket of a dead man . . . Have you ever considered how ridiculous a live person would feel in a world that was finished, and over, but still went on'?[87] Unsurprisingly, especially given its frankness about homosexuality, references to famous people and family members, and horrific vignettes about war, the play was not staged, although Steven Trout sees connections between this play and works by Oscar Wilde and George Bernard Shaw, as well as anticipating characters in Evelyn Waugh's satiric novels of the 1930s.[88]

The theme of 'Enoch Arden' – Tennyson's poem about a sailor who returns home after a long time away to find that his wife has remarried – was unsurprisingly common in post-war writing. Maugham's *Home and Beauty* was an early play based on this idea, and also points towards the new moral laxity. Written in 1915 and directed by Charles Hawtrey at the Playhouse in 1919, it treats the subject with a light touch. Victoria, a vacuous society beauty, waits for her husband to return from war and, after the statutory year she marries his best friend. On her husband's return – he has had amnesia and spent time in a POW camp – both men decide that she is too difficult to live with. Seeing no gain in being married to either, Victoria divorces them both.

Clemence Dane's first play, *A Bill of Divorcement* – written in 1921 but set at the beginning of the 1930s – provided a different perspective. Margaret is desperate to divorce her shell-shocked husband, who has been in a mental hospital for over a decade, so that she can marry another man. On the one hand, this play formed part of the debate about divorce, which continued throughout the interwar years, as well as promoting a woman's right to emotional and sexual satisfaction. On the other hand, though, this is only possible for the mother. Sydney, her daughter, gives up her own chance to get married to look after her father, who has, with perfect melodramatic timing, returned home looking for his wife, not realising that she has divorced him. Worried that she has inherited her father's mental illness, which has been exacerbated by his experiences in the trenches, Sydney turns away from her life as a carefree flapper, a modern woman who pursued a life of freedom and hedonism, to one burdened by moral responsibility, both to her family (taking over her mother's role), and to her country (looking after the returned soldier). It is symptomatic of this complicated period that, although Clemence Dane could project the play forward to the next decade, she could not envisage a more optimistic ending to her story, and so while the mother, technically widowed by the war, could be set free by the new divorce laws, the continuance of past beliefs demanded that another woman take her place.

Shifting social and sexual mores

Gender and sexuality

The social satire in Somerset Maugham's plays became increasingly pointed from the start of the First World War, particularly in terms of the class system. *Our Betters,* written in 1915, first produced in New York in 1917, but not staged in Britain until 1923, is a case in point. This involved adultery between men and women from Britain and America, and was a veiled reference to the affairs of Gordon Selfridge with American heiresses. *The Circle* (1921), a reworking of Wilde's *Lady Windermere's Fan* (1892), is about a married woman who runs off with her lover, regardless of society's disapproval. Her relatives attempt to derail the potential scandal, but in doing so reveal their own adulterous liaisons. As with his earlier *Smith*, it is left to an outsider – a man from the colonies – to point out the skewed morality of the upper classes. At the heart of *The Skin Game* (1920) there is a land dispute, with a clash between Squire Hillcrist's 'old money' and the nouveau riche Hornblowers. The former tries to protect his estate from the latter's attempts to surround it with factories, but neither side is seen as sympathetic. Hornblower wants revenge against Hillcrist for snubbing him and Mrs Hillcrist resorts to blackmail. The title is an American colloquialism for unscrupulous behaviour, but also refers to the activities of Hillcrist's daughter-in-law, who used to support herself by being the 'other party' in divorce cases.

Women dramatists such as Dane, G. B. Stern, Margaret Kennedy and Dodie Smith portrayed how sexuality, family and work became sites of tension between the loss caused by the war, and the gains achieved through female emancipation. Muriel Box's aforementioned *Angels of War* takes up the suffragette cry that society has to accept that if women can do the same jobs as men they need to be treated as full citizens. Most of the all-female cast have nicknames that sound male – Jo, Vic, Nobby – or genderless – Cocky, Moaner, Skinny. They swear, drink and smoke, and Box repeats several of Sherriff's key war myths, such as the naïve newcomer, the cynical old-timer, and the tragic and pointless death.

If Sherriff's play focuses on the 'journey's end' – inevitable death – of the soldiers, Box deliberately sets her play in the last days of the war, so as to raise questions about how women can fit back into society after their time on the Western Front. Jo talks of how 'life has had a purpose out here, even though it has been hell!', and Vic says, 'A lot of us won't be able to marry, and if we don't, I can't see us settling down to fancy needlework or knitting after this, can you?' Like the remaining men of their generation, they wonder what, if anything, the past four years has taught them. Jo knows that, for all its atrocity, the war has opened up new avenues, and she is adamant that it must continue on her return to Britain: 'They sent us out to do men's work . . . I'm hanged if I'll be fobbed off with a nursery maid's job.'[89] Disappointingly, the play does not explore the implications of this socio-political change. Instead, the women are seen as playing their part in making the world a safer place, one where they have forfeited their chances of getting married and having children for service to their country.

As women began to be more visible in society, 'the figure of the spinster acted as a repository during the interwar period for society's fears and anxieties about the loss of so many men, and the perceived growing empowerment of women'.[90] On stage she was sometimes viewed sympathetically, but at other times seen as sexually and economically disruptive. Female dramatists tended to take the former line. Dodie Smith is best known as writer of *The One Hundred and One Dalmatians* (1956) and *I Capture the Castle* (1949), but was also a major female dramatist of the 1930s. Like several other female writers on the time, Smith hid her gender under the pen name of C. L. Anthony, only dropping this with her fourth play. Her first play, *Autumn Crocus* centres Fanny, one of thousands of 'surplus women' who will no longer be unable to marry. The Tyrol mountains and fields of crocuses contrast sharply with the cramped conditions and hard drudgery at home, and for the first time Fanny feels a sense of freedom. Yet, constrained by outmoded morality, she spurns her one moment of passion with Steiner, a married, Austrian inn-keeper, to return instead to her drab life of teaching. Smith had hit upon a subject close to the hearts of a number of those in the audience, receiving letters from middle-aged woman all over the country.[91]

The skittishness of the so-called Gay Twenties, with its shingle-haired flappers, drinking clubs and all-night dancing, may have been more mythical than real, but it certainly pinpointed a shift in social and sexual morality that dramatists were quick to identify. In *A Bill of Divorcement*, Sydney's wartime childhood has led her being 'like the rest of the young women. Hard as nails'![92] This phrase is also repeated in Smith's *Touch Wood* (1934), in which the married Vera's desperate search for 'change and excitement' leads her to become sexually promiscuous.[93] Again, Audrey and Alaric in *Autumn Crocus* have embarked on an experiment in sexual liberation, provocatively based on the teachings of the German psychologist Richard von Krafft-

Ebing, author of an infamous work on sexual pathology, *Psychopathia Sexualis* (1876).

G. B. Stern's *The Man who Pays the Piper* (1931) interrogates further the reality of a transitional society. Here again there is a concern with time, as already discussed in relation to other plays of the interwar years. The prologue is set in 1913, notably a reversal of the date when the play was written in 1931. Acts 1 and 2 are set in 1926, after the first enfranchisement law for women, and Act 3 in 1930, after the second. Subsequent to the Prologue, we learn that Dr Fairley and his eldest son have died in the War, and Daryll has become head of the household. A successful businesswoman, she is nevertheless weighed down by duty and responsibility, as indicated by the play's title. In trying to resolve this seeming contradiction, she gives up work to marry, telling her fiancé to 'smash' her and 'break' her, as if, with these violent methods, she can be returned to a kind of pre-war woman. However, once married, she loses any sense of her identity, and seeking a divorce, bitterly telling her husband, 'I'm no good for marriage . . . it's the war, we had to take over then . . . I expect there's a whole generation of us, ruined for marriage . . . we *fathers* of nineteen fourteen . . . we're all freaks my generation of girls.'[94] As Daryll finds herself increasingly torn between two modes of existence, her husband also finds himself in the same situation. The war has worn him down, making him weary of work and competition and thus the play ends on a tantalising vision of a new type of marital relationship; the wife works in town, returning to her country marital home at weekends. While there are some undoubtedly confused areas in Stern's play, it not only points to the war being the significant watershed in changing male/female roles, a theme most writers had tackled, but to posit an alternative way of living, where gender roles have been refashioned.

Other plays of the period also show this way in which women are caught between pre-1914 sexual customs and post-1918 freedoms. Indeed, the figure of the 'flapper' was 'sexless but libidinous; infantile but precocious; self-sufficient but demographically, economically and socially superfluous'.[95] The heroine of Margaret Kennedy's massive bestseller, *The Constant Nymph* epitomises this figure. It centres on the sexual awakening of the adolescent Tessa who runs away with a much older man, to tragic effect. Although the relationship is never consummated, its implications of free-love and female sexual expression articulated a more generalised feeling that the First World War had triggered a social break with the past, and that the younger generation could no longer believe in the mores, sexual or otherwise, of their elders, who had brought about and prolonged the tragedy of war.

Following the 'Gay Twenties' came the 'Anxious Thirties', when taboo subjects such as sexuality were discussed less openly than in the previous decade. Oscar Wilde's trial in the late 1890s had started a wave of moral horror about homosexuality before this abated, and it was once again relegated to silence. Some playwrights of the time such as J. R. Ackerley and Frith Banbury were openly gay; others took on a persona to hide their personal lives – Coward as an elegant dilettante, Maugham as the Grand Old Man of Letters, Rattigan as a matinee idol and war hero; Coward's persona also helped to hide the fact that he was a spy during the Second World War, while Maugham took on intelligence work. Homosexuality was referred to on stage, albeit within limits. Nicholas de Jongh observes that 'By evasiveness, allusion, ambiguity and innuendo, unrecognised by some audience members, easily identified by others, the homosexual had been a frequent, if shady presence upon the stage.'[96] For example, Coward's operetta, *Bitter Sweet* (1929) had the following stage directions *'four over-exquisitely dressed young men enter. They all wear in their immaculate button-holes green carnations'.*[97] The censor wilfully ignored such obvious encodings.

Audiences delighted in effeminate representations which did not undermine conventional notions of manliness, and these abounded, especially in musicals and farces. More problematical was the allusion to homoeroticism among those who served their country. Ackerley's *Prisoners of War*, which depicted a budding relationship between two young soldiers was examined by the censor but found to be too subtle for audiences to understand its meaning. The play depicts a group of POWs in Switzerland, awaiting their repatriation. Captain Conrad slowly comes to realise that a fellow-soldier, Adelby, has deliberately walked to his death, and when his unrequited love for another soldier is rejected he has a breakdown. Ackerley's work takes on increased resonance when it is known that he was in the Battle of the Somme and suffered from survivor's guilt when his elder brother died two months before the end of the war. The savagery of war is equated with the savagery of social repression: Conrad is as much destroyed by the love that can never be disclosed as he is by his experiences on the battle field.

The Green Bay Tree (1932) by Mordaunt Shairp was far more overt in its presentation of homosexuality. The plot centred on a young man (Julian) caught between his instinctive desire to stay with his rich, older protector (Dulcimer), and convention which demanded that he find a wife. The play managed to evade being banned because there was no direct reference to homosexuality. However, Dulcimer was easily identified as '"homosexual", not simply through the play's action but because he is a man of leisure, effete and opulent', and a connection made with Wilde through the character's "'nimminy-pimminy aestheticism'".[98] Yet, while some parts of the media denounced the Lord Chamberlain's decision to licence the play, others saw it as an 'advertisement . . . of a public opinion that is coming to its senses'.[99]

Race and class

The huge and continuing success of *Chu Chin Chow* showed theatre producers that there was an appetite for the exotic. A host of Oriental plays swept this country during the interwar years, as evidenced by E. M. Hull's *The Sheik* (1919) and its spin-offs: these were further influenced by cinematic representations, particularly those by Rudolph Valentino. In these plays the 'sheik' turns out to be an aristocratic man of European descent but 'the suggestion of interracial romance is used in a way that plays upon British fascination with the exotic "other"' and allows women to fantasise about different forms of sexuality.[100] The researches of Helen Maryam Rajabi have shown that 'the orientalist frames of reference that were used to create this imaginary East were repetitive and changed little over time. Prominent among them were the themes of Exoticism, Barbarism and Miscegenation'.[101] These latter two points were fuelled by eugenics theories, where it was believed that there was a link between race, intelligence and morality, and that 'genetic flaws' in society could be bred out through controlled reproduction. The quest for racial purity would reach its inevitable conclusion with Nazism.

Minstrel shows continued to be popular with music hall audiences. However, actors of colour received limited roles, even though there were many plays written about the colonies during the interwar years. Claire Cochrane has discovered a small number of productions featuring black actors: the Jamaican Una Marson's *At What a Price* (1934) was done in conjunction with members of the League of Coloured People, C. L. R. James's *Toussaint L'Ouverture* was performed in 1936 by the Stage Society, and Paul Robeson worked at Unity Theatre and controversially appeared with Peggy Ashcroft in *Othello* (1930) at the Savoy Theatre, London; this was only the second time that Othello had been played by a black actor in Britain since Ira Aldridge in the early nineteenth century.[102] Mixed-race casts like this aroused long-held prejudices and even after the beginning of mass immigration in the late 1940s this still held true. *The Baker's Daughter* (1950) by Michael and Peggy Walsh was turned down for a licence on political grounds – it was based on the real-life relationship between the chief-designate of the Bamangwato tribe in Bechuanaland and a white woman – but it also attracted aggressive racism.[103] Nevertheless, there was a growing black community in this country. Marson's biographer notes that in 1937 'London, the centre of the empire, was also cradle to the pan-African movement, a sort of boomerang from the horrors of slavery and colonialism, to which Una, like many of her generation, was being steadily drawn.'[104] These colonial and European influences would only increase during the Second World War.

Representation of the working classes continued to be limited. Those with regional accents were also hampered in their career; for example, Molly Urquhart's Scottish accent was considered a disadvantage until it became more acceptable in the post-war period when inequities in the class hierarchy were more frequently exposed. Maltby's *The Temporary Gentleman* (1919), described by *The Morning Post* as 'the best and truest war play we have had', depicts the symbolically named Walter Hope, a clerk who is promoted to Lieutenant during the war due to a lack of officers; after the armistice he is supposed to return to his original station in life.[105] This sharp satire is finely balanced, also exposing the snobbery of Walter and his sister. The last act projects forward to 1921 where, after a period of unemployment, the man finally takes a previously spurned job as a salesman. While approvingly seen by reviewers as against social mobility, the play was also much liked by returning soldiers who saw it as representing their own experiences of class tensions in the services.

During the 1920s there was growing disillusionment with the government's promised better life for returning soldiers and the high levels of unemployment, which lasted until the early part of the Second World War. Steve Nicholson sees 1926 as a 'critical year', where Britain's struggle between the workers and the ruling classes, as played out in the General Strike and capitulation of the TUC to Stanley Baldwin's government, was enacted within the theatrical institution as a whole.[106] May's General Strike severely shook the complacency of the Government. It began with the response to the severe depletion of coal supplies caused by heavy domestic use during the war. Because of this mine owners wanted to lower wages and lengthen working hours, but met resistance. The TUC called for support and the slogan 'Not a penny off the pay, not a minute on the day' brought out several million members in sympathy.

In 1929 stock markets in Wall Street crashed, causing the Great Depression, and two years later British unemployment reached two-and-a-half million. There was widespread poverty and applicants were means tested for eligibility to benefits, leading to much resentment. It was felt in some quarters that capitalism was doomed and many looked to communism as a better political system. Others simply struggled for survival. The industrial unrest continued into the early part of the 1930s, with a series of mass demonstrations and strikes. The Jarrow hunger marches of 1934, 1935 and 1936 physically brought to the poor conditions of the northeast to the more prosperous south.

As I have already demonstrated, the plight of the working classes had been sympathetically portrayed in some parts of the Edwardian theatre. Suffrage dramatists focused not just on enfranchisement but female poverty and the world of work. D. H. Lawrence's plays, which span the first three decades of the century, were perhaps more authentic: his characters, dialect and settings are drawn from first-hand experience of the mining community in which he grew up. However, Christopher Innes argues that Lawrence's work was not overtly political because he 'concentrates exclusively on personal relationships and passions'. Again, Innes sees Lawrence's work dramatically limited by his mythologising of the working classes: 'coalminers and peasants are vital figures, being close to nature or associated metaphorically with the subterranean world of the instincts, while sophistication is suspect and intellectual logic a symptom of decadence'.[107] However, his plays explictly convey the entrapment felt by men and women whose lives are circumscribed by physical hardship and emotional stultification.

A Collier's Friday Night (1909), analogous to chapter 8 of Lawrence's novel, *Sons and Lovers*, opens in a working-class kitchen, with all the accoutrements of ordered domestic labour (washing, ironing) featured alongside those of intellectual and artistic pursuits (books, paintings). Lawrence swiftly undercuts the stereotypical view of the working classes as victimised or dim-witted drudges, but also shows the limitations of their lives through the lack of action and claustrophobic setting. The title is not only about one man's life and death, but also Everyman's as well. *The Widowing of Mrs Holroyd* was a stage adaptation of his short story, 'The Odour of Chrysanthemums', and reminiscent of J. M. Synge's *Riders to the Sea*, much admired by Lawrence for its genuineness. Written in 1911, revised in 1914, and finally given a professional production in this country in 1926, this powerful piece focuses on a brutalised wife of a miner. Her final loving act of laying out his corpse after he has died in a mining accident suggests that her husband had perhaps turned to womanising, alcohol and violence as an escape from his dehumanisation by society. *The Daughter-in-Law* was written in 1913, appearing briefly on the stage in the 1930s as *My Son's My Son* in an adaptation by Walter Greenwood. It relates the tale of an illegitimate pregnancy without judgment or moral repugnance, a far cry from the 'fallen woman' themes of recent years. Instead the main concern is more practical; how to financially provide for the unborn child.

Regional theatres, most notably Annie Horniman's Gaiety Theatre in Manchester, ensured that the working classes were represented on the stage. In a similar vein *Love on the Dole* was adapted by Ronald Gow from Greenwood's successful novel and staged at the Manchester Repertory Theatre in 1934. According to one source more than one million people saw the play in 1935.[108] Greenwood's work appeared just as unemployment reached record levels, at nearly 3 million in 1933 and shows the impact of the economic crisis on the urban poor. It is set in Salford, a place once prosperous through the textile industry and the steam engine and now falling behind in the rapidly expanding global marketplace. Harry Hardcastle, exploited at every turn, joins an apprenticeship at the local engineering plant known to use the workers as cheap labour. When he reaches twenty-one and therefore eligible for a man's wage, Harry and the other apprentices are laid off. His hopes of setting up home with his lover are shattered when she gets pregnant and he cannot claim benefit as the iniquitous Means Test takes his father and sister's earnings into account. Wendy Hiller's first important role was as Sally Hardcastle, Harry's sister, whose fiancé is beaten up during a demonstration against the Means Test. The novel and subsequent stage play did much to stir up working-class resentment, although this was not necessarily its intention; in fact, the tendency of the authors was more towards social documentation rather than an assessment of culpability.

A fractured society

In contrast to working-class lives, Noël Coward wrote about the privileged upper middle classes. He was the most popular dramatist of the age and yet many of his interwar plays dramatised areas of social tension and a generation scarred by war: decadent, self-centred and seeking any form of escape. Two of the most controversial were *The Vortex* and *Design for Living* (1932).

The former clearly depicts a generation fleeing the shadow of war through alcohol, drugs and promiscuity. Florence Lancaster's affair with a younger man is sanctioned by her husband, and their son is a cocaine addict and probable homosexual. Coward's style in *The Vortex* is deliberately chaotic:

the cacophonous gramophone and frenetic dancing represents a society that is no longer at ease with itself:

HELEN	It's much too fast, Nicky.
TOM	Do slow down a bit.
NICKY	It's the pace that's marked on the record.
PAWNIE	I've never danced well since the War, I don't know why.[109]

The confused relationship between Florence and her son and the degradation into which their lives descend is a symptom of the society in which they live. Nicky underlines this when he tells his mother that 'it's not your fault – it's the fault of circumstances and civilisation – civilisation makes rottenness so much easier – we're utterly rotten – both of us – we swirl about in a vortex of beastliness'.[110]

This nightmare scenario is also taken up in the highly successful *Cavalcade*, although the subject matter and staging are different. For some, the play's vast scale provided a release from the Depression. As mentioned, full use was made of the Drury Lane theatre's technology, although it was too expensive ever to stage again in original form.

Domestic scenes alternate with public ones to show the impact of history upon the upper class Marryyot family and their servants, the Bridges. The play is epic in its narration of British history, covering the relief of Mafeking in 1900, through the death of Queen Victoria, sinking of the Titanic, and the First World War to New Year's Eve 1929. Many missed the ironic choice of events: the death of Victoria and coronation of her successor show that it is immaterial which monarch is on the throne: imperialist wars will continue to lead to tragedy. The play has numerous references to the personal cost of war and most of the characters suffer some kind of personal loss: Bridges's pride in his wartime service is undercut as he turns to drink and is run over by a horse-drawn carriage, Joe is unable to marry the woman he loves and is then killed on the battlefield; even the happiness of Edward and Edith does not last as they die on their honeymoon voyage aboard the Titanic.

Staged two weeks before the 1931 General Election, the victorious Conservative Party credited the play's purported patriotism with helping to secure the middle class vote for them, although this was not Coward's intention. He later regretted his first-night speech in which he declared in front of an unfurled Union Jack that 'in spite of the troublous times we are living in, it is still a pretty exciting thing to be English'.[111] Rather than conservative chauvinism, though, Coward's play shares surface similarities with that of T. S. Eliot's *The Wasteland* (1922). The modernist sense that the world had fractured into meaninglessness is invoked throughout, most notably at the end of the play. After 'Twentieth-Century Blues', an '*oddly discordant tune*', the stage directions state:

> *Noise grows louder and louder. Steam rivets, loudspeakers, jazz bands, aeroplane propellers, etc . . .*
> *until the general effect is complete chaos.*
> *Suddenly it all fades into darkness and silence and away at the back a Union Jack glows through the blackness.*[112]

Twentieth-century history, Coward suggests, has got increasingly faster and more out of control, only spurred on by the push for power. The final irony is that the play prefigures Hitler's ascendancy in Germany without realising that this was about to take place.

Coward's plays have been viewed as lightweight fripperies, with no real depth to them, but more recently critics have started to admire his innovations of style and ability to judge the mood of the moment. He is now viewed as a modernist and an absurdist in terms of his linguistic self-reflexivity, instability of meaning, and the performativity of sexual and social identity.[113] *Hay Fever* (1925) has no plot at all; the last act turns on its head every dramatic convention of narrative, suspense and climax. Otto in *Design for Living* says 'Any word's ludicrous if you stare at it long enough. Look at "macaroni"', and Amanda and Elyot's exchange in *Private Lives* (1930) is almost Beckettian:

AMANDA	. . . How was it?
ELYOT	The world?
AMANDA	Yes.
ELYOT	Oh, highly enjoyable.
AMANDA	China must be very interesting.
ELYOT	Very big, China.
AMANDA	And Japan –
ELYOT	Very small.[114]

Coward engaged with a range of theatrical forms, such as Pierrot shows, German expressionism, silent cinema and, most importantly, reinvented the English comedy. This latter can be seen through the way in which 'their dramatic minimalism [reduces] plot to situation, psychology to role-playing, and action to performance'.[115] *Private Lives* is Coward's most accomplished comedy. The action is almost non-existent and trivial, consisting mainly of witty repartee between the leads, played by Coward and Gertrude Lawrence in the original production. The plot, such as it is, concerns the remarriage of Elyot and Amanda to other people; after accidentally meeting on their honeymoons, they decide to get back together and feel that their spouses are better suited to one another. The play is rigidly controlled. There are only four characters and two private settings, and the whole works through a series of redefinitions. Christopher Innes observes how the play reverses the pattern of a romantic comedy, 'opening with a marriage that immediately falls apart – then holding up as the ideal a relationship where quarrels are proof of the passion'.[116]

Interestingly, there was a revival of Restoration comedy at the same time, portraying the fashionably indulgent lifestyle of the 'gay couple'. Yet while Coward's characters are similarly flippant, they point out a serious truth – personal morality is more important than that artificially imposed by society. Elyot and Amanda may be divorced, but they are more bound together than ever. Meanwhile the newly married couples are dull and reticent. The linguistic and physical struggle between the two protagonists shows the strength of their underlying passion, but it also points to the repressive nature of a society desperate to contain dangerous tendencies.

Images of England

If some contemporary drama suggested confusion about the state of society, the mythopoesis of England began in earnest during the interwar years as a counterpoint to the horrors of the battlefield.[117] Additionally, English history and culture – including Shakespeare – was pressed into service as a reminder of what made this nation 'great', shown in the popularity of historical drama and the work of the Old Vic Theatre Company.

Stanley Baldwin, who held the role of Prime Minister three times in the 1920s and 1930s (and was considered by some to be the instrumental figure in the National Government from 1931 to 1935), sought to activate 'a sense of national identity' by appealing 'to what he called the "natural devotion to the land and people of one's birth"'. Known as 'Farmer Stan', he coined the slogan 'England is the country and the country is England'.[118] The image spoke of tradition and endurance, and the interest in national identity would only intensify as the possibility of another world war grew ever nearer.

Pageants

Village pageants are mentioned in numerous novels in the interwar and war years, being an important way to debate notions of Englishness in a country rocked by the Irish situation, internal strife and the war. E. M. Forster wrote two historical pageants: 'The Abinger Pageant' (1934) and 'England's Pleasant Land' (1940). In these he expounded the importance of the English countryside as a place that should not be 'developed', a key word that he uses critically to contrast the development/rape of the land with the development of the human heart.[119] John Cowper Powys's novel *A Glastonbury Romance* (1932) and Anthony Powell's *From a View to a Death* (1933) also invoked the village pageant, but its most significant fictional representation was in Virginia Woolf's last novel, *Between the Acts* (1940). This was 'an attempt to re-establish a vision of national identity based on "pastoral memory" in opposition to the nationalism of Britain's imperial mission'.[120]

As mentioned in Chapter 1, pageants reinforced patriotism by appealing to a sense of history. In an attempt to shore up the Empire on the world stage and as a way of addressing the growing social and political discontent in the country by referring back to Britain's past glories, several large pageants were staged during the 1920s and 1930s. The British Empire Exhibition was held at Wembley Stadium in 1924 and 1925, designed to strengthen trade and cultural ties between Britain and its colonies. Once again Frank Lascelles organised a Pageant of Empire, with music by Edward Elgar. Unwittingly foreshadowing the Blitzkreig, the RAF staged an air display titled 'London Defended'; this ran for six nights and reproduced a bombing attack of the city.

Pageants were also used to commemorate a series of events in the past or a specific place. This had already been done with the Festival of London at the Festival of Empire in 1911. The tradition continued through the interwar years and into the 1950s, but in a more localised form, in places that included Taunton (1928), Salford (1930), Falkirk (1932), Chester (1937) and Manchester (1938).[121] One of the most important of these was the Kennilworth Castle Pageant held on the cusp of war in 1939, and designed to celebrate the gift of the Castle to the nation by Lord Kennilworth. Mick Wallis believes that it 'typifies the inter-war British historical pageant in many ways. It is strictly episodic; predominantly amateur', connects 'ordinary folk to the majesty of high persons and events', and, in its use of large numbers of performers, 'aims to unite and memorialise a community around a sense of local history'.[122] This was particularly important at this time, given the number of villages that had lost their men folk in the war.

Shakespeare

Some of the most experimental work at this time – certainly in terms of space and place – was done in service of that most English of cultural figures: Shakespeare. There were also strong attempts to restore him as a dramatist of the people, rather than the intellectualised and elitist figure he was in danger of becoming. In 1921 Nugent Monck opened the amateur Maddermarket Theatre in Norwich, the first recreation of an Elizabethan stage. Like William Poel, with whom he had previously worked, Monck wanted to mimic the minimalism of Shakespeare's original staging. Ben Greet adapted the dramatist for young people and amateurs, helping to secure the pre-eminence of the dramatist in schools. His productions at the Regent's Park Open Air Theatre – founded by Sydney Carroll and Robert Atkins in 1932 – allowed for a more spontaneous and natural approach to the Bard's work, as did Rowena Cade's vertiginous Minack Theatre, built by hand into the Cornish cliffs.[123] This gave a dramatic backdrop to its first production, *The Tempest*, in 1932.

Lilian Baylis continued her management of the Old Vic in London, rebranding it as 'The Home of Shakespeare and Opera in English'. From the mid-point of the 1920s Baylis started to think of there being a 'natural growth of a National Theatre from the Old Vic', and it is with estimable foresight she questioned the problems of a state supported theatre, believing this would end up being 'mainly supported by the intelligentsia'.[124] Like Joan Littlewood, herself stirred by Shakespearean productions at the Old Vic, Baylis believed in the non-elitism of art, whether that was opera, ballet or theatre, and in 1931 she acquired Sadler's Wells theatre for the exclusive presentation of opera and ballet, under direction of Dame Ninette de Valois.

The most important director of Shakespeare during the interwar years was Tyrone Guthrie, who was artistic director of the Shakespeare Repertory Company from 1937 to 1945. He would go on to recreate the Shakespearean Festival in the Canadian town of Stratford, Ontario. His Appia-influenced staging and fast-paced action emphasised the psychological motivations of the characters, brought to life by a new generation of actors: accompanying Sybil Thorndike and Peggy Ashcroft were John Gielgud and Laurence Olivier, who represented two different styles of Shakespearean acting, Gielgud being softer and romantic, and Olivier more rough and contemporary.

Influenced by the rejection of the proscenium arch by Granville Barker and William Poel, Guthrie strongly advocated the closeness of connection between audience and actor. J. L. Styan states that 'Guthrie believed that the drama makes its effects, not by creating illusion but by means of what he thought of as "ritual", and he planned his stage upon the uncompromising theory that illusion is not the aim of performance.'[125] A serendipitous event during a production of *Hamlet* at Elsinore in Denmark – the rainy weather led to an impromptu performance in a hotel ballroom – led Guthrie to realise the possibilities. Starting his career in radio, Guthrie realised the importance of creating atmosphere through language rather than relying on the *mise en scène*, and he also explored the possibilities of open staging such as theatre-in-the-round. In this way, as Howard Fink has pointed out, he pre-empted Peter Brook's 1969 idea of the 'empty space'; the director famously contested, 'I can take any empty space and call it a bare stage.'[126]

At the Shakespeare Memorial Theatre William Bridges-Adams tried with limited success to move away from old styles of staging. Perhaps his greatest achievement was to collaborate with Theodore Komisarjevsky, originally Director of the Bolshoi Theatre in Moscow. The Russian's productions of Shakespeare in the 1930s were highly stylised, with more emphasis put on the visual effect than on socio-political observations. He had nothing in common with English stagecraft and, like Chekhov, stressed atmosphere rather than realism. His sets were minimalistic, in contrast with his colourful costumes, and both enhanced by subtle lighting that made much of moody shadows and highlights. One of Komisarjevsky's most notable productions was *Macbeth* at Stratford-upon-Avon in 1935. Michael Mullin describes the abstract and expressionistic set: 'The tall scrolls, screens and cylinders "like the interior of a steel prison," formed a "nightmare of twisted aluminium" in which Macbeth finds himself cabin'd, cribb'd, and confin'd.'[127] Unusually, the time and place was not specified. This emphasised the play's enduring themes of ambition and war, and made sense of the soldiers' German officer uniforms and how 'in the battlefield scenes the stark barrels of howitzers fingered the skies'.[128]

Historical drama

While many plays presented a splintered society, the historical or 'bio' play generally worked in the opposite way to draw the country together. This was a popular genre in the 1920s and became even more so in the following decade, highlighting this as a period of intense national consciousness. These plays referred 'more directly to the legend than the fact', a deliberate manipulation of history to suit the times.[129] John Drinkwater was one of the poets associated with Rupert Brook, and a founding member of the Pilgrim Players with Barry Jackson, that evolved into the Birmingham Repertory Theatre. A probable pacifist Drinkwater did not fight in the war, but was nevertheless a loyal patriot and wrote several works based on historical figures. His *Abraham Lincoln* was a standout feature of the 1921 season, and although this was evidently about American history, it was also a more generalised study on war, as had been his Classical-based *X=O*. Several other plays followed: an idealisation of *Oliver Cromwell* (1921), *Mary Stuart* (1922) and *Robert Burns* (1925). All these appeared against growing concerns about the unstable political situation – in 1923, the first National Sociality (Nazi) party rally was held in Munich; a year later Stalin took over power in Russia.

Maggie B. Gale has noted the disjunction between the social move towards placing women back in the home after the First World War, and the rise of historical drama, which in many instances, focused upon the public roles held by women.[130] We see, for example, plays about the lives of Joan of Arc, Elizabeth I, Mary Queen of Scots, Katherine Parr, Queen Victoria, Edith Cavell and the Brontë sisters. There are also disquisitions on the private lives of actress Nell Gwyn and writer Sophie Breszka. Even when female dramatists wrote ostensibly about male figures, their focus is on the women characters, as with Anne Hathaway in Clemence Dane's *Will Shakespeare* (1921) and Elizabeth I and Anne of Bohemia in Gordon Daviot's *Richard of Bordeaux* (1933); Daviot was the pseudonym of the Scottish writer Elizabeth Mackintosh, who also produced mystery novels under the name of Josephine Tey. Thus historical plays became a way of inserting, either consciously or unconsciously, a conception of women as political or public beings into social consciousness, as had happened with the suffrage drama of the Edwardian age.

Shaw's *Saint Joan* draws on original documents of the martyr's trial to provide authenticity lacking in other representations, which would have an impact on later historical dramas. However, he also wanted to use this historical work to draw a parallel with 'a world situation in which we see whole peoples perishing and dragging us towards the abyss which has swallowed them, all for want of any grasp of the political forces that move civilization'.[131] The titular role was written for the young Thorndike, and was considered one of the most 'overwhelming performances of the half century'.[132] She drew out the character's suffering and her passionate belief in humanity, particularly in her final speech:

O God that madest this beautiful earth,
When will it be ready to receive Thy saints?
How long, O Lord, How long?[133]

The inner turmoil felt by Thomas Becket in Eliot's *Murder in the Cathedral* mirrors the author's own spiritual demons, but also alludes to a lost world. Eliot's use of verse was in stark contrast to the romanticised historical drama, like Reginald Berkeley's *The Lady with the Lamp* (1929) and Clifford Bax's *The Rose without a Thorn* (1933). His drama has been described as literary and verbal rather than theatrical and visual, with Niloufer Harben suggesting that 'Climactic moments are expressed in emotive speeches rather than in bold theatrical terms . . . The leaning towards statement rather than suggestion and evocation is strongly felt'.[134]Nevertheless, *Murder in the Cathedral* not only uses liturgy and choric patterning, but like his earlier drama also draws on a typically English genre: the pageant. Written for the Canterbury Festival and performed only a short distance from the original event, Eliot's play is rooted in a sense of place. While evidently an intellectual work, it also demands a collective response from its audience who are already aware of the story. This is presented to them through a series of thematically unified episodes, with the Chorus acting as the voice of the common people. The play also demonstrates the continuum of history, underlined when the Third Priest says with prescience:

For good or ill, let the wheel turn.
For who knows the end of good or evil?[135]

This Greek fatalism is at odds with the surge of aggressive militarism during the 1930s, but at the same time marks an anxiousness about the obliteration of English history.

Conclusion

In 1935 Camillo Pellizzi claimed that 'Half the theatres in London are permanently given over to musical comedy, variety and revue, in fact, to spectacles which have nothing to do with Art with a capital A.'[136] As has been suggested here, however, in terms of subject matter and dramatic technique, the interwar years were ones of considerable variety. Theatrical technique reflected the expanding art scene as well as dramatists' attempts to find a stage language with which to describe trauma. It is too simplistic to say that naturalism was the dominant mode in theatre, and the evidence does not back this up, especially in terms of the easy movement between commercial and radical, and amateur and professional, stages. Some playwrights did struggle with the tension, and the more timid included one experimental section within a naturalistic framework. Others were more forthright in drawing on modernism's stream-of-consciousness or employing allegory and Expressionism. Certainly, as Kate McLoughlin has pointed out, there was at times an inarticulacy in writing about the war, which was 'an ethical-aesthetic response to the challenges of conveying conflict.'[137]

Language reflected post-war uncertainty and at times was fragmentary, artificial, elusive and untrustworthy, foreshadowing the Absurdist drama of Beckett and Pinter. Terms that were once considered steadfast in their meaning – duty, loyalty, honour – now assumed a different intonation as people attempted to remember, commemorate and understand what had taken place. Even when war was not the obvious subject matter, the employment of ghosts, time slips and meta-theatricality all point to a society scarred by the events of 1914–18.

Yet, even as Britain was looking back, the country was undergoing a seismic shift. On stage men were frequently portrayed as physically and mentally incapacitated while stronger female roles reflected women's newly enfranchised position. In some quarters the gendering of war as male led to a new surge in feminist pacifism, as exemplified by Vernon Lee and Cicely Hamilton. Again, even before the Second World War there was a strong impetus towards changing the class system. Although the working classes could still be the butt of the theatrical joke, there was also a greater awareness of their living conditions especially in political and regional theatre; this was furthered through cinematic portrayals of the ordinary man and woman struggling through the Depression.

Politically, the schism between different factions grew apace, with governments made jittery by the Irish troubles, the Russian Revolution and the Spanish Civil War. Several intellectuals saw communism as the way forward, most notably Sidney and Beatrice Webb who wrote *Soviet Communism: A New Civilisation* in 1935. However, the failure of the war in Spain a year later to stop the onrush of fascism led to a growing disenchantment among commentators and writers, most notably expressed in Orwell's *Homage to Catalonia* (1938). The dangers of fascism were not just to be found in Europe but Britain as well, with many figures in elevated positions being supporters of Hitler. The rise of Nazism in Germany finally catapulted the world into war. In 1937, Lord Halifax's meetings with Hitler started the policy of appeasement which was to have disastrous consequences when, after Germany's occupation of Sudentenland in southern Czechoslovakia, Britain was forced to declare hostilities on 3 September 1939. As we will see in the next chapter, this had a monumental effect on British theatre.

CHAPTER 4
SECOND WORLD WAR THEATRE
AND AFTER

Introduction

Britain had been watching the political situation in Europe with growing concern ever since the end of the First World War. The 1919 Treaty of Versailles had done nothing to assuage the Germans, and indeed had exacerbated the delicate political balance in Europe. This, combined with conflicting ideologies of fascism, communism and democracy, led to a series of increasingly volatile events. In 1935, Italy under the rule of Benito Mussolini invaded Ethiopia; the Spanish Civil War raged from 1936 to 1939; Japan invaded China, the Soviet Union and Mongolia between 1937 and 1938; and under Adolf Hitler Germany started to regain lands over which it thought it had a rightful claim.

Hitler had taken up leadership of the National Socialist German Workers' Party in 1921 and twelve years later had inveigled himself into the position of Chancellor. He and his Nazi Party formulated the idea of the Aryan master race, seeking to segregate and destroy all those parts of society not deemed to fit into this idea of national purity: mainly Jews, homosexuals, Romani, blacks and the physically and mentally disabled. In 1936, in violation of the Versailles Treaty, Germany started to expand into the Rhineland, and in 1938 its annexation of Austria led to crisis talks with world leaders. Desperate to avoid another war, Britain and France conceded Sudentenland to Germany on the basis that Czechoslovakia's other territories would be protected. Neville Chamberlain returned from talks with Hitler clutching the Munich agreement and declaring 'peace in our time'. Instead November 1938 saw *Kristallnacht*, an attack on Jewish shops and synagogues in Germany and Austria, and further territories were invaded. Finally, the incursion into Poland on 1 September 1939 forced France, Britain and its Dominions, to declare war two days later.

For the first time in this country fighting was not relegated to some far-off place, and the whole of the nation was under siege. In this Total War 'the morale of the nation was all-important and the process could not be one-sided – especially when the unfulfilled promises bandied around after the First World War were recalled'.[1] Unable to form a government Chamberlain gave up office in 1940 when a wartime coalition administration was put in place, under the leadership of Winston Churchill. Churchill's speeches were designed to rally the country, propaganda and censorship were rife, and – as with the earlier war – all forms of entertainment were utilised to help the war effort. This time, though, there was more Government help available, and an even wider awareness among the population of the importance of the theatre.

Wartime conditions

The impact of the war on the British theatre was enormous. All places where crowds might gather, including theatres, cinemas and music halls, were closed at the outbreak of war. When the expected onslaught did not take place, however, most venues reopened very quickly: one of the first was the Windmill, which claimed that 'we never closed' during the war years. Another was Unity Theatre which put together the revue *Sandbag Follies* within forty-eight hours of the ban being lifted. Richard Fawkes notes that 'By Christmas there were more shows in the West End than there had been the year before with audiences swollen by troops on leave'.[2] Theatres continued to open and close throughout the duration. The most difficult event for London and other major cities was the German Blitzkreig: the bombing raids of 1940–1, and 1944–5, which had an enormous effect on Britain's theatre buildings, and theatre-going in general. Travel was severely disrupted as bombed areas had to be cordoned off for lengthy periods, which meant long round trips to get to one's destination, and there was always the fear of further explosions or gas attacks. In 1944 the V1 'doodlebugs' and V2 'buzzbombs' led once more to closure as audiences stayed away, even from popular shows, and managers realised that musicals and other large-scale shows must be cut if audiences stayed away for more than two weeks.

This was a pattern that continued across the country, with the damage or destruction of, among others, the Coliseum and Prince's Theatre (both in Bristol), Argyle Theatre, Birkenhead, the Grand, Plymouth, the Alexandra Theatre, Hull, the Hippodrome Theatre, Dover and the Birmingham Empire. In London alone these included the Gaiety, Gate, Novelty, Royalty, the original Shaftesbury Avenue, Brixton, Canterbury Hall, Little, St George's

Hall, South London and Stratford Empire.[3] Together with the loss of theatres to cinemas in the pre-war era, this led to a considerable decline in traditional theatre venues that have a marked effect on the development of theatre in the post-war era.

However, as far as possible, business went on as usual, and much was made of the 'wartime spirit', which made light of such difficult and dangerous events where the expectation was that plays would be accompanied by the sound of air raid sirens and falling bombs. Noël Coward gives an evocative image of the surreal quality of theatre-going, in speaking of the opening night of the war's biggest theatrical success, *Blithe Spirit*, at the Piccadilly in July 1941: 'The audience socially impeccable from the journalistic point of view and mostly in uniform, had to walk across planks laid over the rubble caused by a recent air raid to see a light comedy about death.'[4]

Productions shown in 1940 and 1941 have to be read against a background of fear of invasion, which seemed imminent after all Britain's allies had been invaded and occupied, one by one, by fascist forces. Certainly, it is true to say that political and military events had an immediate impact upon theatre-going. George Rowell explains that at the Old Vic, the takings for *Trelawny of the 'Wells'* dropped from £115 to £15 overnight during the Munich Crisis in 1938.[5] The first night of Dodie Smith's *Dear Octopus* during the same event was even more dramatic. As the audiences entered the theatre, the news was that war would break out within six hours unless Chamberlain's talks with Hitler went well. A solution was found and relayed to the audience during the interval and the wave of optimism this unleashed helped the play to become a resounding success.

Whereas runs had been extended during the first war because of the vast numbers of soldiers on leave from the front, the next war brought about shorter runs because of the destruction of many Victorian and Edwardian theatres. Plays were forced to move to one that was vacant, or went on tour. This increased the use of alternative venues and led to a greater spread of entertainment across the country than ever before, augmented by touring companies such as the Pilgrim Players. As well as plays, *in situ* theatre companies also moved location, as when the Old Vic transferred to Burnley, Lancashire and the Sheffield Rep went to Southport. Alternatively, theatres closed down before reinventing themselves a few months later, such as Liverpool and Birmingham Repertory Companies; hit by a bomb, the latter took to performing in local parks.

Thus, wartime conditions allowed for a rethinking of space and place: any available area was opened up for performances, whether a church, a factory, a park or an air raid shelter. An example of this is Unity's Outside Shows Group (later called the Mobile Group), which performed a mixture of sketches, songs and straight drama, with over 1,000 performances put on in total. In 1944 they even ran an all-woman group – the Amazons Company – who staged revues, 'the first since the Actresses' Franchise League to perform "women-only" plays'.[6]

Audiences too were more transient, given that the majority of the population – both male and female – was involved in some kind of war work both in this country and abroad. At any given time, an audience could consist of those who were regular attenders or those who had never seen a production in their life; there could also be local residents, evacuees, refugees, service personnel and foreign troops. In more traditional venues, productions started earlier because of the blackout, which meant that audiences could come straight from work. Beverley Baxter believed that 'the abolishing of that waiting period created a flow, a continuity, which made the theatre a part of the normal life of the day'.[7] They would also often attend in their daily clothes or uniform, rather than evening dress, thus creating a sense of informality.

As well as changes in audiences, the war period also impacted upon the relationship between the state and the theatre, and between London and the rest of the country. The present-day Arts Council sprang from the Council (later Committee) for the Encouragement of Music and the Arts (CEMA), set up in 1940, which was designed to bring culture to all parts of the country. The Theatre Royal, Bristol (now the Bristol Old Vic) became the first theatre to receive state funding via CEMA, and 'it was done in such a way as to emphasize "good drama" as a right of the nation, not just the metropolis'.[8] For the first time, the regions started to be seen as just as important as the capital, with the critic W. A. Darlington observing that 'In stage terms, London had become a "touring date"; and not until after the last severe bombing raid, on 10 May 1941, did she become once more the home of the long run'.[9]

Perhaps learning from mistakes made during the previous war, those involved in the theatre were early on given 'Reserved Occupation' status by the Government. There may have been dissent by those militarists who believed that theatre was too frivolous for such times, and fit young men and women should serve their country in more palpable ways, but the main consensus was that entertainment – especially of service men and women, and later to boost the morale of civilians – was valid work. Hysteria surrounding enlistment was nowhere near as virulent as during the previous war, but while many actors, dramatists and directors had joined the armed forces, such as Terence Rattigan, Laurence Olivier, Ralph Richardson and Alec Guinness, some programmes carried the motto 'All the actors in this production are either unfit for military service or awaiting call-up'.[10]

Both in this country and abroad entertainment was provided for the troops in a much more structured way than previously. As Chapter 2 explains, Basil Dean helped to pioneer troop entertainment and the building of the first Garrison Theatre during the First World War, and drawing on this knowledge, he started talks about entertainment for the troops in 1938 even before the Second World War had broken out. Few were prepared to listen at that point, still clinging to the hope that there would not be a war.

Troop entertainment

While troop entertainment had started during the last war, and the Navy, Army and Air Force Institutes (NAAFI) had continued to provide small concert parties ever since, J. G. Fuller has argued that the lack of proper recognition of its importance had a negative impact on ENSA. Moreover, 'The burgeoning of the film industry and of wireless had both decreased the tolerance for amateur or improvised entertainments'.[11] Nevertheless, there was a marked increase in all aspects of theatrical performances for the troops, both at home and abroad. The Germans too put great store by this, and their troop welfare organisation, 'Truppenbetreuung', was one of the best in the world.

ENSA

At the start of the war Basil Dean was made Director of Entertainments for the NAAFI, but soon after he privately started ENSA with Sir Seymour Hicks and Leslie Henson.[12] Its name was changed to the Department of National Service Entertainment in May 1941, but it continued to be known by its original name for the duration of the war, and this appeared on all its advertising. It was mainly conceived of as a means of organising entertainment for British Services, wherever in the world they might be stationed, but when civilians came under bombardment from German bombers it was agreed that ENSA extend its shows to those in shelters, refuges and factories.

The vast Theatre Royal, Drury Lane, was pressed into service as headquarters, becoming increasingly self-sufficient. The space beneath the stage was turned into an air raid shelter, medical staff was available below the stalls to give vaccinations, and security vetting took place across the street at the Little Fortune Theatre. Fire- watchers also stood guard on the roof, although this did not prevent a bomb from destroying some of the theatre in 1940.

The entertainment put on varied widely, hinted at in Tommy Trinder's infamous quip that the acronym stood for 'Every Night Something Awful'. It could range from a solo performer, either a star of stage or screen, or an unknown, to a small concert party who stopped to give impromptu shows, to a well-advertised production of a West End play (obviously with pared-down staging). Musical comedy fared well, as did singers, comedy and variety acts. Female performers, especially those appearing in the Middle or Far East, came to represent those elements of life missing for men abroad: not only the glamour, femininity and sexuality associated with the female body, but also a deep longing for home and the 'English' way of life. It was also a chance for soldiers to hear what those left in Britain were experiencing, which hardened their resolve to win the war. Straight drama was not always well-received, particularly at the beginning of the war when actors were faced with those who were unused to theatre, and therefore found it difficult to concentrate. To surmount this, John Gielgud wrote a plot outline to each act, delivered by an actor, an idea taken up by others at the time. When victory seemed near, ENSA and other entertainment programmes started to trickle into Europe. ENSA made its European headquarters in Brussels, and the Old Vic Theatre Company and Sadler's Wells Ballet, among others, toured France, Holland and Germany from here.

It proved to be an ambitious but contentious endeavour, from its inception until long after it had been disbanded in August 1946, when the Combined Services Entertainment (CSE) took its place. Criticism was levelled against the patchy provision in this country and abroad, towards muddled organisation, pointless bureaucracy and even Basil Dean's autocratic style, but most of the concerns were with the occasionally poor quality on offer. Nevertheless, it was a huge, and on the whole, successful undertaking, which did much to boost morale and keep theatrical activity alive during the war. It was also to have more far-reaching effects, bringing theatre to new audiences – decommissioned soldiers would often search out those who had entertained them during the war, for example – and locations, and breaking down the artificial barriers between amateur and professional.

In 1941, the United Service Organizations for National Defence (later shortened to the United Services Organizations, or USO) came into existence. This was roughly similar to Basil Dean's ENSA, although lacking the financial backing given in this country and the strategic organisation; that was, until the bombing of Pearl Harbour in 1941, whereupon there was a huge impetus towards entertaining the troops. Once the American soldiers started to come over to Britain, they set up their own premises, such as the Rainbow Corner, set up by the American Red Cross in Piccadilly.

The ABCA play unit

Concerned about dissent in the ranks and the effects of the humiliating defeat at Dunkirk, the Army Bureau of Current Affairs (ABCA) started holding a series of educational events, such as lectures and short courses, designed to interest, entertain and boost morale of the troops. Captain Michael MacOwen, who had run Westminster Theatre before the war, was approached to incorporate drama, and this led to the creation of the ABCA Play Unit, in operation from 1944 to 1946. Ironically, given the Government's concern about political subversion, MacOwen ran this along similar lines to the previously mentioned American Federal Theatre, with its eighteen members acting as a collective. Its writers were drawn from a variety of different political persuasions: MacOwen himself was a Liberal and others included Bridget Boland (Conservative), Ted Willis (Socialist) and Jack Lindsay (Communist). The Communist André von Gyseghem was also involved. It is therefore no surprise that Churchill tried unsuccessfully to close down the Unit.[13] Topics included the roots of fascism (*The Japanese Way*), America's war aid to Britain (*It Started as Lend-Lease*) and post-war reconstruction (*Where Do We Go From Here?*).[14] The Unit had to avoid party politics, but a lot of their work had a socialist undercurrent and Davies argues that 'in the radical context of the war years their plays chimed with the undercurrents which resulted in the substantial Labour Party victory at the 1945 election'.[15]

The Play Unit's first 'try out' was with J. B. Priestley's *Desert Highway* which opened at the Garrison Theatre, Salisbury, in 1943, followed by performances at the Bristol Old Vic, the Playhouse, London, and a tour of army camps and other theatres. Davies points out that Priestley and other 'seasoned observers missed the significance of the novel work that the ABCA Play Unit was doing', viewing *Desert Highway* as 'quite unsuitable for the venue and spectators where the Unit performed'.[16] A better fit was the first 'official' production *What's Wrong with the Germans?* (1944), where cast members were planted in the audience and actors dressed as Nazis entered through the back of the auditorium, almost causing a riot on one occasion. Richard Foulkes notes that 'This development of agit-prop techniques was deliberately designed to draw audiences into the action of the play, to provoke further debate about the central issues.'[17]

The use of '"non-theatrical" locations – Nissan huts, gun sites, factory canteens' – helped to create a more intimate and less elitist connection with its audience and although there were experimental theatrical elements (spotlights on different parts of the stage, spoken blank verse), the quick scene changes, topical subject matter and use of sound and light drew a distinct comparison with the mass medium of cinema.[18] Given that this was often some audience members' first experience of theatre, this had an immediate, visceral effect, which impacted upon expectations of drama in the post-war period.

Other troop entertainment

Apart from ENSA, there were other forms of entertainment put on for the troops, and many initiatives were started by those keen to show their willingness to help out. Within weeks of the outbreak of war, Richard Foulkes tells us, 'church choirs, amateur dramatic societies, operatic groups, Women's Institute revues, YWCA concert parties and troupes of performing children were queuing outside the barracks to give a show'.[19] Various organisations were set up to deal with the dozens of different groups and individuals who came forward. For example, Charles F. Smith, director of Brighton's Theatre Royal set up Mobile Entertainments for the Southern Area. MESA put on plays, concert parties and film shows and helped to launch the career of actors like Donald Sinden. These shows were put on whenever and wherever there was a venue available, be that a theatre, hut, village hall or country house.

Unless they were already in the Services, almost every well-known figure of the time provided individual tours of this country and abroad, including Noël Coward, Vera Lynn, Gracie Fields and Jack Buchanan. This did much to alleviate the boredom, horror and home-sickness of troops abroad. Any professional actors in the Services, or even enthusiastic amateurs, were pressed into putting together entertainment for their Company, often at very short notice and minimal outlay. These concert parties were often ad hoc, with various initiatives set up in far-flung countries, such as the Bengal Entertainment Services Association (BESA) in India.

Ralph Reader had set up the Gang Shows in the 1930s, drawing on his experiences with the Scout movement and, conversely, female chorus lines. Reader belonged to Royal Air Force (RAF) Intelligence, and was asked to utilise his popular Gang Shows as a cover to report back on his travels. Eventually, though, they became an important fund-raising scheme for the RAF, and provided entertainment to flying crew whose morale was badly depleted during the Battle of Britain in 1940. The shows themselves owed much to the Scout shows before the war: comic sketches, drag acts and musical numbers such as 'Crest of a Wave', and were spoofed in the TV series *It Ain't Half Hot Mum*.

When ENSA's reputation started to suffer from the poor quality of some of its output, a new source of entertainment became available. Lieutenant-Colonel Basil Brown, who was involved with the York Repertory Theatre in the pre-war period, started the Central Pool of Artists in 1941, better known as Stars in Battledress. The actor Bill Alexander and impressario George Black were also involved. This was a touring group to be dispersed to more remote areas, and composed of theatre professionals, unlike ENSA that relied to a large part on amateurs. Another difference was that the group was composed of service men and women who could therefore enter war zones. Each of the three armed forces had their own version, and actors were handpicked from ordinary soldiers (i.e. those without a specific trade or role of importance) across the various army units. They were given basic training before being deployed solely for entertainment purposes. Stars in Battledress also contained some of the biggest names of the time, including Charlie Chester, and Black who produced the shows had access to the Crazy Gang routines, and sketches by stars such as Max Miller and Tommy Trinder. However, because the nationwide tours were often placed in the larger established venues in the country, there was a ready and enthusiastic audience which allowed many performers to hone their acts, including Terry Thomas, Kenneth Connor, Harry Secombe, Spike Milligan, Frankie Howerd and Tony Hancock. Later on in the war, tours were organised to Europe, one of which reached Germany in May 1945, shortly after Victory in Europe (VE) day.

Apart from variety-style entertainment, straight plays were also put on. Interestingly, it was deduced that, in an average unit, nearly three-quarters had not been to a theatre, nor did they have a wish to. After initial resistance, however, most were demanding more drama. These included Shaw's *Arms and the Man* (1894), Sherriff's *Journey's End* and Rattigan's *Flare Path* (1942), which was already running successfully in the West End.

As in the first war, soldiers' entertainment for themselves often revolved around all-male drag shows. These were obviously born out of necessity, given that there were no women to take the female roles, and some participants would be aware of the long tradition of cross-dressing in the theatre and music hall. However, this was also an opportunity to assume a different gender and/or sexual identity, and allude to the gay sub-culture in society, as previously described on p. 83. Given that homosexuality was illegal and grounds for immediate dismissal from the forces, theatrical cross-dressing allowed for its very public display. The large pink triangles homosexuals were forced to wear in Nazi Germany point to the dangers surrounding this issue. Significantly, the most popular sketch in the very successful revue *Rise Above It* (1941) was 'The QUEERies', a send-up of ENSA concert parties. Wilfred Hyde-White as compère described these as 'one of the horrors of modern warfare', but 'queers' and 'horrors' also slyly refer to what many would have seen as an unmentionable topic.[20] This is also reinforced by the fact that a number of obvious homosexuals and lesbians were involved in the show, including Frith Banbury, Henry Kendall and a female pianist called 'Bezer'.[21]

Paul Ibell notes the cluster of all-male drag shows which toured in the first ten years after the war: *Soldiers in Skirts*, *Showboat Express*, *Forces Showboat*, *Forces in Skirts* and *Misleading Ladies*. These carried the wartime tradition into the public arena, but escaped censorship because 'the shows were a way of seeing (and in a curious way celebrating) men in the armed services in a fun, and certainly unthreatening way. This was militarism not as in a Nazi propaganda film, but as in a saucy seaside postcard'.[22] Again, these shows were usually based on the loose structure of a revue, avoiding the plot complications that could ensue from a narrative-driven drama, yet could still be a source of considerable merriment for an audience that was conversant with the subject matter.

CEMA

Throughout the late 1930s and war years the Government was highly concerned with the morale of its population, as evidenced by the use made of the Mass Observation social research organisation, initially started in 1937 after the Abdication crisis a year earlier, and the propaganda programme initiated during the war by the Ministry of Information.[23] In 1939 CEMA was set up by the Government. This was to alleviate boredom and apathy (late 1939 to early 1940 was nicknamed the 'Bore War' or the 'Phoney War'), provide employment for those in the entertainment industry, and to raise public morale especially through the assertion of shared cultural values. A less well-advertised objective was to promote and control government views. To this end, activities were as various as lunchtime concerts at the National Gallery by famed pianist Myra Hess, and tours and official photographs of the Ballet Rambert as they visited aircraft factories.

The Pilgrim Trust initially provided financial help in setting up CEMA. This was a private American foundation whose chairman was Lord Macmillan, also Minister of Information in the winter of 1939–40, and its Secretary was Thomas Jones who believed strongly in education and social welfare through the arts. He saw the far-reaching consequences of CEMA, viewing it 'not only as an emergency measure for the benefit of the players and audience in war-time conditions, but as a piece of social policy with big future possibilities'. In particular, children would learn that plays are 'sources of living pleasure, and so to make an eager and intelligent audience for the theatre of to-morrow'.[24]

In 1942 the Pilgrim Trust handed over the reins to the Board of Education and the economist John Maynard Keynes took the helm. With previous experience with founding the Cambridge Arts Theatre in 1936, Keynes would play a major role in shaping, not just wartime CEMA, but arts policy in this country for many years to come. It is also notable that R. A. Butler, soon to instigate sweeping changes through the Welfare State, took a great interest in the work of CEMA after it had been subsumed into his Education Department.

There were three panels: Drama, Music and Visual Arts. Ivor Brown was the first Drama Director, followed by Lewis Casson in 1942. Both were married to formidable women of the theatre: Brown to one of the few female directors of the time, Irene Hentschel; Casson to Sybil Thorndike. One of its stated aims was to 'make a useful contribution to the social life of rural districts and small provincial towns as well as assisting in the maintenance of public morale'.[25] Theatre-less areas such as South Wales and the North-East were particularly targeted, especially by the Old Vic, and James Bridie joined CEMA to speak up for Scottish drama.

Initially, it had been hoped that contributions would also come from private sources, but this quickly foundered, and for the first time in this country, the State became a patron of the arts. Martin and Henzie Browne's Pilgrim Players became, in Peter Billingham's words, 'the first ever theatre company to receive any form of financial subsidy from an official government source'.[26] Again, CEMA – with strong pushing from Herbert Farjeon – helped to save Bristol's Theatre Royal from being sold off as a greengrocery warehouse, making it 'the first major incidence of state support being used to sustain a professional company and it was done in such a way as to emphasize "good drama" as a right of the nation, not just the metropolis'.[27] However, this avowed interest in the regions, along with returning the theatre to the people – views held by Thomas Jones – ran counter to the ideas of Keynes who wanted CEMA to focus on high professional standards. For Keynes, ballet and opera became central to this concept, along with the development of a national theatre, which would bring together all that was best about British drama; all of this should, he believed, take place in the capital.

Yet there was also sterling work done around the country, even if this was controversial. As the first chairman of the Scottish committee CEMA, James Bridie boosted theatre in his country through the founding of the Citizens' theatre, Glasgow, in 1943, 'with a guarantee against loss from CEMA'.[28] Bridie and Thomas [T. J.] Honeyman struggled to wrest control from Keynes, who was against decentralisation of CEMA's management and believed that Scotland was not ready to become autonomous. His comments are cutting and once again stress the partisan, metropolitan bias:

> In my view Scotland is not nearly ready . . . I don't think we can have a National Arts Council without some contemporary national art and it is very doubtful whether there exists in Scotland any considerable body of painters, musicians and writers above a . . . provincial level.[29]

That Scottish drama was at the time dominated by the amateur movement also affected Keynes's views.[30]

While there were considerable problems with the setting up and running of CEMA, the country-wide tours under its auspices allowed new companies to come into existence during and after the war. Yet, although the Arts Council did much to support regional theatre and smaller theatre companies, it cannot be denied that great amounts of funding also went into the larger, more 'prestigious' projects; namely the reopening of Covent Garden Opera House, the Shakespeare Memorial Theatre in Stratford-upon-Avon, and the regeneration of the Old Vic. It also became involved in the development of the country's National Theatre.

Arguments for a National Theatre had rumbled on throughout the century. In 1948 the first British Theatre Conference took place, chaired by J. B. Priestley. Three hundred representatives from across the industry took part and debated the future of theatre, with especial interest in liaising with the Government on issues that needed urgent attention. These included a repeal of the censorship laws and the necessity for a National Theatre. Clement Atlee's socialist government took this a stage nearer to realisation by passing the National Theatre Act (1949). A site had already been purchased on the South Bank in 1946 and a foundation stone was laid five years later but this was repeatedly moved until its final site was agreed upon in 1967. A National Theatre company had already been formed and begun at residency at the Old Vic in 1963 and finally the National Theatre was opened on the South Bank in March 1976. It had been a long-drawn-out process, but at its heart was the belief that the country deserved good quality, affordable theatre for everyone.[31] Nevertheless, Claire Cochrane usefully reminds us that 'There is an ongoing debate about the legitimacy of National Theatres as opposed to the theatres of the nations, i.e., the extent to which expensive, essentially elite prestige institutions actually prove obstacles to nationwide access to theatre.'[32] Linked to this, state funding, which properly started during this period, has been seen as a positive step for the theatre, but at the same time both ideologically and theatrically compromising.

Touring theatre

The Old Vic

In the years before Britain had a national theatre, the Old Vic was closer to being viewed in this light than any other. As a theatre company it was generally held in high regard, because of its specified output of classical work, and it was seen as an example of what could be achieved without state subsidy. Yet, in actuality, the Old Vic had suffered some difficulties during the 1930s, and when Tyrone Guthrie took over the management of the Old Vic after the death of Lilian Baylis in 1937, it was heavily in debt, with no strong audience base.

Guthrie's 1939–40 season was designed to attract a new audience through stars such as Robert Donat, John Gielgud and Fay Compton, and he made the bold move of putting in place a repertory system with plays recurring throughout the season, but not being performed more than two or three times in succession. Even before the Old Vic's Waterloo building was bombed, Guthrie made the decision to move away from London to the town of Burnley in Lancashire before setting up a permanent repertory company at the Liverpool Playhouse. The choice of the Old Vic to remain there (and not a city at that) rather than London was an important factor in destabilising current thought about the centrality of the capital to Britain's theatre. The Old Vic also created several branches to tour areas that normally lacked theatre. Sybil Thorndike and Lewis Casson spearheaded one, visiting Welsh mining villages and Unemployment Clubs, while another went to the North West of England.

Little concession was made to non-theatre-going audiences with a typical repertoire including Shakespeare, Shaw and Euripides. Here we can see a lacuna between what critics' expectations of audience taste and the reality. A good example of this was Casson's decision to show Eugene O'Neill's *Days Without End* (1934). London critics hated it and sniffily remarked, 'What have the poor miners done that they should have this inflicted upon them?' when in fact Casson 'had guessed correctly that its underlying note of religious mysticism would appeal to the Welsh character'.[33]

If the fortunes of the Old Vic had been in trouble prior to the war, its position now underwent a transformation. The company returned to London at the New Theatre in 1944, reassembling again at the war's end under Laurence Olivier and Ralph Richardson and emerging stronger than ever. This was for a number of reasons: they gained national prominence through their national tours and residencies, and the tripling, and more, of the Companies led to greater coverage; support from CEMA and then the Arts Council agitated the debates about the future, and indeed function, of theatre in this country.

It is also reasonable to suggest that audiences had become younger during the war because of the great influx of Service men and women into the theatre and inroads made into Theatre in Education (TIE). This can be seen by changes that took place to the rapidly repaired Waterloo building in London after the war. It reopened with a Theatre Centre alongside, run by three theatrical innovators. Michel St Denis, George Devine and Glen Byam Shaw – or the 'Three Boys' as they became known – incorporated 'an Experimental Stage, a Theatre School and the base for a Children's Theatre Company, the "Young Vic"'.[34] The Arts Council gave funding, and the School opened in January 1947.

Touring companies

Even given Keynes's view, one of the great successes of wartime theatre was its widening participation. For the first time in this country's history, theatre was broadly accessible to the majority of the population. This was partially achieved through the great increase in touring companies at this time. These ventures were disparate, some being free of political intent, others bogged down by idealism or a specific agenda. Because of conscription into the Services or other forms of war work, several of these touring companies mainly consisted of amateurs, some professionals who were protected under the Reserved Occupations Act, and Conscientious Objectors who were allowed to carry out their duty to their country through theatrical work.

Women often took a key role, perhaps freed from conventional and less flexible entrees into the industry. For example, Ruth Spalding founded the Oxford Pilgrim Players, later known as the Rock Theatre Company, which 'claimed to play "any time anywhere", in Welsh miners' halls, schools, universities, once in a garage, in a hospital, in converted stables, in the crypt of St Paul's cathedral, and in East End air-raid shelters'.[35] Nancy Hewins, whose godmother was the Fabian Beatrice Webb, started The Osiris Players, also in Oxford, in 1929, and during the war they performed over 1,500 times, including all-female productions of Shakespeare. The company was run on a shoestring, never having more than seven women in it, meaning that work in local shops and factories had to be fitted around rehearsals and performances.

Significantly, many of those connected to touring theatre were ethically and socially concerned to renegotiate the relationship between the individual and the State, seeing theatre as a tool, not just to entertain the populace, but to educate them as well into the principles of religion, pacifism and/ or Socialism: three such companies were R[ichard] H. Ward's the Adelphi Players, John Crockett's Compass Players and E[lliott] Martin Browne's Pilgrim Players, started with his wife, Henzie.

The Adelphi Players enshrined Ward's Socialist views. His 1941 manifesto, called 'The Theatre of Persons', stated that theatre's function was that of 'illumination' for the 'common man' of 'the whole range of his inward and outward life, his thoughts and sensations and actions'.[36] Thus, *Holy Family* (1942) placed the Nativity story within a contemporary setting, with Jesus's birth being seen as providing hope for a new social order. Staging drew on Greek theatre, namely the Chorus's incantation, to stress the ritualistic aspect of theatre. This was championed under the new leadership of Maurice Browne, the director and theatre manager who produced *Journey's End*, and Paul Robeson's *Othello*, and is credited with starting the Little Theatre Movement. Work by the Adelphi Players, Browne stated, provided a 'new contribution to dramatic structure' that consisted of a sense of 'continuity.

Not only are we free of the front curtain, of scene changes, costume changes, makeup changes and similar obvious breaks in continuity, but even from that sense of a change of "scene" that every entrance or exit provides'.[37]

This searching for theatrical experimentation, in tandem with social experimentation, also formed the bedrock of the Compass Players, started by John and Anne Crockett in 1944. Crockett trained at the Slade School of Art, and took classes run by Saint-Denis and George Devine at the London Theatre Studio, and his wife was a dancer, therefore their style of theatre was both highly visual and physical. Crockett, like Ward and many others connected with touring theatre at this time, was violently opposed to war, and all that had existed in pre-war society. Here it is important to note, as Peter Billingham has done, the connections between the ethics of touring theatre, and its roots in an ideological concept of 'the community'. The Crocketts were connected to the Taena Community, which was based on the 'radical liberal idealism' of William Morris, and brought together people from the Peace Pledge Union, the Independent Labour Party and other left-wing and anti-militarist biased groups.[38]

When the inevitability of war became obvious in 1939, E. Martin Browne (not to be confused with Maurice Browne) devised what were called 'suitcase rackets', the kind of travelling theatre that would be able to reach an 'evacuated population'.[39] These Pilgrim Players travelled around the country on the back of a wagon, similar to the travelling players of the Elizabethan period, so that theatre was taken to the people rather than the other way around. The foundations for all of this had been laid during Browne's early interest with the work of William Poel, the actor and director who believed that the emphasis in theatre should lie with the written and spoken word, rather than spectacle. This was then furthered through Browne's relationship with T. S. Eliot in the 1930s. The war years provided the right kind of opportunity for this, and this pared down, 'pure' theatre, as Billingham states, 'provoked this idealistic response of using theatre in a restorative sense in a time of political and social crisis.'[40]

Easily transportable staging replicated that of the Renaissance period. This was not just because of the material conditions of touring but one based in a completely new ethos of theatre, which was attempting to break down the barriers between audience and performer, and lead to a more 'direct' connection with the basics of drama. Staging techniques such as theatre in the round, rejection of the 'fourth wall', use of masks, improvisation, Choric monologues and allegory, had all been in place in pre-war political and verse drama; the touring companies of the war years expanded upon this and led to even greater experimentation in the 1950s and 1960s.

Community theatre and theatre in education

As can be seen from the above, during the war there was an increase in community theatre, as drama became an important creative outlet with many of these focusing on community issues or those of especial interest to their audiences. Amateur theatre had grown in significance during the interwar years, especially in the suburbs, and in 1936 Robert Graves and Alan Hodge note that there 'were nearly forty thousand amateur dramatic societies, and nearly one million amateur actors in Britain'.[41] Molly Sinclair Urquhart gave her initials to the semi-professional MSU Players, which she started in Scotland in 1939. The company spawned the acting careers of Eileen Herlie, Gordon Jackson and Nicholas Parsons, among others and Urquhart's gift '"of making actors out of people – railway workers, students, teachers, housewives and children", certainly strengthened the indigenous pool of performers'.[42] At the other end of the country, the amateur Questors Theatre in Ealing, London, was inspired by wartime events to write a five-point plan. These coalesced around the notion of theatre as part of the community and as a form of education. In reaching out 'to help local youth groups, short-term drama courses for youth groups were organised, and The Questors helped to establish the Ealing Youth Drama Festival in 1944'; its Student Acting Course was eventually subsidised by the local education authority, adding to the idea of drama as worthy of study.[43]

Mick Wallis cogently argues that amateur theatre was used to 'regenerate village life; and to deliver adult education in rural areas'.[44] The British Drama League grew out of the Village Drama Society, and was started by Geoffrey Whitworth in 1919 in order to put theatre at the centre of the neighbourhood; twenty years later it covered over 600 villages. It vigorously promoted amateur theatre: annual competitions were held, and the winners appeared on the West End stage. From 1948 to 1957, Martin Browne headed the British Drama League. He highlighted the shift in the theatre industry when he stated that 'Acting which had previously been the pastime of a few leisured rich, could become the recreation of the many'.[45]

It worked with CEMA to create a civic theatre scheme as a way to ensure the survival of regional theatre after the war. Olivia Turnbull explains that this 'was based on three major ideals: first, that the development and maintenance of civic theatres would require both state and local financial aid; secondly, repertory would best be served if each theatre had its own resident company, and finally, that theatre companies would need to be of a large enough size to undertake a full repertory programme and simultaneously supply a company to tour the surrounding regions'.[46] The policy was also enshrined in a 1945 Government White Paper on 'Community Centres', which recognised 'the achievements of the non-commercial, independent theatre activities during wartime'.[47]

Many theatre companies toured areas where the Workers Educational Association and the Co-operative Society were particularly rooted in the community, drawing on long associations between the working classes, education and culture. Some companies, like that based at the Century Theatre in Coalville, Leicestershire, continued to serve the community by touring with four trailers – known as 'the Blue Box' – drawn by ex-RAF tractors. It was thought of by John Ridley in 1948 and started on the road four years later. Their repertoire was built on pragmatism and experimentation, so that in any one season they had a popular play, a schools' set text, and a more unusual piece by dramatists as various as Henri Ghéon, André Obey and Gabriel Marcel.

An important element of several theatre companies at this time was the nascent form of TIE that was taking place. Generally speaking, while it was only with Brian Way's Theatre Centre in the 1950s that this began to gain ascendancy, children started to form a distinctive part of the theatre audience during the war years as when the Osiris Players toured schools with their all-female Shakespeare productions. Sometimes this was because schools were the only possible venue available, but at other times companies such as the Compass Players deliberately targeted schools in the immediate post-war period, in order to reach out a younger theatre audience. Evacuee children were also offered theatrical activities to occupy, entertain and educate them in ways that had not happened before.

By 1948 John Crockett, founder of the Compass Players, was able to assert in a programme note that those in education were starting to appreciate that drama must be brought to life in the classroom, not seen as a dry academic subject: 'This, the Company feels, is a justified demand and one to which the theatre must accede if it hopes to combat the spoon-feeding effect of the cinema and help in creating lively and intelligent citizens of the future.'[48] The 1944 Education Act also helped cement the future of TIE, with London Education Authorities (LEA) working to promote and fund widening participation of this through performances and workshops.

The Bristol Old Vic Theatre Company was started in 1946, with its Theatre School (BOVTS) opening a year later. This catered for amateurs and those who wished to go into the profession and was under the directorship of Hugh Hunt and Edward Stanley respectively. Stanley was previously at Perth

Repertory Company and had honed his skills during his military service in the Middle East. He was joined by Raphael (Rudi) Shelly shortly afterwards, an emigré from Hitler's Germany, who also gained much experience during the war, through 'play-reading groups, giving illustrated lectures to British soldiers, and directing amateur Army shows'.[49]

Throughout the war calls had already been made for Drama to be taken seriously as an academic subject worthy of study at University. Glynne Wickham was the first to do this at Bristol in 1948. This put in place 'a famous "triangle" of Theatre school, Repertory Company and University Drama Department, promising a three-sided perspective of vocational training, professional production and theoretical study'.[50] A further Drama Department followed in 1961 at Manchester, set up by Hugh Hunt, who had been the first Director of BOVTS. This was a huge step forward from the interwar years when J. B. Fagan tried to start a University theatre company at Oxford, and received no help whatsoever from the University.

Repertory and regional theatre

The First World War had nearly brought about the closure of the repertory movement, due to loss of staff and support, and there was a fear that this would also happen during the next war. In fact, the Second World War actually strengthened its position. This was partly because of the strange dichotomy imposed by wartime conditions: on the one hand, travel was restricted and so audiences were encouraged to make the best of their local theatres; on the other hand, the population was increasingly mobile so new audiences continued to flow into different areas. Olivia Turnbull argues that the war time conditions 'actually laid the foundations for the establishment, after the war, of a network of regional theatres that came closest to realizing the repertory idea as relates to quality, longer rehearsal periods and new and experimental drama than attempts at any other time'.[51]

Apart from Birmingham and Liverpool, the quality of material put out by repertory theatres had become diluted and thus the growth of new companies and tours of West End productions helped to raise standards. Plays such as Dodie Smith's *Dear Octopus*, Esther McCracken's *Quiet Weekend* (1941), Daphne du Maurier's stage adaptation of *Rebecca* (1940) and later Lesley Storm's *Black Chiffon* (1949) greatly increased ratings because of their appeal to provincial audiences. Again, a mobile population created a new audience base. For example, the Oxford Playhouse – notable for being the only repertory theatre to be built between the wars – struggled to find an audience under normal circumstances. However, a larger audience more receptive to theatre appeared from 1938 as more people moved to what was perceived to be a safer part of the country.[52]

One of its first and most important initiatives of the Arts Council in the immediate post-war period was to move support away from touring companies to the development of regional theatre, as a means of rebuilding communities. Some companies that had toured during the war now moved into permanent lodgings, as with the Adelphi Players, who settled down in Brocklehurst Hall, Macclesfield, rebranding this as The Adelphi Guild Theatre. The Arts Council also turned to supporting the theatre by replenishing the building stock which had been damaged or destroyed by the wartime bombing raids, although this by necessity meant returning to purpose-built structures: Guildford (1946), Ipswich (1947), Kidderminster (1948), Chesterfield (1949), and in 1951, Canterbury, Leatherhead and Derby. The first regional theatre to be built after the war was the Belgrade in 1958, as part of the reconstruction of Coventry. The strong surge of interest led in 1944 to a number of repertory companies coming together to form the Confederation of Repertory Theatres (CORT), and several conferences were held at which CEMA expressed financial support.

The term 'repertory' had become déclassé by the 1950s, being replaced instead by the word 'regional'. Rowell and Jackson believe that 'In the pre-War and inter-War years the word "repertory" had specific, intellectual overtones . . . By the 1950s it was devalued, rightly or wrongly, and associated with "weekly", "seaside", "tatty" and other pejoratives. "Regional" not only stressed the local loyalties of public and programme . . . but emphasized the semi-permanency of those theatres which retained a resident company.'[53] While this may be true, an important distinction needs to be drawn here between repertory theatre and regional drama. While repertory theatres exist in the regions, the repertoire is often generic and interchangeable; regional drama conveys a specific area, be that setting, language, characteristics, subject matter, tone and so on. Thus, Annie Horniman's Gaiety Theatre is both a repertory theatre and one that champions regional drama. More than this, there is a deliberate attempt to construct and defend an indigenous identity, as I suggested in my Introduction.

We can see this with Ewan MacColl; born in Salford, Lancashire, he created the myth that he was Scottish by changing his name from Jimmie Miller. Claire Warden notes that 'This constructed ancestry was central to MacColl's desire to settle in Scotland. It was a search for an authentic homeland, a means of connecting himself with a particular Celtic lineage'.[54] Molly Urquhart, who had been at the Cambridge Festival Theatre, returned to Scotland to set up her own company in Rutherglen. This sprang from her desire to create 'another Little Theatre in Scotland where talented players can be given an opportunity to play in their native country'.[55] When in 1943, Tom Honeyman, James Bridie, and others, started the Citizens Repertory Theatre, its manifesto beseeched its audience: 'London and the other cities are watching our fight. With your regular help and loyalty we can win this battle. Get the regular theatre habit! Come often to the Citizens' Theatre. It is YOUR Theatre'.[56] These examples suggest a strong move towards a finding a sense of connection and meaning within the community, exacerbated I would argue, by two world wars coming so close together. Nevertheless, it was not always easy to find dramatists who could convey a true Scottish identity.

One company that succeeded in this was the Glasgow Unity Theatre, which was formed in 1941 out of four existing groups: the Glasgow Clarion Players, the Workers' Theatre Group, the Transport Players and the Jewish Institute Players. Oddly, the first production was that of an Irish play: Sean O'Casey's *Purple Dust* (1943), but after this there was a succession of plays that were centred on Scottish concerns. Ian Brown sees Ena Lamont Stewart's *Men Should Weep* (1947) and Robert McLeish's *The Gorbals Story* (1948) as 'directly concerned with a Scotland defined in terms of poverty and unemployment, urban and industrialised'.[57]

The former play is described by Nadine Holdsworth as a new form of social realism. It can be connected to the 'pre-war "mass observation" documentary movement, which was concerned to acknowledge and record the life of everyday working people, while Glasgow Unity's staging made the production a precursor to the "kitchen sink" realism of the post-1956 theatrical "revolution"'.[58] Set in a Glaswegian tenement flat in an area known for its acute poverty, Maggie Morrison works to look after her seven children and unemployed husband. The matriarch is supported by her independent sister Lily and a host of female neighbours, but her resources are depleted by the daily battle to survive. By the end of the play her husband has turned to drink, his mother is in the poorhouse, one son has murdered his wife, another succumbs to tuberculosis, and she in turn dies in childbirth. The unremitting tragedy was acceptable to audiences because they recognised its reality, even while the Labour Government in London was attempting to provide a better future for the country. Scottish identity, and more particularly, Glaswegianism, is depicted through the use of language and humour and 'This effect was enhanced by the performers' familiarity with the rhythms and tones of the demotic dialogue, which captured the verbal richness and witty, quick-fire banter of the Glasgow streets.'[59]

McLeish's play has striking similarities with Gorki's *The Lower Depths*, but transfers this to an-altogether Scottish setting. Like Stewart's play it is set in an over-crowded tenement, where eight families share one kitchen. Referencing one of the most pressing concerns of the day – slum housing – it makes a social and political statement, as did the better-known *Love on the Dole*. This was made clear on the opening night which saw 'the civic and literary leadership of the town lectured from the stage before curtain-up by a representative of local squatters who were the group's guests of honour'.[60]

Other parts of the British Isles used regionalism to comment on wider issues to do with colonialism. Although neutral through the war, Ireland was steeped in an awareness of the events just across the water; however, this was fused, as in George Shiels's popular *The Rugged Path* (1940) with an awareness of Ireland's troubled history, most especially its relationship with England. Robert Welch tells us that 'There are continuous references to the Troubles of twenty years back, the War of Independence, and the Civil War ... this is a world given over, to a large degree, to misrule; there are no forms of social cohesion backed up by impartial law.'[61] Provocatively, Shiels suggests that elements of the fascist regime of Germany and Italy can be detected in England as well.

Nationalistic figures at the Abbey Theatre, most notably Ernest Blythe, wanted drama that could 'be representative of the Irish people, and play its part in the continuing development of a distinctively Irish theatrical tradition'.[62] To this end, native dramatists and the Irish language were supported (at that time the first national language of Ireland): from 1942 it was decreed that no non-Irish-speaking actor could be employed at the Abbey, except under special circumstances, and all plays at the Abbey between 1942 and 1946 were directed in Irish by Frank Dermody. Undoubtedly, the wartime conditions affected people's perception of their cultural and geographic identity, and the global conflict had led to a rethinking of colonialism, as had happened in the previous war with Shaw's *O'Flaherty VC*.

Sean O'Casey takes this up in his play, *The Star Turns Red*. This is a political allegory dedicated 'TO THE MEN AND WOMEN WHO FOUGHT THROUGH THE GREAT DUBLIN LOCKOUT IN NINETEEN HUNDRED AND THIRTEEN', but the time is 'To-morrow, or the next day'.[63] The unnamed country is divided into factions: the fascistic Saffron Shirts, supported by the Bishops, and the Christian Front, and the communist Trade Unions led by Red Jim, a character based on real-life Irish trade unionist, Jim Larkin. Written to confront the sweeping tide of Nazism, the play nevertheless also craftily refers to the territorial ambitions of England as well, one of the characters even being named 'English'; this also links with the Christian Front, as the word is from the Irish *'Eaglais'*, meaning church.

Similarly, O'Casey's *The Purple Dust*, only performed five years after being written, is a reworking of Shaw's *John Bull's Other Island*. Two Englishmen buy a decaying Irish property and try to turn it into their vision of a Tudor hall. The satire resides in the interplay between the Irish workers and community, whose Gaelic traditions are more authentic than the interpolators who have no understanding of their rewriting of history and who do not understand their imperialist behaviour. The mansion represents Ireland, broken down through colonisation and the attempts to escape from England's oppression. Its new English owners are named Stokes and Poges, after the village that inspired Thomas Gray's 'Elegy in a Country Churchyard' (1750) and, as Christopher Innes reminds us, 'The flood that drives them out symbolizes the sweeping away of cultural imperialism and capitalism by the river of time.'[64] All that is left is a pile of purple dust, the residue of Ireland's troubled relationship with its coloniser.

Popular genres

Even though there were numerous difficulties with staging theatre during the war, there was a wide variety on offer. At the outbreak of war the theatre critic J. C. Trewin considered that 'London demanded light entertainment, and revival after revival filled the programme.'[65] Nevertheless, in the capital in 1939 alone there might have been Flanagan and Allen in *The Little Dog Laughed* at the Palladium, but there was also Priestley's experimental morality play *Johnson Over Jordan* at the New Theatre, Karel Capek's war allegory *The Mother* at the Garrick, and Eliot's modern tragedy, *The Family Reunion* at the Westminster.

The radio created a new audience for singers, and 'Vera Lynn, billed as "Radio's Sweet Singer of Sweet Songs", would become the Forces' sweetheart.'[66] Tours for the forces kept interest high. Service personnel on leave could go to see operettas and light musicals, particularly those about composers: *Blossom Time* (1942, Schubert), *Waltz without End* (1942, Chopin), *Song of Norway* (1946, Grieg) and so on. Rather than being dismissed, although, these bring to the fore two specific concerns. The first is with a deep concern with old-time (pre-Fascist) Europe, and in that way became talismanic for a life that is both nostalgic of a world without Nazism, and of keeping the plight of Europe to the fore. It can also be seen to link into Britain's concern with its own Empire. 'Foreignness' is exotic and 'different', while any reality of another country's culture is simultaneously flattened out to be non-threatening, stripped of all but the most obvious caricatures.

There were many revivals at the time as these were tried and tested, as well as cheap. *Chu Chin Chow*, so popular during the previous war, made a reappearance, and an influx of American musicals was even more of a success once US soldiers were stationed here. This gathered pace in the immediate post-war years with the arrival of *Oklahoma!* in 1947. The most important figure in British musicals at this time continued to be Ivor Novello, and *The Dancing Years* held a similarly affectionate place in people's hearts that *Chu Chin Chow* had in the previous war. The plot was unusual for a musical, particularly one by Novello, in depicting real-life events as they were unfolding in March 1939. Novello drew on the repression of music by Jewish composers in Nazi-occupied Austria. His own producer Tom Arnold thought the subject matter too difficult to tackle on stage, but although Novello could never be described as a political animal, he felt for the plight of fellow artists, and was prepared to expose the fascism and anti-Semitism in Europe, at a time when Britain's foreign policy was one of appeasement.

Rudi Kleber, played by Novello, is a Jewish composer living in a country under dictatorial rule. The contemporary references are made clear in a prologue and epilogue, referring directly to Kleber's forthcoming execution by the Nazis. The Lord Chamberlain's office refused to licence the play until these specific references were taken out, and the topical commentary toned down: the fear was that this would run counter to the country's attempts at placating Hitler, and even be seen as openly hostile in stirring anti-German feelings. By the time the play returned to the West End in 1941 it was possible for Nazi uniforms to be shown on stage (although the prologue and epilogue were never restored), and the references to the ongoing situation made obvious. Steve Nicholson explores this relationship between politics and censorship more closely in his article on pp. 223–39.

While Kleber can never be with the woman he loves, because she has married a senior figure in the regime, she tells him that his music will live on, even after his death. The play ends with crowds of couples dancing to 'Waltz of my Heart', one of Novello's best-loved songs. As Paul Webb says, 'This final scene may sound rather hackneyed', but there was a strong 'visual and emotional impact' for an audience living through the war.[67]

Similarly, *Perchance to Dream* started its epic run of 1017 performances in April 1945, and has qualities important to an audience worn out by war, but anticipating victory. Set in an English stately home, the couple at its centre are reincarnated from the Regency period into the 1920s, and then to the present day. Kept apart by time and circumstance, they eventually manage to be reconciled. Its smash hit song, 'We'll Gather Lilacs' encapsulated the yearning felt by those waiting at home for their loved ones to return, using the English countryside as a symbol of hope.

At a time when it would be expected that audiences required escapism, twenty-five per cent of West End plays in 1944 were concerned with murder, including two re-enactments of Victorian crimes: Ronald Pertwee's *Pink String and Sealing Wax* and Harold Purcell's *The Rest is Silence*; the latter was based on the infamous Madeleine Smith case, a Victorian woman put on trial for killing her lover. Death is also the prominent theme in the longest running show during the war, Noël Coward's *Blithe Spirit*, as it was in the well-liked American import, Joseph Kesselring's *Arsenic and Old Lace* (1939). One of the most interesting is Agatha Christie's stage adaptation of her 1939 novel, *Ten Little Niggers*; this play went through several title changes before becoming *And Then There Was None*. A seemingly random group of people is brought to an uninhabited island where they are disposed of, one by one, according to the nursery rhyme 'Ten Little Indians'. The island represents Britain, but in direct opposition to the state's view that everyone is working together, and as I have argued elsewhere, 'We are exposed to the exact opposite of a community, one where there is no kinship or cooperative spirit; this is the daily fear of Churchill's government, but here negated by the murder mystery formula.'[68]

Crime writer James Hadley Chase had two notable productions in the theatre during the war. *Get a Load of This* (1941) and *No Orchids for Miss Blandish* (1942). Although British, Chase emulated the hard-boiled style of American pulp fiction, and his brutal depiction of sex and violence won him as many critics as it did fans. However, *Picture Post* was most complimentary about the staging of *Get a Load of This*, describing it as 'London's Most Original Wartime Show'. The London Hippodrome was turned into a replica of the Orchard Room, a New York night club, where the audience sat at tables in the stalls watching the light-hearted murder of gangsters take place around them. Chorus girls in thigh-length uniforms wove in and out of the tables as actors dressed as police officers rushed in to arrest the gangsters. The reviewer noted that 'On the stage, the brutality and crudity of the girls-and-gangster theme loses its sordidness. The audience knows it is all make-believe, and they enjoy the entertainment and novelty of the thing.' [69]

Fear of invasion, so prevalent in the run-up to the First World War, had now become a distinct possibility, especially since the evacuation of the

British Expeditionary Forces from Dunkirk and the occupation of France by German troops in 1940. This, coupled with anxiety over Fifth Columnists and spies, led to a wave of films and plays on the subject. *Cottage to Let* (1940) by Geoffrey Kerr was billed as the first spy thriller of the war, and more British in tone. Appearing at Wyndham's Theatre a few weeks before the Blitz started in earnest, this involved a group of Nazi spies intent on stealing a new invention. One of their agents pretends to be a wounded RAF pilot who parachutes into the village, but the bumbling Charles Dimble foils the plan and he is revealed to be a British undercover agent. The light-hearted tone and casting of Alastair Sim as Dimble help to mitigate anxiety over any German incursion.

Responses to war

Theatre clubs continued to press at the inconsistencies of the censorship laws by presenting challenging work, both in terms of subject matter and in terms of style. This gave cause for concern given the government's determined efforts to keep up morale and mask the realities of the conflict as far as possible. As with the previous war there was still the search for a suitable theatrical language, and dramatic verse, allegory and realism were pressed into service. Christopher Fry attempted to revive poetic drama and, like Eliot, he wanted to return theatre to its religious roots. His Festival plays contained religious subjects and motifs, such as death and resurrection, and written to be performed in ecclesiastical settings. His first big success was *The Lady's Not for Burning* (1948), commissioned by Alec Clunes at London's Arts Theatre. Although set in the 1400s, Fry's verse comedy is actually a plea for present-day pacifism, and John Gielgud for one identified Fry's complex work as expressing 'a real understanding of the inexpressible, tongue-tied, cliché-dreading, desperate vitality of the generations of the two wars'.[70]

In 1949, T. S Eliot's *The Cocktail Party* – a reworking of Euripides' *Alcestis* – depicts characters trapped by almost-pathological indecision. They desperately need companionship and yet are destined to feel alone. Echoing Sartre's *Huis Clos* – which coined the phrase 'Hell is other people' – Edward says

What is hell? Hell is oneself,
Hell is alone, the other figures in it
Merely projections.[71]

J. B. Priestley's immediate response to the imminence of war was his modern morality play, *Johnson Over Jordan*. This follows the journey of Robert Johnson – an allegorical 'Everyman' figure – after he has died. He travels through limbo, first visiting the nightmarish University Insurance Company, and then to a nightclub where he grapples with his baser nature among distorted, bestial figures. Finally he reaches a kind of peace in The Inn at the End of the World, where he is able to correctly assess what is of value in life. In Jude Kelly's acclaimed 2001 revival at the West Yorkshire Playhouse, Leeds, with Patrick Stewart in the lead role, Johnson's gradual disintegration was relayed via the projection of his 'face projected on to a gigantic brick wall that gradually disintegrates as hands, bodies and telephones penetrate its surface'.[72] However, the original production with Ralph Richardson was a critical failure. It was directed by Basil Dean in an Expressionist style that highlighted Johnson's struggle between his id, ego and super-ego, but swamped the narrative. More importantly, Maggie B. Gale considers that Priestley's belief that 'we might take more responsibility for our actions and better understand their impact on others' is 'in the original context of a country on the brink of war . . . a challenging prospect'.[73]

Other playwrights were more straightforward in their representation of war. Terence Rattigan's *Flare Path* was based on the playwright's experiences as an air-gunner in the RAF and later adapted for the cinema as *The Way to the Stars*, directed by Anthony Asquith in 1945. It had a familiar and accessible staging, although the play was initially turned down because producers believed that audiences would shy away from the subject matter; instead it had a long run. Trevor Nunn's 2011 revival at the Theatre Royal, Haymarket, with Sienna Miller, was also a resounding success with audiences and critics alike.

The setting is a hotel adjacent to a Bomber Command airbase. A crew gathers there to meet their loved ones but when they are called back for an emergency night raid on Germany, the women are left behind to wait for their return. As they count the planes taking off and returning the tension becomes almost unbearable when it becomes obvious that one is missing. Winston Churchill was quoted as saying, 'I was very much moved by the play. It is a masterpiece of understatement. But we are rather good at that, aren't we?'[74] During the last war emphasis was put on the heroic nature of those who fight for their country. This is in evidence here as well, but as with Sherriff's *Journey's End* Rattigan also focuses on their fear. Teddy, one of the pilots, breaks down and confesses this to his wife, who makes the decision to stay with him rather than leave with her lover. Several members of the RAF who were in the audience found themselves moved to tears by Rattigan's exposure of their vulnerability and, although the play revolves around the gradual breaking of the great British emotional reserve, its American and Polish characters also shows this as an international experience.

Whereas plays about the first war had dealt with the atrocities of war as well as the bravery, those this time around were more uncompromising in exposing this. One of the most disturbing was James Barke's *The Night of the Big Blitz*, at Glasgow Unity Theatre in 1941. This depicted the terrible decimation of Clydeside in March of that year, once again demonstrating the ability of theatre to swiftly respond to topical events. Rather than shying away from the reality or presenting the propagandist view, Barke's play focused on the physical and emotional trauma suffered by those caught up in the political battle being waged between nations. The 'Mortuary scene' was entirely cut by the censor.[75] This was set in a bombed-out church, where bodies taken from the bombing raids lay in serried rows. After looking in several mortuaries, the working-class Dunlop finds the corpses of his wife and children. He suffers a form of trauma, verbally venting his anger on her, and has to be restrained from physically attacking the body. Eventually he walks away, abandoning his family. This was a direct contradiction to the official line that 'Britain can "take it"'; Barke's rejection of the customary stoical acceptance and faith in a higher duty defamiliarises this scene and renders it deeply troubling.

Rodney Ackland's *The Dark River* (1943) also eschews comforting platitudes. Originally produced as *Remembrance of Things Past* (1938) it is set in 1937 and references both the First World War and the Spanish Civil War. Mrs Merriman's son has died at Ypres and she clings to the hope that his comrade Maltby will be able to offer information. However, what she hears is that 'you wouldn't have recognised him – he was so burnt'. When Gwen tries to temper this news by suggesting that he died quickly, Maltby once again refuses this consolation: 'Oh, no, miss, he lingered on for two days'.[76] Shortly before Gwen has shut her ears to the horrors of a German raid on Barcelona in 1937, and Mrs Merriman will not let her young ward read about the horrors of Guernica. Noises from the river bank outside are of political meetings now being held there; Mrs Merriman says, 'Communists or Bolsheviks, Fascists or Pashists, I don't know what they're called, I never read the papers', echoing the characters' denial of the larger world in Shaw's *Heartbreak House*. This is reinforced by the sounds of gunfire and aeroplanes which continue throughout the play. Ackland's message that reality must be faced, not ignored nor sugar-coated, is underlined by Catherine's last words:

'don't let's turn away – let's try to face whatever's coming and not *pretend* any more'.[77]

Coward's *Peace in our Time* (1946), taking as its title the common misquotation from Chamberlain's 1938 visit to Munich, posits that Britain has lost the war and is occupied by Germans. This was a shocking situation given that the country had come close to this reality, and the image of Nazis mixing with English people in a London pub was unpalatable for many; for this reason it was not a hit. This alternative slice of history presented the audience with differing responses, from those who collaborate to those who resist, with Coward drawing his inspiration from the occupation of France. He asks difficult questions about whether life could continue as normal when living with the enemy and how far political and moral values needed to be compromised.

Later plays about the war include *Cockpit* (1948) by Bridget Boland. Drawing on her experiences with the ABCA Play Unit during the war, she utilised the whole theatre space, transforming it into a facsimile of a German Playhouse that is being used as a Displaced Persons Assembly Centre. The unsuspecting audience was given a taste of the refugees' bewilderment as they surveyed signs in foreign languages and attempted to listen to women onstage arguing in Polish. The chaotic situation symbolised a Europe ripped apart by war, where the émigrés have to choose between being sent eastbound or westbound. Reactions were mixed, with some thinking that it was unable to offer any solutions to the problems in European unification, and it only ran for a couple of months. Criticisms of plays such as those by Coward and Boland suggest that audiences were unwilling to be presented with difficult subject matter with the war so recently over, yet dramatists continued to confront the almost unimaginable.

The Holocaust and nuclear war

The genocide of Jews was denied by many, even when it became fully known to the British Government in 1942, and the word 'Holocaust' only came into usage in the later 1950s. Aware of the dangers of propaganda, many were sceptical about the scale of what had happened. It was only in the final weeks of the war as news footage of the liberation of the concentration camps began to sink in that first-hand testimony began to be taken seriously. John Lennard astutely points out, 'tens of thousands had witnessed *something*' but what that was remained unquantifiable.[78] In the immediate post-war period drama from this country and abroad dealt with the subject of bearing witness, however painful that might be: John Van Druten's *I am a Camera* (1951), an adaptation of Christopher Isherwood's earlier Berlin stories was an early work; others included Arthur Miller's *After the Fall* and *Incident at Vichy* (both 1964) and Peter Weiss's *The Investigation* (1965). Not surprisingly, in the wake of the Nuremberg trials, there was also a strong interest in justice: for example, *Crime and Punishment* (1946) adapted by Rodney Ackland from Dostoyevsky's novel, Rattigan's *The Winslow Boy* (1946), Joan Temple's *No Room at the Inn* (1946), Priestley's *An Inspector Calls* (1946) and Miller's *All My Sons* (1948). How the Holocaust could be assessed was still in process, but the residual desecration of humanity lingered in terms of Existentialism. Life's absurdity was explored in plays such as Sartre's *Huis Clos* and Beckett's *Waiting for Godot*, both of which were staged in Britain in 1946 and 1955 respectively.

Most of these plays do not directly tackle the Holocaust, but others are more forthright. As mentioned, J. B. Priestley was persuaded to write *Desert Highway* for Michael MacOwen at the War Office, but the result was not as MacOwen expected. The structure once again takes up Priestley's interest in time. It starts with British soldiers led by a Jewish sergeant who are lost in the desert with a broken-down truck; strafed by German bombers the youngest member loses his life. In the middle there is a flashback to a caravan lost in the same spot 2,000 years ago when the Assyrians invaded the Middle East; once again, the youngest soldier is killed. The play ends with the approach of an aeroplane, but the audience are unsure as to whether it is an ally or enemy. In this play Priestley deliberately subverted clichés of war literature: the insertion of a central 'Interlude' shows the connections between past and present conflict, and the way in which common foot soldiers have been stereotyped. The appearance of a Jewish sergeant is designed to shock audiences into understanding the reasons for the war by describing the genocidal crimes against Jews across Europe:

> Old men, women, children have been packed into sealed trucks and gassed to death . . . girls have been raped and then butchered . . . children have been buried alive or had their brains bashed out.[79]

This shocking description was a truth that the government sought to deflect, and it is significant that it was first produced abroad for the ABCA Play Unit in 1943, where it was toured around military bases, with roles being taken by soldiers.

Rodney Ackland's *The Pink Room* was written in 1945, not staged until 1952, and rewritten as *Absolute Hell* in 1987.[80] While latterly this play has been analysed in terms of its brave depiction of sexuality, it also includes an early depiction of trauma caused by watching the liberation of concentration camps. In the play, Douglas Eden brings news back of Elizabeth's friend who has died in Ravensbruck camp. Elizabeth refuses to listen, until she is forced to confront it when she sees a photograph. Even then, she never fully commits to the United Nations' Refugee Relief Association (UNRRA), suggesting that the cycle of violence will continue until it is confronted head-on. The reality of the horror of human behaviour is more than they can bear.

Another character, Crowley, had spent eighteen months in a prison camp, and ends by shooting his service revolver at the ceiling, before collapsing with the words 'England for ever . . . !' on his lips.[81] As the Labour celebrations are heard taking place across the road, Christine repeatedly cries out the word 'Hell!' Tyrone Guthrie saw it as a brave piece, which would contradict the legend he anticipated growing up around the Second World War. Instead, 'The play exposes a little corner of London where conduct was not entirely heroic, not at all patriotic; and treats the conventional and traditional patterns of behaviour with less reverence than is usually, and probably rightly, accorded to them.'[82]

On 6 August 1945 an atomic bomb was dropped on Hiroshima, followed by another three days later in Nagasaki. The publishing of the Smythe Report, which detailed the making of the atomic bomb and destruction of these two places led to Theatre Workshop's *Uranium 235* (1946). This was first performed at Newcastle's People's Theatre, and its radical roots was highlighted in a later production when it was described by a critic as a play 'with a message' and who noted the selling of pamphlets at the end about germ warfare in Korea.[83] *Uranium 235* covered 2,500 years of atomic discovery and concluded with the social and political ramifications of fissure. Initially running for sixty-five minutes long, this was then extended to include an 'atomic ballet' and elements of previous agit prop productions. It incorporated styles borrowed from the Greek chorus, historical pageant, radio documentary, modern dance and burlesque. This creates a jazz-like structure 'in which, after the theme has been stated, solo instruments take turns in exploring the theme's chordal structure, each one restarting the theme in a different way'.[84]

Although in his nineties, Shaw's *Buoyant Billions* (1947) and *Far Fetched Fables* (1948) stage the debate for and against atomic weapons. His preface to the 1945 *Geneva* categorically states the ridiculousness of countries *consoling* themselves 'with the hope that the atomic bomb has made war impossible'.[85] This satire on the League of Nations had to be constantly altered to keep pace with political events, but this still did not stop it becoming outdated. Priestley – a spokesman for the Campaign for Nuclear Disarmament – was more optimistic. His play, *Summer Day's Dream* (1949) depicts a world destroyed by an atomic war, now replaced by an ideal state of existence, where humankind is forced back to a pre-industrial age, dependent on non-competitive agrarian communities.

Concerns about the impact of war, the importance of remembering, and the dangers of ideological differences were all to be found in MacColl's *The Travellers*. This was first performed as part of the Edinburgh Festival in 1952. An anti-war, anti-American political thriller, it can be seen as an early Cold War drama. A seemingly random group of people embark on a train journey across Europe on their way to America. They include the damaged, displaced and dispossessed. Among them are three Jewish and Polish survivors of Nazi concentration camps, and a bigoted American soldier who blatantly denies the others their experiences. All are seeking a new life, but as they debate differing ideological positions, most realise that America is not perhaps the land of opportunity after all. Nadine Holdsworth summarises that 'the play accuses the West of historical amnesia and of hurtling headlong into the path of further death and destruction. It rails against apathy and advocates the importance of ethnical witnessing, responsibility and human agency through the choices the travellers face between communism and capitalism, individualism and collectivity, peace and war'.[86]

As in *The Pink Room*, John Whiting's *Saint's Day* depicts the breakdown of society. Whiting wrote it after the first atomic bomb had been dropped but it only surfaced when he entered it for the 1951 Festival of Britain drama competition and won. His octogenarian poet-hero, Paul Southman, has spent decades in exile, inhabiting an isolated house deep in the woods. Undercurrents of anger and violence erupt with the arrival of another poet, Robert Procathren and three army deserters in the nearby village. The play ends with an almost apocalyptic vision as Southman is executed and the village burnt down as civilisation collapses into barbarism. The play looks back to the work of T. S. Eliot and forward to that of Harold Pinter, John Arden and Edward Bond, and in his review of Richmond's Orange Tree revival in 2002, Michael Billington proposes that 'there is also something deeply and unconsciously Beckettian about Procathren's vision of life as a progression from "darkness to darkness"'.[87]

Political plays

Political plays of the interwar period had mainly been concerned with capitalism, class warfare and social inequality. This continued with some groups, most notably with Unity and companies run by MacColl and Littlewood. MacColl's *Landscape with Chimneys* (1951) depicts soldiers returning to a street in the North of England; it moves from celebration to a sense of personal and political loss. Ginger welcomes back to Salford the soldiers by chalking up messages on the wall that refer back to the strikers of 1933. In doing this he is inscribing them into the very fabric of the city and, as Claire Warden says, 'the regional space becomes a collective territorial myth infused with politics'.[88] Time for MacColl's characters is organised by the mechanised sounds of the factory which can be seen as 'a political construct rather than an apolitical given, a constant dictatorial power associated with capitalist hegemonic forces'.[89]

However, most political plays during the war were about government policy or the forces of fascism and communism. In 1940 an Emergency Regulation was brought in to make 'it an offence for anyone to distribute any statement about the war "likely to cause alarm or despondency"'.[90] Anti-Nazi plays sorely tested the censorship rule about not disturbing relations with Foreign Powers. Either it was thought best to ignore what was happening abroad or, later, it was important not to jeopardise the precarious negotiations. Terence Rattigan's *Follow My Leader* (1938) mocks German aggression in a way that was threatening to the process of appeasement taking place by Neville Chamberlain's Government. The three leading characters were thinly disguised characterisations of Hitler, Goering and Goebbels, and it was banned outright until after the start of war when it was no longer a threat. In contradistinction, by 1942 Joe Corrie's *Dawn* was rebuked for not being anti-German enough. Corrie gave a bilateral view of war from the perspective of two families, one English and the other German. Both were dealt with sympathetically, particularly the two sons, neither of which wanted to go to war. The censor saw this as championing pacifism and therefore being unpatriotic. Again, there was an unsuccessful production of Shakespeare's *Henry V* in September 1938, not just because of Ivor Novello's miscasting but because the theatre-going public were hoping that war would be averted. However, by 1944 Laurence Olivier's film version was hailed as a major hit. Dedicated 'To the Commandos and Airborne Troops of Great Britain, the spirit of our Ancestors', it jingoistically sought to remind audiences of their duty to their country.

Many European and American dramatists dealt with the threat of fascism both overtly and in more codified ways. One of the first plays to confront the persecution of Jews in Nazi Germany was Freidich Wolf's *Professor Mamlock* (1933), written immediately after the Reichstag fire. Karel Čapek's *The White Disease* (1937) depicts the German threat to Czechoslovakia through the symbolic spread of an incurable plague, and Brecht's *The Resistible Rise of Arturo Ui* (1941) parodies Hitler as a ruthless Chicago gangster. Both Robert Ardrey's *Thunder Rock* (1940) and Lillian Hellman's *Watch on the Rhine* (1941) were propaganda pieces designed to alert Americans to the dangers of fascism and the urgent need for the country to enter the war.

However, it was left to the radical theatre companies to be more critical in their stance. Unity Theatre continued to be a political irritant during the war years, proudly claiming that 'We are the first theatre to attack the war policy of a government in war time since Euripides' *Trojan Women* was performed in Athens in 415 BC.'[91] The carnivalesque elements of the revue meant that it teetered on the edge of disobedience, which led to problems with the censor, especially given its ad hoc nature.

As the last chapter described, in the late 1930s the theatre put on a series of Living Newspapers, utilising agitprop methods such as placards, cartoon action and symbolic costumes. One of these pieces was *Living Newspaper 2: Crisis* (also known as *Czechoslovakia*), which opened on the day that Chamberlain flew to Munich. This 'drew on documentary material – BBC broadcasts, politicians' speeches, military statistics – to explain the difference between democracy and fascism and British responsibility for the spread of fascism'.[92] Audience members could watch this, and other political pieces, as German forces marched across Europe as it became evident that appeasement had failed. Merseyside Unity's *The Spectre that Haunts Europe* (1941) was refused a licence because it attempted to go further in pointing the finger of blame. Establishment figures in the Cliveden set (Unity Mitford and the Asquith family) are portrayed as vultures and crows, provocatively saying of Hitler, 'We've built him up, financed his storm troops, helped him to create his army and his fleet'.[93]

As well as Living Newspapers, Unity also specialised in political pantomimes, the most famous being *Babes in the Wood* (1938). This was a veiled satire on Britain's betrayal of Czechoslovakia; the wicked uncle (Chamberlain) wants to hand over the Babes' lands to two robbers (Hitler and Mussolini, and George V is portrayed as King Eustace the Useless. Unity provided 'an alternative to formal theatre, and the company's amateur status paradoxically became a source of marginal cultural power'. Not tied to stringent censorship laws 'enabled the company to present a reading of contemporary history beyond the scope of censored theatre professionals'.[94]

Other works were less obviously subversive. *Sandbag Follies*, one of the first theatre productions after the outbreak of war, veered between approval for the war ('This time we won't be bitten; we know for what we fight') and comments on how war perpetuates the class system ('the brass hats sit where the bombs can't hit/While the tin hats win the war').[95] The revue *Get Cracking* (1942) with its mixture of 'low' and 'high' culture encouraged audience interaction with its repertoire of songs, sketches and monologues, but is also subtitled 'a revue in Unity's tradition of Musical Shows with a Political Point'; this gestures towards a more radical tradition.[96]

Get Cracking was written after the Anglo-Soviet Pact in 1942, with the Government reluctantly turning to left-wing theatre companies for help with its pro-Russia propaganda. We can also see this with a number of large-scale pageants held as part of country-wide events to celebrate the founding of the Red Army and the new political alliance. *An Agreement of the People* was held in 1942 and *Alliance for Victory* a year later. Basil Dean's pro-Soviet *Salute to the Red Army* (1943), held at the Royal Albert Hall, is the most spectacular of all.[97] The Ministry of Information was in a difficult position, needing to introduce the idea of Russia as an ally while not being seen to support Communism.[98] Indeed, Angus Calder asserts that class warfare was still seen as dangerously prevalent and the belief was 'that the defeat of Britain would create chaos in which a Communist coup would be possible'.[99]

Nevertheless Dean was approached to put on a pro-Russia pageant. This ran for over two hours without an interval and there were over 2,000 participants, including several orchestras, choirs and regimental bands. Solidarity between the countries is shown through the pageant's juxtaposing scenes: for example, a Russian folk song is followed by a Welsh one, an Announcer makes connections between different cultures, and Service personnel stand shoulder to shoulder. However, Soviet values are also privileged, most dangerously when the Communist Manifesto is echoed in the words, 'Workers of the world unite! You have nothing to lose but your chains'![100]

The script was written by the poet Louis MacNeice and the speed with which it was rushed through – less than a month from commission to production – shows the zealousness of Government propaganda.[101] Undoubtedly, if more time had been given to the project, its marked political staging could well have run into considerable problems with the censor. As it stands, Claire Warden sees the work as closely resembling 'the constructivist experiences of Meyerhold ... *Salute to the Red Army* amounted to a political pageant that used agitprop declamation – or, as the playtext suggested, "staccato commentary" as its primary method of dialogue. It promoted a clear agenda that attempted to encourage a spirit of solidarity between stage and auditorium, participant and spectator. In this sense, it sought to fulfil the original goals of agitprop theatre'.[102] These pageants, then, teetered between censorship and propaganda, showing how political events could draw together the establishment and radical theatre in ways that would have been unthinkable before the war.

Reinscribing national identity

Cate Haste has written on how propaganda was 'rationalized and modernized' during the First World War. At this time it mainly revolved around the restriction and structuring of information in order 'to justify the war and assist recruitment'.[103] Propaganda during this war was more inclusive and subtle than before, focusing on the home front and relying on a general dissemination of images of England that, while not always realistic, presented a concern with land, history, family and community: this emphasised the idea that the war was being fought to preserve the English way of life from obliteration. National identity was therefore stressed across all cultural forms: feature films (Michael Powell and Emeric Pressburger's *A Canterbury Tale*, 1944), documentaries (Humphrey Jennings and Stewart McAllister's *Listen to Britain*, 1942), public service broadcasting ('London Can Take It'!, 1940), radio programmes (Priestley's 'Postscript on Dunkirk'), music ('The White Cliffs of Dover') and posters ('Your Britain. Fight for it *now*'). As Colls said of *Listen to Britain*, this 'stressed the collective defence of the country and transmitted a strong impression of the best of what was being defended, from Blake and Browning to Flanagan and Allen'.[104]

In the theatre this was done in a number of different ways. There were plays that extolled the virtues of the common people. Emlyn Williams's *The Morning Star* (1941) became a 'Tribute to the courage and humour of the Cockneys during the London Blitz', Noël Coward's play, *This Happy Breed* (1943) focused on a 'typical' lower-middle-class family struggling through the decades leading up to the present day, and Esther McCracken's *No Medals* (1944) showed the day-to-day existence of an ordinary woman working through the obstacles of rationing and air-raids.[105] While there are occasional subversive messages, these commercial works do little to challenge the status quo, and certainly they do not expose what Angus Calder has seen as a fabricated narrative of the war.[106]

Scenes of the English countryside continued to proliferate as a kind of pastoral idyll of pre-industrial life, although this also charted the changing class hierarchy of the time. This can be seen through the image of the country house: literary examples include D. H. Lawrence's *Lady Chatterley's Lover* (1928), Vita Sackville-West's *The Edwardians* (1930), Daphne du Maurier's *Rebecca* (1938), Virginia Woolf's *Between the Acts* (1941), and Evelyn Waugh's *Brideshead Revisited* (1944). As I have said elsewhere, 'The country house has often been depicted as representative of the aristocracy, but beyond this it is also a paternalistic and patriarchal institution. In the drama of the middle part of the twentieth century, though, the country house increasingly began to be related to the middle classes and the matriarchal' and there was a gradual shift away from the country house 'as representative of the aristocracy', and 'a paternalistic and patriarchal institution' towards the domestic femininity of the middle-class family.[107] By the end of the war, the focus was more on 'a house in the country rather than a country house'.[108] This view of the 'cosy middle class family' thus stressed the importance of the home at the heart of English society.

Du Maurier's own stage adaptation of her novel *Rebecca* came in 1940, the same year that Alfred Hitchcock's celebrated film appeared and she made a number of significant changes to it. The most important of these was the ending. In the novel, Maximillian de Winter kills his wife, and Manderley, his stately home, is burnt to the ground. In rewriting the play for the wartime stage, du Maurier ensured that Max was not a murderer but an innocent victim who eventually triumphs over evil, and the house is saved for posterity, 'a visible sign of "the ancient social order"'.[109]

Again, plays from the late 1930s, such as Dodie Smith's *Dear Octopus*, as well as Esther McCracken's *Quiet Weekend* (1941), were successfully staged for wartime audiences because they presented idealised visions of England and the family. The former play is set, not in a stately home, but in a country house where the '*furniture is heavy and old-fashioned*' but '*the general atmosphere is pleasant and comfortable*'.[110] Here the extended family of Charles and Dora Randolph gather for their Golden Wedding Anniversary, embracing its warmth and comfort, as well as its sense of continuity with the past. John Gielgud, in his role as the son, gives a toast at the end describing the tenacity of the family, and with that, England itself: 'It is, like nearly every British institution, adaptable. It bends, it stretches – but it never breaks.'[111]

Quiet Weekend was a sequel to McCracken's *Quiet Wedding* (1938), and reunites the Royd family as they spend time in their country cottage in the village of Throppleton. Unlike Manderley which was aristocratic and exclusive, this house is deliberately troped as inclusive as servants, neighbours, relatives and friends meet in an idealistic representation of village life. Set before the war, *Quiet Weekend* celebrates simple country pursuits such as fishing and jam making, and the community comes together in a concert at the end of the play to sing traditional English folk songs. The reviewer in *Theatre World* postulated that 'Its real charm lies in the contrast it presents to the life most of us are forced to live these days. This glimpse of a very human and typically English family week-ending it at their cottage in the country in peace-time has an appeal of almost fairy-tale quality. To see it is to vow never again to take the simple pleasures of life for granted.'[112]

Historical drama was also a way to conjure up and celebrate a sense of the country's past, but this had to be presented in the right kind of way. The Lord Chamberlain's Office rebuked the Gate Theatre for its 1940 private production of *The Jersey Lily*, 'a historical play which focused on the "not very elevating story of Edward, Prince of Wales". The Office considered "That it is not in the public interest, especially in these critical times, to stage a play which may in any way undermine the dignity of the crown".'[113] The Gate was even threatened with a reconsideration of the legal basis of private performances, so fearful was the establishment of anything that could lower public morale.

Several other dramatists plundered the history books to write more appropriate works. There were plays on Charles II (*In Good King Charles's Days*, 1940), Disraeli (*The Prime Minister*, 1941) and William Pitt (*The Young Mr Pitt*, 1942). Clemence Dane wrote a number of historical plays. Jenny Hartley notes that 'In a war a nation needs strong leaders and this became the hallmark of Dane's wartime output. She wrote about Queen Elizabeth and Nelson, and a series of radio plays called *The Saviours* dramatising legends of heroes such as Arthur, Alfred and Robin Hood, who help their people in times of need.'[114]

On a larger scale open-air pageants did much to connect communities together through religious values, and these were usually performed in and around churches and cathedrals. In many cases, several features were borrowed from Medieval Mystery Plays: an epic scale, promenade audience and casts mixed with amateur and professional players. These contrasted with the enormous, well-drilled Nazi rallies that took place in Germany, most notably in Nuremberg from 1933 to 1938. After the Blitz had finished in 1944, and when it became clear that Britain was winning the war, Basil Dean put on a large-scale pageant on the steps of St Paul's Cathedral, to pay tribute to Londoners.

Thousands of people turned out to see what Jenny Hartley describes as an 'exuberant pageant of virtue to counter the dark pageants of Nazi Germany'.[115] The script of *Cathedral Steps* was by Clemence Dane, staging several scenes from British history, and Sir Henry Wood conducted the massed bands of the Household Cavalry and the Brigade of Guards. It was also performed in the ruins of Coventry Cathedral after the terrible destruction inflicted on that city by the Luftwaffe.

Shakespeare was also co-opted as a way of reinscribing national identity, most notably in Olivier's film of *Henry V* as well as G. Wilson Knight's stage production of *This Sceptred Isle* (1941). Indeed the Shakespeare Memorial Theatre in Stratford-upon-Avon became talismanic for all that was English. Anthony Eden, then Dominions Secretary, gave a speech on the stage here in 1940 about 'The Progress of the War', claiming that this is where 'our history is enacted . . . We stand at the very heart of England, and we can have little doubt what it is we must do battle to defend'.[116] Donald Wolfit's 'Lunch Time Shakespeare' was presented at the Kingsway Theatre with minimal staging in a way that contrasted sharply with Shakespearean productions of just a few years ago, as did Tyrone Guthrie's Old Vic touring companies. Along with Nancy Hewins's Osiris Players, these ensured that Shakespeare reached as many parts of the country as possible.[117] ENSA also took abroad abridged versions of plays such as *The Merry Wives of Windsor* and *Twelfth Night*.

Radio and television

At the start of the war the British Broadcasting Service moved from regional medium wave channels to a simultaneous one called the Home Service; this was to prevent German aircraft from using the radio for direction finding. Dubbing itself 'the voice of Britain' – the name of the 1935 documentary about the BBC – information and light entertainment was now brought to the majority of the population. A mixture of comedy and music, similar to revues and variety, could be heard in the most popular shows, including *Workers' Playtime*, *Garrison Theatre*, *ITMA*, *Hi Gang!* and *Variety Bandbox*, Programmes 'For the Forces' were also broadcast.

This mass culture went against the policies of John Reith, the BBC's first managing director, who believed in public service rather than commercial concerns. However, this could also be seen as a fruitful clash of ideologies. As Simon Frith has observed, it posed 'questions that other intellectuals avoided. What did it mean to *construct* a national culture? Who were "the people"? What did it mean to "please" the public?'[118] Nowhere was this more obvious than in 'Postscripts', a series of Sunday broadcasts by a range of speakers on topical subjects, and set up as a response to Lord Haw-Haw's counter-intelligence broadcasts from Germany. J. B. Priestley's contributions in particular were designed to generate homogeneity and collectivism. His talks stressed several key factors: the enduring English countryside, the strength of the cities and towns, English culture (Shakespeare, Tennyson, Hardy) and the courage and community spirit of the English people. Nevertheless, they were also controversial because of his socialist views, where the war was treated 'as an opportunity to change life in a way that had failed after WWI'.[119]

Radio did much to create a new audience for drama. Originally known as the BBC Repertory Company, the Radio Drama Company (RDC) – or Rep, as it was known – was founded in 1939–40. Because of the difficulties of travelling, this company of actors camped out in Broadcasting House's Concert Hall to deliver radio drama on a regular basis without fear of interruption; as with the stage, productions went out 'live'; again, BBC's Empire Entertainments Unit took up residence at the Criterion Theatre. Herbert Farjeon wrote a series of reviews of radio plays, 'Critic on the Hearth' for *The Listener* from 1943 to 1945, and he himself also presented a series on Shakespeare's Characters in 1943, thus helping a wide audience to critically respond to drama.

During the 1930s the BBC had started broadcasting excerpts from West End shows every fortnight, which acted as a form of advertising for those in the provinces who wanted to take in a show when visiting London. Graves and Hodge note how this was a distinct advantage for a number of productions, most notably *Me and my Girl* at the Chelsea Palace in 1937, which was due to end its short run: a broadcast of Lupino Lane singing 'The Lambeth Walk' turned it into one of the smash hits of the time.[120] A broadcasting studio was even set up in the Drury Lane Stalls bar, which transmitted a show for two years without a break titled 'London Carries On'. The history of the playhouse, with its statues of Edmund Kean and David Garrick, lay behind each broadcast, subtly underpinning the historical lineage and cultural value of British theatre.

By 1949, 'about 2.5 per cent of the UK population owned a combined radio and TV licence . . . and the vast majority of them were concentrated in London and parts of the Midlands (where the limited signal, at that stage, was strongest).[121] Radio, therefore, was still the more important medium in the war and post-war periods. Nevertheless, because of the advancing technology television began to take off in the 1950s, and the many performers who came to recognition in Garrison theatres and ENSA tours were in a good position to transfer from theatres to TV. Television did not start to become more widely used until Queen Elizabeth II's coronation in 1952. However, before then the BBC began to be aware of the potential for televising drama. In 1937 a scene from *The Merry Wives of Windsor* was presented by Robert Atkins's Bankside Players, featuring Violet Vanbrugh as Mistress Ford and Irene Vanbrugh as Mistress Page.[122] The first complete play was televised live from a theatre in 1946; this was George Savory's comedy, *George and Margaret*, staged at the Intimate Theatre, Palmers Green. Geoff Bowden explains that 'The BBC was keen to set up a television set on the premises so that West End managers such as Hugh "Binkie" Beaumont, doyen of impresarios and manager of the powerful H. M. Tennent organisation, could see what the viewers were seeing and hopefully encourage other theatres to allow cameras in'.[123] By the end of the decade plays were televised from the Intimate Theatre at almost monthly intervals.

Refugee theatre

Robert Graves and Alan Hodge have estimated that 'By 1939 it was calculated that some 25,000 refugees had entered the country from Germany and Austria, some of them illegally, since 1933.'[124] By the start of the war most of them were classified as 'enemy aliens', and were either put into internment camps or allowed to remain at large under supervision. The British theatre already housed a number of émigrés, with some of the most important actors of the Second World War arriving from abroad, including Elisabeth Bergner. German workers had been banned by the Nazis and several practitioners fled to Britain. These refugees set up their own groups or joined those already in existence, such as Proltet, who performed in Yiddish in London's East End between 1932 and 1934.[125]

Prior to the Second World War, some performers had already gained theatre experience within European companies: Greta Newell, who toured with the Adelphi Players during the war, had trained with Michel Saint-Denis at the London Theatre Studio as had John Crockett, and the founders of the Compass Theatre were influenced by dancers who had fled from the Ballet

Jooss in Germany; again, the producer Basil Dean had visited Russia on a number of occasions to study its theatre and was a follower of Meyerhold.[126] There was also an interest in movement, which became a large part of Joan Littlewood's rehearsal process and now spilled out into productions such as their free version of Molière's *The Flying Doctor* (1945).

Refugees would go on to have a noticeable impact upon the development of theatre in this country, and there was a rich cross-cultural fertilisation, especially in wartime London. The Lantern Theatre in Hampstead was set up by Viennese exiles, while the Free German League of Culture (FGLC) opened the Klein Buhne (Little Theatre) in Belsize Park; launched in 1938/9 this continued until beyond the end of the war. This and other venues were used to bring together refugees – 'enemy aliens' – fleeing from fascist forces. Meetings, concerts and theatre performances were held; the latter events included satirical revues and plays, introducing many British people to European theatrical fare, long before the arrival of Brecht's Berliner Ensemble in 1956. In fact, Brecht was virtually unknown in this country at the start of the war; *Mother Courage*, written in 1939, was only translated into English two years later. Always under the careful watch of the British government, many members of the FGLC were interned, leaving them at times bereft of performers and audience, but benefits to raise money were held by the League's supporters, including Sybil Thorndike, Beatrix Lehmann and Roger Livesey.

Here audiences could see exciting new works from abroad, with pioneering staging techniques. As well as promoting European culture, these productions also drew on more home-grown talent: so, revues such as *Mr Gulliver Goes to School* (1942) followed the style of Herbert Farjeon's topical skits, and productions of plays by J. M. Barrie and Oscar Wilde were given a foreign twist. The FGLC also adapted pieces seen at other London venues, as with *Calling Erna Krämer* (1941), taken from a one-act play at the left-wing Unity Theatre.[127]

Although it falls outside the remit of this book, it is also important to note the existence of concentration camp drama. Michael Balfour makes the astute comment about performances under extreme conditions: this is theatre 'as a politically and socially malleable medium for cultural expression, as conducive to supporting the structures and ideologies of power as to challenging and overthrowing them'.[128] Much as we have seen with soldiers between 1914–18 and 1939–45, POWs are empowered by making a creative space out of inauspicious surroundings, thereby resisting the situation into which they have been forcibly put.

Post-war Britain

The war was declared over in Europe on 8 May and in the East on 14 August 1945.[129] In between these dates was sandwiched the General Election, and it was expected that Winston Churchill's Conservative Party would win. Instead the Labour Party won a landslide victory under Clement Atlee; its manifesto had been titled *Let Us Face the Future* and this was, it seemed, what the country wanted to do. Many 'people refused to believe that they could go through the violent discontinuity of war and yet find themselves back in the 1930s at its conclusion'.[130] Key elements of the Socialist agenda were the promise of full employment, new housing, nationalisation, wider education (already instigated by the 1944 Butler Education Act) and in 1947 the start of the Welfare State. By the time of the next election in 1950, Labour was still laboriously instigating various reforms, but these were not quick enough for a country in the midst of austerity measures. Their majority was slashed and they lost another election the following year, with the new Prime Minister Harold Macmillan presiding over a further series of far-reaching changes for the country, including the dismantling of the Empire. Later in the decade Macmillan confidently announced that 'most of our people have never had it so good' with the official line being that 'this country is today a more united and stabler society than it has been since the "Industrial Revolution" began'.[131] This ran counter to the fact that Britain was on the brink of bankruptcy, a growing generation gap, fears about the atomic bomb, and the start of the Cold War.

Two distinct modes of thought existed in the immediate post-war period. The first was that the war had provided an opportunity to rethink society, especially in terms of class and gender. This thinking had been happening from the late 1930s onwards, with the 'fear that the conditions of the last post-war period may be repeated'. Voters did not so much want a Labour Party as not want a Conservative one, 'in so far as this represents "vested interests", "privilege", and "the old gang"'.[132] Others were more forward in their radical thinking, looking to Soviet Russia as providing a new blueprint for society. For example, in *The Night of the Big Blitz* the left-wing Scottish dramatist James Barke shows how the classes can unite under socialist rule. It ends with a plea: 'Now we in our terror and torment must reach for the Soviet Star and hold it aloft as a banner to rally from near and from far.'[133] His play *When the Boys Come Home* (1945) interrogates this in more detail. Set in the office of Foreman Steel Checkers a debate is set up between differing union members, including a communist and a nationalist, although all are agreed that as returning soldiers they will no longer countenance pre-war conditions.

The second view looked back with nostalgia to the past and saw the war as a disruption to normality. The Golden Age of Empire continued to be attractive, with its paternalistic perspective. In line with this, the sweeping changes made by first wave feminism were put under pressure and it was expected that women give up their jobs to bring up the next generation. Hence it is significant that there was a resurgence of interest in the Edwardian period. Ironically, the youth fashion for Edwardian dress – lending its name to the term 'Teddy boy' – took place during 1950s, a period poised between the future and the past. Several dramatists would set their work in the first decade of the twentieth century as a way of making a link between the two periods, or as a form of wistfulness.

This dichotomy was marked by the 1951 Festival of Britain held on London's South Bank, which became a way of looking back to the country's previous successes, as well as paving the way for a new future. On the one hand it referenced the zenith of the British Empire: the Great Exhibition of 1851. On the other hand it marked its demise. John M. MacKenzie notes that it 'was designed principally to propagate the ideas of the post-war Labour government on social and economic change. There was little direct imperial content, imperial exhibits being concentrated at another site, the Imperial Institution.'[134] By the 1950s the country had lost India, Ceylon and Burma, and it would receive a further battering with the Suez crisis of 1956, when Britain lost control of the Egyptian territory. Again, the coronation of Queen Elizabeth II two years later supposedly gave rise to the 'new Elizabethan' age but this continued to reinscribe old values about the establishment.

Post-war theatre

Political lines were drawn among the theatre old-guard in complex ways. Although Noël Coward was a rebel, he was also a die-hard conservative. He loathed socialism and the idea of a welfare state, saying of the battle lines drawn over Suez that 'The good old imperialism was a bloody sight wiser and healthier than all this woolly-headed, muddled, "all men are equal" humanitarianism, which has lost us so much pride and dignity and prestige in the modern world.'[135] His *Relative Values* was a misfiring class satire, harking back to those of the earlier twentieth century. The countess of Marshwood House is dismayed to find her son about to marry an American movie star who she deems to be of much lower status, and her maid Moxie is even more upset by this possible attack on the 'natural' order. Written just before the Conservatives were returned to power in 1951, the word 'change' is treated with scorn and the play ends with the butler toasting 'the final inglorious disintegration of the most unlikely dream that ever troubled the foolish heart of man – Social Equality'.[136] More in tune with the earlier plays of Barrie and Maugham than contemporary drama, Coward's later plays never managed to equal the success of his previous ones.

In contrast, although Rattigan gave the appearance of a wealthy socialite, he had sympathies with the Labour Party. His *Love in Idleness* (1944), originally named *Less than Kind*, centres on an idealistic young Labourite. Michael Brown returns home from Canada where he has been based during the war, only to find his mother living with a man who has strong Conservative views and was once part of the war cabinet. Michael's political beliefs drive him to try and break up her relationship with this ex-industrialist. However, it was rewritten at the request of the popular stage couple, Alfred Lunt and Lynn Fontanne, and Rattigan was forced to water down his reaction to the new socialist government. *The Winslow Boy* (1946) was subtler by being historically distant. Based on an Edwardian scandal when a naval cadet was accused of theft, the play is seemingly about an individual's struggle against the powers-that-be. In fact Rattigan's choice of subject at this particular time in history is significant. He looks back to the Edwardian period that is envisaged as stable, but threatens liberty through the Establishment's tyrannical behaviour and lack of humanity; there is also a veiled political commentary about the very recent defeat of fascism and start of a new order.

Another stalwart of the theatre also shared Rattigan's socialist principles. Described by John Baxendale as 'some kind of conservative ruralist', J. B. Priestley was actually more concerned with the future rather than the past, the urban landscape, not the countryside, and the common people instead of the privileged.[137] Many of his plays focused on the creation of a new society that has learnt from the pre-war social and political problems. *They Came to a City* was written in 1942, staged a year later, and filmed by Ealing Studios in 1944. The eponymous conurbation is based on a Welfare State ideal where people work together for the common good, unmarked by competition or commercialism. The allegorical set-up allows a broad spectrum of 'types' to debate whether they wish to embrace or reject this utopian vision, and to challenge the audience on their views as well.

Priestley's earlier plays such as *The Good Companions* (1929) and *Eden End* (1934) had presented the Edwardian period in a rosy light, but *An Inspector Calls* (1946), his best known play, condemns the lack of progress that had been made in the country during the last thirty years. For those in authority, lack of responsibility and blind materialism was still evident. The well-named Inspector Goole visits a well-to-do Northern household in 1912, asking questions about the suicide of Eva, a young working-class woman. All members of the Birling family have brought about Eva's social ruin through a series of unthinking actions. By the end of the play, some characters have admitted their culpability in Eva's death, while others remain blind to the truth. Inspector Goole is both a realistic figure and a symbolic one: the Birlings receive a telephone call saying that a woman's body has been found and the local police are on the way to start the investigation.

Significantly the play was first performed in Soviet Russia in 1945, and some critics have seen the confrontation between Birling and Goole as an ideological standoff between conservative Victorian values and the socialist Welfare State. The corrupting power and necessary destruction of the former was highlighted in Stephen Daldry's ground-breaking 1992 revival for the National Theatre when the Edwardian house (designed by Ian MacNeil) spectacularly collapsed in on itself. This action, as well as a Second World War framing device, makes the point that historical events (both wars, the Holocaust, a Labour Government) have led to a violent break with the past and a reassessment of society is urgently required.

This idea of a world breaking down is also seen in Ackland's *The Pink Room*. Its first public appearance at the Lyric Theatre, Hammersmith was a critical failure, coming one year after the triumphalist vision of Britain in the Festival of Britain. The play is located in a London West End drinking club, La Vie en Rose, on the eve of the 1945 general election. The club has been condemned after a nearby explosion and Stephen Lacey likens it to Chekhov's *The Cherry Orchard*, where 'La Vie en Rose functions both as a metonym of postwar London and as a metaphor for Britain, faded and crumbling, and its demise, like that of the Ranyevskaya estate, is symbolic of the end of an era.'[138] As with Chekhov's cherry trees, La Vie en Rose falls at the end of the play, but hope exists in Labour's success, achieved at exactly the same time. All the characters are there to escape the outside world – the war, the new socialism – which constantly intrudes on the sequestered clique, and suggests a society bewildered by the past and uncertain about the future. They block out reality through drink and sex, and are apathetic to the election, even though they are mainly pro-Labour. This stems partly from their collective and individual lack of identity. One character talks about 'the young guy [who] catches sight of himself in the mirror and kinda realizes he can't prove that anybody's real except himself and he doesn't know who the hell he is anyway – or why'.[139] Statements such as these gesture towards the existentialism of Beckett and Theatre of the Absurd, not yet making its presence felt in this country.

As with the First World War, society had undergone a radical change in terms of views about gender, sexuality and class. Daphne du Maurier's *The Years Between* (1945), directed by Irene Hentschel, is a prime example of the former. The original title – *The Return of the Soldier* – echoes narratives at the end of the previous war. Diana Wentworth is crushed when her husband goes missing and presumed dead, but persuaded to take over Michael's career as an MP she blossoms with new-found confidence, and is on the brink of remarrying her neighbour, Richard. At this point her husband returns, now seen as a war hero for his secret spying missions. Embittered by the changes he sees in the country he fought for, Michael believes that his wife has turned from the woman who 'had a quality of stillness' to 'One of those managing, restless women'.[140] Their pointed exchange goes to the heart of the debate:

DIANA	But Michael – you wouldn't have us put back the clock, and return to where we were before?
MICHAEL	Why not?
DIANA	I thought we were fighting for a new world.
MICHAEL	Was the old one so very bad?
DIANA	Well – I don't know . . . but I think we all feel rather differently about it, here at home.[141]

The ending of the play is ambiguous: husband and wife work towards a reunited Europe, but separately, not together, while Diana hopes for a world based on equality rather than duty. As with the previous war, women were no longer content to return to the old world, and growing dissatisfaction would eventually lead to the second wave feminism of the 1960s and 1970s.

So-called unsavoury subjects became increasingly common on the British stage in the immediate post-war period. *Pick-Up Girl* (1946) by the American writer Elsa Shelley exposed under-age promiscuity. It was an early example of the soon-to-be-common term 'juvenile delinquency', and 'caught the censorship process at a point of transition'.[142] Older playwrights also picked up on the mood of the moment. Both du Maurier and Lesley Storm wrote plays about potential incestuous relationships – *September Tide* (1948) and *Black Chiffon* respectively – showing women forced to sublimate their sexual desires and straining under oppressive gender roles. A recurring theme in Rattigan's *Separate Tables* (1954) and *The Deep Blue Sea* (1952) is the tension between public codes of behaviour and private sexual passion, stimulated by Rattigan's need to keep his own homosexuality hidden at a time when it was an illegal act. *Separate Tables* consisted of two short plays: *Table by the Window* and *Table Number Seven*. Major Pollock in the latter play is accused of sexually harrassing women in the cinema, but in an earlier draft, he was found guilty of homosexual importuning. Andrew Wyllie explains that 'Critical to the legitimization of homosexuality as a topic for debate was the formation in the mid-1950s of the Wolfenden Committee.' Thus, in the theatre, it moved from Rattigan's 'sympathetic but covert treatment' . . . through a neutral but overt representation in Shelagh Delaney's *A Taste of Honey* (1958), to a sympathetic *and* overt characterization in the 1960s'.[143]

Rattigan specialised in creating neurotic, possessive women and emotionally frozen men whose inner and outer personae are at odds with one another as they live in fear of shame and humiliation. Thus, Hester Collyer, the runaway wife of a High Court Judge, is caught between the devil and the deep blue sea: that is, between lust/self-destruction and drowning/escape; between convention/non-conformity; and between social duty/individual pleasure. Her adulterous affair with the younger Freddie Page, a former RAF pilot, leads her to the brink of suicide but, unlike the heroines of former well-made plays, Hester does not have to kill herself. There is muted optimism (women no longer have to be punished with death) but also stoicism: life goes on but without the expectation of happiness.

Moreover, *The Deep Blue Sea* exposes a post-war society in flux. The boarding house setting distances itself from pre-war drawing room drama and prefigures the gritty kitchen sink plays to come. Hester and Freddie live in a Victorian building now divided into separate units, where people of different backgrounds are thrown together. On one level this describes the housing shortage and concomitant sense of impermanence. On another level, it shows the breakdown of hierarchy. As Nicholas de Jongh claims, the Second World War 'precipitated the erosion of the symbolic barriers dividing one class from another' and the automatic deference to authority – law, military, religious – was dissipating.[144]

Enid Bagnold's *The Chalk Garden* (1956) is a symbolic disquisition on this topic, in a style that is both middlebrow and modernist. Appearing one month before *Look Back in Anger*, it portrays a social world that is in decline, symbolised by the unhealthy lime soil in the garden that cannot nurture life. Mrs St Maugham clings to the past habits and customs of another – pre-war – world, even while acknowledging that it no longer exists. Throughout the play she shows an acute awareness about the fragility of her class-ridden existence, and learns to look forward rather than be dragged back into memories of her previous role as a glamorous Edwardian society hostess. Other characters are less perceptive. Pinkbell, the never-seen and destructive butler, represents the emptiness of social custom, and Mrs St Maugham's friend, the Judge, likens his ritualistic entrance into the courtroom as similar to 'a dried saint carried in festival'.[145] He is shown as representative of a world in which the force of tradition is more important than justice, and each of these two men is in some way (literally in the case of Pinkbell) dying or bringing about death because they try to hold on to something that no longer exists.

During the 1950s, Kenneth Tynan ridiculed the continuance of middlebrow drama, labelling it as 'Life in Loamshire . . . a glibly codified fairy-tale world' that had no place in post-war society.[146] The slow reconstruction of the country also prompted an attack on past modes of behaviour and value systems, and, ironically, the changes instigated by the Second World War in terms of theatre-going (e.g. no formal dress, mixed audiences, different venues), all helped to prepare the way for a more relaxed theatre experience in the 1950s. Thus, with the championing of playwrights such as John Osborne and Arnold Wesker, the cultural focus moved towards youth, masculinity, and the working classes: the so-called Angry Young Men of the late 1950s and early 1960s.

Conclusion

The general critical view has been that until 1956 and the appearance of John Osborne's *Look Back in Anger* the British theatre largely lived on its past both in subject matter and in staging. Audiences continued as before with their lavish first-nighters, rituals of evening dress and traditional playhouses, and light entertainment was produced for the middle classes, such as musicals, comedies and thrillers. In contrast startling new work was being forged in America by Arthur Miller and Tennessee Williams, and on the Continent, work by Jean Anouilh, Jean-Paul Sartre and Samuel Beckett challenged the boundaries of theatre.

However, the seeds of this kind of theatre had been sown earlier, and the more democratic, egalitarian, younger and theatrically innovative experiments of the war gradually filtered through to find presence in the development of the working-class drama of the 1950s and the fringe theatre from that decade onwards. The freeing up of theatre during the Second World War would have massive ramifications in terms of how theatre is conceived, funded and consumed in this country. Far from being a period of conservative timidity within the theatre, the war years saw instead a degree of experimentation that both reached into the past and presaged changes in the post-war period. A number of theatre practitioners saw the unusual wartime conditions as a means to devise, develop and enact their individual agenda, and the various types of theatre seen during the war led to a generation realising that it was not just the perquisite of the rich or the intellectual. In many ways, the lack of purpose-built theatre venues, the fusion of amateur and professional, the expansion of geographical access, all led to an increase in theatre going, in whatever form. The post-war era started with a resurgence of interest in the new audiences that had been opened up. This all fed into the concern with creating a more just and egalitarian Britain from the one at the beginning of 1939.

To this we can also add a whole range of theatre-based initiatives: the first Drama Department at the University of Bristol, a rise in the opening of Drama Schools, the Society of Theatre Research, Confederation of Repertory Theatres (CORT) to support repertory theatres, and in 1948 the Entertainments Tax reduced to half its level for live theatre, and removed for small rural areas. Along with the support of CEMA, the Arts Council, the Rural Development Commission and even such initiatives as the British Theatre Exhibition held in Birmingham at the end of the 1940s, everything was in place for a renaissance in British theatre.

CHAPTER 5
'PRODUCING THE SCENE': THE EVOLUTION OF THE DIRECTOR IN BRITISH THEATRE 1900–50

Claire Cochrane

The idea of the director as a single authority figure with a distinctive set of skills evolved quite slowly in British theatre during the first half of the twentieth century. Every actor-manager of any importance since the seventeenth century had attempted to harness and control resources to shape the artistic product to a personal artistic vision. What distinguishes twentieth-century practice is that the role starts to separate off from the leading actor in performance, with much greater control exercised at the pre-performance stage. As Simon Shepherd points out in his book *Direction*, the uncertainty about what precisely this new individual was responsible for was reflected in shifting nomenclature.[1] In British theatre, the job title 'producer' given to the artistic co-ordinator now known as the director was the most widely used term right up until the early 1960s. However, from the beginning of the twentieth century, 'director', 'stage director' and 'stage manager' were also used interchangeably for the same function. Also, while within the academy there has been so much emphasis on the director as a charismatic, transformative agent of artistic change, it has been forgotten that the producer/director is a necessary functionary within quotidian theatre practice. The role evolved in the twentieth century alongside structural changes in company and stage management, and the growing importance of technical and scenographic innovation. Key concepts derived from a very disparate range of influences gradually gathered weight mediated by individuals often working in relatively isolated or short-term circumstances.

It should be emphasised, however, that the old model of the actor-manager remained a familiar figure in the British theatre landscape despite the fact that historically well-known metropolitan celebrities, such as Henry Irving and Herbert Beerbohm Tree, died between 1905 and 1918.[2]

Harley Granville Barker who, Dennis Kennedy has claimed, 'created and defined the position of the modern director in England', stopped acting in his own productions in 1911 and William Bridges-Adams, as the director of the New Shakespeare Company at the Shakespeare Memorial Theatre may just possibly have been the first director to sign a contract in 1919 specifically binding him not to act, but many directors continued to act in their own productions because they wanted to or, out of sheer necessity.[3] The actor John Gielgud in management was an actor-manager albeit with the theatrical entrepreneur Bronson Albery as a commercial partner.[4] Donald Wolfit who founded his own company in 1937, which he toured for thirty years, was considered the quintessential English actor-manager.[5] In 1951, at the Shakespeare Memorial Theatre, Anthony Quayle directed Shakespeare's *Richard II* to *Henry V* history cycle and played Falstaff himself.[6] This was five years after Peter Brook, arguably the only British director to achieve the international status accorded to his European contemporaries, directed his celebrated Watteau-inspired 1946 production of *Love's Labours Lost* at the Shakespeare Memorial Theatre (SMT).[7]

Perhaps the most significant legacy of the most flamboyant of the actor-managers was the example of the artistic power they wielded over all aspects of their productions. Henry Irving's legendary management at the Lyceum Theatre in London is perhaps the best-known example. In 1905, Gordon Craig's imagined stage director explained the range of skills which his ideal 'captain' of the theatrical ship needed to have acquired:

> the right use of actors, scene, costume, lighting, and dance, and by means of these had mastered the crafts of interpretation, he would then gradually acquire the mastery of action, line, colour, rhythm, and words, this last strength developing out of all the rest.[8]

Although Craig clearly states that it is the role of the perfect stage manager [sic] to be in front of the stage 'that he may view it as a whole' and that 'if we found our perfect actor who was our perfect stage manager, he could not be in two places at the same time', he is challenging what was time-honoured practice.[9] From the humblest touring company to the metropolitan star ensemble it was understood that the actor-manager could and should be capable of being in two places at the same time.

A. E. W. Mason, best known for his novel *The Four Feathers*, wrote three plays between 1909 and 1913 for the actor George Alexander whose management at the St James's Theatre had made it one of the most prestigious in London. Mason's account of the methods a star actor deployed to shape his new play *The Witness for the Defence* provides an illuminating insight into how the dual role could be achieved. It took roughly two years from the first discussion of preliminary ideas for the play to the delivery of the script in late 1910 when it was immediately accepted and casting agreed. In the boardroom of St James's Theatre, Mason was shown a small toy stage with a set of draughtsmen labelled with the names of the different characters. 'For the better part of two days we arranged and marked in the script the various movements and positions of all the characters throughout the progress of the play. Alexander had analysed the dialogue sentence by sentence, and every now and then he would turn upon me with a quite disconcerting abruptness and say, "What did you mean by that?" . . . When the movements had been arranged, what is known as a stage cloth with the doors and entrances painted upon it was prepared. Thus, before a single rehearsal was called we had a complete plan to work upon'.[10]

The entire production process took three weeks. Strictly controlled three-hour rehearsals, which gave actors respite for travelling or evening performances, culminated in a four-day theatre closure when morning and evening rehearsals were followed by two dress rehearsals prior to the first performance. Alexander and his leading lady Ethel Irving also worked separately: 'he suggested to her such movements, such small pieces of business, and even such intonations of the voice as seemed to him helpful to establish the individual authority of her part'.[11]

Origins and obstacles

What emerges from Mason's account is the emphasis on careful preparation and attention to detail, especially at the pre-rehearsal stage, combined with speed and efficiency once the intensive production process began. Throughout the period under review in this chapter, economic imperatives together with the relentless time pressures demanded of professional practice right across the theatrical spectrum determined that much the same priorities had to be observed even by the most ambitious of the new breed of directors. While the ideals of intensive textual and physical exploration and training advanced by key European directors such as Konstantin Stanislavski, Vsevolod Meyerhold and Jacques Copeau gradually infiltrated British consciousness, there was rarely sufficient time or resources to exploit them adequately. In the 1920s the Russian émigré director and designer Theodore Komisarjevsky overcame

British resistance to Chekhov with productions of five plays, all of which achieved a winning lightness of tone within major constraints, especially at the tiny Barnes Theatre where he staged *Uncle Vanya*, *Three Sisters* and *The Cherry Orchard* from 1925–6.[12] Between 1932 and 1936 at the Shakespeare Memorial Theatre his iconoclastic, highly original productions of seven of Shakespeare's plays were permitted little more than ten days' rehearsal within the punishing season schedule.[13]

That said, European modernist experiments with challenging new drama, new stagecraft and new models of company organisation certainly provided the impetus for the intellectual and aesthetic innovations introduced by home-grown directors. It is well-known that European naturalism as represented by the plays, for example, of Émile Zola, Henrik Ibsen and Eugène Brieux and staged in small independent theatres such as André Antoine's Théâtre Libre in Paris and Otto Brahm's Freie Bühne in Berlin, would have immensely influential long-term effects.[14] Drama which dealt with the underlying social and sexual tensions of everyday life and moreover was written to be performed in settings which aimed to replicate 'real' life offered exciting opportunities for a generation of young British actors increasingly radicalised by emerging socialism and political movements such as the campaigns for universal suffrage and women's rights. The sheer effort required to overcome obstacles such as the Lord Chamberlain's refusal to grant full public performance licenses to the most controversial plays, the limited access to performance venues, and the need for actors to juggle income-generating employment with more professionally satisfying experiment, created the conditions for the necessary emergence of a directorial figure. What was most vital was an intellectual understanding of the kind of inward-facing performance style required to represent the enclosed social milieu created by the dramatists.

The Scottish-born critic William Archer who worked with Harley Granville Barker on the first private publication of their jointly authored *A National Theatre: Schemes and Estimates* in 1904, was never explicitly credited as a director and always worked collaboratively. However his determined advocacy of Ibsen in the 1880s and 1890s not only resulted in what became the standard English translations of the plays for the best part of thirty years, but was also the driving force behind the most significant early attempts at London production. The results of his detailed notes to actors based on meticulous rehearsal observation began to reveal the possibilities of externally shaped naturalism in the hands of skilled actors especially Elizabeth Robins in the 1891 production of *Hedda Gabler*.[15]

Arguably the most dominant characteristic of Granville Barker's directorial approach lay in the same meticulous approach to textual understanding and ensemble delivery, an overall objective which was not lost on the actors who worked with him between 1904 and 1907 in the celebrated Vedrenne-Barker [Royal] Court Theatre seasons, who would themselves go on to direct.[16] Dennis Kennedy quotes both the future Old Vic director Harcourt Williams who described 'the whole thing at his fingers' ends at the first rehearsal' and Lewis Casson who subsequently directed in Manchester and Glasgow. Casson's biographical entry on Barker for the *Dictionary of National Biography* concludes:

> He was a perfectionist but no dictator, criticizing to the last inch and the last rehearsal, always with good humour, every tiniest movement or vocal inflection, until the whole play became a symphony in which every phrase, rhythm, melody and movement reached as near perfection as he could make it.[17]

Although the best-known products of the Vedrenne-Barker management were new British plays which could be broadly classified as social-realist – *The Silver Box* by John Galsworthy, Elizabeth Robins's *Votes for Women*, Barker's own *The Voysey Inheritance*, and of course and pre-eminently eight plays by George Bernard Shaw – directorial strategies were applied way beyond the confines of naturalism. In any case Shaw's plays required a significantly more robust performance style. What was in fact a quite eclectic programme of plays included Greek tragedy and modern poetic drama by contemporary dramatists such as W. B. Yeats and John Masefield. Barker was consolidating the *idea* of the director, but primarily in the interests of creating a new ideal company structure which could enable a strongly grounded repertoire of what was considered to be the best of modern and classical drama.

The director in the regions

Barker's efforts to create a sustainable 'exemplary' theatre management in London ultimately failed.[18] The economic obstacles were too great and the outbreak of the First World War in 1914 called a halt to much fruitful cross-European creative exchange especially with the German avant-garde. But it is quite clear that the co-ordinating 'stage manager' was increasingly seen as necessary to effective play production. In his autobiography *A Life in a Wooden*

O, Ben Iden Payne describes how directing and managerial work had been thrust upon him as a young actor with a small touring company which then led, in 1907, to an appointment as 'stage director' at the Abbey Theatre in Dublin and then the task of establishing as 'general manager' at the Manchester Repertory Company under the patronage of Annie Horniman.[19] The founding of a small number of autonomous producing 'repertory' theatres outside London (The Abbey Theatre, Dublin, 1904; Manchester Repertory Company, 1908; Glasgow Repertory Company, 1909; Liverpool Repertory Theatre, 1911; Birmingham Repertory Theatre, 1913) ensured radical ideas kept circulating.[20] Payne had been recommended to W. B. Yeats by Barker himself, but he had also experienced the painstaking and lengthy rehearsal methods of Frank Benson.[21] Essentially Benson was an archetypal and often unfairly derided actor-manager, but his Shakespearean and Old English Comedy Company was in theory, at least, run on the ensemble principles introduced across Europe by the Meiningen Company as early as the 1870s and 1880s.[22]

What was increasingly desirable, if not always achievable, was not just that well-rehearsed, evenly balanced actor ensembles could commit to tackling a range of genres, but that audiences could witness performances within stage environments which had been shaped by a controlling visual aesthetic. In this respect innovative ideas were coming for the most part from outside the constraints of the professional theatre industry. Edward Gordon Craig had been a professional actor and indeed actor-manager, but immensely influential scenographic experiments conducted with amateurs – at once more easily malleable and willing to devote the necessary time to realising his vision – demonstrated the value of powerful suggestion and evocative use of colour enhanced by new lighting technology. Almost pathologically incapable of working in a sustained way with theatre professionals, the gradual dissemination of his ideas, which could be reproduced with very basic materials to create simple architectural scenic frameworks, would transform approaches to non-naturalistic drama.[23] At the Abbey Theatre where Yeats's primary objective was the production of new Irish poetic drama, a scenography which could enhance symbolic, emotionally and linguistically enriched drama could potentially as he put it create 'an ideal country where everything was possible, even speaking in verse or in music'.[24]

The other major agent of transformation was William Poel. Eccentric, wayward and determined to return Shakespeare and other early modern drama to his version of 'original' staging conditions, sometimes literally erected inside conventional proscenium stages, his productions with his Elizabethan Stage Society drew in, either as actors or audience, the majority of the early radicals. Granville Barker played Shakespeare's Richard II for Poel in 1899 and Marlowe's Edward II in 1903. Lewis Casson played in both a production of Ben Jonson's *The Alchemist* and Shakespeare's *Much Ado About Nothing*.[25] In 1908 Payne's invitation to Poel to direct a production of the rarely performed *Measure for Measure* with the Manchester Repertory Company helped to introduce to wider audiences his principles of non-illusionistic, uncluttered staging and rapidly spoken, free-flowing texts.[26]

The dissemination of Poel's influence continued with Basil Dean, as a member of the Manchester company trained in Poel's verse-speaking methods, subsequently appointed as the first 'Controller and Producer' at the Liverpool Repertory Theatre.[27] In Birmingham, having seen Poel's *Measure for Measure* presented at the Shakespeare Memorial Theatre, the young wealthy theatre enthusiast, Barry Jackson, already well-versed in Craig's ideas, began a series of Shakespeare experiments within simple 'draped' stages with his amateur company the Pilgrim Players.[28] When Jackson opened his purpose-built Birmingham Repertory Theatre in 1913, the transition to professional practice still firmly adhered to the fundamental principles learnt from both Craig and Poel. In Norwich, however, in 1921, where Nugent Monck who had acted and stage-managed for Poel, installed his amateur Norwich Players in a replica Elizabethan-style theatre, the Maddermarket, the creative freedom of amateur status was retained.

The consolidation of the repertory, or rather the short-run system of play production where plays were mounted weekly, or more exceptionally fortnightly, in rapid succession, extended right across the theatre industry by the 1920s.[29] At its most relentless in resident commercial companies often employed on a seasonal basis in regional receiving houses, the system was 'twice-nightly' so that plays were cut to permit time for two performances. A producer was appointed to select, edit, cast and direct plays with the core company, which represented an appropriate range of gender, age and physical types. At its most basic with many commercially popular plays characters were effectively formulaic. Nevertheless it was essential that the producer even within limited artistic horizons had to ensure good quality control to maintain audience confidence in the product on offer.[30]

In the gradually developing regional producing theatres, run as limited companies on a not-for-profit basis by boards of directors, the producer had to balance his own artistic instincts with the tastes of local audiences. In Liverpool, where it had proved impossible to sustain the kind of avant-garde policy originally envisaged in 1911 by Basil Dean, William Armstrong became producer in 1922. As an actor he had been in Benson's company and acted with the Glasgow and Birmingham Repertory Companies. Formally titled 'Director and Producer', he led the Liverpool Playhouse until 1941 with plays very largely drawn from the 'new drama' first introduced in the Edwardian period: Shaw, Galsworthy, J. M. Barrie, Harold Brighouse, for example, with newer playwrights represented by W. Somerset Maugham and J. B. Priestley. There was also a sprinkling of women dramatists, especially the American playwright Susan Glaspell, four of whose plays were staged between 1925 and 1930. While never in any sense an 'art theatre', it attracted ambitious young actors in the early stages of their careers such as Michael Redgrave, Rachel Kempson, Diana Wynyard and Robert Donat.[31] The director in this context was effectively laying the foundations for an accepted canon of late-nineteenth- and twentieth-century drama and establishing the principle that regional producing theatre could function as a legitimate training ground.

Liverpool, like Birmingham Rep could afford to run plays for at least a fortnight, allowing more rehearsal time, but a more punishing production schedule did not automatically mean low standards even in the twice-nightly system. The presence of a long-term resident designer working in partnership with the producer could enable contemporary design trends to add a consistently strong visual style especially to non-naturalistic drama. At the Northampton Royal Theatre, for example, the appointment of Tom Osborne Robinson as in-house designer in 1928, working initially alongside Herbert Prentice as producer, brought a highly trained scene-painter, influenced in his striking use of colour and form by exposure to Leon Bakst's designs for the Ballet Russes, into a relationship with the Royal Theatre which lasted nearly fifty years.[32]

Prentice's work as a director had begun with amateur actors in Sheffield in 1919. Employed in 1921 as a producer for the amateur Sheffield Repertory Company, Prentice had the freedom to experiment with more challenging plays including Greek tragedy, Shakespeare and, in line with a growing interest in German expressionism, the English premiere of Ernst Toller's *The Machine Wreckers*. With no previous experience as an actor, in a modest and now largely forgotten way, Prentice could be regarded as a Craig-like model stage manager/director. Not only did he exhibit as a set and costume designer at the 1923 International Theatre Exhibition, but with his Sheffield associate Harold Ridge, metallurgist, amateur actor and stage lighting expert, he also developed innovative approaches to stage lighting.[33]

In 1926 Ridge partnered Terence Gray in the founding of the Cambridge Festival Theatre. This saw Prentice employed as resident producer to realise practically Gray's vigorous assault on any kind of naturalism in drama which ranged from Aeschylus and Sophocles to Strindberg, Capek and Pirandello. Prentice spent two years in Cambridge before leaving, perhaps because of Gray's maverick personality, to go to the rigours of weekly rep in Northampton where he directed more than 200 plays.[34] At the Festival Theatre, Gray's construction of a radically non-illusionist open stage, his elevation of the producer's conceptual and scenographic vision over the playwright's intentions and his promotion of masked, physical performance all saw him aligned with contemporary avant-garde European practice. In 1947 Norman Marshall, reflecting on Gray's experiment which he abandoned in 1933, concluded that there had been 'practically no effect upon the English theatre' – an opinion he might have overturned had he experienced the 'director's theatre' perceived to be so dominant later in the century.[35]

Relatively speaking, Birmingham Rep in the interwar years provided the most stable regional environment for the development of directorial and scenographic skills. The Craig-influenced architectural stage design practised by Barry Jackson up until 1919 gave way after the arrival of Paul Shelving as resident designer to the work of another highly skilled scene painter distinguished by a stunning use of colour and frank stylisation. The appointment of H. K. Ayliff as Stage Director in 1922 brought together the South-African-born former actor with Shelving to stage in both Birmingham and London a series of ground-breaking productions. These included in 1923 the British premiere of Bernard Shaw's *Back to Methusaleh*, *Cymbeline*, the very first production of Shakespeare in modern-dress, and an ambitious, if poorly attended, production of Georg Kaiser's expressionist play *Gas*. Jackson's decision in 1925 to exploit the Rep's artistic capital by maintaining companies in London as well as Birmingham ensured maximum exposure for Ayliff and Shelving. The 1925 modern-dress *Hamlet*, followed in 1928 by modern-dress productions of *Macbeth* and *The Taming of the Shrew*, initiated a profound shift in Shakespeare production values. It was in effect, the logical outcome of Poel's Elizabethanism, utilised in the interests of highlighting the contemporary relevance of a classic text.

Directing women

Thus far the discussion of the development of the role of the director has been primarily male-focused. If a substantial proportion of the individual male directors referred to above were marginalised in their own time or have since been consigned to oblivion by historians, their female equivalents were even more marginalised – a gender imbalance which would continue to characterise British theatre as a whole for most of the century. Maggie Gale in her 1996 book *West End Women* drew attention not only to the prolific, but ignored, output of women playwrights on the London stage between 1918 and 1962, but also the female managers, administrators and directors who facilitated the work of male theatre-makers as well as women.[36]

Of course Annie Horniman in Dublin and Manchester, Lady Gregory in Dublin and Lilian Baylis at the Old Vic, did achieve historical status as important patrons and managers who had the power to progress the careers of the new directors. Relatively few will have heard of the redoubtable Maud Carpenter who managed the Liverpool Playhouse from 1923 until 1962.[37] But before this in 1914, the actress Madge McIntosh, appointed as producer in Liverpool on the basis of her previous directorial record with the Glasgow Repertory Theatre, found herself saving the theatre from closure. She and fellow actress Estelle Winwood set up a two-year 'Commonwealth' where the company was committed to work for only a guaranteed minimum living wage.[38]

Within metropolitan theatre at the more high profile end of the spectrum of actual directorial activity, there were Irene Hentschel and Esmé Church. Between 1934 and 1943 Hentschel directed three of J. B. Priestley's plays in West End theatres. Perhaps most significantly she was the first of a very sparse number of women to direct at the Shakespeare Memorial Theatre. In 1939 Iden Payne, by then director of the theatre, invited Hentschel to direct *Twelfth Night*. Bringing with her the trio of women designers known as Motley who had developed their scenographic methods based on simple, basic materials working with John Gielgud in London, Hentschel's production gave the play an eclectic Victorian-style setting and most controversially flouted tradition by casting Olivia as unusually young and skittish. For the Old Vic Company under Tyrone Guthrie, Esmé Church directed three Shakespeare productions, most memorably her 1937 *As You Like It* which featured Edith Evans and Michael Redgrave as Rosalind and Orlando and which, nine years before Peter Brook, drew on Watteau's painting for visual inspiration.[39]

Both Hentschel and Church had been protégées of Lena Ashwell, the actress-turned-manager and director who had made her name as a West End actress, but moved into London management at the Kingsway Theatre in 1907. Her hugely ambitious First World War Concert Party venture which took thousands of play extracts and musical recitals to troops fighting on battle fronts across Europe and the Middle East was followed in 1919 with the founding of the Lena Ashwell Players. As her biographer, Margaret Leask has emphasised Ashwell's leadership of the Players which toured round the London suburbs and undertook residences in theatres across England created a team of women directors and repertory companies focused on presenting a substantial repertoire of plays in difficult non-conventional venues and frequently hard-to-reach audiences.[40]

That record of working outside the mainstream in relative obscurity is characteristic of the majority of the women who assumed directorial roles with both professionals and amateurs. Edith Craig, the daughter of Ellen Terry and Edward Gordon Craig's sister began directing in 1908 and directed her last production, a pageant, in 1946. Throughout her life as costume maker and designer as well as director she worked across sectors in the regions as well as in London. As a leading figure in the Actresses' Franchise League and the founder in 1911 of the Pioneer Players, she was a prolific director of the London-produced suffrage plays. Overall, however, the variety of drama tackled, ranging from medieval to modern American, with some staged briefly in commercial West End venues such as the Criterion and Shaftesbury theatres, is extraordinary. Working with Norman MacDermott who founded the experimental Hampstead Everyman Theatre in 1920, her productions included eight plays by Shaw. As a widely travelled advocate of the British Drama League she became heavily engaged in promoting the amateur theatre movement serving as Art Director of the Leeds Art Theatre and directing in York for the York Everyman Theatre.[41]

Craig prioritised feminist principles, rather than any specific political affiliation. But her work with community actors, interest in non-conventional playing spaces and simple scenography serves to link her, albeit tangentially, with the socialist amateur groups who were gradually introducing the next wave of avant-garde experimentalism drawn from German, Russian and American political theatre. Indeed in 1930 Craig was invited to direct Upton Sinclair's *Singing Jailbirds* presented as the first production of the Masses' Stage and Film Guild.[42] Although undoubtedly marginalised, Craig was well-known within the metropolitan theatrical elite. In complete contrast Joan Littlewood, who is now recognised as the most important woman director of her generation, spent most of the 1930s and 1940s working in complete obscurity with Ewan MacColl as joint leaders of the socialist Theatre Union. Meticulous research and practical exploration of a raft of European theory and practice encompassing Stanislavsky, Piscator, Brecht, Meyerhold, Laban and others, and conducted with actors functioning as effectively pre-professional rather than amateur, laid the foundations for

Littlewood's pioneering initiatives in ensemble improvisation and devised theatre which were to prove so influential in the 1950s and 1960s.[43]

The Oxbridge factor

By the time in the late 1950s that Littlewood's genius had achieved some measure of recognition, if not much in the way of institutional financial support, the kind of journey her career represented could well be seen as belonging to a bygone era. She and MacColl, despite the rigorous education they devised for themselves, were not university graduates. As a new generation of directors emerged post-Second World War, more and more had been university educated and in the case of the most powerful individuals, that university was Oxford or Cambridge. To conclude this chapter, I want to consider the roots of this phenomenon.

As I have pointed out elsewhere that the end of the nineteenth century saw the growth in the numbers of actors from middle-class backgrounds including a proportion who were also university graduates. While it would be 1947 before the first degree-offering drama department was opened at Bristol University, the extracurricular student theatricals represented by the Cambridge Amateur Dramatic Club (ADC founded in 1855), the Oxford University Dramatic Society (OUDS founded in 1885), and then from 1908 in Cambridge, the Marlowe Society, meant that highly educated, socially advantaged young men could indulge a passion for theatre which through relative ease of access to influential networks could convert quite rapidly to professional opportunity.[44] J. B. Fagan, whose directorial record before setting up the Oxford Playhouse in 1923 included five Shakespeare productions (1918–21) at the Court Theatre and the British premiere in 1921 of Shaw's *Heartbreak House*, had acted with both Benson and Beerbohm Tree after a brief period as an Oxford undergraduate.[45] As a student, William Bridges-Adams acted with the OUDS, but learnt his craft as a director while also employed as a professional actor by among others, Barker, Poel and Alexander.[46]

In the 1920s, although both operated on the physical fringes of their university cities, the Oxford Playhouse and the Cambridge Festival Theatre undoubtedly contributed to an ambience of heightened, if short-lived experimentalism. Terence Gray, also a distinguished and wealthy Egyptologist, was an Oxford graduate.[47] Norman Marshall who witnessed six of Fagan's seasons as a student recalled in *The Other Theatre* his astonishment that 'theatre could be so varied, so amusing, so provocative' and in his opinion ideally suited to an undergraduate audience.[48] Moreover while the exponents of late-nineteenth-century realism were represented in the repertoire, the staging, partly because of the limitations of the first adapted Playhouse building, aimed to be 'Presentational'. In the early seasons plays were 'presented' in white – and wholly impractical-draped curtains. Part of Fagan's legacy, after he left the Playhouse in 1929, was not only the by-then-expected repertory nurturing of future star actors such as Flora Robson, but also his 1925 production of *The Cherry Orchard* with John Gielgud as Trofimov which confirmed Chekhov's play as a masterpiece. Fagan also inspired at least two more Oxford-spawned directors: Marshall himself, and Tyrone Guthrie both of whom were later invited to direct their own seasons at the Cambridge Festival Theatre.

Oxford in the 1920s and 1930s was a particularly powerful means of creating interpersonal 'magic circles' of influence. E. Martin Browne who went up to Oxford to read history and theology in 1919, would eventually in 1935 direct the premiere of T. S. Eliot's *Murder in the Cathedral* casting his Oxford friend Robert Speaight as Thomas Becket. Thereafter directing all of Eliot's verse plays, and a leader in the attempt to promote a revival of poetic drama, Browne was also committed to the cultural value of amateur theatre. In York in 1951 he directed the first revival of the York Mystery Play cycle since the sixteenth century.[49] His near-Oxford contemporary Tyrone Guthrie spent two years from 1926 being 'taught [his] job' employed as the director of the amateur Scottish National Players.[50] Arguably the most dynamic of the mid-century generation of directors, his career included two periods as Director of the Old Vic Company. The legacy of Poel's 'apron' or thrust stage ventures, and Gray's open stage were just two of the factors contributing to Guthrie's later collaboration with the designer Tanya Moiseiwitsch on thrust stages in Canada and America which would strongly influence new British theatre architecture in the 1960s.[51]

Guthrie's first encounter as an inept actor and assistant stage manager with Fagan arose because of the OUDS's tradition of employing professional directors. In 1932, George Devine as President of the OUDS, was directed by John Gielgud in a student *Romeo and Juliet* which also featured Peggy Ashcroft as an invited Juliet. Given immediate entrée into the metropolitan nexus, Devine played for Komisarjevsky, was introduced to the Motleys, and eventually formed a fruitful, long-term friendship with Copeau's nephew, Michel Saint-Denis. This in turn led to the founding in 1936 of the London Theatre Studio, which began the process of the kind of intensive training necessary to sustain the intellectual and artistic mission of the English Stage Company which Devine was invited to set up at the Royal Court Theatre in 1955.[52] The two young directors most associated with Devine, Tony Richardson and William Gaskell, were yet again Oxford graduates, and Peter Brook – like Terence Gray, a 'Magdalene man' – began his stratospheric professional directorial career at the age of only twenty launched by Barry Jackson at Birmingham Rep in 1945.[53]

Clearly to reduce a multifaceted record of the work of many individuals to a neat linear transmission of influence risks a charge of historical distortion. But it is difficult to ignore the origins of the fully fledged directors who would emerge after 1950 to take control of the major theatrical institutions. In his autobiography *Making an Exhibition of Myself* Peter Hall describes the Cambridge theatre culture of his undergraduate years from 1950 to 1953. George 'Dadie' Rylands, an English don at King's College, shaped the verse-speaking skills of generations of student actors in the Marlowe Society while remaining an enthusiastic amateur and occasional professional director. John Barton, whom Hall would appoint as one of his co-directors after he founded the Royal Shakespeare Company in 1961, dominated the ADC as both director and actor. 'The productions', Hall wrote, were regarded by the arts editors of the national papers as news, and first-string critics often travelled from London to see them. It was thought I suppose, that anyone who survived the university rat race stood a good chance of making a mark in the profession.[54]

Making a mark for individuals such as Devine, Brook, Richardson, Hall et al., not only served to reinforce the growing authority of the director in British theatre, it also, in the context of the post-1945 era of state and civic subsidy, led to the creation of new enabling institutions. What was to follow after 1950 in terms of new British drama, the re-visioning of the classical canon, especially Shakespeare, new dynamic approaches to ensemble acting and scenography all built on the work of the first 'directors'. As I have tried to show, this constrained, piecemeal and often frustrated record left a legacy of incalculable value to British theatre in the second half of the century and beyond.

CHAPTER 6
'MASCULINE WOMEN AND EFFEMINATE MEN': GENDER AND SEXUALITY ON THE MODERNIST STAGE

Penny Farfan

The centrality of female characters in modern drama has been widely recognised, and also the complexity of the figure of the 'New Woman' in both her conservative and progressive aspects, but the modernist period saw corresponding transformations in the representation of masculinity, along with shifts in the staging of sexuality as well as gender.[1] Works such as Henrik Ibsen's *Hedda Gabler*, *Rosmersholm* and *Little Eyolf* (1894) had queer as well as feminist dimensions,[2] and reviewers of the 1889 London productions of *A Doll's House* and *Pillars of Society* (1877) described the spectators in attendance as 'unnatural-looking women [and] long-haired men' and as 'masculine women and effeminate men',[3] underscoring the vital role that modern drama and theatrical performance played in the articulation of new gender and sexual roles and the circulation of new ideas about gender and sexuality in the late nineteenth and early twentieth centuries. Katherine Kelly has described late-nineteenth-century Ibsenism as a 'pandemic',[4] but Ibsen's plays in their early London productions were only one part of how theatre, drama and performance figured in the modernist subversion of gender and sexual norms and the staging of new gender and sexual identities. Centering on selected works of British drama and key figures in British theatre in the early twentieth century, this chapter traces out points of intersection between feminist and queer drama, performance and modes of reception as they played out on and around, and contributed to the development of, the modernist stage as it both reflected and shaped broader social and cultural transformations. Instead of focusing on figures who have typically dominated accounts of British theatrical and dramatic modernism, I approach the subject from an angle that aligns with Eve Kosofsky Sedgwick's sense of *queer* as meaning *across*.[5] More specifically, I bring my examples into view from *across* customary boundaries of the field of British modernism, drawing them in from various positions that have typically rendered them marginal or beyond the pale: rather than focusing on scenographer Edward Gordon Craig, for example, I focus on his sister, the director, designer and sometime-performer Edith (Edy) Craig, and her suffragist collaborators Cicely Hamilton and Christopher St John; I look at British reactions to Canadian-born dancer Maud Allan, and, through her, to Oscar Wilde, who died in 1900 but remained a queer presence haunting the social and cultural imagination into the early twentieth century and beyond; and I consider the work of Noël Coward, whose popularity has caused him to seem peripheral to modernist experiment and critique but whose frivolity, as John Lahr has noted, was in its own way 'profound'.[6] In bringing together these examples of some of the 'bad modernisms' that have been increasingly encompassed by the so-called new modernist studies, with its expansions in 'temporal, spatial, and vertical directions',[7] and in suggesting points of contact both among them and to a wider domain of British modernism, I hope to suggest a kind of field within a field, intuited by those reviewers who saw in the London Ibsen audiences 'unnatural-looking women [and] long-haired men', 'masculine women and effeminate men'.

Long identified first and foremost as the daughter of actress Ellen Terry and the sister of Edward Gordon Craig but more recently reappraised as a central figure within the suffrage theatre movement, Edith Craig first came to modernism through secondary roles in the Independent Theatre's 1897 tour of Ibsen's *A Doll's House*, in which she played the role of Mrs Linden (*sic*), and in George Bernard Shaw's *Candida*, in which she played Proserpine.[8] Both of these characters might be construed as 'odd women', a term of the period that described unmarried women but that, as Elaine Showalter has noted, 'conflated elements of the lesbian, the angular spinster, and the hysterical feminist' and that, as Yopie Prins observes, could describe 'a working woman, a suffragette, a single woman living outside the sphere of the family, a woman living with other women, a celibate woman, a mannish woman, a sexually autonomous woman, an "odd" woman not to be paired with a man'.[9] In *A Doll's House*, the widow Mrs Linde, an 'odd woman' of sorts, is perhaps inordinately interested in the marriage of her friend Nora, despite being paired off with Krogstad at the end, while in *Candida*, Prossy, a typist, has a crush on her boss, the Reverend James Morrell, but is at the same time the prosaic counterpart of the poetical Eugene Marchbanks, who is described in the text as 'effeminate' and 'queer'.[10]

From these male-authored 'odd woman' roles, Craig went on to develop her skills as a director and costume designer and eventually to found her own company, the Pioneer Players, which, from 1911 to 1920, specialised in staging plays by and/or about women, as well as English translations of continental modernist works.[11] Along the way, Craig paired up with Cicely Hamilton and Christopher St John, who became her life companion, to create some of the key theatrical works of the suffrage campaign, including *How the Vote Was Won* and *A Pageant of Great Woman*, both of which were first performed in 1909. St John was among the early wave of women to attend university and her Oxford education may have been reflected in her recovery of women's theatre history in *The First Actress*, which the Pioneer Players staged in 1911, as well as in her translation of Hrotsvit's *Paphnutius*, staged by the Pioneer Players in 1914. Hamilton had a background as an actress but turned to writing and political activism, authoring the socialist-feminist tract *Marriage as a Trade* (1909) and becoming the first female member of the British Society for the Study of Sex Psychology, for which she reportedly translated an abridged essay by German sexologist and homosexual rights advocate Magnus Hirschfeld titled 'What Should the People Know about the Third Sex?'[12] Later, in the lead-up to the 1928 obscenity trial of Radclyffe Hall's lesbian novel *The Well of Loneliness*, Hamilton published an article in *Time and Tide* in which she suggested that the 'special, inherited horror of the vice we call unnatural' was a holdover from pre-modern times when there was a 'primal need for children' to ensure the well-being of the tribe, and in which she surmised that '"unnatural" offenders . . . may be judged more leniently in an era convinced of the need for a regular birth-rate'.[13]

I have elsewhere discussed the queer dimensions of *A Pageant of Great Women*, which featured Craig, Hamilton and St John in cross-dressed roles, but *How the Vote Was Won* was in certain ways also queer as well as feminist.[14] In it, Hamilton and 'Miss "Christopher St. John"' (as one reviewer referred to her) rewrote the role of the 'odd woman', showing that she was not so 'odd' after all but was in fact in the majority and essential to the smooth operation of society, and that without her labour and economic contributions, the day-to-day functioning of all aspects of British public and domestic life would grind to a halt.[15] Premised on the fantastical idea of a women's strike whereby all working women give up their paid occupations and present themselves to their nearest male relatives to be supported until they are granted the vote and the rights of citizenship that are their due as self-supporting, tax-paying members of society, *How the Vote Was Won* is *Lysistrata* without the sex.[16] Still, as young Horace Cole's near and distant female relations descend on his household, they transform the heterosexual nuclear home into a homosocial world of 'unwomanly women' who do not conform to the feminine ideal exemplified by Horace's wife Ethel. Her 'pretty, fluffy' hyperfemininity is denaturalised as it is set against the less conventional gender performances of her husband's female relatives and as she finds herself, with comic ineptness, having to take up chores, such as preparing a chop for Horace's tea, that her cook would be doing if she too had not vacated her post to present herself to her nearest male relative for economic support.[17] Edith Craig directed the premiere of How the Vote Was Won at the Royalty Theatre in London as part of a suffrage fair in April 1909 and also acted the role of Horace's Aunt Lizzie, a lodging-house keeper. In a production by the Play Actors at the Court Theatre the following month, Hamilton played the role of Horace's suffragist sister-in-law Winifred.

In 1908, St John wrote a withering critique of a performance by the Canadian-born, American-raised dancer Maud Allan at the Palace Theatre music hall in London.[18] While St John's review focused on Allan's work as derivative of and inferior to that of Isadora Duncan, who had formerly been involved with Edward Gordon Craig and was thus a kind of family connection of St John's through her companion Edith Craig, the hearty homosociality of the female characters in How the Vote Was Won the following year was distinctly different from the decadent staging of perverse female desire in Allan's Oscar Wilde-inspired work The Vision of Salome, which she presented in Germany, Austria and France before bringing it to London, where it played for more than 250 performances. As Amy Koritz and Judith Walkowitz have noted, Allan elicited more attention from British audiences and critics than Duncan or Ruth St Denis, who both performed in London that same year and are now widely regarded as more important figures in the historical development of modern dance, or Loïe Fuller, who created Salome dances in 1895 and 1907.[19] Given Allan's extraordinary success in London, Koritz makes a case for 'an approach to [her] dance that focuses more on the specificity of the English cultural context than that of dance as an art form'.[20] For Walkowitz, Allan's popularity was related largely to the key role that she played in the 'double-edged cosmopolitanism' that pervaded and defined early-twentieth-century London. This cosmopolitanism, Walkowitz explains, 'conveyed a fascination with . . . cultural imports but also a suspicion of them as tainted', and thus it 'confirmed some existing hierarchies, but . . . disrupted others, altering the social and sexual spaces of the city and challenging Victorian constructions of corporeality that were central to ideas of nation, gender, sexuality, and class'.[21]

Attempting to exploit Allan's Canadian background, an advance publicity notice described the dancer as 'belong[ing] to a land where the fires of the French temperament glow ardently through the icy purity of the People of Snow'.[22] Canada was an unusual recruit to the orientalist project; commentators more often focused on Salome's Middle Eastern origins, and Koritz notes with reference to Edward Said's analysis of orientalism as 'a Western style for dominating, restructuring, and having authority over the Orient' that Allan's performance of Salome as exotic, sexually transgressive Other functioned as a gauge against which to mark British national identity.[23] Thus, one reviewer remarked of Allan's performance:

> We have the largest Eastern Empire the world has ever seen, and yet we not only neglect to study Eastern thought and custom, we even shrink with horror, which is instinctive, but which we like to believe virtuous, from anything Eastern. That is the real reason why such dancing as that now being exhibited by Miss Maud Allan at the Palace has never before been received with even lukewarm sentiment in England. Racial instinct, island prejudice, and national conceit have kept our eyes closed to a whole garden of beauties, and have condemned to flow in a narrow channel an art which should spread its beneficent charms over all fields of life.[24]

In this reviewer's assessment, Allan's performance of 'Eastern' dance enhanced British imperial power, providing knowledge while offering a 'garden of beauties' for consumption. Reviewer Walter Higgins also remarked on the 'Eastern' aura of Allan's work but was less appreciative in his assessment of it, complaining that 'London has never seen such a glorification of the flesh' and that '[i]n the soft blue light Miss Allan's white limbs, gleaming through the clinging draperies of dusky gauze, reminded me of nothing so much as the pestilential mists rising from Eastern tropical swamps'.[25]

Walkowitz has noted that Allan, as a North American, occupied an 'insider/outsider role within the Imperial Nation', a hybrid status that was reflected in the critical reception of her work.[26] The comforting fact that Allan's dance was only, in Max Beerbohm's words, 'quasi-Oriental'– or in another reviewer's phrasing, 'Eastern, though Miss Allen [sic] has never been to the East' – co-existed alongside the emasculating threat posed by the figure of Salome as the quintessential *femme fatale* who desires, demands and engages erotically with the head of John the Baptist.[27] One reviewer attempted to reconcile these two aspects of Allan's work by asserting that her 'dancing as Salome, though Eastern in spirit through and through, [was] absolutely without the slightest suggestion of the vulgarities so familiar to the tourist in Cairo or Tangier. She achieves the distinction – we admit it risks being a nice distinction, but she achieves it – between the lascivious and the voluptuous'.[28] Allan herself worked to allay the threat that Salome posed while at the same time exploiting the character's appeal for British audiences. Thus, although Salome was, throughout the late nineteenth and early twentieth centuries, related to the figure of the New Woman, with her feminist and queer associations, Allan took pains to distance herself from the suffragists, explaining in her 1908 autobiography *My Life and Dancing* that while she was in favour of advances in women's education and of opening some professions to women, she was 'not convinced . . . that the vote [was] at present necessary'.[29] As well, while Allan's performance relied upon orientalist fantasies for its appeal with London audiences, she attempted to de-emphasise the salaciousness of the Salome story by staging it as a dream rather than actual waking experience (the 'vision' of Salome) and by describing it, somewhat disingenuously, as a narrative of a young girl's 'spiritual awakening'.[30] Also, as Koritz points out, Allan endeavoured to acquire a reputation for 'aesthetic seriousness and feminine respectability' that enabled her to maintain her distance, as a Western woman, from the exotic sexualised Other that she performed on stage, giving lectures on the classical origins and spiritual dimensions of dance, beginning her autobiography with a chapter tracing the origins of dance to the classical world and situating herself within that classical lineage, and preceding her performance of *The Vision of Salome* with less controversial and more classically flavoured dances to Mendelssohn's 'Spring Song' and Rubinstein's 'Valse Caprice'.[31]

For reviewer Walter Higgins, though, the more innocent dances on Allan's concert programs '[threw] the other dance into a startling and cruel contrast', and he traced the provenance of Allan's Salome to queer proponents of decadent art, specifically Wilde and Aubrey Beardsley, whose illustrations accompanied an 1894 edition of Wilde's play.[32] Elaine Showalter has noted that Wilde's *Salome* was, from the outset, 'understood as an avant-garde text that represented perverse sexuality' and that, throughout its critical history, it has 'been linked with Wilde's homosexuality'.[33] Allan's associations with what Higgins called 'the incarnation of the bestial' in Wilde and Beardsley came back to haunt her in 1918 when a scandal erupted in the British press and courts following a notice in the *Sunday Times* advertising a private performance of Wilde's *Salome* featuring Allan in the title role and produced by J. T. Grein's Independent Theatre.[34] An extreme right-wing member of parliament and publisher, Noel Pemberton-Billing, seized upon this notice to generate war-time paranoia, announcing in his journal *The Vigilante*, under the headline 'The Cult of the Clitoris', that Allan and Grein were at the vanguard of a queer alien threat to the nation, colluding with the German enemy by spreading sexual perversion and moral corruption and enlisting some 47,000 British converts to their secret degenerate ranks. Allan sued Pemberton-Billing for libel but lost her case as he and his witnesses succeeded over the course of the bizarre trial in insinuating that she was a lesbian, if only by virtue of her understanding of the word *clitoris*, with its associations with transgressive, non-reproductive, masculinised female sexuality.[35] The scandal and failed libel suit ended Allan's career and reasserted the dangers of association with Wilde, even years after his death, as his interlinked aesthetics, sexuality and fate were invoked throughout the trial in defense of Pemberton-Billing's claims regarding Allan's degenerate life and art.[36] The obscenity trial of Radclyffe Hall's 1928 novel *The Well of Loneliness* has been regarded as 'a crucial stage in the evolution of a public image of lesbianism' and as having had 'for women an equivalent social impact to the one the Wilde trial had for men', but Jodie Medd has rightly argued that the Pemberton-Billing trial 'introduced the specter of female (homo)sexuality as a locus of national anxiety'.[37]

When Steven Berkoff set his 1989 production of Wilde's *Salome* in the 1920s, some reviewers were reminded of Noël Coward and the 'bright young things' who people his plays of that period.[38] With its overwrought emotions, tortured relationships and decadent ambience, Coward's early social problem play *The Vortex* had more in common with *Salome* than with Wilde's society dramas or comedies of manners, but later works such as *Design for Living* were more on the comic model. Cole Lesley acknowledges that '[t]he brilliant wit of [Wilde's] plays ... appealed to Noël', yet Coward also wanted to set himself apart from Wilde, causing Terry Castle to suggest that his 'whole career might be considered an "improved" version of Wilde's – a Wildean life without the final unhinging tragedy'.[39]

Design for Living took as its theme 'love among the artists' and the relation between modernist artistic practice and the transformation of conventional heterosexual relationships.[40] The play's self-reflexive engagement with modernism is clear from the opening scene when art dealer Ernest Friedman enters with a painting by Matisse that he later succeeds in selling for a high price. The two young artists in the play, Otto and Leo, are both on the brink of success, the former with '[p]opular portraits at popular prices', the latter with a hit play (84). Gilda, an interior designer, is in love with both Leo and

Otto, who are in turn in love with her, but also with each other. As Leo says to Gilda, 'I love you. You love me. You love Otto. I love Otto. Otto loves you. Otto loves me' (21). As a designer, Gilda's struggle to find the right 'design for living' constitutes the play's central action. Desiring conventionality – 'I wish I were a nice-minded British matron, with a husband, a cook, and a baby' (7) – and troubled by the queer triangulation of desire among herself, Leo and Otto, she initially describes her situation to Ernest as freakish: 'Look at the whole thing as a side show . . . Walk up and see the Fat Lady and the Monkey Man and the Living Skeleton and the Three Famous Hermaphrodites!' (15). To escape her discomfort, she runs away to New York and marries Ernest, 'selling out' by designing other people's lives until, like the uncanny return of the repressed, Leo and Otto come to claim her, their queerness figured in an earlier scene when they collapse into each other's arms consoling each other for the loss of Gilda, but also by their twinning when they turn up at Ernest's apartment in evening dress to fetch Gilda back and then come downstairs together the following morning wearing Ernest's pyjamas. Ernest himself is coded as gay, described as 'sterile' (61) and 'rather precise in manner' (3), as 'a respectable little old woman in a jet bonnet' (9), and as having gone on 'a world cruise with a lot of old ladies in straw hats' (60), but despite this coding, he is too conservative to cope with 'love among the artists', condemning Gilda, Otto and Leo as 'unscrupulous, worthless degenerates' involved in a 'disgusting three-sided erotic hotch-potch' (123). Throughout the play, there are recurring references to Norway (56–8, 66, 72), perhaps recalling the gloom of Ibsen's dramas and the young painter Oswald Alving's doomed quest in *Ghosts* for the 'joy of life'. In finally leaving Ernest for Otto and Leo, Gilda embraces 'love among the artists', electing to enact a modernist redesign of the art of living through her own experimental social arrangements rather than creating 'artistically too careful, but professionally superb' designs for non-artists to consume (103). As Otto tells her, 'Life is for living first and foremost. Even for artists, life is for living' (57).

Written in 1932, *Design for Living* premiered in New York in 1933 but was not licensed for production in England until 1938. In his review of the 1933 New York premiere, in which Coward played Leo, Brooks Atkinson wrote, 'Mr. Coward . . . has a way of his own with the familiar triangle . . . It is a decadent way, if you feel obliged to pull a long moral face over his breezy fandango. It is an audacious and hilarious way if you relish the attack and retreat of artificial comedy that bristles with wit.'[41] The hysterical laughter of the three lovers with which *Design for Living* ends, and which figures gestically throughout the play, suggests the power of comedy to represent that which might not be staged or stated through less 'flippant' means.[42] As the reader for the Lord Chamberlain wrote in approving *Design for Living* for its 1939 London premiere, 'the play is pure Coward and despite the immorality of its theme, the Public would not, in my opinion, be justified in raising any serious objections to what is, after all, only an artificial Comedy of Manners'.[43]

Radclyffe Hall, an avid theatre-goer who was friends with Coward as well as Edith Craig and Christopher St John, regarded audience members at 'first nights' as being like select members of a special club, united by their dedication to theatrical adventure.[44] As the quotations from the early Ibsen performances in London indicate, however, there was within the coterie of modernist theatre-goers a subset of feminist and queer spectators in attendance at, reflected in, and in formation through engagement with modernist theatrical events. A letter from Bloomsbury writer Lytton Strachey to artist Duncan Grant about a 1907 revival of Wilde's *A Woman of No Importance* (1893) provides a vivid example of queer reception:

It was rather amusing, as it was a complete mass of epigrams, with occasional whiffs of melodrama and drivelling sentiment. The queerest mixture! Mr [Beerbohm] Tree is a wicked Lord, staying in a country house, who has made up his mind to bugger one of the other guests – a handsome young man of twenty. The handsome young man is delighted; when his mother enters, sees his Lordship and recognises him as having copulated with her twenty years before, the result of which was – the handsome young man. She appeals to Lord Tree not to bugger his own son. He replies that that's an additional reason for doing it (oh! he's a *very* wicked Lord!) She then appeals to the handsome young man, who says, 'Dear me! What an abominable thing to do – to go and copulate without marrying! Oh no, I shall certainly pay no attention to anyone capable of doing *that*,' and then suddenly enters (from the garden) a young American millionairess, with whom (very properly) the handsome young man is in love. Enter his Lordship. Handsome Y. M.: 'You devil! You have insulted the purest creature on God's earth! I shall kill you!' But of course he doesn't, he contents himself with marrying the millionairess, while his mother takes up a pair of gloves, and slashes the Lord across the face. It seems an odd plot, doesn't it? But it required all my penetration to find out that this was the plot, as you may imagine.[45]

Other evidence of queer and feminist reception is less direct and explicit than Strachey's reading of Wilde's play. Newspaper coverage of suffrage performances suggests the homosocial feminist ambience in the auditorium, reporting '[f]eminine cheers and a few that were masculine resounding throughout the Royalty Theatre' and 'an enthusiastic call for "Author"' following a performance of *How the Vote Was Won* in April 1909, and that the play had 'evoked a storm of cheering and hissing from the ladies in the theatre'.[46] Walkowitz's research on Allan's Salome includes fascinating details of queer as well as feminist sub-cultures in London. Allan attracted a large female audience, with one reviewer reporting that at least ninety per cent of the audience for one of her concerts was female and observing that '[i]t might have been a suffragist meeting', but Walkowitz further notes that Allan received fan mail from a male dancer who performed '"always as a lady"'; that the Palace Theatre and her performances there were associated with gay male cruising; that Radclyffe Hall attended a performance by one of Allan's many Salome imitators in 1910; and that Allan's work helped to create the conditions of possibility for a private feminist production of Wilde's *Salome* in 1911 that featured the honorary secretary of the Actresses' Franchise League, Adeline Bourne, in the title role and attracted a predominantly female audience.[47] In language reminiscent of that used by the early Ibsen critics, one reviewer described this 1911 production as 'a sorry spectacle' suitable only for 'sexless women and pussycat men'.[48] As for Coward, Alan Sinfield argues that he 'manage[d] to attract two audiences: a general boulevard audience that [found] naughtiness titillating, and a more specialised audience of sexual dissidents for whom he and his work were actively constitutive of a newly emergent gay subculture. Coward's plays . . . did not merely reflect ideas of gayness: they afforded a reference point through which many men cultivated their own ideas of who they were'.[49] As such evidence of queer and feminist reception makes clear, theatre, drama and performance played a key role in the formation of modern gender and sexual identities, and feminist and queer artists and spectators played a no-less crucial part in the production of modernism, both on the British stage and beyond.

CHAPTER 7
STAGING HITLER, NOT STAGING HITLER
Steve Nicholson

Introduction

In July 1939, a few weeks before Britain declared war on Germany, the Lord Chamberlain's Office, which had responsibility for licensing and censoring stage plays, rejected a translation of Ernst Toller's *Pastor Hall* as 'a violently prejudiced piece of special pleading' which 'spares no pains to vilify the Nazis and exalt the Jews'.[1] Over the previous six years they had regularly intervened to suppress stage criticism of Germany. The primary aim of this chapter is to recover some of these anti-fascist texts, now largely invisible in theatre and performance history, which bear powerful testament to the politics of the period, and to the determination of some theatre writers to inject a world dominated by make-believe escapism with a sense of the European catastrophe.

Although this chapter will foreground the plays themselves, we need also to be aware of the impact of the decisions made by the Lord Chamberlain about what could and could not be spoken and shown in public theatres.[2] Indeed, he regularly consulted not only the British Foreign Office but also the German Embassy, which was always ready to complain. There was, for example, a direct and absolute embargo on the direct representation of Hitler. This came to a head in early 1937 when a theatre manager and a comedian were actually prosecuted over a pantomime version of Robinson Crusoe:

> Bold, bad pirate Will Atkins (Hal Bryan) thundered down the stairs with one lock of hair over his forehead, and wearing a little black moustache.
> 'Heil!' 'Heil!' 'Heil!' he shouted, and the house rocked with laughter. It was looked upon as one of the best gags in the show.[3]

The German Embassy objected, and since the gag had been illegally added after the script was licensed, the judge found them guilty and imposed fines. It was an important precedent, and a leading journal for the theatre profession warned that other performers should 'Take heed'.[4] The standard advice and escape clause for playwrights was to remove all overt references and 'ruritanianise' their texts. But as we shall see, policies were not fixed; rather, they were susceptible to events, government strategies, public attitudes and subjective opinion.

1933–4

Attempts to expose the reality of life in Nazi Germany began soon after Hitler came to power. In the summer of 1933 a Jewish doctor and novelist from Leeds set *Who Made the Iron Grow* in a country called Nordia, which is ruled by a dictator named Hacker and his anti-semitic Yellow Shirts. However, the playwright told the *Daily Express* that his script was 'based entirely on first-hand information', and the article was explicitly headlined 'LIFE UNDER THE REGIME OF HITLER', so the mask of fiction could hardly have been thinner.[5] The play centres on the family of a medical professor, who has always hidden his Jewish background even from his wife. She now blames the Jews for all her country's problems, telling a friend that she 'would gladly see the whole cursed race wiped out' and her husband that 'our very existence depends upon the extermination of the Jews'. The professor is sacked from his University post, and an official sticks labels saying 'Jew' throughout their apartment. The professor's wife is advised that she can annul the marriage, while their son is directly involved in the brutal murder of one of the father's former colleagues, a brilliant Jewish scientist. The professor denounces Hacker: 'It is his voice that has stirred up the people. It is his teaching that has turned Nordia into an armed camp'. The population, he declares, has been 'doped, drugged, anaesthetised with words'. But he believes that people will eventually wake from their 'delirium', and in a final image of optimism his wife does just that, expressing her solidarity by holding up one of the 'Jew' labels in front of herself.[6] Initially, the Lord Chamberlain, supported by the Foreign Office, turned the play down: 'Whatever one may think of the Hitler regime, the prosecution of Jews etc. they are no direct concern of ours.' However, a revised version was licensed the following year after the removal of anything (including costumes and a Nazi salute) which referenced Germany too overtly.[7]

Like *Who Made the Iron Grow*, Leslie Reade's *Take Heed* – originally *Achtung!* – was first performed privately, without the need for licensing. Staged at the Piccadilly Theatre in January 1934, the *Daily Telegraph* called Reade's play an 'indictment of the Hitler regime in Germany', while some referred disparagingly to its 'anti-Nazi and pro-Jewish bias', criticising the writer's 'unwillingness to allow his opponents a shred of decent feeling'.[8] Again, the narrative centres on a professor and his wife, but this time it is she who is Jewish, and who is eventually driven to suicide. *Take Heed* exposes the hate-filled rhetoric of the fascists ('the Jew is slowly eating us up and getting fat on us') and the ruthless brutality of the regime ('The Marshall himself has promised to stamp out Judaism like syphilis or any other filthy disease'). Most of the physical violence is reported rather than shown – although the second Act ends with stones being thrown through the windows, and off-stage voices shouting 'death to the Jews'. It is also made explicit that the regime has designs which extend beyond Germany. 'We are not yet ready to deal with the British swine' warns a storm troop leader; 'Their turn is after the French'. In the final moments of the play he issues an ominous warning, standing over the corpses of the Professor and his wife:

> Here lie our internal enemies, vanquished by our lion hearts and nerves of steel. The dirty foreign democracies will be harder, but their day will also come. When we are ready, we shall do the same to them . . . Let the world beware.[9]

Critics were inclined to assume that Reade's play overstated the situation, but when it was staged in New York a couple of months later as *The Shattered Lamp*, the *New York Times* reported that it 'seems overwrought merely because it is true'.[10] Similarly, when a revised version was eventually approved for Britain three years later, *The Times* noted that what had once appeared to be 'the melodramatic exaggeration of propaganda' seemed very different now: 'In 1938 the facts have so far outstripped Mr Reade's imagined horrors that one is more inclined to suppose that they have been deliberately toned down.'[11]

One of the sub-themes of *Take Heed* is its depiction of a lifelong friend and colleague of the professor gradually turning against him and becoming a paid-up storm trooper. A similar attempt to chart how apparently decent and reasonable people were succumbing to the allure of Fascism was at the heart of *Heroes*, a play by the Austrian dramatist Theodor Tagger, who had himself fled Germany when Hitler came to power.[12] *Heroes* shows how anti-semitism and the violent persecution of Jews become normalised almost overnight in a German University and city. Its central character is Karlanner, a liberal medical student who is unable to resist the psychological pressure of mob mentality, or the increasingly confident rhetoric and nationalistic fervour of the student leaders: 'A whole nation of masters have allowed themselves to be twisted round the fingers of a handful of slaves, just because they didn't realise that they were of a ruling race. That's all over.'[13] Karlanner abandons the Jewish girlfriend who has stood by him through his studies, and participates in violent raids and the abject humiliation of a former Jewish friend. Bruckner's play could have been a powerful piece of propaganda, but in March 1934 the Lord Chamberlain turned it down. As his own Reader dryly commented: 'To those who take the theatre seriously it must seem a pity that matters which have stirred public feeling should be excluded from it.'[14]

The texts discussed so far were built on realism and authenticity, but a rather more fanciful play which was also refused a licence in the autumn of 1934 was Henry Daniell's *Lucid Interval*. The central character is Anton Shindler – another thinly disguised version of Hitler – who finds himself in a sanatorium and treated as insane after his plane crashes during a secret foreign mission. Mistakenly identified as a regular patient subject to self-hallucinations, there is some fairly gentle comedy against Shindler ('an overgrown boy scout without his pole'), especially when he becomes irate in his attempts to convince the nurses and doctors that he is a dictator and a national leader ('If Matron hears you she'll scold you'). But Daniell's play is not only a comedy; in the opening scene, we hear about the brutality and oppression of Shindler's regime and witness the making of a propaganda film in which Shindler issues a chilling warning to foreign enemies: 'Out of the ashes and from the charred cinders that you have left of our territory I have risen . . . Nothing can stop me.' When he makes a final speech at the end of the play, a stage direction informs us that he 'becomes instantly the terrific mob orator', using 'every trick of elocution and platform glamour', while 'His eyes, as always when addressing his followers, become enormous and hypnotic'. *Lucid Interval* also makes reference to rumours about Hitler's own racial background, when he is shown to revert under hypnosis to a previous incarnation in which he is himself a Jew, tortured and killed by the Spanish Inquisition. 'The curious thing is that today my patient has a strong racial antipathy to the Jews', explains the doctor: 'Dying, he carried over in excruciating pain the resolve to be revenged.'[15]

1935–7

By November 1934 the Lord Chamberlain was warning the Foreign Office that 'It is not easy to go on shielding the Germans from their misdeeds being depicted on the stage in this country'. The Foreign Office agreed that he should loosen the reins: 'we cannot object on political grounds to all plays about

Nazis'.[16] As a result, more criticisms of the German state began to appear on the public stage. *The Crooked Cross* was an adaptation by Sally Carson of her own 1934 novel, staged at Birmingham Repertory Theatre in 1935 under the direction of Sir Barry Jackson, and reaching London two years later.[17] Set in Germany in early 1933, this was a fast-moving and heightened drama in which a young couple (Lexe and Moritz) are forced apart by the violent anti-semitism developing in the society around them. In the final scene, Moritz is shot as he tries to escape across a mountain, and Lexe chooses to jump to her own death. Despite the tragedy which unfolds, and the innocence of its victims, many of the critics praised its 'restraint from propaganda' and the fact that it was not 'a pro-Jew, anti-Nazi, pamphleteering, tub-thumping sermon'. The abusers were 'not, in origin, vile or evil, but children perverted by hysterical delight in power', and Carson 'interprets understandingly the side of the swashbuckling Nazi', emphasising 'the faith, the devotion and the purpose it gives to its adherents'.[18] Such comments may tell us more about the reviewers than the play, but there is certainly a sense that some of those who buy into fascist culture are playing games which get out of hand rather than acting from deep-seated convictions: 'all you really care about is the uniform and the noise and the flagwaving and the girls', as Lexa tells one of her brothers. When Erich returns to the family house after committing an act of brutal violence, we see him happily consuming the lemonade and biscuits thoughtfully left out for him by his mother. Lexa can only find one way to explain her brother's actions: 'You're drunk. That's it . . . You're all drunk. You can't help it.'[19] Yet in the end, she and the play both know that the Nazis are not about to sober up any time soon.

Other texts staged at this time included Eleanor Elder's *Official Announcement*, again focusing on discrimination against a German professor and his non-Aryan wife, and Michael Walsh's *Son of Judea*, which shows us stormtroopers committing gratuitous acts of violence against the occupants of a Berlin apartment whom they suspect of having Jewish connections and sympathies.[20] *Do We Not Bleed*, by George H. Grimaldi, was a somewhat old-fashioned and implausible melodrama set in 'an imaginary Totalitarian State' named Galania, where Rabias Strafen is the owner of an anti-semitic newspaper and the State Governor. Strafen is outwitted by an impeccably cool English journalist, called – inevitably – Drake, who tells him the truth about life in his country:

> men walk your streets with the look of hunted animals. The women creep from their poor home at dusk, their faces atwitch with fear. The

children run weeping from your schools where their school fellows are taught to revile them . . . And what is their crime? That they are Jews.

Strafen insists that all the nation's problems can be laid at the door of 'these cunning, cringing hordes of Israel', the 'parasites who poison our race and suck the life from us'. But Drake – who is himself Jewish – has the killer card up his sleeve – the knowledge that Strafen has Jewish blood in his veins following a trip to England during which his life was saved by an emergency blood transfusion from none other than Drake himself.[21]

In *Death of a Ghost*, a German opera singer and Nazi supporter, Margarete Engelbrecht, marries and has a child – Adolf – with Anthony, a liberal Englishman. When their marriage breaks up she moves in with Gerhardt Sturm, a German composer whose approach to music embodies Fascist aesthetics, and whose operas preach Nazi propaganda. Anthony is desperate to bring up the child himself, to prevent him growing up as a 'little Nazi, a little robot in uniform – to believe all their devil's drivel about the Aryan race, and the glories of war, and splendour of spitting in Jews' faces'. Finally, it is revealed that Margarete has herself been banned from the stages of the Reich for having distant Jewish connections of which she had been unaware. 'I believed in the Fatherland – the Fatherland has flung me out', she declares; 'I am the blind who has just begun to see.' When her husband turns on her as 'a crow disguised in eagle's feathers' carrying 'poison in your veins!', she replies (in a line carefully deleted by the Lord Chamberlain) that this accusation has been levelled at 'the Leader' himself.[22]

1938–9

In May 1938, following Hitler's effective annexation of Austria, the Lord Chamberlain again wrote to the Foreign Office: 'I can foresee that we shall receive an increasing number of plays bearing on Germany and the Nazi regime.'[23] The next fifteen months did indeed produce some sharp and intelligent scripts which led to confrontations with the Lord Chamberlain – and also within his own office. The title of Jack Duval's *Lorelei* alluded to the significance of Germanic myths in the Nazi construction of national identity, but more specifically, to the tale of a beautiful maiden, transformed after death into a siren, eternally luring sailors on the Rhine. The narrative centres on a brilliant scientist, Eric Rumpau, who has fled from Germany not because he himself is under threat, but out of solidarity with victims of the regime. Now based in a French resort in the Vosges Mountains some thirty miles from the German border, he produces anti-Nazi leaflets to be dropped by plane in his homeland, targeting in particular the women of Germany: 'those who are asked to beget breathing missiles and bleeding targets ... who are pregnant with manure for foreign pastures'. Yet he declines invitations to ally himself with international campaigns, believing that in the end the nation's own people will reject the Nazis and that he will see 'the gates of Germany re-opened from the inside'. Desperate to punish him for his betrayal, the German government sends a siren – Karen – to lure him back, but their mutual respect – and attraction – inspires an honest exchange of views. Eric tells her that she is serving 'a Germany of barracks and prisons'; yet through Karen's defence of Hitler, the playwright again tries to suggest some of the reasons for his appeal:

If a man has become our Leader, it was not because he was right or wrong, for the poor or for the rich. It is because at his baton's stroke, young men have marched in harmonious formations, with new rhythms and uniforms; young women have assembled in choirs and parades ... He has been the first ruler to order girls to learn swimming and riding, boys to harvest and plough!

Karen also declares that Germany is bound to something deeper and more profound than their current leader: 'We obey ten centuries of ancestors!' But Eric quashes her seductive claim with a simple but telling image which captures how the past is manipulated by the present: 'How pleasant to obey the dead, once we have crowded their silent mouths with orders of our choice.'[24]

When the Lord Chamberlain sought the advice of the Foreign Office on Duval's play, they recommended that it might be considered if it could be ruritanianised; but in fact he chose to inform the producer simply that in his view 'England would be better served by not putting on such plays during this time of international stress.' We have no way of knowing the views of the playwright, since the negotiation was always between the Lord Chamberlain and the producer, or the theatre manager who was thinking of staging the play. In this instance, the producer agreed that 'as the father of children, he did not consider it advisable to put on the stage, or to make money out of anything that might possibly prejudice the future lives of people in this country'.[25]

The production which generated the most press hype in 1938 was *Trumpeter, Play!*, written by Vere Sullivan, a childhood friend and correspondent of Katherine Mansfield. Promoted when it opened at London's Garrick Theatre as 'a play of vital concern to everybody',[26] the opening night audience included Sir Thomas Inskip, the Minister for Co-ordination of Defence, and Duff Cooper, the first Lord of the Admiralty and former Secretary of State for War. An earlier version of the text had been staged the previous year under the title *Code of Honour*, when it was not just passed but positively lauded by the Censorship for the 'great understanding and sympathy' it showed towards Germany. 'The Teutonic point of view, and its justification, is treated with as much sympathy, if not more, as the British', wrote the Lord Chamberlain's reader, approvingly; 'I think the play, far from doing any harm, may do good.' [27] Yet *Code of Honour* had subsequently attracted considerable public hostility for being supposedly anti-British, and Sullivan felt compelled to rewrite it.

As the play's producer, Leon Lion, informed the Lord Chamberlain, 'my author is very distressed' by suggestions that her play 'smacks of propaganda for Nazism'. While Lion said that he himself did not agree with such a reading, he had 'received too many protests and reproaches to ignore', and now accepted 'that if there is to be any bias in such a sympathetic presentment of two Peoples, it should fall definitely to our own country rather than seem against it'. Remarkably, and most unusually, the Lord Chamberlain told Lion he was himself 'distressed' that the original text was being withdrawn, since 'rather well-informed people' had indicated to him that they were 'impressed with its fairness and helpfulness', and considered it 'a helpful play in the present continuous crisis'. He urged Lion not to bow to pressure: 'Do please persuade your author not to rewrite the play full of "jingo" spirit.' When the script of *Trumpeter, Play!* was submitted for licensing, regret was expressed that she had been 'persuaded that too great sympathy with the Teutonic point of view is unlikely to prove popular', and had therefore 'made concessions to national amour-propre'.[28]

Sullivan's play seeks to draw comparisons between the national characteristics and contemporary outlook of typical British and German middle-class families, using the marriage between a German Air Force Officer, Karl, and an English woman, Peggy, to take us into both family homes. The event on which the plot hinges is that Peggy becomes so unwell during childbirth that Karl must choose whether to save the life of his wife or that of the unborn child; 'He decides that the Fatherland must not be robbed of a son to defend it, or a daughter to breed more sons, and that Peggy must be sacrificed.'[29] The message is clearly that Germans love their country more than their family. As Karl's uncle himself declares:

The Englishman dies for his country with the greatest gallantry . . . but he doesn't live for England – he forgets her until he is called on to die for her again. The German not only dies for Germany – he lives for her.

In the play's original incarnation, when Karl decides that his primary duty is to the child and the nation 'the brave girl agrees with this decision and dies'. In *Trumpeter, Play!* she takes a much more critical attitude towards German priorities: 'Any woman would be morbid who was giving a son to Germany today' Peggy tells her English family; 'Germany is hypnotised by one thought. Every baby is born with one idea. Germany must be mighty. Germany must be united. Germany must be avenged.' Indeed, the younger generation in Germany are shown from the start to be itching for war and revenge; those who remember 1914–18 are more circumspect, but in the end they, too, are unable to resist the mood, and become caught up in the fervour and adulation as 'the Leader' passes in the street, and the crowd's choruses of 'Sieg Heil' grow ever louder.

KARL: (*His eyes lighting up, his whole mood changing*). You hear! Uncle Nik! The soul of Germany! Germany's calling to her sons!

COUNT NIKOLAUS: Yes. It's stronger than ourselves – a radiant light is shining, Heil! Heil! Heil!.. (*Ecstasy seizing him, flings away his sticks, groping forward with his hands towards the window. He is utterly carried away by the intensity of the cheering*).

KARL: God bless the Leader! God bless the Fatherland![30]

The Lord Chamberlain's Office – sensitive, still, to the need not to antagonise the German Embassy – deleted a reference to 'the madness of a whole people', along with accusations that 'the German is a Barbarian' and that 'Germany's mind is unhinged'.[31] The production proved something of a damp squib, closing within two weeks. 'It is an excellent play so far as it goes', wrote one reviewer; 'though it may easily be objected that it goes no distance at all.'[32] To some it seemed as if the energy of the play had become dissipated by its determination 'to be fair to Germans, English, militarists, pacifists, and anyone else who turns up'.[33] Soon afterwards, Sullivan had another play – 'the central theme of which is the persecution of the Jews by a European State' – turned down by the Lord Chamberlain on the explicit request of the Foreign Office.[34]

'We have always maintained that the playwright has no business to don the preacher's stole, using the stage for a pulpit.' So declared the authors Anthony Heckstall-Smith and E. P. Hare in their programme notes for the 1939 production of *Juggernaut*, an ambitious if laboured historical chronicle which focused on one family to chart key political developments in Austria between 1913 and the present. 'Rather', they continued, 'it is his duty like that of the landscape painter, to present a picture of a scene as he sees it', and the playwrights were adamant that their play had 'no message to give nor moral to point'.[35] As we have already seen, the wish to be 'fair' to both sides permeates through many of the newspaper reviews, and also the discussions in the Lord Chamberlain's Office. Certainly, *Juggernaut* allowed the Nazis a voice:

> Before I joined the party I was useless living without a purpose . . . think what a hopeless outlook it was for me, growing up in this country after the war . . . Look what we've done in Germany already. Look what she was ten years ago and what she is now! Look at the youth camps where thousands of boys and young men are being trained to be useful to be constructive.[36]

'I do not believe that any reasonable German would object to the play', wrote the Lord Chamberlain's Reader; for it was not 'a real genuine anti-Nazi play' but 'a fair and detached statement of historical fact'.[37]

Private theatre clubs were not, of course, subject to the same level of scrutiny or restrictions as public theatres since they were permitted to function outside the control of the Lord Chamberlain .The most politically active of these clubs was the left-wing Unity Theatre. *Crisis*, a 'living newspaper' which juxtaposed narration, songs, sketches, naturalism and verbatim material to interpret political events in Europe, opened with an actor in Nazi costume reading aloud from Hitler's *Mein Kampf*, and was full of undisguised references to Germany and Hitler throughout.[38] Group Theatre, whose artistic contributors included Spender, Auden, Isherwood, Doone, Britten and Piper, had a reputation for being more committed to aesthetic experimentation than ideological analysis or agitation, but their repertoire also had a strong political dimension. Spender's verse tragedy

Trial of a Judge, for example, centres on a group of Fascists who are released from prison, despite being convicted for the brutal murder of a Jew:

JUDGE:
The precedent
Licenses their acts to flourish like a tree
Spreading murder which grows branches
Above that soil where the law is buried . . .
BLACK TROOP LEADER: Comrade, comrade see
How everything is altered.
We who did violence stand here free. And honoured . . .
. . . as what the law approves.[39]

In 1938, Group Theatre staged Auden and Isherwood's *On the Frontier*, in which the two nations of Westland and Ostnia confront each other and finally go to war. The play was to be presented publicly rather than privately, and the script was only approved after deleting references which hinted too strongly at the real, and following disagreements and argument within the Lord Chamberlain's Office: 'To forbid this would be to subscribe to fascist ideology', insisted one of his readers. But what ultimately saved the play in the eyes of the censors was that it was more an anti-war than an anti-Hitler play, with the two nations, and their rulers and systems of government, both engaging in war-mongering and nationalistic propaganda. As the play's supporter in the Lord Chamberlain's Office realised, it was 'equally critical of both philosophies', and the portrait of Westland's dictator was 'not unsympathetic'.[40] The play can also be seen as attack on capitalism, with the dictator shown as a puppet in the hands of business and industry magnates who tell him 'you will never know what's happening nor who pulls the strings'. He even confides that 'I never wished to be Leader. It was forced upon me'.

Auden and Isherwood's writing gives the play a distinctive and at times poetic style, very different from the forms which continued to dominate and limit much theatrical expression. One scene in *On the Frontier* powerfully adapts the meeting of the witches in *Macbeth*:

FIRST JOURNALIST: Where have you been?
SECOND JOURNALIST: Watching the frightened die
          As bombs fell from the Asiatic sky . . .
    And untrained peasants facing hopeless odds.

FIRST JOURNALIST: The rattle of Spain's execution squads . . .
SECOND JOURNALIST: When by telephone and wire
    Come reports of flood or fire.
THIRD JOURNALIST: Where the wounded's frantic cry
    Crawls upon the midnight sky.
FOURTH JOURNALIST: Where the words of hate are spoken
    And the will of children broken.
FIRST JOURNALIST: Where the homeless stare aghast
    Thither we must travel fast.
FOURTH JOURNALIST: And where terror's famished drum
    Swallows reason, we must come . . .
SECOND JOURNALIST: When shall we four meet again?
THIRD JOURNALIST: In the midst of human pain.
FOURTH JOURNALIST: Where women weep as soldiers die
    We shall gather by and by.[41]

With music by Benjamin Britten, the staging also broke with naturalistic convention, not least by splitting the stage in two so that the focus cuts instantly between characters in the two countries – or allows us to view them simultaneously. However, most critics found that the production was 'spoilt by the anti-realistic elements' and the 'atmosphere of pretentiousness so tiresome to the average playgoer.'[42]

'I would rather be sworn at than laughed at' wrote one of the Lord Chamberlain's officials in relation to Auden and Isherwood's play.[43] But On the Frontier was not alone in trying to use comedy and satire to mock the Nazis. In Unity's celebrated 'pantomime with political point' – Babes in the Wood – Hitler and Mussolini are robbers, while Austria and Czechoslovakia are the babes, and the British Prime Minister, Neville Chamberlain, a wicked uncle who more or less conspires with the robbers.[44] Political pantomime even reached the West End in December 1939, when Who's Taking Liberty – an adaptation of Cinderella by the popular novelist Pamela Frankau – was staged at the Whitehall Theatre. In one scene, the ugly sisters – Gretchen and Katinka (or Hitler and Stalin) – sing a duet which comments on the Soviet/German alliance:

KATINKA: Oh, what would I do without you? . . .
             You're planning to cheat me.
GRETCHEN: You're out to defeat me.
BOTH: You've got to belong to me now.

BOTH:	Oh, what would I do without you?
	When splitting up Europe in two?

GRETCHEN:	For I'll take the west bit.
KATINKA:	But I'll have the best bit!
GRETCHEN:	Oh, what would I do without you?[45]

The final text I want to discuss also aimed to use humour as a weapon. *Follow My Leader* was a witty and in some ways a brilliant anti-Nazi farce, written in 1938 by Terence Rattigan in collaboration with Tony Goldschmidt, but – courtesy of the Lord Chamberlain – not staged until January 1940.[46] It has never been seen again, nor published; and yet in some respects *Follow My Leader* invites comparison with the work of a later political farceur such as Dario Fo. Politically, it got some things badly wrong. But reading it even at a distance of three quarters of a century, it is not hard to agree with the memory of one of the original cast, Frith Banbury, who in an interview given in his nineties remembered the script as having been 'really, really funny'.[47] It is certainly like no other play about the Nazis written during the 1930s – and probably no other play written by Rattigan.

Although Rattigan was still in the early stages of his career when he wrote *Follow My Leader*, he had already enjoyed considerable commercial and critical success with *French Without Tears*, which had run for over a thousand performances in the West End. The suppression of this play has therefore been described by biographers as a 'bad blow to Rattigan's morale', which left him 'bitter and angry', while the failure of the production when it was finally staged left him with a 'sense of despair and bewilderment'.[48] By 1940, critics and audiences found the tone inappropriate – perhaps even offensive – since 'The foolishness of dictators was no longer something the British audience felt like laughing about'.[49] One reviewer compared it to 'fiddling while Warsaw burns', and the very notion of 'A farce about concentration camps, faked propaganda, jackasses in jack-boots' was certainly highly questionable. 'The authors seem to have no burning anger in them' complained the critics.[50] Yet Rattigan had come close to joining the Communist Party during the Spanish Civil War, and the possibility of a political satire against Fascism had been in his mind for a couple of years before he sat down in the spring of 1938 to write one.

Follow My Leader takes place in the offices of the Moronian Patriots' Party. In the first Act, they are in opposition with no apparent prospect of power, although their ambitions are clear from two maps on the wall:

'One, which is uncoloured, save for a small blue patch in Central Europe, bears the label, MORONIA TODAY. The other, which is entirely coloured blue, except for the Gobi desert and Australia is called, MORONIA TOMORROW.'[51] Field Marshall Baratsch and Karl Slivovitz (doubtless inspired by Goering and Goebbels) spend most of the Act arguing about which of them should be party Leader. They then hit on the idea of appointing a figurehead whom they can manipulate between them. Enter a plumber – 'a mild-looking little man with a drooping moustache, in workman's clothes' – who is mending the radiators. 'He's got everything we want. Good appearance, knows nothing of politics – easily controlled – fine voice – wonderful war record.' They bribe Zedesi with an increase in salary and then, in a scene reminiscent of Brecht's *Arturo Ui*, instruct him on how he must present himself:

BARATSCH: Stand up straight and throw out your chest. (*The little man does so*) Now raise your right hand. (*He obeys and Slivovitz pulls the little man's hair over his eyes*) . . . Look angry. (*Gives him a sharp blow in the stomach. The little man turns angrily on Baratsch. Slivovitz seizes his right hand, which he has lowered, and pulls him back into position*) . . . Now say after me . . . 'I demand a place in the sun for Moronia'.

LITTLE MAN: (*mildly*) I demand a place in the sun for Moronia . . .

SLIVOVITZ: Now bang the desk with your left hand while saying it, and shout as loud as you can.

LITTLE MAN: (*Shouting at the top of his voice and banging the desk*) I demand a place in the sun for Moronia!

BARATSCH: Magnificent! Couldn't do better myself.

The second Act opens on the first anniversary of the day when 'our glorious Leader made the historic decision to take into his own hands the supreme direction of the State', ensuring that 'Moronia was saved from the horrors of democracy'. Baratsch summarises some of the party's achievements:

We are making bigger and deadlier shells than any other nation . . . We have suppressed fifteen newspapers; we've got rid of no less than twenty-five thousand dangerous Liberal agitators: we've eliminated the Trade Unions: we've abolished the Constitution, and we've resigned from the League of Nations. Not bad going for one year, eh?

The curtain then opens to reveal Zedesi on the balcony, arm raised, speaking to the crowds, while another official, supposedly invisible, dictates the text for him to repeat. Afterwards, their real relationship becomes clear:

QUETSCH	How often have I got to tell you, leader, to relax the muscles when you're making a gesture? You looked a perfect fool, standing there with your arm as stiff as a poker. . .
ZEDESI	(*putting on his coat and muttering to himself*) I'm hot as hell and hoarse as a crow. It's been talk, talk, talk – chatter, chatter, chatter – the whole blooming day . . .
QUETSCH	(sharply) That's quite enough from you, Leader. We don't want to hear any more grumbling.

It is also revealed that there is still widespread opposition to the government within the country and that 'we may easily be driven from power within a month'. The solution the officials come up with is to start a war by 'findin' some piddlin' little country and just walking into it', and they agree to invade the neighbouring Neurasthenia:

QUETSCH:	If I might raise a point, Mr Slivovitz, we don't seem to have any excuse for taking their country.
BARATSCH:	Excuse? What a duffer you are, Quetsch! You don't need excuses for taking people's countries these days – you just take 'em.
QUETSCH:	Yes, but we've got a pact of non-aggression with them.
BARATSCH:	(still chuckling) So we have, by Jove. What a chance to catch 'em napping!

The justification they then concoct for this invasion mocks the German argument for invading Czechoslovakia: 'most fortunately, it appears that there is an oppressed Moronian minority in the western province'; although, as they privately admit, the oppression amounts to little more than a requirement to pay taxes. Slivovitz invites the entire Neurasthenian cabinet and the monarch to visit Moronia, so he can bomb the embassy where they will be staying. This task is given to an enthusiastic ('Oh, goody-goody! An Embassy! That will be fun') but incompetent hitman, Riszki, who makes a mistake and accidentally blows up the British Embassy instead. This in turn leads to one of the play's funniest and most pointed scenes when the

British Ambassador arrives – dressed in the battered remains of his pinstripe trousers and top hat – to register the mildest of complaints concerning the 'untoward circumstance that has just arisen in connexion with my embassy'. He apologises for the fact that 'it will be necessary for me to report the matter to His Majesty's Government', and Rattigan's target is clearly those members of the British government and establishment who continue to kowtow to Hitler: 'Whitehall will take no hasty decisions, and the matter will be viewed from every angle', says the British Ambassador; 'it is conceivable that they may instruct me to deliver a formal protest'.

Meanwhile, Zedesi escapes, and although he is arrested for supposedly imitating himself, he has already revealed the truth to a female investigative journalist with whom he has instantly fallen in love. In the final scene, Zedesi abandons the text of another speech written and dictated for him to deliver to the crowds, and – urged on by the female journalist – tells them what is really going on. To loud cheers and general agreement he then denounces 'all these parades, rallies in uniforms and Youth Movements and speeches and Secret Police', cancels the war, dissolves the Patriots' Party, and promises to reinstate the old Constitution, and arrange new elections. He himself will return to his life as a plumber, and the play ends with Slivovitz, Baratsch and Quetsch fleeing abroad – 'It was a good racket while it lasted, but it couldn't go on for ever', they concede.

While *Follow My Leader* was superficially ruritanianised, too much of it was too clearly identifiable for the Lord Chamberlain's Office to accept this 'light-hearted burlesque of fascism'. The playwrights then considered the possibility of a private performance, incorporating genuine newsreel footage between scenes to draw the parallels more closely. This idea seems to have come to nothing, and a year later Rattigan tried again – arguing to the Censors that the political situation had changed and offering to remove any passages still considered 'objectionable'. But even in August 1939 the German Embassy was consulted, and they replied that Rattigan's play would not 'be helpful in improving Anglo-German relations'.[52] The script was licensed soon after the outbreak of war, but its moment had gone. 'I wish Rattigan's play ... had been put on earlier', wrote the *Daily Mail* 'before the time was out of joint'.[53] It wasn't that the performance was necessarily unfunny; 'those who think the times appropriate to an elongated jest of this kind will get plenty of laughs', said the *Daily Mirror*.[54] But as James Agate put it, 'I just personally don't see that you can write a full-length burlesque about, say, the Plague when the plague is in full visitation.'[55] Such criticisms are surely valid – although it could be argued that similar points could have been made about Charlie Chaplin's film *The Great Dictator*, which was released nearly a year later to be met with considerable acclaim. Interestingly, one review of Rattigan's play had even described the performance of the actor playing Zedesi, Reginald Beckwith, as 'Chaplinesque'.[56]

Viewed in retrospect, there are certainly other problems with Rattigan's text – even if they are not unique to it. For one, it cannot bring itself to believe fully in the danger and power of Nazism, preferring to see it as so inherently absurd that it cannot survive. Then it might be argued that the comedy seems to be directed less against the political ideology of the Nazis, and more at their incompetence. As one review put it, they come across as 'not unlikeable buffoons'.[57] Also it is hard to think of anything more misjudged than characterising Hitler as 'a complete nonentity'[58] and 'a sort of doll figure',[59] or, most especially, the total absence of reference to Jewish persecution. Nevertheless, there are aspects of the play which still make it seem odd that *Follow My Leader* should have almost completely disappeared from theatre and Rattigan history.

Follow My Leader is one of a perhaps surprising number of playtexts from the 1930s which sought to place Hitler or the Nazis on stage, either explicitly or in thinly veiled representations. Those discussed in this chapter do not amount to a complete catalogue, and I have largely ignored notable texts by foreign playwrights which came to Britain, including *Judgment Day* (1934) by Elmer Rice, *Till the Day I Die* (1935), by Clifford Odets, *Professor Schelling* by Leivick Halpern and *Professor Mamlock* by Friedrich Wolf. Moreover some of the plays discussed here were probably never performed because they were refused licences, while others were delayed or had significant changes imposed by the censors. Again, most of those which were staged had relatively short runs, or were presented in small and relatively obscure venues. No one, I think, would argue that direct engagement with international political issues was at the heart of British theatre during the 1930s. Yet, as this chapter shows, there were plenty of playwrights, directors and theatre managers – including some who worked in the commercial sector – who did seek to use it for such purposes, and specifically to attack what was occurring in Nazi Germany. Even at this distance, it is impossible to miss the urgency and commitment of these plays.

CONCLUSION

The first fifty years of the twentieth century contained two of the most devastating clashes known to humanity. Scores of people were killed, physically and mentally maimed, made homeless or even nationless. Competing ideologies of capitalism, communism, fascism and democracy led to a fight for global power, with America, Germany and Russia attempting at various points to wrest control. By the start of the 1950s a Cold War was in full swing and there were fears about the destruction of the world.

Throughout this period there were attempts by many countries to reshape society. These ranged from a belief in genetic engineering to massive shifts in political ideology. Britain did not undergo such radical changes but after 1918 there was a surge towards starting a new social order that was more egalitarian and dealt with the problems of before: poverty, illiteracy, disease. After 1945 there was a determined quest for a 'New Jerusalem' that would sweep away the unjust hierarchies of the past. In Britain, minorities such as women and the working classes began the process to get equal opportunities. Although the Empire was gradually being dismantled, mass immigration shifted the country towards a multi-cultural society, even if conversely parts of the kingdom such as Scotland and Ireland were pressing for independent recognition. The technological advances of cinema, radio and television began to democratise culture on a scale not seen before, and artistic experimentation led to new ways of representing life; this ranged from realism and naturalism to modernism and expressionism.

These bare facts describe a decisive change between the Edwardian age and that of the post-war era, one that could not have been imagined in the dying days of Queen Victoria. It is hardly surprising therefore that British theatre was extraordinarily varied in the way that it responded to socio-political events. During the period under investigation playhouses, the theatre industry, and views about theatre workers underwent a remarkable transformation. Indeed, essential elements of contemporary theatre, whether the use of empty space, state funding, theatre-in-education, or regionalism – to name a few – were already firmly in place before 1950.

Certainly there were still vestiges of nineteenth-century theatre, and the period has often been criticised for producing staid, superficial and antediluvian drama; staging had also generally been inherited from the late Victorian model. Radical changes propounded by Edward Gordon Craig and others had no major impact upon the big theatres, which were still dominated by 'realistic' box sets based around the upper-middle-class drawing room. The proscenium arch acted as a frame for this and the audience formed the fourth wall, exactly as it had done in the previous century. Older theatre buildings were demarcated according to class – generally speaking those who sat in the gallery were mainly working class, and those who sat in the stalls and circle were middle- or upper class – but increasingly these artificial barriers were challenged.

The Court Theatre, place of the first burst of repertory theatres in Britain, began to alter people's perceptions of the function of the stage, as well as the whole process from writing, directing and rehearsal through to the role of the audience. After transmuting into the Royal Court Theatre, the English Stage Company under the leadership of George Devine played host to some of the most innovative and shocking work of the second half of the twentieth century: debuts included John Osborne's *Look Back in Anger*, Edward Bond's *Saved* (1965), Caryl Churchill's *Top Girls* (1982) and Sarah Kane's *Blasted* (1995).

The Lord Chamberlain's office, in place since the eighteenth century, attempted to control the theatre via stringent censorship laws that refused to license plays on religious, political and moral grounds. Again, theatre clubs made a mockery of the laws by putting on private productions, and it was obvious that more ad hoc performances in revues or on the battlefield, for example, could not be restrained in the same way. Problem plays, instigated by Ibsen and carried forward by Shaw, exposed social hypocrisy, leading to a continued tension between what needed to be said and what was allowable. This was also obvious during the wars where national security and public morale was at the forefront of the government's mind. For example, in the previous chapter Steve Nicholson has argued that representations of Hitler and Nazism were dependent on the government's prevailing relationship with Germany, and attempted to keep pace with rapidly changing foreign policy; what was allowable in one year – or even one month – could be outmoded by the next. In fact, throughout these years there was a constant pushing of moral and political taboos across the board: from Frank Matcham's semi-naked spectacles to drug taking and sexual deviance in the work of Coward, and from Maugham and Shaw's searing condemnations of war to Unity Theatre's exposure of governmental incompetence and class corruption. With the new wave of dramatists from the 1950s onwards, the situation became increasingly untenable and theatre censorship was finally abolished in 1968.

Looking beyond traditional playhouses leads us to awareness of street theatre, pageants, touring companies, wartime concert parties and the like. These were frequently given a political agenda. Suffrage drama, although largely a middle- and upper-middle-class enterprise, was produced not only in theatres but alternative spaces such as skating rinks and outside factory gates. Attendance was seen as a communal activity, drawing the audience together in a shared objective. This resurfaced during 1960s' and 1970s' second-wave feminism, which similarly found impetus in public spectacles and street demonstrations: the 1970 Miss World protest springs to mind.[1] The two world wars, particularly the latter one, also did much to destroy divisions between actor and audience, as well as the notion of venue. Performance became available to everyone and any location could be transformed into a theatrical space, whether that was the trenches, bomb shelters, school halls or cathedral steps.

Little, regional and amateur theatres, generally overlooked in standard histories, were at the forefront of theatrical change. Not as hidebound by commercial interests as mainstream stages, these smaller spaces were freer to draw on European influences, notably the plays of Ibsen, the acting techniques of Stanislavski and the staging of Appia, Piscator and Brecht. The influx of refugees into Britain during the 1930s and 1940s aided this process but, even before this, practitioners were aware of major dramatic trends that ranged from Yeats's use of Japanese Noh theatre and Rupert Doone's total spectacle to Priestley's allegorical plays and Unity Theatre's Living Newspapers. Again, as Penny Farfan has shown in her chapter, modernist performances helped to shape gender and sexual identities in a way that spoke to the continued renegotiation of male, female and queer identities sharpened by Oscar Wilde's trial, the New Woman, and the First World War.

Smaller theatres helped to reinscribe regional identity. In specific areas such as Scotland, Ireland, Wales, theatre was used to expose England's political and cultural colonialism at home, a view that would continue long into the century and beyond: Brian Friel's *Translations* (1980) and Gregory Burke's *Black Watch* (2006) are cases in point. The use of social realism was particularly prevalent in regional theatre as a means of depicting the hardship of mainly working-class lives during a time of large-scale unemployment and poverty in all corners of the country, and this also allowed for the use of dialect which countered the received pronunciation of the more mainstream stage.

Acting as a professional career was pursued by more people than ever before, with opportunities for training afforded by a plethora of stage schools, drama was beginning to be seen as worthy of academic study through theatre-in-education initiatives and university departments. As Claire Cochrane has pointed out in this book, the actor-manager, so prevalent in the Victorian and Edwardian period, was gradually being replaced by the producer/director, many of who had sharpened their talents in university drama productions. There were still actor-managers – most notably John Gielgud and Donald Wolfit – but with the growing complexity of running a theatre (technical, fiscal, artistic) came the separation of roles. In turn there was a further interest in ensembles and collectives, which would lead to the development of fringe theatre in the 1960s and 1970s.

While the notion of state subsidised theatre had been debated since the end of the nineteenth century, it became enshrined during the Second World War, not surprising given the Government's concern with guiding and monitoring the audience's belief systems. In 1944 new laws were passed so that companies funding touring work no longer had to pay Entertainment Tax, if this was non-profit making, and the following year Community Centres were recognised for their work with 'non-commercial, independent theatre initiatives during wartime'.[2] However, the closer relationship between the theatre and the state has not always been viewed as advantageous. On the one hand, CEMA and its successor, the Arts Council of Great Britain, pursued subsidised culture for all, with the Second World War ushering in 'a new era where the artistic objectives of theatre pursued on a not-for-profit basis assumed the ideological high ground'.[3] On the other hand, it also brought about a theatre highly dependent on the vagaries of funding and a greater interference by the establishment, as with the Thatcherite policies of the 1980s.[4]

It is reductive to suggest that the First World War swept away the certainties of the Edwardian age as of course that period was fraught with its own difficulties. However, there was a real sense that something had been broken by 1918, further underscored by the next war. The advancement of technological warfare led to a number of plays on this theme, most of which warned against its dangers unless its potential was harnessed in the correct manner. The apocalyptic vision conjured up by the atom bomb joined those of the concentration camps to fuel despair about the future of the human race. It is therefore not surprising that three of the bleakest styles of theatre – Antonin Artaud's Theatre of Cruelty, Jerzy Grotowski's Poor Theatre, and Theatre of the Absurd – all arose out of a period marked by such horrors. In particular, Martin Esslin's explanation of latter demonstrates the enormous shift in belief systems from the turn of the century to its mid-point. Theatre of the Absurd expresses, Esslin says, 'the anxiety and despair that spring from the recognition that man is surrounded by areas of impenetrable darkness, that he can never know his true nature and purpose, and that no one will provide him with ready-made rules of conduct'.[5] The idea that there was a divine plan for the world was now seen as incredible in many quarters, leading to the existentialist view that the meaninglessness of life could only be countered by personal responsibility.

British theatre between 1900 and 1950 can be seen as one of great range and variety. Middle-class drawing room drama jostled for space with lavish representations of the exotic East. Ivor Novello's sentimental musicals were as popular as the Scottish romanticism purveyed by Harry Lauder. The political plays of the suffragists and working classes drew in audiences, as did the social satires of Shaw and Galsworthy. While this period saw theatre becoming more professionalised, with an increase in stage schools, academic study and specialist bodies, there was a concomitant rise in amateur and community-based activities. Two world wars within the same generation helped to loosen ties to the Victorian and Edwardian heritage, leading to a greater exploration of space and place, as well as underpin awareness of the fundamental necessity for theatre that lies at the core of society. Growing out of ancient ritual, it brings magic, provides a means of understanding the chaos of life and death, and brings people together through the sharing of a common sense of humanity. All of this was nowhere more obvious – or needed – than in the tumultuous first half of the twentieth century.

CHRONOLOGY

NB: All events refer to Britain unless otherwise stated.

Date	Historical Events	Theatrical Events
1900	Second Boer War: 1899–1902.	Stephen Phillips, *Paolo and Francesca* and *Herod*. Henry Arthur Jones, *Mrs. Dane's Defence*. Edward Gordon Craig directs *Dido and Aeneas*. Oscar Wilde dies in Paris.
1901	Death of Queen Victoria. Accession of Edward VII. Founding of the Labour Party by Keir Hardie.	London Hippodrome opened by Frank Matcham. *A Geisha Girl* and *A Chinese Honeymoon* continue the fashion for exotic musical comedy. Edward Gordon Craig's production of *Dido and Aeneas*. Walter Melville's *That Wretch of a Woman* is part of series of plays that are a backlash to the appearance of the 'New Woman' in society. W. B. Yeats collaborates with George Moore on *Diarmuid and Grania*.
1902		David Belasco's *The Darling Buds* becomes one of first important transfers from America's Broadway to London's West End. John Galsworthy's first play, *The Silver Box*. J. M. Barrie, *The Admirable Crichton*. W. B. Yeats and Augusta Gregory, *Cathleen ni Houlihan*.
1903	Women's Social and Political Union (WSPU) founded by Emmeline Pankhurst	First part of George Bernard Shaw's *Man and Superman* staged. *In Dahomey*, first all-black revue, imported from America. Publication of Synge's first play, *Riders to the Sea*; produced a year later.

Date	Historical Events	Theatrical Events
1904	St Louis World Fair in America.	The Abbey Theatre set up in Dublin by W. B. Yeats and Lady Augusta Gregory, with funding from Annie Horniman. Court Theatre started by Granville Barker and J. E. Vedrenne. J. M. Barrie's *Peter Pan*. George Bernard Shaw, *John Bull's Other Island*. Royal Academy of Dramatic Art (RADA) founded by Herbert Beerbohm Tree. Granville Barker and William Archer publish National Theatre scheme. Anton Chekhov dies.
1905		Start of Shakespeare Annual Festival, organised by Herbert Beerbohm Tree. Edward Gordon Craig publishes *The Art of Theatre*. George Bernard Shaw, *Major Barbara*. Granville Barker, *The Voysey Inheritance*. Henrik Ibsen dies. Henry Irving dies.
1906	Liberal Government in power. SS *Dreadnought* built.	Elsie Fogerty starts the Central School of Speech and Drama (CSSD). *The Girl Behind the Counter* is one of many plays about women working in department stores. First public performance of George Bernard Shaw's *Caesar and Cleopatra* (written in 1898). Samuel Beckett born.
1907		Granville Barker's *Waste* banned; rewritten in 1927 and publicly performed in 1936. J. M. Synge's *The Playboy of the Western World* causes riots at Abbey Theatre, Dublin. St John Hankin, *The Cassilis Engagement*. Elizabeth Robins, *Votes for Women!* Gaiety Theatre founded in Manchester by Annie Horniman. Lena Ashwell manages Kingsway Theatre.

Date	Historical Events	Theatrical Events
1908		The Actresses' Franchise League (AFL) started. Edward Gordon Craig publishes *The Actor and the Über-Marionette.* Le Théâtre du Grand-Guignol tours Britain. Cicely Hamilton, *Diana of Dobson's.* George Bernard Shaw, *Getting Married.* Annie Horniman starts Manchester Repertory Company.
1909	Launch of Futurist Movement by Filippo Tommaso Marinetti in Italy. Series of strikes by dock, railway and mining workers between 1909 and 1912. Gladstone imposes forcible feeding for imprisoned suffragettes.	Herbert Beerbohm Tree second actor to be knighted after Henry Irving in 1895. Arthur Wareing founded Glasgow Repertory Company. Guy du Maurier, *An Englishman's Home.* D. H. Lawrence, *A Collier's Friday Night.* John Galsworthy, *Strife.* Elizabeth Baker, *Chains.* Cicely Hamilton and Christopher St. John, *How the Vote was Won.* Cicely Hamilton's *A Pageant of Great Women* produced from 1909 until the start of the First World War.
1910	Manet and the Post-Impressionists exhibition in London. King Edward VII dies. Accession of George V.	Variety Theatres Controlling Company Ltd started by Alfred Butt. Publication of Edward Gordon Craig's *A Note on Masks.* Little Theatre in London started by Gertrude Kingston as a venue to stage suffrage drama. John Galsworthy, *Justice.* Granville Barker, *The Madras House.*
1911	Festival of Empire at Crystal Palace and Coronation Durbar in Delhi to celebrate coronation of George V.	Oscar Asche, *Kismet.* Edith Craig starts the Pioneer Players. Allan Monkhouse, *Mary Broome.* Basil Dean sets up Liverpool Repertory Theatre.
1912	Sinking of the Titanic. Outbreak of war in Balkans.	First Royal Command performance for George V and Queen Mary. Stanley Houghton, *Hindle Wakes.* Lilian Baylis becomes manager of Royal Victoria Hall (later known as the Old Vic). José Levy's *Seven Blind Men* at the Palladium, London. Githa Sowerby, *Rutherford and Son.* Lilian Baylis inherits Old Vic Theatre, London.

Date	Historical Events	Theatrical Events
1913		Diaghilev's *L'après-midi d'un faune* first performed in Britain.
		Harry M. Vernon and Harold Owen, *Mr. Wu*.
		Granville Barker's ground-breaking productions of *The Winter's Tale* and *Twelfth Night*.
		John Galsworthy, *The Fugitive*.
		Inez Bensusan sets up Women's Theatre Company at the Coronet Theatre, London.
		Barry Jackson and John Drinkwater open Birmingham Repertory Theatre.
1914	Britain declared war against Germany on 4 August 1914 and on Austria-Hungary on 10 August.	Charles Cochran's first revue, *Odds and Ends*, with Alice Delysia.
		E. Temple Thurston, *The Cost*.
	The Defence of the Realm Act.	John Galsworthy, *The Mob*.
	Publication of Wyndham Lewis's Vorticist magazine, *Blast*.	Women's Emergency Corps (WEC) set up by Lena Ashwell, Decima and Eva Moore, and Eva Haverfield.
		Title of suffrage newspaper changes from *The Suffragette* to *The Britannia*.
		Ban on public performances of Ibsen's *Ghosts* ended.
		Old Vic starts cycle of Shakespeare's complete repertoire, ending in 1923.
		George Bernard Shaw, *Pygmalion*.
1915	Field Marshall Douglas Haig commands British Expeditionary Force until end of war.	Harold Brighouse, *Hobson's Choice*.
		Walter W. Ellis, *A Little Bit of Fluff*.
	Setting up of Women's International League for Peace and Freedom.	Frank Price, *Mother's Sailor Boy*.
		Edgar Wallace, *The Enemy in our Midst*.
	Sinking of RMS. Lusitania.	Dreda Boyd, *John Feeney, Socialist*.
		George Bernard Shaw, *O'Flaherty V.C.: A Recruiting Pamphlet*.
		Miles Malleson, *'D' Company*.
		Fred Karno, *All Women*.
		Lena Ashwell's concert party tours France.

Date	Historical Events	Theatrical Events
1916	Conscription introduced in Britain. Cabaret Voltaire club opened in Zurich. Irish Easter Uprising begins on 24 April. The Battle of the Somme.	Entertainment Tax introduced for theatres. Entertainments Department set up by armed services with involvement of Basil Dean. Allan Monkhouse, *Shamed Life*. Miles Malleson, *Black 'Ell*. Rudolf Besier and Sybil Spottiswoode, *Kultur at Home*. *The Bing Boys are Here*. *Flying Colours* revue. Albert P. de Courville, *Razzle Dazzle*.
		Oscar Asche's *Chu Chin Chow* runs until 1921. On 23 April, celebrations to mark Shakespeare's Tercentenary.
1917	Russian Revolution and Civil War (1917–21).	Bruce Bairnsfather, *The Better 'Ole*. Oscar Asche's production of *The Maid of the Mountains*. Mrs Horace Porter, *Patriotic Pence; or, The Home Fairy*. Henry Arthur Jones, *The Pacifists*. John Drinkwater, *X = 0*. Basil Dean becomes head of War Office theatres. Cicely Hamilton's *The Child in Flanders* performed in Abbeville. H. F. Maltby, *Petticoats*. J. E. Harold Terry, *General Post*. J. M. Barrie, *Dear Brutus*. Herbert Beerbohm Tree dies.
1918	First World War ends on Signing of Armistice on 5 November. Propaganda centralised under Ministry of Information. Tsar Nicholas II and family killed; Vladimir Lenin establishes Soviet Union. Kaiser Wilhelm II abdicates.	Unionisation of the acting profession. Seymour Hicks and Arthur Shirley, *Jolly Jack Tar*.

Date	Historical Events	Theatrical Events
	Coalition Government; Liberal Party's David Lloyd George becomes prime minister. League of Nations Union set up. Women granted partial vote.	
1919	Constructist movement started in Russia. Sex Disqualification Removal Act. Treaty of Versailles. Jallianwala Bagh massacre in Amritsar, India.	Basil Dean founded production company, ReandeaN, with Alec Rea. George Bernard Shaw, *Heartbreak House*; first performed in New York before appearing in London in 1921. Maugham's *Home and Beauty*, written in 1915, staged at the Playhouse, London. E. M. Hull, *The Sheik*. H. F. Maltby, *The Temporary Gentleman*. Village Drama Society, a forerunner of the British Drama League, started by Geoffrey Whitworth.
1920	Oxford University degrees conferred on women. National Insurance introduced for all. Irish Civil War.	Karel Čapek's *RUR (Rossum's Universal Robots)* produced in Czechoslovakia. José Levy starts his Grand Guignol Theatre in London. Vernon Lee, *Satan the Waster*. J. M. Barrie, *Mary Rose*. Somerset Maugham, *The Skin Game*.
1921	Creation of the Irish Free State. Hitler becomes leader of National Socialist German Workers' Party.	Nugent Monck opens Maddermarket Theatre, Norwich. Luigi Pirandello's absurdist *Six Actors in Search of an Author*, opens in Italy. Ernst Toller's *Masses and Man* written while imprisoned in Germany. Publication of W. B. Yeats's *Four Plays for Dancers*. Scottish National Players runs from 1921–47. Gerald du Maurier creates the stage role of Sapper's fictional hero, Captain Hugh 'Bulldog' Drummond.

Date	Historical Events	Theatrical Events
		Christopher Holland's *The Old Women* and H. F. Maltby's *The Person Unknown* at London's Grand Guignol Theatre.
		Clemence Dane's first play, *A Bill of Divorcement*.
		Somerset Maugham, *The Circle*.
		Clemence Dane, *Will Shakespeare*.
1922	British Broadcasting Company (BBC) founded under directorship of John Reith. Conservatives win General Election; Stanley Baldwin is prime minister.	First drama transmission from BBC is scene from *Julius Caesar*. George Blake, *Clyde-Built*. Basil Dean produces James Elroy Flecker's *Hassan*. The musical *Lilac Time* arrives in London's West End, after appearing in Europe and America. Scottish National Theatre Society founded.
1923	First National Socialist (Nazi) party rally held in Munich.	Allan Monkhouse, *The Conquering Hero*. J. B. Fagan founded Oxford Playhouse. Sanders Lewis, *Blodeuwedd* (1923–5). Sean O'Casey's *Dublin Trilogy* (1923–6). Ernst Toller's *The Machine Wreckers*, directed by Nugent Monck for the Stage Society. Ben Travers's series of Aldwych farces (1923–33).
1924	Great Empire Exhibition, Wembley. Ramsey MacDonald's Labour Party in power for only nine months. Taken over by Stanley Baldwin and the Conservative Party. Stalin assumes power in Russia.	*St Joan*, George Bernard Shaw. Richard Hughes's *Comedy of Danger* is first radio play. Council for Proletarian Art became Workers' Theatre Movement before being taken over by Tom Thomas's Hackney People's Players. Noël Coward, *The Vortex*. Barry Jackson's modern-dress *Hamlet*.
1925		Gate Theatre opened in London by Peter Godfrey. Hubert Griffiths, *Tunnel Trench*. J. R. Ackerley, *Prisoners of War*. Arnold Ridley, *Ghost Train*.
1926	General Strike for nine days in May.	Cambridge Festival Theatre started by Terence Gray and Harold Ridge. Scottish Community Drama Association founded.

Date	Historical Events	Theatrical Events
		Sean O'Casey's *The Plough and the Stars* causes riots at Abbey Theatre, Dublin.
		Joe Corrie, *In Time o' Strife*.
		Margaret Kennedy's stage adaptation of her 1924 novel, *The Constant Nymph*.
		D. H. Lawrence, *The Widowing of Mrs. Holroyd* (written 1911, revised 1914).
		Workers' Theatre Movement founded.
1927	British Broadcasting Company (BBC) formed.	Jerome Kern's *Show Boat* transfers from New York's Broadway to London's West End.
		Velona Pilcher and Peter Godfrey set up the Gate Theatre Studio in London.
1928	Equal Franchise Act.	R. C. Sherriff, *Journey's End*.
		Gate Theatre Company, Dublin, established by Hilton Edwards and Micheál MacLiammóir.
		Sean O'Casey, *The Silver Tassie*.
		Moscow Arts Theatre (MAT) visit London.
		League of Welsh Drama started.
1929	America's Wall Street Crash sparks Great Depression. First talking pictures. Labour win election with a minority; Ramsay MacDonald is prime minister.	Basil Dean and Reginald Baker found Associated Talking Pictures Ltd which later becomes Ealing Studios.
		Velona Pilcher, *The Searcher*; staged at the Grafton Theatre, London, in 1930.
		Noël Coward, *Bitter Sweet*.
		Osiris Players started by Nancy Hewins.
		Barry Jackson starts Malvern Festival
1930	Coalition national government under MacDonald.	British Actors' Equity Association started.
		Noël Coward, *Post Mortem*.
		Robert Graves, *But It Still Goes On*.
		Noël Coward, *Private Lives*; *Bitter Sweet*.
		Paul Robeson appears alongside Peggy Ashcroft in *Othello* at the Savoy Theatre, London.
1931	Glasgow Exhibition. Multi-party National Government.	Noël Coward, *Cavalcade*.
		Ewan MacColl starts the Red Megaphones in Manchester; with Joan Littlewood, this becomes Theatre of Action (1934), Theatre Union (1936) and Theatre Workshop (1945).
		Agatha Christie's first play, *Black Coffee*.
		Dodie Smith's first play, *Autumn Crocus*.
		G. B. Stern, *The Man who Pays the Piper*.

Date	Historical Events	Theatrical Events
		Lilian Baylis takes over Sadler's Wells theatre for opera and ballet, under direction of Ninette de Valois. First English performance of Oscar Wilde's *Salome*.
1932	Oswald Mosley's New Party merges with British Union of Fascists. Hunger marches in London.	W. Somerset Maugham, *For Services Rendered*. Robert Medley and Rupert Doone found the Group Theatre in London. Hans Chlumberg, *Miracle at Verdun*. Mordaunt Shairp, *The Green Bay Tree*. Noël Coward, *Design for Living*. Rowena Cade opens the open-air Minack Theatre, Cornwall, with a production of *The Tempest*. New Shakespeare Memorial Theatre opens. Lady Augusta Gregory dies.
1933	Adolf Hitler becomes Chancellor of Germany.	Howard De Walden's bi-lingual Welsh National Playhouse runs from 1933–9. T. S. Eliot's *Fragment of a Prologue* (1926) and *Fragment of an Agon* (1927) first published and performed together as *Sweeney Agonistes*. Maugham's last play, *Sheppey*, is poorly received. John Gielgud directs and stars in Gordon Daviot's *Richard of Bordeaux*. Tyrone Guthrie directs the Old Vic Company. Regent's Park Open Air Theatre established.
1934	Jarrow hunger marches take place in 1934, 1935 and 1936.	Eliot's *The Rock* staged by E. Martin Browne. Auden and Isherwood, *The Dog Beneath the Skin* (1934–6). Ewan MacColl, *John Bullion*. Dodie Smith, *Touch Wood*. Una Marson, *At What a Price*. *Love on the Dole*, adapted by Ronald Gow from Walter Greenwood's novel, and staged at Manchester Repertory Theatre

Date	Historical Events	Theatrical Events
1935	General Election sees first Communist Party MP in Parliament; Stanley Baldwin becomes Prime Minister Italy under rule of Benito Mussolini invades Ethiopia.	Eliot's *Murder in the Cathedral* performed in Canterbury Cathedral. Auden's *The Dance of Death*. Clifford Odets, *Waiting for Lefty* staged by Group Theatre, New York. American Federal Theatre Project (1935–9) started as part of Roosevelt's New Deal. Cole Porter's *Anything Goes* transfers from New York's Broadway to London's West End. Ivor Novello's *Glamorous Night* at Drury Lane, London. Publication of Muriel Box's *Angels of War*, with first professional production in 1981. Theodore Komisarjevsky's production of *Macbeth* at Stratford-upon-Avon.
1936	George V abdicates the throne in favour of his brother who becomes George VI. Battle of Cable Street. Spanish Civil War (1936–9). German expansion into Rhineland. Television introduced on BBC.	Michel Saint-Denis establishes London Theatre Studio with George Devine, Marius Goring and Glen Byam Shaw. Auden and Isherwood, *The Ascent of F6* (written in 1935, performed a year later). Unity Theatre, London, begins. Jack Lindsay, *Who are the English?* C. L. R. James's *Toussaint L'Ouverture* performed by the Stage Society. John Maynard Keynes founds Cambridge Arts Theatre.
1937	Neville Chamberlain becomes prime minister. Lord Halifax's meetings with Hitler start policy of appeasement. Japan invades China, Soviet Union and Mongolia between 1937 and 1938. Mass Observation social research *Windsor* project started by Government.	Lupino Lane creates the dance craze, The Lambeth Walk, in *Me and My Girl*. J. B. Priestley, *Time and the Conways*. Tyrone Guthrie becomes artistic director of the Shakespeare Repertory Company until 1945. Death of Lilian Baylis. BBC televises scene from *The Merry Wives of Windsor* by Robert Atkins's Bankside Players. Laurence Olivier and Ralph Richardson join the Old Vic.
1938	German annexation of Austria. Kennilworth Castle Pageant. Neville Chamberlain meets Hitler in Munich.	*The Death of Cuchulain* is Yeats's last play. Swansea Stage Society put on Jack Jones's *Land of My Fathers: A Play of the Distressed Area*. Emlyn Williams, *The Corn is Green*. Unity Theatre's *Living Newspaper 1: Busmen*;

Date	Historical Events	Theatrical Events
	Germany invades Poland Republic of Ireland established.	*Living Newspaper 2: Crisis.* George Bernard Shaw, *Geneva.* Dodie Smith, *Dear Octopus.* Terence Rattigan, *Follow My Leader.* Free German League of Culture (FGLC) open Klein Buhne (Little Theatre) in Belsize Park, London.
1939	Germany's occupation of Sudentenland in southern Czechoslovakia leads to declaration of war by Britain on 3 September 1939.	Places of entertainment closed on outbreak of war; most open within a couple of weeks. Unity's *Sandbag Follies* put on within 48 hours. Entertainments National Service Association (ENSA) set up by Basil Dean and run from Drury Lane Theatre, London. Ivor Novello's *The Dancing Years* runs until 1944. J. B. Priestley, *Johnson over Jordan.* Eliot's *The Family Reunion.* E. Martin Browne's Pilgrim Players tour the United Kingdom. Molly Urquhart founded the MSU Players in Scotland. W. B. Yeats dies.
1940	Chamberlain gives up office; wartime coalition administration put in place under the leadership of Winston Churchill. German bombing raids (Blitzkreig) on key locations in Britain 1940–1 and 1944–5.	Sean O'Casey, *The Star Turns Red.* Council for the Encouragement of Music and the Arts (CEMA), set up. Old Vic Theatre moves to Burnley, Lancashire, until 1943, when it returns to London. Creation of several Old Vic touring companies. Daphne du Maurier's stage adaptation of *Rebecca.* George Shiels, *The Rugged Path.* Geoffrey Kerr, *Cottage to Let.*
1941	Bombing of Pearl Harbour by Japan brings USA into war. Germany invades Soviet Union.	Glasgow Unity Theatre started. Noël Coward, *Blithe Spirit.* United Service Organizations for National Defence (later known as the United Services Organizations, or USO). Basil Brown starts up Central Pool of Artists in 1941 (Stars in Battledress). Old Vic Theatre bombed. Old Vic tours country under auspices of CEMA.

Date	Historical Events	Theatrical Events
		Rise Above It revue.
		R. H. Ward publishes his manifesto, 'The Theatre of Persons'.
		Glasgow Unity Theatre formed.
		Esther McCracken, *Quiet Weekend*.
		James Hadley Chase, *Get a Load of This*.
		James Barke, *The Night of the Big Blitz*.
1942	Anglo-Soviet Pact.	Terence Rattigan, *Flare Path*.
		John Maynard Keynes takes over leadership of CEMA.
		Bristol's Theatre Royal receives state support from CEMA.
		The Adelphi Players stage *Holy Family* by R. H. Ward.
		James Hadley Chase, *No Orchids for Miss Blandish*.
		Joe Corrie, *Dawn*.
1943	Meeting of Churchill, Roosevelt and Stalin.	Agatha Christie, *Ten Little Niggers* (retitled *And Then There were None*).
		J. B. Priestley, *Desert Highway*.
		James Bridie and Thomas [T. J.] Honeyman found Citizens Theatre, Glasgow.
		CEMA provides financial subsidy for Theatre Royal, Bristol.
		Sean O'Casey, *Purple Dust*.
		Rodney Ackland, *The Dark River*.
		Noël Coward, *This Happy Breed*.
		J. B. Priestley, *They Came to a City*.
		Basil Dean directs *Salute to the Red Army* at the Royal Albert Hall.
1944	Butler Education Act.	ABCA Play Unit set up by Michael MacOwen; first official production is *What's Wrong with the Germans?*
		Compass Players started by John and Anne Crockett.
		Ronald Pertwee, *Pink String and Sealing Wax*.
		Harold Purcell, *The Rest is Silence*.
		Esther McCracken, *No Medals*.
		Terence Rattigan, *Love in Idleness*.
		Conference of Repertory Theatres (CORT) founded.

Date	Historical Events	Theatrical Events
		Basil Dean produces Clemence Dane's *Cathedral Steps* outside St Paul's Cathedral and in the ruins of Coventry Cathedral.
1945	6 August: atomic bomb dropped on Hiroshima, followed one on Nagasaki on 9 August 8 May: Victory in Europe (VE day). 15 August: Victory in Japan (VJ day). Labour Party wins General Election; Clement Atlee becomes Prime Minister. Start of Welfare State.	Ivor Novello, *Perchance to Dream*. Rodney Ackland, *The Pink Room* (not staged until 1952). James Barke, *When the Boys Come Home*. Daphne du Maurier, *The Years Between*. Arts Council of Great Britain grows out of CEMA.
1946		ENSA disbanded in place of Combined Services Entertainment (CSE). Site purchased for National Theatre on London's South Bank. Bristol Old Vic Theatre Company started. Noël Coward, *Peace in our Time*. Terence Rattigan, *The Winslow Boy*. J. B. Priestley, *An Inspector Calls*. Theatre Workshop's *Uranium 235*. George Savory's *George and Margaret* televised live from the Intimate Theatre, Palmers Green.
1947		Michel Saint-Denis, Glyn Byam Shaw and George Devine open Old Vic Theatre Centre. Ena Lamont Stewart, *Men Should Weep*. *Oklahoma!* imported from America. First Edinburgh Festival opens. Granville Barker dies.
1948	National Health Services begins.	First British Theatre Conference. Founding of Society for Theatre Research. Robert McLeish, *The Gorbals Story*. Christopher Fry, *The Lady's Not for Burning*. Bridget Boland, *Cockpit*. Daphne du Maurier, *September Tide*.

Date	Historical Events	Theatrical Events
1949		Britain's first university drama department started in Bristol by Glynne Wickham. Bristol Old Vic Theatre School (BOVTS) opens. Lesley Storm, *Black Chiffon*. T. S. Eliot, *The Cocktail Party*. National Theatre Act.
1950	Labour lose election to Conservatives; Harold Macmillan declared prime minister.	Michael and Peggy Walsh, *The Baker's Daughter*. George Bernard Shaw dies.

NOTES

Introduction

1 Alan Sinfield, *Literature, Politics and Culture in Postwar Britain*, London: Continuum, 1997, p. 30.

2 Johanna Alberti, 'A Time for Hard Writers: The Impact of War on Women Writers', in Nick Hayes and Jeff Hill (eds), *Millions Like Us? British Culture in the Second World War*, Liverpool: Liverpool University Press, 1999, pp. 156–78 (p. 156).

3 John Keegan, *The First World War*, London: Pimlico, 1999, p. 3.

4 Nicoletta F. Gullace, *'The Blood of Our Sons': Men, Women, and the Renegotiation of the British Citizenship during the Great War*, Basingstoke: Palgrave Macmillan, 2002, pp. 4, 6.

5 Dan Todman, *The Great War: Myth and Memory*, London: Hambledon and London, 2005, p. 180.

6 The notion of the Angel in the House came from an 1854 poem by Coventry Patmore that extolled the virtues of the self-sacrificing woman at home.

7 Claire Warden, *British Avant-Garde Theatre*, Basingstoke: Palgrave Macmillan, 2012, p. 3.

8 See Terence Rattigan, 'Preface', *Collected Plays, Volume II*, London: Hamish Hamilton, 1953, pp. vii–xxi; Kenneth Tynan, *A View of the English Stage 1944–65*, London: Methuen, 1984, pp. 148–9.

9 Gary Day, 'Introduction', in Gary Day (ed.), *Literature and Culture in Modern Britain, Volume Two: 1930–1955*, London: Longman, 1997, pp. 1–27 (p. 19).

10 Nicola Beauman, *A Very Great Profession: The Woman's Novel 1914–1939*, London: Virago, 1983, p. 5.

11 Quoted in Susan Bennett, 'A Commercial Success: Women Playwrights in the 1950s', in Mary Luckhurst (ed.), *A Companion to Modern British and Irish Drama 1880–2005*, Oxford: Blackwell, 2006, pp. 175–87 (p. 184).

12 Dave Russell, 'The Making of the Edwardian Music Hall', in Michael R. Booth and Joel H. Kaplan (eds), *The Edwardian Theatre: Essays on Performance and the Stage*, Cambridge: Cambridge University Press, 1996, pp. 61–85 (p. 75).

13 Jen Harvie, *Staging the UK*, Manchester: Manchester University Press, 2005, p. 2.

14 Michael Woolf, 'In Minor Key: Theatre 1930–55', in Gary Day (ed.), *Literature and Culture in Modern Britain*, pp. 86–106 (p. 90).

15   David Thomas, David Carlton and Anne Etienne, *Theatre Censorship: From Walpole to Wilson*, Oxford: Oxford University Press, 2007, p. 78.

16   The term comes from a series of novels by Anthony Hope, including *The Prisoner of Zenda* (1894), which was set in a fictionalised central European country.

Chapter 1

1   See Benjamin Seebohm Rowntree's 1899 study in York, published as *Poverty, A Study of Town Life*, Bristol: Policy Press, 2001 [1901].

2   Samuel Hynes, *The Edwardian Turn of Mind*, Princeton, NJ: Princeton University Press, 1971, p. vii.

3   Virginia Woolf, 'Mr. Bennett and Mrs. Brown', London: Hogarth Press, 1924, p. 4.

4   Claire Cochrane, *Twentieth-Century British Theatre: Industry, Art and Empire*, Cambridge: Cambridge University Press, 2011, p. 28.

5   Ibid., pp. 39–40.

6   See George R. Sims (ed.), *Living London: Its Work and Its Play: Its Humour and Its Pathos: Its Sights and Its Scenes*, Vol. 1, London: Cassell, 1901, p. 248.

7   See Heidi J. Holder, 'The East-End Theatre', in Kerry Powell (ed.), *The Cambridge Companion to Victorian and Edwardian Theatre*, Cambridge: Cambridge University Press, 2004, pp. 257–76 (p. 261).

8   See Jim Davis, 'The East End', in Michael R. Booth and Joel H. Kaplan (eds), *The Edwardian Theatre: Essays on Performance and the Stage*, Cambridge: Cambridge University Press, 1996, pp. 201–19.

9   Tracy C. Davis, 'Edwardian Management and the Structures of Industrial Capitalism', in Powell (ed.), *The Cambridge Companion to Victorian and Edwardian Theatre*, pp. 111–29 (p. 120).

10   Granville Barker changed his name to Harley Granville-Barker in his published work after the First World War.

11   Bruce McConachie, 'Theatre and Performance in Modern Media Cultures, 1850–1970', in Phillip B. Zarrilli, Bruce McConachie, Gary Jay Williams and Carol Fisher Sorgenfrei (eds), *Theatre Histories: An Introduction*, 2nd edition, London: Routledge, 2010, pp. 299–326 (p. 302).

12   See Lucie Sutherland, 'The Actress and the Profession: Training in England in the Twentieth Century', in Maggie B. Gale and John Stokes (eds), *The Cambridge Companion to the Actress*, Cambridge: Cambridge University Press, 2007, pp. 95–115.

13   Katherine Newey, 'Ibsen in the English Theatre in the *Fin de Siècle*', in Mary Luckhurst (ed.), *A Companion to Modern British and Irish Drama*, Oxford: Blackwell, 2006, pp. 35–47.

14   Christopher Innes, *Modern British Drama: 1890–1990*, Cambridge: Cambridge University Press, 1992, p. 8.

15   For more information on the New Woman in the theatre, see Sally Ledger, 'New Woman Drama', in Mary Luckhurst (ed.), *A Companion to Modern British and Irish Drama*, pp. 48–60; and Jean Chothia, 'The New Woman and Theatre in 1894', in Hubert Hermans, Wessel Krul and Hans van Maanen (eds), *1894: European Theatre in Turmoil*, Amsterdam: Rodopi, 1996, pp. 27–40.

16   David Mayer, 'Encountering Melodrama', in Kerry Powell (ed.), *The Cambridge Companion to Victorian and Edwardian Theatre*, pp. 145–63 (p. 145).

17   Michael R. Booth, Richard Southern, Frederick and Lise-Lone Marker and Robertson Davies (eds), *The Revels History of Drama in English: Volume VI 1750–1880*, London: Methuen, 1975, p. 33.

18   Mayer, 'Encountering Melodrama', p. 161.

19   Sos Eltis, 'The Fallen Woman On Stage: Maidens, Magdalens, and the Emancipated Female', in Powell (ed.), *The Cambridge Companion to Victorian and Edwardian Theatre*, pp. 222–36 (p. 223).

20   Dave Russell, 'The Making of the Edwardian Music Hall', in Booth and Kaplan (eds), *The Edwardian Theatre*, pp. 61–85 (p. 63).

21   Paul Maloney, '"Wha's Like Us?" Ethnic Representation in Music Hall and Popular Theatre and the Remaking of Urban Scottish Society', in Ian Brown (ed.), *From Tartan to Tartanry: Scottish Culture, History and Myth*, Edinburgh: Edinburgh University Press, 2010, pp. 129–50 (p. 149).

22   Laurence Senelick, 'Politics as Entertainment: Victorian Music-Hall Songs', *Victorian Studies*, Vol. 19 (1975–6), pp. 149–80 (p. 156).

23   Jacky Bratton, 'The Music Hall', in Powell (ed.), *The Cambridge Companion to Victorian and Edwardian Theatre*, pp. 164–82 (pp. 173–4).

24   See Gordon Williams, *British Theatre in the Great War: A Revaluation*, London: Continuum, 2003, p. 116.

25   Mary Ann Doane, *Femmes Fatales: Feminism, Film Theory, Psychoanalysis*, London: Routledge, 1991, p. 24.

26   Williams, *British Theatre in the Great War*, p. 93.

27   See J. S. Bratton, 'Gender Play and Role Reversal in the Music Hall', in Booth and Kaplan (eds), *The Edwardian Theatre*, pp. 86–110 (p. 98).

28   See Jacqueline Rose, *The Case of Peter Pan: Or the Impossibility of Children's Fiction*, Philadelphia, PA: University of Pennsylvania Press, 1992.

29   J. M. Barrie, *The Plays of J. M. Barrie in One Volume*, London: Hodder & Stoughton, 1928.

30   Ibid., p. 99.

31   Ibid., p. 278.

32   Peter Bailey, '"Naughty but Nice": Musical Comedy and the Rhetoric of the Girl, 1892–1914', in Booth and Kaplan (eds), *The Edwardian Theatre*, pp. 36–60 (p. 40).

Notes

33 Len Platt, *Musical Comedy on the West End Stage, 1890–1939*, Basingstoke: Palgrave Macmillan, 2004, pp. 4, 7.

34 Peter Bailey argues that '*A Gaiety Girl*, written by Sidney Jones and Owen Hall, [was] the first work to be termed "musical Comedy", and the definitive hit of the new form', '"Naughty but Nice"', p. 37. There was also a lesser trend for 'boy musicals' as well.

35 For example, Lily Elsie's collaboration with the designer Lucile, led to a fad for plumed hats after the major success of *The Merry Widow* (1907).

36 Sos Eltis, 'Private Lives and Public Spaces: Reputation, Celebrity and the Late Victorian Actress', in Mary Luckhurst and Jane Moody (eds), *Theatre and Celebrity in Britain, 1660–2000*, London: Palgrave Macmillan, 2005, pp. 169–88 (p. 179).

37 David Mayer, 'The Actress as Photographic Icon: From Early Photography to Early Film', in Gale and Stokes (eds), *The Cambridge Companion to the Actress*, pp. 74–94 (p. 80).

38 See Helen Day, 'Female Daredevils', in Viv Gardner and Susan Rutherford (eds), *The New Woman and Her Sisters: Feminism and Theatre 1850–1914*, Hemel Hempstead: Harvester Wheatsheaf, 1992, pp. 137–57.

39 Jeffrey Richards, *The Ancient World on the Victorian and Edwardian Stage*, Basingstoke: Palgrave Macmillan, 2009, p. 152.

40 David Mayer, 'Introduction', in David Mayer (ed.), *Playing Out the Empire: 'Ben-Hur' and Other Toga Plays and Films, 1883–1908 – A Critical Anthology*, Oxford: Clarendon, 1994, pp. 1–22 (p. 9).

41 Dennis Kennedy, 'British Theatre, 1895–1946', in Baz Kershaw (ed.), *The Cambridge History of British Theatre. Volume 3 Since 1895*, Cambridge: Cambridge University Press, 2004, pp. 3–33 (p. 9).

42 Innes, *Modern British Drama*, p. 19.

43 See John MacKenzie, *Propaganda and Empire: The Manipulation of British Public Opinion, 1880–1960*, Manchester: Manchester University Press, 1984.

44 *New York Times*, http://query.nytimes.com/mem/archive-free/pdf?res=F70616 FE3D5E12738DDDAD0894DA415B828CF1D3

45 See Edward Said, *Orientalism*, New York: Vintage, 1979.

46 MacKenzie, *Propaganda and Empire*, pp. 53–4.

47 See Ayako Yoshino, *Pageant Fever: Local History and Consumerism in Edwardian England*, Tokyo: Waseda University Publications Department, 2011.

48 Baz Kershaw, 'Curiosity or Contempt: On Spectacle, the Human and Activism', *Theatre Journal*, Vol. 55, No. 4 (2003), pp. 591–611 (p. 595).

49 McConachie, 'Popular Entertainments', p. 339.

50 See MacKenzie, *Propaganda and Empire*, pp. 110–11.

51 Ibid., p. 112.

52   Bruce McConachie, 'Theatres of the Avant-Garde, 1880–1940', in Phillip B. Zarrilli, Bruce McConachie, Gary Jay Williams and Carol Fisher Sorgenfrei (eds), *Theatre Histories: An Introduction*, 2nd edition, London: Routledge, 2010, pp. 354–87 (p. 357).

53   McConachie, 'Theatre and Performance', p. 320.

54   See Jennifer Buckley, '"Symbols in Silence: Edward Gordon Craig and the Engraving of Wordless Drama', *Theatre Survey*, Vol. 54, No. 2 (May 2013), pp. 207–30.

55   Gordon Craig, *On Movement and Dance*, Arnold Rood (ed.), London: Dance Books, 1978, p. 50.

56   See Raphaël Ingelbien, 'Symbolism at the Periphery: Yeats, Maeterlinck, and Cultural Nationalism', *Comparative Literature Studies*, Vol. 42, No. 3 (2005), pp. 183–204.

57   Michael McAteer, *Yeats and European Drama*, Cambridge: Cambridge University Press, 2010, p. 128.

58   Christopher Innes, 'Modernism in Drama', in Michael Levenson (ed.), *The Cambridge Companion to Modernism*, Cambridge: Cambridge University Press, 1999, pp. 130–56 (p. 135).

59   Innes, *Modern British Drama*, p. 363.

60   Ibid., p. 138.

61   Nicholas De Jongh, *Politics, Prudery and Perversions: The Censoring of the English Stage 1901–1968*, London: Methuen, 2000, p. 44.

62   Carolyn Tilghman, 'Staging Suffrage: Women, Politics, and the Edwardian Theater', *Comparative Drama*, Vol. 45, No. 11 (2011), pp. 339–60 (p. 340).

63   Peter Raby, 'Theatre of the 1980s: Breaking Down the Barriers', in Powell (ed.), *The Cambridge Companion to Victorian and Edwardian Theatre*, pp. 183–206 (p. 185).

64   Quoted in Cary M. Mazer, 'Granville Barker and the Court Dramatists', in Mary Luckhurst (ed.), *A Companion to Modern British and Irish Drama*, pp. 75–86 (p. 79). William Archer, *The Old Drama and the New*, London: Heinemann, 1923, p. 25.

65   Stuart E. Baker, 'Shavian Realism', *Shaw*, Vol. 9, No. 2989, 1989, pp. 79–97 (p. 89).

66   Innes, *Modern British Drama*, p. 25.

67   Michael R. Booth, 'Comedy and Farce', in Powell (ed.), *The Cambridge Companion to Victorian and Edwardian Theatre*, pp. 129–44 (p. 137).

68   Quoted in ibid., p. 135.

69   John Galsworthy, *Galsworthy: Five Plays*, London: Methuen, 1984, p. 149.

70   Benedict Nightingale, 'Introduction', in ibid., pp. vii–xxvii (p. xv).

71   Innes, *Modern British Drama*, p. 67.

72 J. M. Barrie, *The Admirable Crichton*, Fairford, Gloucestershire: Echo Library, 2007, p. 13.

73 Emma Goldman, *The Social Significance of Modern Drama*, New York: Applause Theatre Books, 1987, p. 106.

74 Awam Amkpa, 'Drama and the Languages of Postcolonial Desire: Bernard Shaw's *Pygmalion*', *Irish University Review*, Vol. 29, No. 2 (1999), pp. 294–304 (p. 294).

75 Mazer, 'Granville Barker and the Court Dramatists', p. 82.

76 Granville Barker, *Granville Barker: Plays Two*, London: Methuen Drama, 1994, p. 167.

77 Joel H. Kaplan and Sheila Stowell, *Theatre and Fashion: Oscar Wilde to the Suffragettes*, Cambridge: Cambridge University Press, 1995, p. 10.

78 Innes, *Modern British Drama*, p. 61.

79 Barker, *Granville Barker: Plays Two*, p. 198.

80 Linda Fitzsimmons, 'Typewriters Enchained: The Work of Elizabeth Baker', in Gardner and Rutherford (eds), *The New Woman and Her Sisters*, pp. 189–201 (p. 194).

81 See Maggie B. Gale, *West End Women: Women and the London Stage 1918–1962*, London: Routledge, 1996, p. 11.

82 Githa Sowerby, *Rutherford and Son*, Central, Hong Kong: Forgotten Books, 2012, p. 188.

83 Gary Farnell, 'The New Woman (Which Is Not One) in Githa Sowerby's *Rutherford and Son*', *Women's Writing*, Vol. 21, No. 3 (2014), pp. 1–14 (p. 7).

84 Christine Dymkowski, 'Case Study: *Diana of Dobson's*, 1908', in Kershaw (ed.), *The Cambridge History of British Theatre*, pp. 110–26 (p. 115).

85 Quoted in ibid., p. 115.

86 Quoted in Sheila Stowell, 'Drama as a Trade: Cicely Hamilton's *Diana of Dobson's*', in Gardner and Rutherford (eds), *The New Woman and Her Sisters*, pp. 177–88 (p. 180).

87 The play appeared a few weeks after Oscar Wilde's *A Woman of No Importance*, with which it has much in common. Sos Eltis sees Pinero's play as 'finding a lucrative middle-ground between Ibsenite radicalism and conventional melodrama', 'The Fallen Woman on Stage', p. 228.

88 Quoted in Viv Gardner, 'Introduction', in Gardner and Rutherford (eds), *The New Woman and Her Sisters*, pp. 1–14 (p. 9).

89 Michael Billington, 'The Marrying of Ann Leete', *Guardian*, 7 September 2004. http://www.guardian.co.uk/music/2004/sep/07/popandrock

90 George Bernard Shaw, 'Preface', *Mrs Warren's Profession*, New York: Cosimo, 2006, p. 181.

91 Lisa Tickner, *The Spectacle of Women: Imagery of the Suffrage Campaign 1907–14*, Chicago: University of Chicago Press, 1988, p. 10.

92 Julie Holledge has counted over 400 female dramatists between 1900 and 1920, *Innocent Flowers: Women in the Edwardian Theatre*, London: Virago, 1981, p. 3.

93 Edy Craig quoted in Sheila Stowell, *A Stage of Their Own: Feminist Playwrights of the Suffrage Era*, Manchester: Manchester University Press, 1992, p. 40.

94 See Maroula Joannou, '"Hilda, Harnessed to a Purpose": Elizabeth Robins, Ibsen, and the Vote', *Comparative Drama*, Vol. 44, No. 2 (2010), pp. 179–200.

95 Apart from enfranchisement, suffragettes wanted to overturn the view that men were 'naturally' superior, provide better conditions for all classes of women and children, and expose the invisibility of women in history, as well as equality within marriage and to their sexuality out of it as well. These issues were all explored in suffrage drama.

96 Elizabeth Robins, *Votes for Women!!*, in Jean Chothia (ed.), *The New Woman and Other Emancipated Woman Plays*, Oxford: Oxford University Press, 1998, p. 162.

97 Susan Carlson, 'Suffrage Theatre', in Mary Luckhurst (ed.), *A Companion to Modern British and Irish Drama*, pp. 99–109 (p. 100).

98 Katharine Cockin, 'Women's Suffrage Drama', in Maroula Joannou and June Purvis (eds), *The Women's Suffrage Movement: New Feminist Perspectives*, Manchester: Manchester University Press, 1998, pp. 127–39 (pp. 128–9).

99 Penny Farfan, *Women, Modernism and Performance*, Cambridge: Cambridge University Press, 2004, p. 82.

100 See Viv Gardner, 'Provincial Stages, 1900–1934: Touring and Early Repertory Theatre', in Kershaw (ed.), *The Cambridge History of British Theatre*, pp. 60–85.

101 Quoted in Kate Dunn, *Exit Through the Fireplace: The Great Days of Rep*, London: John Murray, 1998, p. 3.

102 L. J. Collins, *Theatre at War, 1914–18*, Basingstoke: Palgrave Macmillan, 1998, p. 1.

103 Quoted in Hugh Hunt, Kenneth Richards and John Russell Taylor (eds), *The Revels History of Drama in English. Volume VII 1880 to the Present Day*, London: Methuen, 1978, p. 25.

104 It is also important to acknowledge Yeats's attempts to restore Shakespeare as a 'British' dramatist, and not an 'English' one.

105 Lauren Arrington, *W. B. Yeats, the Abbey Theatre, Censorship, and the Irish State: Adding the Half-pence to the Pence*, Oxford: Oxford University Press, 2010.

106 Robert Welch, *The Abbey Theatre, 1899–1999: Form and Pressure*, Oxford: Oxford University Press, 2003, p. vii.

107   Quoted in Innes, *Modern British Drama*, p. 224.

108   Gregory's work also drew upon Irish myth, but her dramatic retellings often differed from her male counterparts by incorporating feminist elements. Her adaptation of the Diarmuid and Grania tale, *Grania* (pub. 1912) focuses more on Grania's intelligence than her beauty: 'Her heroine's psychology is more like that of a modern woman, struggling to define herself against conventional strictures and realising that breaking with these will cost her a great deal of pain', Maureen Waters, 'Lady Gregory's "Grania": A Feminist Voice', *Irish University Review*, Vol. 25, No. 1 (1995), pp. 11–24 (p. 17).

109   This play was mainly written by Gregory but publicly credited to Yeats.

110   Victor Morrison, 'Domestic and Imperial Politics in Britain and Ireland: The Testimony of Irish Theatre', in Luckhurst (ed.), *A Companion to Modern British and Irish Drama*, pp. 7–12 (p. 9).

111   Bruce McConachie, 'The *Playboy* Riots: Nationalism in the Irish Theatre', in Zarrilli et al. (eds), *Theatre Histories*, pp. 292–8 (p. 296).

112   See Christopher Innes, 'Defining Irishness: Bernard Shaw and the Irish Connection on the English Stage', in Julia M. Wright (ed.), *A Companion to Irish Literature, vol 2*, Oxford: Wiley Blackwell, 2010, pp. 35–49.

113   George Bernard Shaw, *John Bull's Other Island*, London: Penguin, 1984, p. 69.

114   Brad Kent, 'Shaw's Everyday Emergency: Commodification in and of *John Bull's Other Island*', *SHAW*, Vol. 26 (2006), pp. 162–179 (p. 164).

115   Andrew Davies, *Other Theatres: The Development of Alternative and Experimental Theatre in Britain*, Basingstoke: Macmillan, 1987, p. 46.

116   Elaine Aston, 'The "New Woman" at Manchester's Gaiety Theatre', in Gardner and Rutherford (eds), *The New Woman and Her Sisters*, pp. 205–20 (p. 216).

117   Stanley Houghton, *Hindle Wakes*, London: Oberon Books, 2012, p. 104.

118   Harold Brighouse, *Hobson's Choice*, London: Heinemann, 1992, p. 82.

119   Nina Auerbach, 'Before the Curtain', in Powell (ed.), *The Cambridge Companion to Victorian and Edwardian Theatre*, pp. 3–14 (p. 9).

Chapter 2

1   Bruce McConachie, 'Theatre and Performance in Modern Media Cultures', pp. 299–326 (p. 322).

2   Frank Field, *British and French Writers of the First World War: Comparative Studies in Cultural History*, Cambridge: Cambridge University Press, 1991, p. 105.

3   Quoted in ibid., p. 142.

4   Paul Fussell, *The Great War and Modern Memory*, Oxford: Oxford University Press, 2000, p. 193.

5   Williams, *British Theatre in the Great War*, p. 11.

6   Jay Winter, 'Popular Culture in Wartime Britain', in Aviel Roshwalt and Richard Stites (eds), *European Culture in the Great War: The Arts, Entertainment and Propaganda, 1914–1918*, Cambridge: Cambridge University Press, 2002, pp. 330–48 (p. 331).

7   Hunt, Richards and Taylor (eds), *The Revels History of Drama in English*, p. 30.

8   Quoted in Collins, *Theatre at War*, p. 34, pp. 33–4.

9   Williams, *British Theatre in the Great War*, p. 149.

10 Herbert Farjeon, *Era* (1918), p. 43.

11 Fussell, *The Great War and Modern Memory*, p. 17.

12 Philip M. Taylor, *The Projection of Britain: British Overseas Publicity and Propaganda, 1919–1939*, Cambridge: Cambridge University Press, 1981, p. 4.

13 Collins, *Theatre at War*, p. 202,

14 Williams, *British Theatre in the Great War*, p. 22.

15 'Jingle', 'The Bairnsfather Touch', *The Bystander*, 27 September (1916), p. 568.

16 Quoted in Fussell, *The Great War and Modern Memory*, p. 194.

17 Williams, *British Theatre in the Great War*, p. 82.

18 Some figures put this as 2,238 performances.

19 F. Hadland Davis, '"Chu Chin Chow" and the "Arabian Nights"', *Saturday Review of Politics, Literature, Science and Art*, Vol. 132, No. 3431, 30 July (1921), pp. 147–8 (p. 147).

20 Graham Sutton, 'Chu Chin Chow' to 'Hassan', *The Bookman*, September (1924), pp. 306–7.

21 Williams, *British Theatre in the Great War*, p. 92.

22 Edward Knoblock, *Round the Room*, London: Chapman & Hall, 1939, p. 201.

23 Winter, 'Popular Culture in Wartime Britain', p. 332.

24 MacKenzie, *Propaganda and Empire*, p. 40.

25 Williams, *British Theatre in the Great War*, p. 122.

26 See ibid., pp. 101–2.

27 Siegfried Sassoon, 'Blighters', *The Old Huntsman, and Other Poems*, New York: E. P. Dutton & Company, 1918, p. 31.

28 Williams, *British Theatre in the Great War*, p. 11.

29 Ibid., p. 12.

30 Quoted in Collins, *Theatre at War*, p. 32.

31 See ibid., p. 29.

32 See ibid, p. 189.

33 Williams, *British Theatre in the Great War*, p. 19.

Notes

34 See Collins, *Theatre at War*, p. 205.

35 Quoted in Richard J. Hand and Michael Wilson, *London's Grand Guignol and the Theatre of Horror*, Exeter: University of Exeter Press, 2007, p. 6.

36 Quoted in Collins, *Theatre at War*, p. 180.

37 Quoted in Robert Tanitch, *London Stage in the 20th Century*, London: Haus Publishing, 2007, p. 54.

38 Collins, *Theatre at War*, p. 188.

39 E. Temple Thurston, *The Cost: A Comedy in Four Acts*, London: Chapman & Hall, 1914, p. 33.

40 Collins, *Theatre at War*, pp.184–5.

41 W. A. Darlington, *Six Thousand and One Nights: Forty Years a Critic*, London: Harrap, 1960, p. 73.

42 See Fussell, *The Great War and Modern Memory*, pp. 191–230.

43 Marion Wentworth, *War Brides*, New York: Century, 1915, p. 31.

44 Quoted in Heinz Kosok, *The Theatre of War: The First World War in British and Irish Drama*, Basingstoke: Palgrave Macmillan, 2007, p. 32.

45 Cited in Tanitch, *London Stage in the 20th Century*, p. 53.

46 See Field, *British and French Writers of the First World War*, chapter 5.

47 George Bernard Shaw, *O'Flaherty V.C.: A Recruiting Pamphlet*, in *Heartbreak House, Great Catherine, Playlets of the War*, London: Constable, 1931, p. 202.

48 Mary Luckhurst, 'Drama and World War 1', in Mary Luckhurst (ed.), *A Companion to Modern British and Irish Drama*, Oxford: Blackwell, 2006, pp. 301–15 (p. 305). See also Kathleen Devine (ed.), *Modern Irish Writers and the Wars*, Gerards Cross: Colin Smythe, 1999.

49 Miles Malleson, *'D' Company* and *Black 'Ell*, London: Hendersons, 1916, p. 9.

50 Ibid., pp. 27, 31.

51 Ibid., p. 45.

52 J. G. Fuller, *Troop Morale and Popular Culture in the British and Dominion Armies 1914–1918*, Oxford: Clarendon Press, 2006, p. 95.

53 See Collins, *Theatre at War*, Chapter 4 for more information.

54 See Margaret Leask, *Lena Ashwell: Actress, Patriot, Pioneer*, Herfordshire: University of Hertfordshire Press and The Society for Theatre Research, 2012, p. 109.

55 The words belong to Lady Smith-Dorrien, wife of General Sir H. Smith-Dorrien, quoted in Collins, *Theatre at War*, p. 161.

56 Ibid., p. 62.

57 Ibid., *Theatre at War*, p. 92.

58 Ibid., p. 96.

59 Williams, *British Theatre in the Great War*, p. 7.

60   Kosok, *The Theatre of War*, p. 4.

61   Luckhurst, 'Drama and World War 1', p. 303.

62   Fussell, *The Great War and Modern Memory*, p. 192.

63   Winter, 'Popular Culture in Wartime Britain', p. 332.

64   Quoted in Collins, *Theatre at War*, p. 132.

65   Fuller, *Troop Morale and Popular Culture in the British and Dominion Armies*, p. 24.

66   Cited in Collins, *Theatre at War*, p. 13.

67   See Fuller, *Troop Morale and Popular Culture in the British and Dominion Armies*, pp. 105–6.

68   David A. Boxwell, 'The Follies of War: Cross-Dressing and Popular Theatre on the British Front Lines, 1914–18', *Modernism/Modernity*, Vol. 9, No. 1 (2002), pp. 1–20.

69   Ibid., p. 11.

70   Ibid., p. 10.

71   Samuel Hynes, *A War Imagined: The First World War and English Culture*, London: Bodley Head, 1990, pp. 88, 379.

72   Krisztina Robert, 'Constructions of "Home", "Front", and Women's Military Employment in First-World-War Britain: A Spatial Interpretation', *History and Theory*, Vol. 52, No. 3 (2013), pp. 319–43 (p. 320).

73   Clive Barker, 'Theatre and Society: The Edwardian Legacy', in Clive Barker and Maggie B. Gale (eds), *British Theatre between the Wars 1918–1939*, Cambridge: Cambridge University Press, 2000, pp. 4–37 (p. 12).

74   Williams, *British Theatre in the Great War*, p. 103.

75   Ibid., pp. 103, 160.

76   Ibid., p. 74.

77   Quoted in ibid., p. 110.

78   Quoted in Tanitch, *London Stage in the 20th Century*, p. 47.

79   Quoted in Williams, *British Theatre in the Great War*, fn. 217, p. 209.

80   Adrian Barlow, '"The Word is Said": Rereading the Poetry of John Drinkwater'. www.johndrinkwater.org/jdpages/. . ./Thewordissaid-Drinkwaterlecture.pdf

81   See Collins, *Theatre at War*, p. 117.

82   Kennedy, 'British Theatre, 1895–1946', p. 28.

83   Christopher McCullough, 'Harley Granville Barker: A Very English *avant-garde*', *Studies in Theatre and Performance*, Vol. 27, No. 3 (2007), pp. 223–35 (p. 231).

84   See Kennedy, 'British Theatre, 1895–1946'; Richard Halpern, *Shakespeare Among the Moderns*, New York: Cornell University Press, 1997; Cary M. Mazer, *Shakespeare Refashioned: Elizabethan Plays on Edwardian Stages*, Ann Arbor: UMI Research Press, 1981.

85 Coppèlia Kahn, 'Remembering Shakespeare Imperially: The 1916 Tercentenary', *Shakespeare Quarterly*, Vol. 52, No. 4 (2001), pp. 456–78 (p. 456).

86 Fuller, *Troop Morale and Popular Culture in the British and Dominion Armies*, p. 5.

87 Quoted in Clive Barker, 'Theatre and Society', p. 7.

88 Trudi Tate, 'The First World War: British Writing', in Kate McLoughlin (ed.), *The Cambridge Companion to War Writing*, Cambridge: Cambridge University Press, 2009, pp. 160–74 (p. 170).

89 Claire Cochrane, *Twentieth-Century British Theatre: Industry, Art and Empire*, Cambridge: Cambridge University Press, 2011, p. 54.

90 Quoted in Collins, *Theatre at War*, p. 209.

Chapter 3

1 Barry Day (ed.), *The Essential Noël Coward Compendium: The Very Best of His Work, Life and Times*, London: Methuen Drama, 2009, p. 193.

2 See Gary Wharton, *Suburban London Cinemas*, Stroud, Gloucestershire: Sutton Publishing, 2008, p. 17; and John Earl and Michael Sell (eds), *The Theatres Trust. Guide to British Theatres 1750–1950: A Gazetteer*, London: A & C Black, 2000, p. x.

3 See Ernest Reynolds, *Modern English Drama: A Survey of the Theatre from 1900*, Oklahoma: University of Oklahoma Press, 1951, p. 22.

4 J. C. Trewin, *The Turbulent Thirties: A Further Decade of Theatre*, London: Macdonald, 1950, p. 32.

5 Stephen C. Shafer, *British Popular Films 1929–1939: The Cinema of Reassurance*, London: Routledge, 1997, p. 2.

6 Cochrane, *Twentieth-Century British Theatre*, p. 101.

7 Quoted in ibid., p. 100.

8 Maggie B. Gale, 'Women Playwrights on the London Stage: 1918–1968', *Europa*, Vol. 1, No. 4 (1995), pp. 77–84 (p. 77).

9 Norman Marshall, *The Other Theatre*, London: John Lehmann, 1947, p. 46.

10 Ibid., p. 47.

11 Viv Gardner, 'Provincial Stages, 1900–1934', in Baz Kershaw (ed.), *The Cambridge History of British Theatre*, Cambridge: Cambridge University Press, 2004, pp. 60–85.

12 See Raphael Samuel, 'Theatre and Socialism in Britain (1880–1935)', in Raphael Samuel, Ewan MacColl and Stuart Cosgrove (eds), *Theatres of the Left, 1880–1935: Workers' Theatre Movements in Britain and American*, London: Routledge and Kegan Paul, 1985, pp. 3–76; Colin Chambers, *The Story of*

Unity Theatre, London: Lawrence and Wishart, 1989; Peter Billingham, *Theatre of Conscience 1939–53: A Study of Four Touring British Community Theatres*, London: Routledge, 2013; Cochrane, *Twentieth-Century British Theatre*, pp. 8–10.

13 Billingham, *Theatres of Conscience*, p. 32.

14 Pamela Dellar and Gillian Holtby (compilers), and Barbara Robinson (ed.), *The Swelling Scene: The Development of Amateur Drama in Hull from 1900*, Beverly, Hull: Highgate Publications, 1996, p. 4.

15 For more information, see Claire Warden, 'Ewan MacColl, "The Brilliant Young Scots Dramatist": Regional Mythmaking and Theatre Workshop', *International Journal of Scottish Theatre and Screen*, Vol. 4, No. 1 (2011), http://journals.qmu.ac.uk/index.php/IJOSTS/article/view/112

16 Claire Cochrane, 'The Pervasiveness of the Commonplace: The Historian and Amateur Theatre', *Theatre Research International*, Vol. null, No. 3 (2001), pp. 233–42 (p. 238).

17 Adrienne Scullion, 'Scottish Theatre and the Impact of Radio', *Theatre Research International*, Vol. 17, No. 2 (1992), pp. 117–31 (p. 120).

18 Ian Brown, *Scottish Theatre: Diversity, Language, Continuity*, Amsterdam: Rodopi, 2013, pp. 138, 140.

19 For information on *Blodeuwedd* see Hazel Walford Davies, 'Case Study: Refashioning a Myth, Performances of the Tale of *Blodeuwedd*', in Kershaw (ed.), *The Cambridge History of British Theatre*, pp. 273–87.

20 Emlyn Williams, *The Corn is Green: A Comedy in Three Acts*, London: William Heinemann, 1938, p. 27.

21 Mary Trotter, 'Gregory, Yeats and Ireland's Abbey Theatre', in Mary Luckhurst (ed.), *A Companion to Modern British and Irish Drama*, Oxford: Blackwell, 2006, pp. 87–98 (p. 96).

22 Colbert Kearney, 'The Voice of the Man in *The Plough and the Stars*', in C. C. Barfoot and Rias van den Doel (eds), *Ritual Remembering: History, Myth and Politics in Anglo-Irish Drama*, Amsterdam: Rodopi, 1995, pp. 97–104 (p. 99).

23 Sean O'Casey, *Collected Plays 1*, London: Macmillan, 1971, pp. 1–89 (p. 87).

24 Ronald Ayling, *Sean O'Casey's Theater of War*, Vernon, BC: Kalamalka Press, 2004, p. 35.

25 Jean Chothia, 'Sean O'Casey's Powerful Fireworks', in Mary Luckhurst (ed.), *A Companion to Modern British and Irish Drama*, Oxford: Blackwell, 2006, pp. 125–37 (p. 126).

26 Sean O'Casey, *Plays Two*, London: Faber and Faber, 1998, p. 84.

27 McConachie, 'Theatres of the Avant-Garde', p. 371.

28 Quoted in Warden, *Avant-Garde Theatre*, p. 12.

29 Innes, *Modern British Drama*, p. 349.

30 See Howard Goorney, *The Theatre Workshop Story*, London: Eyre Methuen, 1981, p. 25.

31 Robin Grove, 'Auden and Eliot: Theatres of the Thirties', in Mary Luckhurst (ed.), *A Companion to Modern British and Irish Drama*, Oxford: Blackwell, 2006, pp. 138–50 (p. 138).

32 John Worthen, *T. S. Eliot: A Short Biography*, London: Haus Publishing, 2009, pp. 205–6.

33 Quoted in Peter Edgerly Firchow, *W. H. Auden: Contexts for Poetry*, Delaware: University of Delaware Press, 2002, p. 59.

34 W. H. Auden and Christopher Isherwood, *The Dog Beneath the Skin, or, Where is Francis?* London: Faber and Faber, 1986, p. 17.

35 For specific information on Auden and Isherwood's play, see Nicholson, *The Censorship of British Drama 1900–1968, Volume Two 1933–1952*, Exeter: University of Exeter Press, 2005, p. 31.

36 Raphael Samuel, 'Workers' Theatre 1926–36', in David Bradby, Louis James and Bernard Sharratt (eds), *Performance and Politics in Popular Drama: Aspects of Popular Entertainment in Theatre, Film and Television 1800–1976*, Cambridge: Cambridge University Press, 1981, p. 215.

37 See Ros Merkin, 'The Religion of Socialism or a Pleasant Sunday Afternoon?: The ILP Arts Guild', in Clive Barker and Maggie B. Gale (eds), *British Theatre Between the Wars*, Cambridge: Cambridge University Press, 2000, pp. 162–89.

38 Chambers, *The Story of Unity Theatre*, p. 29.

39 David Bradby and John MacCormick, *People's Theatre*, London: Taylor & Francis, 1978, p. 98.

40 Chambers, *The Story of Unity Theatre*, p. 64.

41 Quoted in Innes, *Modern British Drama*, p. 73.

42 Camillo Pellizzi, *English Drama: The Last Great Phase*, London: Macmillan, 1935, p. 288.

43 J. C. Trewin, *The Gay Twenties: A Decade of the Theatre*, London: MacDonald, 1958, p. 32.

44 William Poel, *What is Wrong with the Stage?*, London: George Allen & Unwin, 1920, p. 10.

45 For more information on the staging of these Aldwych character types, see Leslie Smith's *Modern British Farce: A Selective Study of British Farce from Pinero to the Present Day*, Basingstoke: Palgrave Macmillan, 1989.

46 See Barker, 'Theatre and Society', p. 31.

47 See Claire Warden, '*Hassan*: Iraq on the British stage', *Theatre Notebook*, Vol. 66, No. 3 (December 2012), pp. 160–80, http://www.questia.com/library/journal/1G1-325174135/hassan-iraq-on-the-british-stage

48 Ibid., n.p.

49   John Stokes, 'Body Parts: The Success of the Theatre in the Inter-War Years', in Clive Barker and Maggie B. Gale (eds), *British Theatre between the Wars*, Cambridge: Cambridge University Press, 2000, pp. 38–62 (pp. 46–7).

50   Ibid., p. 57.

51   Hand and Wilson (eds), *London's Grand Guignol and the Theatre of Horror*, p. 24.

52   See Alison E. Wheatley, 'Laughing Anne: An Almost Unbearable Spectacle', *Conradiana*, Vol. 34, Nos 1–2 (2002), pp. 63–76.

53   Hand and Wilson (eds), *London's Grand Guignol and the Theatre of Horror*, p. 40.

54   Eliot Crawshay-Williams, *The Nutcracker Suite*, in Richard J. Hand and Michael Wilson (eds), *London's Grand Guignol and the Theatre of Horror*, Exeter: University of Exeter Press, 2007, p. 218.

55   H. F. Maltby, *The Person Unknown*, in Richard J. Hand and Michael Wilson (eds), *London's Grand Guignol and the Theatre of Horror*, Exeter: University of Exeter Press, 2007, p. 158.

56   St. John Ervine, *The Organised Theatre: A Plea in Civics*, London: George Allen & Unwin, 1924, p. 123.

57   Quoted in Tanitch, *London Stage in the 20th Century*, p. 63.

58   Hynes, *A War Imagined*, pp. ix, 442.

59   Trudi Tate, 'The World War: British Writing', in Kate McLoughlin (ed.), *The Cambridge Companion to War Writing*, Cambridge: Cambridge University Press, 2009, p. 168.

60   R. C. Sherriff, *Journey's End*, Harmondsworth: Penguin, 2000, p. 95.

61   *Sydney Morning Herald*, 30 July 1937. http://trove.nla.gov.au/ndp/del/article/17395554

62   For more information on Atkinson's play, see Claire Buck, 'Women's Literature of the Great War', in Vincent Sherry (ed.), *The Cambridge Companion to the Literature of the Great War*, Cambridge: Cambridge University Press, 2005, pp. 85–112 (p. 99).

63   Muriel Box, *Angels of War*, in Claire M. Tylee, with Elaine Turner and Agnes Cardinal (eds), *War Plays by Women: An International Anthology*, London: Routledge, 1990, p. 120.

64   Luckhurst, 'Drama and World War 1', p. 313.

65   J. R. Ackerley, *The Prisoners of War*, London: Chatto and Windus, 1925, pp. 2, 99.

66   Warden, *British Avant-Garde Theatre*, p. 35. For O'Casey's contradictory views on war, see Bernice Schrank, 'The Politics of O'Casey's War Plays: Pacifism and Progress in *The Silver Tassie* and *Oak Leaves and Lavender*', in C. C. Barfoot and van den Doel (eds), *Ritual Remembering: History, Myth and Politics in Anglo-Irish Drama*, Amsterdam: Rodopi, 1995, pp. 75–83.

67   O'Casey, *Plays Two*, pp. 198–9.

68   Elena Gualtieri, ''Three Guineas* and the Photograph: The Art of Propaganda', in Maroula Joannou (ed.), *Women Writers of the 1930s: Gender, Politics and History*, Edinburgh: Edinburgh University Press, 1998, pp. 165–78 (p. 165).

69   Elizabeth Rye, *Five New Full-length Plays for All-Women Casts*, London: Lovat Dickson & Thompson, 1935, p. 241.

70   Clemence Dane, *Shivering Shocks or, The Hiding Place: A Play for Boys*, in Philip Wayne, *One-Act Comedies*, London: Longmans, 1935, p. 124.

71   Steve Nicholson, '1930s Drama', in Tony Sharpe (ed.), *W. H. Auden in Context*, Cambridge: Cambridge University Press, 2013, pp. 217–27 (p. 220).

72   Vernon Lee, *Satan the Waster: A Philosophic Trilogy with Notes and Introduction*, New York: John Lane, 1920, p. vii. For critical readings of this play see, for example, Gillian Beer, 'The Dissidence of Vernon Lee: Satan the Waster and the Will to Believe', in Suzanne Raitt and Trudi Tate (eds), *Women's Fiction and the Great War*, Oxford: Clarendon Press, 1997, pp. 107–31; Gill Plain, 'The Shape of Things to Come: The Remarkable Modernity of Vernon Lee's Satan the Waster (1915–1920)', in Claire Tylee (ed.), *Women, the First World War and the Dramatic Imagination: International Essays (1914–1999)*, New York: Edwin Mellen Press, 2000, pp. 5–21.

73   Lee, *Satan the Waster*, pp. 31, 41.

74   Clive Barker, 'The Ghosts of War: Stage Ghosts and Time Slips as a Response to War', in Clive Barker and Maggie B. Gale (eds), *British Theatre between the Wars, 1918–1939*, Cambridge: Cambridge University Press, 2000, pp. 215–43 (p. 229).

75   Maggie B. Gale, *J. B. Priestley*, London: Routledge, 2008, pp. 94–95.

76   Ibid., p. 77.

77   J. B. Priestley, *Time and the Conways*, London: W. Heinemann, 1938, p. 36.

78   Innes, *Modern British Drama*, p. 373.

79   Gerwin Strobl, *The Swastika and the Stage: German Theatre and Society, 1933–1945*, Cambridge: Cambridge University Press, 2007, p. 61.

80   Noël Coward, *Collected Plays: 2*, London: Methuen Drama, 1999, p. 285.

81   Luckhurst, 'Drama and World War 1', p. 310.

82   Alan Burton, 'Death or Glory? The Great War in British Film', in Claire Monk and Amy Sargeant (eds), *British Historical Cinema: The History, Heritage and Costume Film*, London: Routledge, 2002, pp. 31–46 (p. 32); Claire M. Tylee, *The Great War and Women's Consciousness: Images of Militarism and Womanhood in Women's Writing, 1914–64*, Basingstoke: Palgrave Macmillan, 1990, p. 255. See also Fussell, *The Great War and Modern Memory*; Robert Wohl, *The Generation of 1914*, London: Weidenfeld, 1980.

83   Peter Clarke, *Hope and Glory: Britain 1900–2000*, 2nd edition, Harmondsworth: Penguin, 2004, p. 81.

84   W. Somerset Maugham, *Plays: Two*, London: Methuen Drama, 1999, p. 83.

85   Robert Graves, *Goodbye to All That,* Harmondsworth: Penguin, 1988, p. 188.

86   Steven Trout, *Robert Graves: Goodbye to All That and Other Great War Writings*, Manchester: Carcanet Press, 2007, p. xviii.

87   Ibid., p. 310.

88   See ibid, p. xxx.

89   Box, *Angels of War*, p. 138.

90   Rebecca D'Monté, 'Drama, 1920–1945', in Maroula Joannou (ed.), *The History of British Women's Writing, 1920–1945*, Basingstoke: Palgrave Macmillan, 2013 pp. 182–98 (p. 188).

91   See Dodie Smith, 'Legion of Loveless Women', *Pearson's Weekly*, 6 May (1931).

92   Clemence Dane, *A Bill of Divorcement*, London: Heinemann, 1922, p. 92.

93   Dodie Smith, *Touch Wood*, in *Three Plays by Dodie Smith*, London: Heinemann, 1939, p. 334.

94   G. B. Stern, *The Man Who Pays the Piper*, London: William Heinemann, n.d. [1931], p. 96.

95   Billie Melman, *Women and the Popular Imagination in the Twenties: Flappers and Nymphs*, Basingstoke: Palgrave Macmillan, 1988, p. 1.

96   De Jongh, *Politics, Prudery and Perversions*, p. 83.

97   Noël Coward, *Plays: Two*, London: Eyre Methuen, 1979, p. 169.

98   John Deeney, 'When Men were Men and Women were Women', in Clive Barker and Maggie B. Gale (eds), *British Theatre between the Wars*, Cambridge: Cambridge University Press, 2000, pp. 63–87 (pp. 79, 80).

99   Quoted in Nicholson, *The Censorship of British Drama 1900–1968, Volume Two: 1933–1952*, p. 99.

100 Helen Maryam Rajabi, 'The Idea of Race in Interwar Britain: Religion, Entertainment and Childhood Experiences', unpublished thesis, University of Manchester, 2013, p. 70.

101 Ibid., p. 62.

102 See Cochrane, *Twentieth-Century British Theatre*, pp. 106–8.

103 See Nicholson, *The Censorship of British Drama*, pp. 370–3.

104 Delia Jarrett-Macauley, *The Life of Una Marson 1905–1965*, Manchester: Manchester University Press, 1998, p. 54.

105 Quoted in Tanitch, *The London Stage*, p. 58.

106 Steve Nicholson, 'A Critical Year in Perspective: 1926', in Baz Kershaw (ed.), *The Cambridge History of British Theatre*, Cambridge: Cambridge University Press, 2004, pp. 127–42.

107 Innes, *Modern British Drama*, p. 69.

Notes

108   See Chris Hopkins, *English Fiction in the 1930s: Language, Genre, History*, London: Continuum, 2006, p. 44.

109   Noël Coward, *Plays: One*, London: Eyre Methuen, 1979, p. 129.

110   Ibid., p. 169.

111   Noël Coward, *Present Indicative*, London: Methuen, 1986, pp. 239–40.

112   Noël Coward, *Plays: Three*, p. 199.

113   See, for example, Jackson F. Ayres, 'From to Pleasure to Menace: Coward, Pinter and Critical Narratives', *Journal of Dramatic Theory and Criticism*, Vol. 24, No. 1 (Fall 2009), pp. 41–58; Penny Farfan, 'Noël Coward and Sexual Modernism: *Private Lives* as Queer Comedy', *Modern Drama*, Vol. 48, No. 4 (Winter 2005), pp. 677–88.

114   Noël Coward, *Plays: Three*, p. 89; *Private Lives*, London: A & C Black, 2013, p. 36.

115   Innes, *Modern British Drama*, p. 257.

116   Ibid., p. 254.

117   See Alun Hawkins, 'The Discovery of Rural England', in Robert Colls and Philip Dodd (eds), *Englishness: Politics and Culture 1880–1920*, Beckenham, Kent: Croom Helm, 1987, pp. 62–88 (p. 80).

118   Clive Bloom, *Bestsellers: Popular Fiction Since 1900*, Basingstoke: Palgrave Macmillan, 2002, p. 95.

119   See Patrick Parrinder, *Nation and Novel: The English Novel from Its Origins to the Present Day*, Oxford: Oxford University Press, 2008, p. 298.

120   Ibid., p. 313.

121   See Mark Freeman, 'Splendid Display; Pompous Spectacle: Historical Pageants in Twentieth-Century Britain', *Social History*, Vol. 38, No. 4 (2013), pp. 423–55.

122   Mick Wallis, 'Delving the Levels of Memory and Dressing up in the Past', in Clive Barker and Maggie B. Gale (eds), *British Theatre Between the Wars*, Cambridge: Cambridge University Press, 2000, pp. 190–214 (p. 194).

123   See Michael Dobson, *Shakespeare and Amateur Performance: A Cultural History*, Cambridge: Cambridge University Press, 2011, chapter 4.

124   Elizabeth Schafer, *Lilian Baylis: A Biography*, Hertfordshire: University of Hertfordshire Press, 2006, pp. 167, 168.

125   J. L. Styan, 'Elizabethan Open Staging: William Poel to Tyrone Guthrie', *Modern Language Quarterly*, Vol. 37, No. 3 (1976), pp. 211–20 (p. 217).

126   Howard Fink, 'Beyond Naturalism: Tyrone Guthrie's Radio Theatre and the Stage Production of Shakespeare', *Theatre Research in Canada* (1981), http://journals.hil.unb.ca/index.php/TRIC/article/view/7519/8578; Peter Brook, *The Empty Space*, London: Penguin, 2008, p. 9.

127   Michael Mullin, 'Augures and Understood Relations: Theodore Komisarjevsky's', *Macbeth*, *Educational Theatre Journal*, Vol. 26, No. 1 (1974), pp. 20–30 (p. 23).

128 Ibid., p. 25.

129 Niloufer Harben, *Twentieth-Century English History Plays: From Shaw to Bond*, Basingstoke: Macmillan, 1988, p. 7.

130 See Maggie B. Gale, *West End Women: Women and the London Stage 1918–1962*, London: Routledge, 1996, p. 139.

131 Quoted in Harben, *Twentieth-Century English History Plays*, p. 41.

132 J. C. Trewin, quoted in Brian Tyson, *The Story of Shaw's Saint Joan*, Montreal: McGill-Queen's Press, 1982, p. 96.

133 George Bernard Shaw, *Saint Joan*, London: Penguin, 2001, p. 159.

134 Harben, *Twentieth-Century English History Plays*, p. 67.

135 T. S. Eliot, *The Complete Poems and Plays of T. S. Eliot*, London: Faber and Faber, 1969, p. 243.

136 Pellizzi, *English Drama*, trans. Roman Williams, p. 288.

137 Kate McLoughlin, 'War and Words', in Kate McLoughlin (ed.), *The Cambridge Companion to War Writing*, Cambridge: Cambridge University Press, 2009, pp. 15–24 (p. 17).

Chapter 4

1 Andrew Davies, 'The War Years', in Michael Balfour (ed.), *Theatre and War 1933–1945: Performance in Extremis*, New York: Berghahn Books, 2001, p. 54.

2 Richard Fawkes, *Fighting for a Laugh: Entertaining the British and American Armed Forces 1939–1946*, London: Macdonald and Jane's, 1978, p. 17.

3 See Earl and Sell (eds), *The Theatres Trust*, 2000.

4 Noël Coward, *Future Indefinite*, London: Methuen Drama, 2004, p. 191.

5 George Rowell, *The Old Vic Theatre: A History*, Cambridge: Cambridge University Press, 1993, p. 128.

6 Davies, 'The War Years', p. 58.

7 Beverley Baxter, *First Nights and Noises Off*, London: Hutchinson, 1949, p. 143.

8 Olivia Turnbull, *Bringing Down the House: The Crisis in Britain's Regional Theatres*, Bristol: Intellect, 2008, p. 23.

9 W. A. Darlington, *The Actor and His Audience*, London: Phoenix House, 1949, p. 170.

10 Quoted in Jonathan Croall, *John Gielgud: Matinee Idol to Movie Star*, London: Bloomsbury, 2011, p. 278.

11 Fuller, *Troop Morale and Popular Culture*, p. 177.

12 For more information, see Andy Merriman, *Greasepaint and Cordite: How ENSA Entertained the Troops during World War II*, London: Aurum Press, 2013.

Notes

13   See Billingham, *Theatres of Conscience*, p. 68.

14   For information about the former play, see Don Watson, 'The ABCA Play Unit and the Far East, 1945–1946', *Labour History Review*, Vol. 60, No. 3 (1995), pp. 39–42.

15   Davies, 'The War Years', p. 61.

16   Ibid., p. 61.

17   Fawkes, *Fighting for a Laugh*, p. 106.

18   Davies, 'The War Years', p. 60.

19   Fawkes, *Fighting for a Laugh*, p. 25.

20   Quoted in Tanitch, *The London Stage*, p. 121.

21   See Charles Duff, *The Lost Summer: The Heyday of the West End Theatre*, London: Nick Hern, 1995, p. 42.

22   Paul Ibell, *Theatreland: A Journey through the Heart of London's Theatre*, London: Continuum, 2009, p. 34.

23   On Mass Observation see Nick Hubble, *Mass Observation and Everyday Life: Culture, History, Theory*, Basingstoke: Palgrave Macmillan, 2010, and James Hinton, *The Mass Observers: A History, 1937–1949*, Oxford: Oxford University Press, 2013. On the Ministry of Information see Ian McLaine, *Ministry of Morale: Home Front Morale and the Ministry of Information in World War II*, London: Allen & Unwin, 1979, and Paul Addison and Jeremy A. Crang, *Listening to Britain: Home Intelligence Reports on Britain's Finest Hour, May-September 1940*, London: Vintage, 2011.

24   Quoted in Jörn Weingärtner, *The Arts as a Weapon of War: Britain and the Shaping of National Morale in the Second World War*, London: Tauris Academic Studies, 2006, p. 74.

25   Rees Llewellyn, 'The Arts Council', in John Andrews and Ossia Trilling (eds), *Dobson's Theatre Year-book 1948/49*, London: Dennis Dobson, 1949, pp. 64–71 (p. 64).

26   Billingham, *Theatres of Conscience*, p. 42.

27   Turnbull, *Bringing Down the House*, p. 23.

28   Euan McArthur, *Scotland, CEMA and the Arts Council, 1919–1967*, Aldershot: Ashgate, 2013, p. 61.

29   Ibid., p. 82.

30   See Jan McDonald, 'Towards National Identities: Theatre in Scotland', in Baz Kershaw (ed.), *The Cambridge History of British Theatre*, pp. 195–227 (p. 200).

31   For more information, see Daniel Rosenthal, *The National Theatre Story*, London: Oberon, 2013.

32   Cochrane, 'The Pervasiveness of the Commonplace', p. 238.

33   Charles Landstone, *Offstage: A Personal Record of the First Twelve Years of State Sponsored Drama in Great Britain*, London: Elek, 1953, p. 54.

34 Rowell, *The Old Vic Theatre*, p. 139.

35 Joan Thirsk, 'Obituary: Ruth Spalding', *The Independent*, 26 May 2009.

36 R. H. Ward, 'The Theatre of Persons', *The Adelphi*, 1941, pp. 122–6 (p. 122).

37 Quoted in Cecil Davies, *The Adelphi Players: The Theatre of Persons*, London: Routledge, 2014, p. 25.

38 Billingham, *Theatres of Conscience*, p. 93.

39 Pamela Keily, quoted in ibid., p. 37.

40 Ibid., p. 27.

41 Robert Graves and Alan Hodge, *The Long Week-End: A Social History of Great Britain 1918-1939*, London: Cardinal 1991 [1940], p. 348.

42 Jan McDonald, 'Theatre in Scotland', p. 204.

43 Gwenan Evans and others, *A Few Drops of Water: The Story of the Questors Theatre 1929-1989*, London: Mattock Press, 1989, p. 14.

44 Mick Wallis, 'Drama in the Villages: Three Pioneers', Paul Brassley, Jeremy Burchardt and Lynne Thompson (eds), *The English Countryside 1918-39: Regeneration or Decline?*, Woodbridge, Suffolk: The Boydell Press, 2006, pp. 102–15 (p. 102).

45 E. Martin Browne, 'The British Drama League', *Educational Theatre Journal*, Vol. 5, No. 3 (October, 1953), pp. 203–6 (p. 203).

46 Turnbull, *Bringing Down the House*, p. 29.

47 Davies, *The Adelphi Players*, p. 5.

48 Cited in Billingham, *Theatres of Conscience*, p. 106.

49 Shirley Brown, *Bristol Old Vic Theatre School: The First 50 Years 1946-1996*, Bristol: BOVTS Productions, 1996, p. 21.

50 Ibid., p. 25.

51 Turnbull, *Bringing Down the House*, p. 20.

52 See Marshall, *The Other Theatre*, p. 28.

53 Rowell and Jackson, *The Repertory Movement*, p. 87.

54 Warden, 'Ewan MacColl', http://journals.qmu.ac.uk/index.php/IJOSTS/article/view/112

55 Quoted in McDonald, 'Towards National Identities', p. 204.

56 Paul Vincent Carroll, Citizens' Theatre Programme for *Shadow & Substance*, 15 November 1943.

57 Brown, *Scottish Theatre*, p. 149.

58 Nadine Holdsworth, 'Case Study: Ena Lamont Stewart's *Men Should Weep*, 1947', in Baz Kershaw (ed.), *The Cambridge History of British Theatre*, pp. 228–41 (p. 230).

59 Ibid., p. 231.

60   Chambers, *The Story of Unity Theatre*, p. 282.

61   Robert Welch, *The Abbey Theatre 1899–1999: Form and Pressure*, Oxford: Oxford University Press, 1993, p. 139.

62   Ibid., p. 141.

63   Sean O'Casey, *Collected Plays, Volume Two*, London: Macmillan, 1950, pp. 239, 240.

64   Innes, *Modern Drama*, p. 87.

65   Trewin, *The Turbulent Thirties*, p. 131.

66   Tanitch, *London Stage in the 20th Century*, p. 121.

67   Paul Webb, *Ivor Novello: Portrait of a Star*, London: Haus Books, 1999, p. 160.

68   Rebecca D'Monté, 'Moving Back to "Home" and "Nation": Women Dramatists, 1938–1945', in Teresa Gómez-Reus and Terry Gifford (eds), *Women in Transit Through Literary Liminal Spaces*, Basingstoke: Palgrave Macmillan, 2013, pp. 139–50 (p. 148).

69   *Picture Post*, 'A New Way to Use a Theatre', 6 December 1941, pp. 16–18 (p. 18).

70   John Gielgud, with Richard Mangan (ed.), *Sir John Gielgud: A Life in Letters*, New York: Arcade, 2011, p. 125.

71   Eliot, *The Complete Poems and Plays*, p. 397.

72   Michael Billington, *The Guardian*, 14 September (2001).

73   Maggie B. Gale, *J. B. Priestley*, London: Routledge, 2008, p. 168.

74   Quoted in Tanisch, *London Stage in the 20th Century*, p. 124.

75   See Nicholson, *The Censorship of British Drama*, p. 184.

76   Rodney Ackland, *The Dark River*, London: French, 1942, pp. 56–7.

77   Ibid., p. 103.

78   John Lennard 'Staging "the Holocaust" in England', in Mary Luckhurst (ed.), *A Companion to Modern British and Irish Drama*, Oxford: Blackwell, 2006, pp. 316–28 (p. 317).

79   J. B. Priestley, *The Plays of J. B. Priestley, Vol. III*, London: Heinemann, 1950, p. 258.

80   See Joanna Townsend, 'Aftermath: Rodney Ackland's *The Pink Room*', in Tony Howard and John Stokes (eds), *Acts of War: The Representation of Military Conflict on the British Stage and Television Since 1945*, Cambridge: Scolar Press, 1996, pp. 61–81 (p. 61).

81   Quoted in ibid., p. 71.

82   Quoted in ibid., p. 62.

83   See 1952 review of Theatre Workshop's *Uranium 235* at the Embassy Theatre, http://www.vam.ac.uk/users/node/8814

84   Ewan MacColl, 'Introduction: The Evolution of a Revolutionary Theatre Style', in Goorney and MacColl (eds), *Agit-Prop to Theatre Workshop*, pp. ix–lvii (p. liv).

85   George Bernard Shaw, *Collected Plays with Their Prefaces*, London: Bodley Head, 1974.

86   Nadine Holdsworth, *Joan Littlewood's Theatre*, Cambridge: Cambridge University Press, 2011, p. 64.

87   Michael Billington, '*Saint's Day*', *The Guardian*, 25 October (2002).

88   Warden, 'Ewan MacColl, http://journals.qmu.ac.uk/index.php/IJOSTS/article/view/112

89   Ibid.

90   Nicholson, *The Censorship of British Drama*, p. 175.

91   Quoted in Davies, 'The War Years', p. 58.

92   Chambers, *The Story of Unity Theatre*, p. 164.

93   Quoted in Steve Nicholson, 'Theatre Pageants in the Second World War', *Theatre Research International*, Vol. 18, No. 3 (1993), pp. 186–96 (p. 186).

94   Ben Harker, 'Mediating the 1930s: Documentary and Politics in Theatre Union's *Last Edition* (1940)', http://usir.salford.ac.uk/12133/3/Chapter_2_-_Ben_Harker.pdf

95   Ibid., p. 193.

96   Quoted in Claire Warden, *Avant-Garde Theatre*, Basingstoke: Palgrave Macmillan, 2012, p. 47.

97   For more information see Nicholson, 'Theatre Pageants in the Second World War'.

98   For further examples of communism on stage, see Steve Nicholson, *British Theatre and the Red Peril: The Portrayal of Communism 1917–1945*, Exeter: Exeter University Press, 1999.

99   Angus Calder, *The People's War, Britain, 1939–45*, London: Random House, 2012, p. 245.

100 Quoted in Claire Warden, '"We are Here to Salute the Red Army": Basil Dean and His Russian Adventures', *Theatre Survey*, Vol. 54, No. 3 (2013), pp. 347–66 (p. 359).

101 For more information, see Nicholson, *British Theatre and the Red Peril*, pp. 128ff.

102 Ibid., p. 355.

103 Cate Haste, *Keep the Home Fires Burning*, London: Viking, 1977, pp. 2, 3.

104 Robert Colls, *The Identity of England*, Oxford: Oxford University Press, 2002, p. 129.

105 Tanitch, *London Stage in the 20th Century*, p. 123.

106 See Calder, *The People's War* and *The Myth of the Blitz*, London: Jonathan Cape, 1991.

107 Rebecca D'Monté, 'Feminizing the Nation and the Country House: Women Dramatists 1938–1940', in David James and Philip Tew (eds), *New Versions of*

Pastoral: Post-Romantic, Modern, and Contemporary Responses to the Tradition, New Jersey: Fairleigh Dickinson University Press, 2009, pp. 139–55 (p. 139).

108 Mark Girouard, *Life in the English Country House: A Social and Architectural History*, London: Penguin, 1980, p. 302.

109 Malcolm Kelsall, 'Manderley Revisited: *Rebecca* and the English Country House', in *Proceedings of the Bristol Academy, 83* (no eds), 1993, pp. 303–15 (p. 303).

110 Dodie Smith, *Dear Octopus*, London: Samuel French, 1938, p. 7.

111 Ibid., p. 88.

112 Quoted in Tanitch, *London Stage in the 20th Century*, p. 122.

113 Quoted in Nicholson, *The Censorship of British Drama*, p. 172.

114 Jenny Hartley, 'Clothes and Uniform in the Theatre of Fascism: Clemence Dane and Virginia Woolf', in Angela K. Smith (ed.), *Gender and Warfare in the Twentieth Century: Textual Representations*, Manchester: Manchester University Press, 2004, pp. 96–110 (p. 108).

115 Ibid., p. 108.

116 Quoted in Simon Barker, 'Shakespeare, Stratford, and the Second World War', in Irena R. Makaryk and Marissa McHugh (eds), *Shakespeare and the Second World War: Memory, Culture, Identity*, Toronto: University of Toronto Press, 2012, pp. 199–217 (p. 209).

117 See Peter Billingham, 'Rosalinds, Violas, and Other Sentimental Friendships: The Osiris Players and Shakespeare, 1939–1945', in ibid., pp. 218–32.

118 Simon Frith, 'The Pleasures of the Hearth: The Making of BBC Light Entertainment', in *Formations of Pleasure* (no eds), London: Routledge and Kegan Paul, 1983, pp. 101–23 (p. 105).

119 Neil Hanson (ed.), with Tom Priestley, *Priestley's Wars*, Ilkley, Yorkshire: Great Northern Books, 2008, p. 8.

120 Graves and Hodge, *The Long Week-End*, p. 389.

121 Graham McCann, *Bounder! The Biography of Terry-Thomas*, London: Aurum, 2008, p. 51.

122 See the University of Westminster's web project, 'Screen Plays: Theatre Plays on British Television', http://screenplaystv.wordpress.com/about/

123 Geoff Bowden, *Intimate Memories: The History of the Intimate Theatre*, Palmers Green, Westbury, Wiltshire: The Badger Press, 2006, p. 73.

124 Graves and Hodge, *The Long Week-End*, p. 438.

125 See Ray Waterman, 'Proltet: The Yiddish-Speaking Group of the Workers' Theatre Movement', *History Workshop*, No. 5 (Spring 1978), pp. 174–8.

126 See Billingham, *Theatre of Conscience*, p. 65.

127 See Charmian Brinson and Richard Dove, *Politics By Other Means: The Free German League of Culture in London 1939–1946*, Middlesex: Vallentine Mitchell, 2010.

128 Michael Balfour (ed.), *Theatre and War 1933–1945: Performance in Extremis*, New York: Berghahn Books, 2001, p. 4. See also Len Crome, *Unbroken: Resistance and Survival in the Concentration Camps*, London: Lawrence & Wishart, 1988.

129 In some places, 15 August is declared VJ day.

130 McLaine, *Ministry of Morale*, p. 179.

131 Quoted in Stephen Lacey, *British Realist Theatre: The New Wave in its Context 1956–1965*, London: Routledge, 1995, p. 11.

132 Paul Addison, *The Road to 1945, British Politics and the Second World War*, 2nd edition, 1977.

133 James Barke, *The Night of the Big Blitz*, Barke Papers, Mitchell Library, Glasgow, Box 10.

134 MacKenzie, *Propaganda and Empire*, p. 98.

135 Quoted in David Cannadine, *In Churchill's Shadow: Confronting the Past in Modern Britain*, London: Allen Lane, 2002, p. 269.

136 Noël Coward, *Coward Plays: 5*, London: Methuen Drama, 2006, p. 113.

137 John Baxendale, *Priestley's England: J. B. Priestley and English Culture*, Manchester: Manchester University Press, 2014, p. 2.

138 Stephen Lacey, 'When Was the Golden Age? Narratives of Loss and Decline: John Osborne, Arnold Wesker and Rodney Ackland', in Mary Luckhurst (ed.), *A Companion to Modern British and Irish Drama*, pp. 164–74 (p. 171).

139 Rodney Ackland, *Absolute Hell*, London: Oberon, 1995, p. 48.

140 Daphne du Maurier, *The Years Between*, in Fidelis Morgan (ed.), *The Years Between: Plays by Women on the London Stage 1900–1950*, London: Virago, 1994, p. 373.

141 Ibid., p. 367.

142 De Jongh, *Politics, Prudery & Perversions*, pp. 166–7.

143 Andrew Wyllie, *Sex on Stage: Gender and Sexuality in Post-War British Theatre*, Bristol: Intellect, 2009, p. 15.

144 De Jongh, *Politics, Prudery & Perversions*, p. 169.

145 Enid Bagnold, *The Chalk Garden*, London: William Heinemann Ltd, 1956, p. 57.

146 Tynan, *A View of the English Stage*, pp. 148–9.

Chapter 5

1 Simon Shepherd, *Direction*, Basingstoke: Palgrave Macmillan, 2012, pp. 9–13.

2 Henry Irving died in 1905, Herbert Beerbohm Tree died in 1917, George Alexander died in 1918.

Notes

3   Dennis Kennedy, *Granville Barker and the Dream of Theatre*, Cambridge: Cambridge University Press, 1985, p. 21; Sally Beauman, *The Royal Shakespeare Company A History of Ten Decades*, Oxford: Oxford University Press, 1982, p. 72.

4   John Gielgud, *Early Stages*, London: Macmillan, 1939.

5   Donald Wolfit, *First Interval*, London: Odhams, 1954.

6   Beauman, *The Royal Shakespeare Company*, pp. 206–9.

7   Ibid., pp. 176–7.

8   Edward Gordon Craig, 'The Art of the Theatre. The First Dialogue', in J. Michael Walton (ed.), *Craig on Theatre*, London: Methuen, 1983, pp. 52–71 (p. 70).

9   Ibid., p. 68.

10 A. E. W. Mason, *Sir George Alexander & the St James' Theatre*, London: Macmillan, 1935, p. 24.

11 Ibid., p. 25.

12 Laurence Senelick, *The Chekhov Theatre A Century of the Plays in Performance*, Cambridge: Cambridge University Press, 1999, pp. 154–62.

13 See Beauman, *The Royal Shakespeare Company*, pp. 125–7.

14 See Edward Braun, *The Director and the Stage From Naturalism to Grotowski*, London: Methuen, 1982, pp. 11–36.

15 See Peter Whitebrook, *William Archer A Biography*, London: Methuen, 1993, pp. 73–143.

16 See Kennedy, *Granville Barker*, pp. 18–27.

17 Harcourt Williams, *Old Vic Saga*, London: Winchester Publications, 1949; Lewis Casson, 'Harley Granville Barker, *The Dictionary of National Biography*, 1941–1950, Oxford: Oxford University Press, 1959; quoted in Kennedy, *Granville Barker*, pp. 36–7.

18 I have discussed Barker's concept of the exemplary theatre and his managerial history in Cochrane, *Twentieth Century British Theatre*, pp. 46–57.

19 See Ben Iden Payne, *A Life in a Wooden O: Memoirs of the Theatre*, New Haven: Yale University Press, 1977, pp. 58–9; pp. 78–9.

20 See George Rowell and Anthony Jackson, *The Repertory Movement A History of Regional Theatre in Britain*, Cambridge: Cambridge University Press, 1984, pp. 16–53.

21 See Payne, *A Life in a Wooden O*, pp. 27–31; pp. 63–6.

22 See Beauman, *The Royal Shakespeare Company*, pp. 26–34.

23 For a detailed discussion of Craig's 1900–02 experiments with the Purcell Society, see Christopher Innes, *Edward Gordon Craig*, Cambridge: Cambridge University Press, 1983, pp. 35–83.

24   Ibid., p. 42.

25   Robert Speaight, *William Poel and the Elizabethan Revival*, London: William Heinemann, 1954.

26   See Payne, *Life in a Wooden O*, pp. 84–8.

27   Speaight, *William Poel*, p. 96.

28   Claire Cochrane, *Shakespeare and the Birmingham Repertory Theatre 1913–1929*, London: Society for Theatre Research, 1993, pp. 36–46.

29   Cecil Chisholm, *Repertory: An Outline of the Modern Theatre Movement*, London: Peter Davies, 1934.

30   See details of commercial company management and type casting in M. F. K. Fraser, *Alexandra Theatre, The Story of a Popular Playhouse*, Birmingham: Cornish Brothers Ltd, 1948, pp. 43–9.

31   See Grace Wyndham Goldie, *The Liverpool Repertory Theatre 1911–1934*, Liverpool: Liverpool University Press, 1935, pp. 135–222.

32   See Richard Foulkes, *Repertory at The Royal Sixty-Five Years of Theatre in Northampton 1927–92*, Northampton: The Northampton Repertory Players, 1992, pp. 31–2.

33   Ibid., p. 21.

34   See ibid., pp. 21–37.

35   Marshall, *The Other Theatre*, pp. 53–71. See also Richard Cave, *Theatre in Focus Terence Gray and the Cambridge Festival Theatre*, Cambridge: Cambridge University Press, 1980.

36   See Gale, *West End Women*, pp. 58–66.

37   See Ros Merkin, *Liverpool Playhouse: A Theatre & Its City*, Liverpool: Liverpool University Press, 2011, pp. 33–8, pp. 52–4.

38   See Goldie, *The Liverpool Repertory Theatre*, pp. 95–111.

39   Elizabeth Schafer, *Ms-Directing Shakespeare Women Direct Shakespeare*, London: The Women's Press, 1998, pp. 215–17.

40   See Leask, *Lena Ashwell*, Chapter 5.

41   Katharine Cockin, *Edith Craig (1869–1947): Dramatic Lives*, London: Cassell, 1998.

42   See ibid., pp. 159–60.

43   See Holdsworth, *Joan Littlewood's Theatre*, pp. 6–15.

44   See Cochrane, *Twentieth Century British Theatre*, pp. 89–92.

45   Don Chapman, *Oxford Playhouse High and Low Drama in a University City*, Hatfield: University of Hertfordshire Press/The Society for Theatre Research, 2008, p. 32.

46   Beauman, *The Royal Shakespeare Company*, pp. 73–4.

47 Norman Marshall provides detailed accounts of both theatres from his experience as audience member and director in *The Other Theatre*, pp. 17–29; pp. 53–71.

48 Ibid., p. 20.

49 E. Martin Browne with Henzie Browne, *Two in One [by] E. Martin Browne with Henzie Browne*, Cambridge: Cambridge University Press, 1981.

50 Tyrone Guthrie, *A Life in the Theatre*, London: Hamish Hamilton, 1961, p. 43.

51 Rowell and Jackson, *The Repertory Movement*, p. 102.

52 Irving Wardle, *The Theatres of George Devine*, London: Jonathan Cape, 1978.

53 See J. C. Trewin, *The Birmingham Repertory Theatre 1913–1963*, London: Barrie and Rockcliff, 1963, pp. 136–40.

54 Peter Hall, *Making an Exhibition of Myself*, London: Sinclair-Stevenson, 1993, pp. 68–73.

Chapter 6

1 On women and modern drama, see, for example, Gail Finney, *Women in Modern Drama: Freud, Feminism, and European Theater at the Turn of the Century*, Ithaca: Cornell University Press, 1989; Katherine E. Kelly (ed.), *Modern Drama by Women 1880s–1930s: An International Anthology*, London: Routledge, 1996; and Farfan, *Women, Modernism, and Performance*, and 'Women's Modernism and Performance', in Maren Tova Linett (ed.), *The Cambridge Companion to Modernist Women Writers*, Cambridge: Cambridge University Press, 2010, pp. 47–61. On the New Woman, see, for example, Elaine Showalter, *Sexual Anarchy: Gender and Culture at the Fin de Siècle*, New York: Viking, 1990, pp. 38–58; Jan McDonald, 'New Women in the New Drama', *New Theatre Quarterly*, Vol. 6, No. 21 (February 1990), pp. 31–42; Viv Gardner and Susan Rutherford (ed.), *The New Woman and Her Sisters: Feminism and Theatre 1850–1914*, Ann Arbor: University of Michigan Press, 1992; and Ledger, in Mary Luckhurst (ed.), 'New Woman Drama'. For studies of dissident sexualities in modern drama, see, for example, Nicholas de Jongh, *Not in Front of the Audience: Homosexuality on Stage*, London: Routledge, 1992; Laurence Senelick, *Lovesick: Modernist Plays of Same-Sex Love, 1894–1925*, London: Routledge, 1999; Alan Sinfield, *Out on Stage: Lesbian and Gay Theatre in the Twentieth Century*, New Haven: Yale University Press, 1999; and Deeney, 'When Men were Men and Women were Women'.

2 For a brief discussion of the queer associations of hysteria as they may relate to *Hedda Gabler*, see Farfan, *Women, Modernism, and Performance*, pp. 73–4. Rosmer in *Rosmersholm* feels deep aversion to female sexual desire. In *Little Eyolf*, Allmers's half-sister Asta, to whom he is attracted and who is eventually revealed to be not biologically related, used to cross-dress for him in his boyhood clothes while he would call her 'Eyolf'.

3 Quoted in Tracy C. Davis, 'Ibsen's Victorian Audience', *Essays in Theatre*, Vol. 4, No. 1 (November 1985), p. 24; quoted in Powell (ed.), *Women and Victorian Theatre*, Cambridge: Cambridge University Press, 1997, p. 71.

4 Katherine E. Kelly, 'Pandemic and Performance: Ibsen and the Outbreak of Modernism', *South Central Review*, Vol. 25, No. 1 (Spring 2008), pp. 12–35.

5 For example, in his chapter on 'Modernism in Drama', Christopher Innes focuses on English and Irish modernists Wyndham Lewis, W. B. Yeats, Edward Gordon Craig and George Bernard Shaw, along with August Strindberg, Oskar Kokoschka, Eugene O'Neill, Antonin Artaud, T. S. Eliot, Vsevolod Meyerhold and Bertolt Brecht. As Sedgwick notes, *queer* derives 'from the Indo-European root – *twerkw*, which also means the German *quer* (transverse), Latin *torquere* (to twist), English *athwart*'; 'Foreword: T times', *Tendencies*, Durham: Duke University Press, 1993, p. xii.

6 John Lahr, *Coward the Playwright*, London: Methuen, 1982, p. 3.

7 Douglas Mao and Rebecca L. Walkowitz, 'The New Modernist Studies', *PMLA*, Vol. 123, No. 3 (2008), pp. 737; 737–48. By 'vertical' expansions, Mao and Wolfowitz refer to the fact that 'once quite sharp boundaries between high art and popular forms of culture have been reconsidered' (pp. 737–8). See also Mao and Walkowitz's 'Introduction: Modernisms Bad and New', *Bad Modernisms*, ed. Mao and Walkowitz, Durham: Duke University Press, 2006, in which they explain that 'the new modernist studies has extended the designation "modernist" beyond such familiar figures as Eliot, Pound, Joyce, and Woolf . . . and embraced less widely known women writers, authors of mass cultural fiction, makers of the Harlem Renaissance, artists from outside Great Britain and the United States, and other cultural producers hitherto seen as neglecting or resisting modernist innovation' (p. 1).

8 See, for example, Cockin, *Edith Craig (1869–1947): Dramatic Lives*, London: Cassell, 1998.

9 Showalter, *Sexual Anarchy*, p. 23; Yopie Prins, 'Greek Maenads, Victorian Spinsters', in Richard Dellamora (ed.), *Victorian Sexual Dissidence*, Chicago: University of Chicago Press, 1999, p. 47.

10 George Bernard Shaw, *Candida*, New York: Penguin, 1952, pp. 22, 24, 45.

11 The Pioneer Players staged one final production in 1925: Susan Glaspell's *The Verge* (1921).

12 Eileen Barrett, 'The British Society for the Study of Sex Psychology: Bloomsbury and the Medicalization of Same-Sex Love', in Laura Davis and Jeanette McVicker (eds), *Virginia Woolf and Her Influences: Selected Papers from the Seventh Annual Conference on Virginia Woolf*, New York: Pace University Press, 1998, pp. 111–16 (p. 112).

13 Cicely Hamilton, 'Morals through the Centuries; IV. The Sins We Do Not Speak of: An Attempt to Consider an Ugly Subject Dispassionately', *Time and Tide* (2 November 1928), p. 1035.

14 See Farfan, *Women, Modernism, and Performance*, pp. 79–84.

15 'Woman Suffrage', *The Times*, 16 April 1909, p. 8.

16 See Stowell, *A Stage of Their Own*, on this comparison to Aristophanes, p. 58.

17 Cicely Hamilton and Christopher St. John, 'How the Vote Was Won', in Carole Hayman and Dale Spender (eds), *How the Vote Was Won and Other Suffragette Plays*, London: Methuen, 1985, p. 23.

18 Christopher St. John, 'All We Like Sheep', *The Academy*, 2 May 1908, pp. 735–6.

19 Amy Koritz, 'Dancing the Orient for England: Maud Allan's "The Vision of Salome"', *Theatre Journal*, Vol. 46, No. 1 (March 1994), pp. 63–78 (p. 66); Judith R. Walkowitz, 'The "Vision of Salome": Cosmopolitanism and Erotic Dancing in Central London, 1908–1918', *The American Historical Review*, Vol. 108, No. 2 (April 2003), pp. 350–1.

20 Koritz, 'Dancing the Orient', p. 66.

21 Walkowitz, 'The "Vision of Salome"', p. 339.

22 Quoted in 'A New Dancer. Maud Allan at the Palace Theatre', *Pall Mall Gazette*, 7 March 1908, p. 8.

23 Edward Said, *Orientalism*, New York: Vintage, 1979, p. 3; quoted in Koritz, 'Dancing the Orient', p. 63.

24 J. C. F., 'Miss Maud Allan's Salome Dance', *The Academy*, 21 March 1908, p. 598.

25 Walter Higgins, '"The Vision of Salome"', *Labour Leader*, 26 June 1908, p. 404.

26 Walkowitz, 'The "Vision of Salome"', p. 355.

27 Max Beerbohm, 'At the Palace Theatre', *The Saturday Review*, 4 July 1908, p. 11; J. C. F., 'Miss Maud Allan's Salome Dance', p. 599.

28 'The Drama. The New Dancer', *Times Literary Supplement*, 26 March 1908, p. 102.

29 Maud Allan, *My Life and Dancing*, London: Everett, [1908], p. 112.

30 Koritz, 'Dancing the Orient', p. 67. For Allan's interpretation of Salome, see *My Life and Dancing*, pp. 120–8.

31 Koritz, 'Dancing the Orient', p. 69.

32 Higgins, '"The Vision of Salome"', p. 404.

33 Elaine Showalter, 'It's Still Salome', *Times Literary Supplement*, 2 September 1994, p. 13.

34 Higgins, '"The Vision of Salome"', p. 404. Written in 1891, Wilde's *Salomé* was denied a stage license in England in 1892. The Théâtre de l'Oeuvre's production of the play in Paris in 1896 began a revival of Wilde's artistic reputation following his conviction and imprisonment on charges of gross indecency in 1895 and there were private performances of *Salome* in London like the 1911 feminist production mentioned in this chapter, but the play

was not publicly staged there until 1931, when it was presented at the Savoy Theatre.

35 Allan may, in fact, have been involved with Margot Asquith, wife of the prime minister, around the time of the trial. In later life, she had a relationship with her secretary-companion Verna Aldrich.

36 For accounts of the Pemberton-Billing trial, see, for example, Philip Hoare, *Oscar Wilde's Last Stand: Decadence, Conspiracy, and the Most Outrageous Trial of the Century*, New York: Arcade, 1997; Jodie Medd, "'The Cult of the Clitoris": Anatomy of a National Scandal', *Modernism/Modernity*, Vol. 9, No. 1 (2002), pp. 21–49; and Walkowitz, 'The "Vision of Salome"'.

37 Jeffrey Weeks, *Coming Out: Homosexual Politics in Britain, from the Nineteenth Century to the Present*, London: Quartet, 1977, p. 101; Medd, "'The Cult of the Clitoris"', p. 25.

38 Showalter, 'It's still Salome', p. 13.

39 Quoted in ibid., p. 113; Terry Castle, *Noël Coward and Radclyffe Hall: Kindred Spirits*, New York: Columbia University Press, 1996, p. 10.

40 Noël Coward, *Collected Plays: Three*, London: Methuen, 1999, pp. 57, 62, 82; subsequent references to the play will be given parenthetically in the text.

41 Brooks Atkinson, 'The Play: Alfred Lunt, Lynn Fontanne, Noel Coward and an Artificial Comedy titled "Design for Living"', *New York Times*, 25 January 1933, p. 13.

42 'Flippancy' is a key strategy for Coward's primary characters as they challenge conventional morality. Near the end of *Design for Living*, Leo makes a crack to defuse Ernest's tirade about 'disgusting three-sided erotic hotchpotch', and his crack in turn provokes Ernest to complain that Leo's 'ill-timed flippancy is only in keeping with the rest of [his] execrable taste' (p. 123). For a discussion of flippancy in *Private Lives*, see my essay 'Noël Coward and Sexual Modernism', p. 684.

43 Quoted in Philip Hoare, *Noël Coward: A Biography*, New York: Simon & Schuster, 1995, p. 292.

44 Radclyffe Hall, 'The "First Night"', Radclyffe Hall and Una Troubridge Collection, Harry Ransom Humanities Research Center, The University of Texas at Austin.

45 Quoted in Richard Ellmann, *Oscar Wilde*, New York: Vintage, 1988, p. 378n.

46 'A Suffragist Play', *The Era*, 17 April 1909, p. 21; 'Court Theatre. The Play Actors', *Times*, 10 May 1909, p. 12.

47 Quoted in Walkowitz, 'The "Vision of Salome"', p. 360. Ibid., pp. 363, 363–4, 362, 368–9.

48 Quoted in ibid., p. 369.

49 Alan Sinfield, 'Noël Coward and Effeminacy', in Joel Kaplan and Sheila Stowell (eds), *Look Back in Pleasure: Noël Coward Reconsidered*, London: Methuen, 2000, pp. 33–43 (pp. 39–40); see also Sinfield, *Out on Stage*, pp. 98–113.

Notes

Chapter 7

1 Ernst Toller, *Pastor Hall*, LCP CORR: 1939/3083.

2 For a detailed discussion which foregrounds this, see Nicholson, *The Censorship of British Drama*, pp. 9–54.

3 As reported in the *Star*, 20 January 1937, reviewing the production at the Kin's Theatre, Hammersmith.

4 *Performer*, 11 February 1937.

5 *Daily Express*, 1 August 1933.

6 Quotations taken from the unpublished manuscript of *Whither Liberty* in the Lord Chamberlain's Plays archive. It was written under the name of Alan Peters, although the real identity of the playwright was probably Doctor Hipshon (identified in one newspaper as Dr Ibsen!).

7 See LCP CORR: *Who Made the Iron Grow* LR (1933). The revised version was staged in Bradford in 1934 by the Civic Players, under the title *Whither Liberty*.

8 *The Daily Telegraph*, 29 January 1934; *The Morning Post*, 29 January 1934; *The Times*, 29 January 1934.

9 Quotations taken from Leslie Reade, *Take Heed*, unpublished manuscript, Lord Chamberlain's Plays archive.

10 *New York Times*, 22 March 1934, p. 26.

11 *The Times*, 7 December 1938.

12 Tagger wrote under the pseudonym of Ferdinand Bruckner. *Die Rassen*, was translated by Gladys Henrietta Schütze under the ironic title of *Heroes*, but was more usually translated as 'Race'. Schütze herself was a writer and political activist, and the author of a novel based on her experiences of prejudice as a supposed foreign alien in Britain during the First World War.

13 Quotations taken from the unpublished manuscript of *Heroes* in the Lord Chamberlain's Plays archive.

14 See LCP CORR: *Heroes* LR 1934.

15 Quotations taken from the unpublished manuscript of *Lucid Interval* in the Lord Chamberlain's Plays archives.

16 See LCP CORR: 1934/13372: *The Crooked Cross*.

17 It opened at the Westminster Theatre in January 1937.

18 Catholic Herald, 22 January 1937. http://archive.catholicherald.co.uk/article/22nd-january-1937/10/thc-play and *The Times*, 14 January 1937, p. 10.

19 Quotations taken from the published text. Sally Carson, *The Crooked Cross*, London: Jonathan Cape, 1938, pp. 80, 98.

20 *Official Announcement* was first staged at Bexhill in February 1935. *Son of Judea* opened at the Festival Theatre, Cambridge, in May 1935.

21 Quotations taken from the unpublished manuscript of *Do We Not Bleed* in the Lord Chamberlain's Plays archives. The play was staged in a hall in Iver, Buckinghamshire in the summer of 1936.

22 Quotations taken from the unpublished manuscript of *Death of a Ghost* in the Lord Chamberlain's Plays archives. The play was first staged at Roath Church House, Cardiff, in September 1936.

23 See LCP CORR: *Lorelei* WB 1938.

24 Quotations taken from Jack Duvall, *Lorelei*, unpublished manuscript in the Lord Chamberlain's Plays archives.

25 See LCP CORR: *Lorelei* WB 1938.

26 *Daily Mail*, 15 June 1938, p. 3.

27 See Vere Sullivan, LCP CORR: 1937/650: *Code of Honour*. The play opened at the Arts Theatre, Cambridge, in September 1937.

28 See Vere Sullivan, LCP CORR: 1937/1597: *Trumpeter, Play!* The play opened at London's Garrick Theatre in June 1938.

29 Ibid.

30 Quotations taken from the unpublished manuscript of *Trumpeter, Play!* in the Lord Chamberlain's Plays archives.

31 See LCP CORR: 1937/1597: *Trumpeter, Play!*

32 *Glasgow Herald*, 14 June 1938, p. 13.

33 *The Times*, 14 June 1938, p. 14.

34 See LCP CORR: *We, the Condemned.* WB 1938.

35 'A Word from the Authors' in the programme for the 1939 production of *Juggernaut* at the Saville Theatre.

36 Quotations taken from the unpublished manuscript of *Juggernaut* in the Lord Chamberlain's Plays archives. The play was first staged privately at the Aldwych Theatre in January 1939 and opened at the Saville Theatre in June.

37 See Anthony Heckstall-Smith and E.P. Hare, LCP CORR: 1939/2282: *Juggernaut.*

38 See unpublished manuscript of *Crisis* in the Lord Chamberlain's Plays archives. Unity's first performance was on 29 September 1938 – coinciding with the day Chamberlain flew to Munich for talks with Hitler.

39 Stephen Spender, *Trial of a Judge*, London: Faber and Faber, 1938. The play's first performance by Group Theatre took place at Unity Theatre in March 1938.

40 See W. H. Auden and Christopher Isherwood, LCP CORR: 1938/1978: *On the Frontier*. The play was first performed at Cambridge Arts Theatre in November 1938.

41 W. H. Auden and Christopher Isherwood, 'On the Frontier', in Edward Mendelson (ed.), *Plays and Other Dramatic Writings 1928–1938*, London: Faber and Faber, 1989, pp. 357–418 (pp. 413–14).

42 *Observer*, 19 February 1939.

43 See LCP CORR: 1938/1978: *On the Frontier*.

44 See unpublished manuscript of *Babes in the Wood* in the Lord Chamberlain's Plays archives. The production opened in November 1938 and ran until May 1939.

45 Quotations taken from the unpublished manuscript of *Who's Taking Liberty* in the Lord Chamberlain's Plays archives.

46 The production had a try out in Cardiff before transferring to St James's Theatre, London, in January 1940. Rattigan's collaborator on the text was a friend from School and University who wrote under the pseudonym of Anthony Maurice.

47 See http://sounds.bl.uk/related-content/TRANSCRIPTS/024T-1CDR0032282X-0100A0.pdf

48 See Geoffrey Wansell, *Terence Rattigan*, London: Fourth Estate, 1995, pp. 91, 103.

49 Ibid., pp. 91, 102.

50 *News Chronicle*, 17 January 1940.

51 Quotations taken from the unpublished manuscript of *Follow My Leader* in the Lord Chamberlain's Plays archives.

52 See LCP CORR: 1940/3219: *Follow My Leader*.

53 *Daily Mail*, 25 January 1940.

54 *Daily Mirror*, 17 January 1940.

55 Cited in Wansell, *Terence Rattigan*, p. 103.

56 The *Bystander*, 31 January 1940, p. 133.

57 Ibid.

58 The *Observer*, 21 January, 1940, p. 11.

59 Description in interview by Frith Banbury, who acted in the production. See http://sounds.bl.uk/related-content/TRANSCRIPTS/024T-1CDR0032282X-0100A0.pdf

Conclusion

1 See Lizbeth Goodman, *Contemporary Feminist Theatres: Each to Her Own*, London: Routledge, 1993, p. 24.

2 Billingham, *Theatres of Conscience*, p. 85.

3 Cochrane, *Twentieth-Century British Theatre*, p. 12.

4 See D. Keith Peacock, *Thatcher's Theatre: British Theatre and Drama in the Eighties*, London: Greenwood Press, 1999.

5 Martin Esslin, *Theatre of the Absurd*, 3rd edition. London: Penguin, 1968, pp. 415–16.

BIBLIOGRAPHY

Plays

Ackerley, J. R., *The Prisoners of War*, London: Chatto and Windus, 1925.

Ackland, Rodney, *The Dark River*, London: French, 1942.

—, *Absolute Hell*, London: Oberon, 1995.

Anon, 'Death of a Ghost', Unpublished Manuscript, LCP.

Auden, W. H. and Christopher Isherwood, *On the Frontier*, LCP CORR: 1938/1978.

— *The Dog Beneath the Skin, or, Where Is Francis?* London: Faber and Faber, 1986.

—, 'On the Frontier' in Edward Mendelson (ed.), *Plays and Other Dramatic Writings 1928–1938*, London: Faber and Faber, 1989.

Bagnold, Enid Bagnold, *The Chalk Garden*, London: William Heinemann, 1956.

Barke, James, *The Night of the Big Blitz*, Barke Papers, Mitchell Library, Glasgow, Box 10.

Barker, Granville, *Granville Barker: Plays Two*, London: Methuen Drama, 1994.

Barrie, J. M., *The Plays of J. M. Barrie in One Volume*, London: Hodder & Stoughton, 1928.

—, *The Admirable Crichton*, Fairford, Gloucestershire: Echo Library, 2007.

Box, Muriel, *Angels of War*, in Claire M. Tylee, with Elaine Turner and Agnes Cardinal (eds), *War Plays by Women: An International Anthology*, London: Routledge, 1990.

Brighouse, Harold, *Hobson's Choice*, London: Heinemann, 1992.

Carson, Sally, *The Crooked Cross*, LCP CORR: 1934/13372.

—, *The Crooked Cross*, London: Jonathan Cape, 1938.

Coward, Noël, *Plays: One*, London: Methuen, 1979.

—, *Plays: Two*, London: Eyre Methuen, 1979.

—, *Plays: Three*, London: Methuen, 1979.

—, *Plays: Two*, London: Methuen Drama, 1999.

—, *Collected Plays: Three*, London: Methuen, 1999.

—, *Coward Plays: 5*, London: Methuen Drama, 2006.

—, *Private Lives*, London: A & C Black, 2013.

Crawshay-Williams, Eliot, *The Nutcracker Suite*, in Richard J. Hand and Michael Wilson (eds), *London's Grand Guignol and the Theatre of Horror*, Exeter: University of Exeter Press, 2007.

Dane, Clemence, *A Bill of Divorcement*, London: Heinemann, 1922.

—, *Shivering Shocks or, The Hiding Place: A Play for Boys*, in Philip Wayne (ed.), *One-Act Comedies*, London: Longmans, 1935.

Daniell, Henry, 'Lucid Interval', Unpublished Manuscript, LCP.

Bibliography

Du Maurier, Daphne, *The Years Between*, in Fidelis Morgan (ed.), *The Years Between: Plays by Women on the London Stage 1900–1950*, London: Virago, 1994.

Duval, Jack, *Lorelei*, LCP CORR: *Lorelei* WB 1938.

Eliot, T. S., *The Complete Poems and Plays of T.S. Eliot*, London: Faber and Faber, 1969.

Frankau, Pamela, 'Who's Taking Liberty', Unpublished Manuscript, LCP.

Galsworthy, John, *Galsworthy: Five Plays*, London: Methuen, 1984.

Graves, Robert, *Goodbye to All That*, Harmondsworth: Penguin, 1988.

Grimaldi, George H., 'Do We Not Bleed', Unpublished Manuscript, LCP.

Hall, Radclyffe, 'The "First Night"', Radclyffe Hall and Una Troubridge Collection, Harry Ransom Humanities Research Center, The University of Texas at Austin.

Hamilton, Cicely and Christopher St. John, *How the Vote Was Won*, in Carole Hayman and Dale Spender (eds), *How the Vote Was Won and Other Suffragette Plays*, London: Methuen, 1985.

Heckstall-Smith and E. P. Hare, *Juggernaut*, LCP CORR: 1939/2282.

Houghton, Stanley, *Hindle Wakes*, London: Oberon Books, 2012.

Lee, Vernon [Violet Page], *Satan the Waster: A Philosophic War Trilogy with Notes and Introduction*, New York: John Lane, 1920.

Malleson, Miles, *'D' Company* and *Black 'Ell*, London: Hendersons, 1916.

Maltby, H. F., 'The Person Unknown', in Richard J. Hand and Michael Wilson (eds), *London's Grand Guignol and the Theatre of Horror*, Exeter: University of Exeter Press, 2007.

Maugham, W. Somerset, *Plays: Two*, London: Methuen Drama, 1999.

Nightingale, Benedict, 'Introduction', *Galsworthy: Five Plays*, London: Methuen, 1984, pp. vii–xxvii.

O'Casey, Sean, *Collected Plays, Volume Two*, London: Macmillan, 1950.

—, *Collected Plays 1*, London: Macmillan, 1971.

—, *Plays Two*, London: Faber and Faber, 1998.

Peters, Alan, 'Whither Liberty', Unpublished Manuscript, LCP, British Library.

—, *Who Made the Iron Grow*, LR (1933), LCP CORR.

Priestley, J. B., *Time and the Conways*, London: W. Heinemann, 1938.

Priestley, J. B., *The Plays of J. B. Priestley Volume II*, London: William Heinemann, 1949.

—, *The Plays of J. B. Priestley, Vol. III*, London: Heinemann, 1950.

Rattigan, Terence, 'Follow My Leader', Unpublished Manuscript, LCP CORR: 1940/3219: *Follow My Leader*.

—, *The Collected Plays of Terence Rattigan. Volume II*, London: Hamish Hamilton, 1953.

Reade, Leslie, 'Take Heed', Unpublished Manuscript, LCP.

Robins, Elizabeth, *Votes for Women!*, in Jean Chothia (ed.), *The New Woman and Other Emancipated Woman Plays*, Oxford: Oxford University Press, 1998.

Rye, Elizabeth, *Five New Full-length Plays for All-Women Casts*, London: Lovat Dickson & Thompson, 1935.

Shaw, George Bernard, *O'Flaherty V.C.: A Recruiting Pamphlet*, in *Heartbreak House, Great Catherine, Playlets of the War*, London: Constable, 1931.

—, *Candida*, New York: Penguin, 1952.
—, *John Bull's Other Island*, London: Penguin, 1984.
—, *Saint Joan*, London: Penguin, 2001.
—, *Mrs. Warren's Profession*, New York: Cosimo, 2006.
Sherriff, R. C., *Journey's End*, Harmondsworth: Penguin, 2000.
Smith, Dodie, *Dear Octopus*, London: Samuel French, 1938.
—, *Three Plays by Dodie Smith*, London: Heinemann, 1939.
Sowerby, Githa, *Rutherford and Son*, Central, Hong Kong: Forgotten Books, 2012.
Spender, Stephen, *Trial of a Judge*, London: Faber and Faber, 1938.
Stern, G. B., *The Man Who Pays the Piper*, London: William Heinemann, n.d. [1931].
Sullivan, Vere, *Code of Honour*, LCP CORR: 1937/650.
—, *Trumpeter, Play!* LCP CORR: 1937/1597.
—, *We, the Condemned*, WB 1938, LCP CORR.
Tagger, Theodor, [Ferdinand Bruckner], *Heroes* LR 1934, LCP CORR.
Thurston, E. Temple, *The Cost: A Comedy in Four Acts*, London: Chapman & Hall, 1914.
Toller, Ernst, *Pastor Hall*, LCP CORR: 1939/3083.
Unity Theatre, *Crisis*, Unpublished Manuscript, LCP.
—, 'Babes in the Wood', Unpublished Manuscript, LCP, 1938.
Wentworth, Marion, *War Brides*, New York: Century, 1915.
Williams, Emlyn, *The Corn Is Green: A Comedy in Three Acts*, London: William Heinemann, 1938.

Primary sources

Allan, Maud, *My Life and Dancing*, London: Everett, [1908].
Andrews, John and Ossia Trilling (eds), *Dobson's Theatre Year-book 1948/49*, London: Dennis Dobson, 1949.
Atkinson, Brooks, 'The Play: Alfred Lunt, Lynn Fontanne, Noël Coward and an Artificial Comedy Entitled "Design for Living"', *New York Times*, 25 January 1933, p. 13.
Baxter, Beverley, *First Nights and Noises Off*, London: Hutchinson, 1949.
Beerbohm, Max Beerbohm, 'At the Palace Theatre', *The Saturday Review*, 4 July 1908, p. 11.
Browne, E. Martin, 'The British Drama League', *Educational Theatre Journal*, Vol. 5, No. 3 (October 1953), pp. 203–6.
Browne, E. Martin with Henzie Browne, *Two in One [by] E.Martin Browne with Henzie Browne*, Cambridge: Cambridge University Press, 1981.
Bystander, 31 January 1940, p. 133.
Carroll, Paul Vincent, Citizens' Theatre Programme for *Shadow & Substance*, 15 November 1943.
Casson, Lewis, 'Harley Granville Barker', *The Dictionary of National Biography*, 1941–1950, Oxford: Oxford University Press, 1959.

Catholic Herald, 22 January 1937, http://archive.catholicherald.co.uk/article/22nd-january-1937/10/thc-play

Chisholm, Cecil, *Repertory: An Outline of the Modern Theatre Movement*, London: Peter Davies, 1934.

Craig, Edward Gordon, *On Movement and Dance*, Arnold Rood (ed.), London: Dance Books, 1978.

—, 'The Art of the Theatre. The First Dialogue', in J. Michael Walton (ed.), *Craig on Theatre*, London: Methuen, 1983, pp. 52–71.

Daily Express, 1 August 1933.

Daily Mail, 15 June 1938.

—, 25 January 1940.

Daily Mirror, 17 January 1940.

Daily Telegraph, 29 January 1934.

Darlington, W. A., *The Actor and His Audience*, London: Phoenix House, 1949.

—, *Six Thousand and One Nights: Forty Years a Critic*, London: Harrap, 1960.

Davis, F. Hadland, '"Chu Chin Chow" and the "Arabian Nights"', *Saturday Review of Politics, Literature, Science and Art*, Vol. 132, No. 3431 (30 July 1921), pp. 147–8.

Ervine, St. John, *The Organised Theatre: A Plea in Civics*, London: George Allen & Unwin, 1924, p. 123.

Farjeon, Herbert, *Era*, 1918.

Fraser, M. F. K., *Alexandra Theatre: The Story of a Popular Playhouse*, Birmingham: Cornish Brothers, 1948.

Gielgud, John, *Early Stages*, London: Macmillan, 1939.

Glasgow Herald, 14 June 1938, p. 13.

Goldman, Emma, *The Social Significance of Modern Drama*, New York: Applause Theatre Books, 1987 [1914].

Goldie, Grace Wyndham, *The Liverpool Repertory Theatre 1911–1934*, Liverpool: Liverpool University Press, 1935.

Graves, Robert and Alan Hodge, *The Long Week-End: A Social History of Great Britain 1918–1939*, London: Cardinal 1991 [1940].

Guthrie, Tyrone, *A Life in the Theatre*, London: Hamish Hamilton, 1961.

Hamilton, Cicely, 'Morals through the Centuries; IV. The Sins We Do Not Speak of: An Attempt to Consider an Ugly Subject Dispassionately', *Time and Tide*, 2 November 1928.

Higgins, Walter, '"The Vision of Salome"', *Labour Leader* 26 June 1908, p. 404.

J. C. F., 'Miss Maud Allan's Salome Dance', *The Academy*, 21 March 1908.

'Jingle', 'The Bairnsfather Touch', *The Bystander*, 27 September (1916), p. 568.

Knoblock, Edward, *Round the Room*, London: Chapman & Hall, 1939.

Landstone, Charles, *Offstage: A Personal Record of the First Twelve Years of State Sponsored Drama in Great Britain*, London: Elek, 1953.

Llewellyn, Rees, 'The Arts Council', in John Andrews and Ossia Trilling (eds), *Dobson's Theatre Year-Book 1948/49*, London: Dennis Dobson, 1949, pp. 64–71.

Marshall, Norman, *The Other Theatre*, London: John Lehmann, 1947.

Mason, A. E. W., *Sir George Alexander & the St James' Theatre*, London: Macmillan, 1935.

Morning Post, 29 January 1934.

News Chronicle, 17 January 1940.

New York Times, 22 March 1934, p. 26.

Observer, 19 February 1939.

Observer, 21 January, 1940, p. 11.

Pall Mall Gazette, 'A New Dancer. Maud Allan at the Palace Theatre', 7 March 1908, p. 8.

Pellizzi, Camillo, *English Drama: The Last Great Phase*, London: Macmillan, 1935.

Performer, 11 February 1937.

Picture Post, 'A New Way to Use a Theatre', 6 December (1941), pp. 16–18.

Poel, William, *What is Wrong with the Stage?*, London: George Allen & Unwin, 1920.

Reynolds, Ernest, *Modern English Drama: A Survey of the Theatre from 1900*, Oklahoma: University of Oklahoma Press, 1951.

Rowntree, Benjamin Seebohm, *Poverty, A Study of Town Life*. Bristol: Policy Press, 2001 [1901].

Sassoon, Siegfried, *The Old Huntsman, and Other Poems*, New York: E. P. Dutton & Company, 1918.

Seebohm Rowntree, Benjamin, *Poverty, A Study of Town Life*, Bristol: Policy Press, 2001 [1901].

Sims, George R. (ed.), *Living London: Its Work and Its Play: Its Humour and Its Pathos: Its Sights and Its Scenes*, Vol. 1, London: Cassell, 1901.

Smith, Dodie, 'Legion of Loveless Women', *Pearson's Weekly*, 6 May 1931.

Speaight, Robert, *William Poel and the Elizabethan Revival*, London: William Heinemann, 1954.

St. John, Christopher, 'All We Like Sheep', *The Academy*, 2 May 1908, pp. 735–6.

Star, 20 January 1937.

'A Suffragist Play', *The Era*, 17 April 1909, p. 21.

Sutton, Graham, '"Chu Chin Chow" to "Hassan"', *The Bookman*, September (1924), pp. 306–7.

Theatre Workshop's *Uranium 235*, 1952 Review, http://www.vam.ac.uk/users/node/8814

Times Literary Supplement, 'The Drama. The New Dancer', 26 March 1908, p. 102.

Times, 'Woman Suffrage', 16 April 1909, p. 8.

Times, 29 January 1934.

Times, 14 January 1937, p. 10.

Times, 14 June 1938, p. 14.

Times, 7 December 1938.

Times, 'Court Theatre. The Play Actors', 10 May 1909, p. 12.

Trewin, J. C., *The Turbulent Thirties: A Further Decade of Theatre*, London: Macdonald, 1950.

—, *The Birmingham Repertory Theatre 1913–1963*, London: Barrie and Rockcliff, 1963.

Ward, R. H., 'The Theatre of Persons', *The Adelphi*, 1941, pp. 122–6.

Williams, Harcourt, *Old Vic Saga*, London: Winchester Publications, 1949.

Wolfit, Donald, *First Interval*, London: Odhams, 1954.

Woolf, Virginia Woolf, 'Mr. Bennett and Mrs. Brown', London: Hogarth Press, 1924.

Secondary sources

Addison, Paul, *The Road to 1945: British Politics and the Second World War*, 1977.

Addison, Paul and Jeremy A. Crang, *Listening to Britain: Home Intelligence Reports on Britain's Finest Hour, May-September 1940*, London: Vintage, 2011.

Alberti, Johanna, 'A Time for Hard Writers: The Impact of War on Women Writers', in Nick Hayes and Jeff Hill (eds), *Millions Like Us? British Culture in the Second World War*, Liverpool: Liverpool University Press, 1999, pp. 156–78.

Amkpa, Awam, 'Drama and the Languages of Postcolonial Desire: Bernard Shaw's *Pygmalion*', *Irish University Review*, Vol. 29, No. 2 (1999), pp. 294–304.

Arrington, Lauren, *W. B. Yeats, The Abbey Theatre, Censorship, and the Irish State: Adding the Half-Pence to the Pence*, Oxford: Oxford University Press, 2010.

Aston, Elaine, 'The "New Woman" at Manchester's Gaiety Theatre', in Viv Gardner and Susan Rutherford (eds), *The New Woman and Her Sisters: Feminism and the Theatre 1850–1914*, London: Harvester Wheatsheaf, 1992, pp. 205–20.

Auerbach, Nina, 'Before the Curtain', in Kerry Powell (ed.), *The Cambridge Companion to Victorian and Edwardian Theatre*, Cambridge: Cambridge University Press, 2004, pp. 3–14.

Ayling, Ronald, *Sean O'Casey's Theater of War*, Vernon, BC: Kalamalka Press, 2004.

Ayres, Jackson F., 'From to Pleasure to Menace: Coward, Pinter and Critical Narratives', *Journal of Dramatic Theory and Criticism*, Vol. 24, No. 1 (Fall 2009), pp. 41–58.

Bailey, Peter, '"Naughty but Nice": Musical Comedy and the Rhetoric of the Girl, 1892–1914', in Michael R. Booth and Joel H. Kaplan (eds), *The Edwardian Theatre: Essays on Performance and the Stage*, Cambridge: Cambridge University Press, 1996, pp. 36–60.

Baker, Stuart E, 'Shavian Realism', *Shaw*, Vol. 9, No. 2989, pp. 79–97.

Balfour, Michael (ed.), *Theatre and War 1933-1945: Performance in Extremis*, New York: Berghahn Books, 2001.

Barfoot, C. C. and Rias van den Doel (eds), *Ritual Remembering: History, Myth and Politics in Anglo-Irish Drama*, Amsterdam: Rodopi, 1995.

Barker, Clive, 'Theatre and Society: The Edwardian Legacy', in Clive Barker and Maggie B. Gale (eds), *British Theatre between the Wars 1918–1939*, Cambridge: Cambridge University Press, 2000, pp. 4–37.

—, 'The Ghosts of War: Stage Ghosts and Time Slips as a Response to War', in Clive Barker and Maggie B. Gale (eds), *British Theatre between the Wars 1918–1939*, Cambridge: Cambridge University Press, 2000, pp. 215–43.

Barker, Clive and Maggie B. Gale (eds), *British Theatre between the Wars 1918–1939*, Cambridge: Cambridge University Press, 2000.

Barker, Simon, 'Shakespeare, Stratford and the Second World War', in Irena R. Makaryk and Marissa McHugh (eds), *Shakespeare and the Second Word War: Memory, Culture, Identity*, Toronto: University of Toronto Press, 2012, pp. 199–217.

Barrett, Eileen, 'The British Society for the Study of Sex Psychology: Bloomsbury and the Medicalization of Same-Sex Love', in Laura Davis and Jeanette McVicker (eds), *Virginia Woolf and Her Influences: Selected Papers from the Seventh*

Annual Conference on Virginia Woolf, New York: Pace University Press, 1998, pp. 111–16.

Baxendale, John, *Priestley's England: J. B. Priestley and English Culture*, Manchester: Manchester University Press, 2014.

Beauman, Nicola, *A Very Great Profession: The Woman's Novel 1914–1939*, London: Virago, 1983.

Beauman, Sally, *The Royal Shakespeare Company A History of Ten Decades*, Oxford: Oxford University Press, 1982.

Beer, Gillian, 'The Dissidence of Vernon Lee: Satan the Waster and the Will to Believe', in Suzanne Raitt and Trudi Tate (eds), *Women's Fiction and the Great War*, Oxford: Clarendon Press, 1997, pp. 107–31.

Bennett, Susan, 'A Commercial Success: Women Playwrights in the 1950s', in Mary Luckhurst (ed.), *A Companion to Modern British and Irish Drama 1880–2005*, Oxford: Blackwell, 2006, pp. 175–87.

Billingham, Peter, *Theatres of Conscience 1939–53: A Study of Four Touring British Community Theatres*, London: Routledge, 2002.

—, 'Rosalinds, Violas, and Other Sentimental Friendships: The Osiris Players and Shakespeare, 1939–1945', in Irena R. Makaryk and Marissa McHugh (eds), *Shakespeare and the Second Word War: Memory, Culture, Identity*, Toronto: University of Toronto Press, 2012, pp. 218–32.

Billington, Michael, 'Johnson Over Jordan', *The Guardian*, 14 September 2001.

—, 'Saint's Day', *The Guardian*, 25 October 2002.

Bloom, Clive, *Bestsellers: Popular Fiction Since 1900*, Basingstoke: Palgrave Macmillan, 2002.

Booth, Michael R., 'Comedy and Farce', in Kerry Powell (ed.), *The Cambridge Companion to Victorian and Edwardian Theatre*, Cambridge: Cambridge University Press, 2004, pp. 129–44.

Booth, Michael R. and Joel H. Kaplan (eds), *The Edwardian Theatre: Essays on Performance and the Stage*, Cambridge: Cambridge University Press, 1996.

Booth, Michael R., Richard Southern, Frederk Marker, Lise-Lone Marker and Roberston Davies (eds), *The Revels History of Drama in English: Volume VI 1750–1880*, London: Methuen, 1975.

Bowden, Geoff, *Intimate Memories: The History of the Intimate Theatre, Palmers Green*, Westbury, Wiltshire: The Badger Press, 2006.

Boxwell, David A., 'The Follies of War: Cross-Dressing and Popular Theatre on the British Front Lines, 1914–18', *Modernism/Modernity*, Vol. 9, No. 1 (2002), pp. 1–20.

Bradby, David and John MacCormick, *People's Theatre*, London: Taylor & Francis, 1978.

Bradby, David, Louis James and Bernard Sharratt (eds), *Performance and Politics in Popular Drama: Aspects of Popular Entertainment in Theatre, Film and Television 1800–1976*, Cambridge: Cambridge University Press, 1981.

Brassley, Paul, Jeremy Burchardt and Lynne Thompson (eds), *The English Countryside Between the Wars: Regeneration or Decline?*, Woodbridge, Suffolk: The Boydell Press, 2006.

Bibliography

Bratton, Jacky, 'Gender Play and Role Reversal in the Music Hall', in Michael R. Booth and Joel H. Kaplan (eds), *The Edwardian Theatre: Essays on Performance and the Stage*, Cambridge: Cambridge University Press, 1996, pp. 86–110.

—, 'The Music Hall', in Kerry Powell (ed.), *The Cambridge Companion to Victorian and Edwardian Theatre*, Cambridge: Cambridge University Press, 2004, pp. 164–82.

Braun, Edward, *The Director and the Stage from Naturalism to Grotowski*, London: Methuen, 1982.

Brinson, Charmian and Richard Dove, *Politics by Other Means: The Free German League of Culture in London 1939–1946*, Middlesex: Vallentine Mitchell, 2010.

Brook, Peter, *The Empty Space*, London: Penguin, 2008.

Brown, Ian, *Scottish Theatre: Diversity, Language, Community*, Amsterdam: Rodopi, 2013.

Brown, Shirley, *Bristol Old Vic Theatre School: The First 50 Years 1946–1996*, Bristol: BOVTS Productions, 1996.

Buck, Claire, 'Women's Literature of the Great War', in Vincent Sherry (ed.), *The Cambridge Companion to the Literature of the Great War*, Cambridge: Cambridge University Press, 2005, pp. 85–112.

Buckley, Jennifer, '"Symbols in Silence": Edward Gordon Craig and the Engraving of Wordless Drama', *Theatre Survey*, Vol. 54, No. 2 (May 2013), pp. 207–30.

Burton, Alan, 'Death or Glory? The Great War in British film', in Claire Monk and Amy Sargeant (eds), *British Historical Cinema: The History, Heritage and Costume Film*, London: Routledge, 2002, pp. 31–46.

Calder, Angus, *The People's War: Britain, 1939–45*, London: Random House, 2012.

—, *The Myth of the Blitz*, London: Jonathan Cape, 1991.

Cannadine, David, *In Churchill's Shadow: Confronting the Past in Modern Britain*, London: Allen Lane, 2002.

Carlson, Susan, 'Suffrage Theatre', in Mary Luckhurst (ed.), *A Companion to Modern British and Irish Drama 1880–2005*, Oxford: Blackwell, 2006, pp. 99–109.

Castle, Terry, *Noël Coward and Radclyffe Hall: Kindred Spirits*, New York: Columbia University Press, 1996.

Cave, Richard, *Theatre in Focus: Terence Gray and the Cambridge Festival Theatre*, Cambridge: Cambridge University Press, 1980.

Chambers, Colin, *The Story of Unity Theatre*, London: Lawrence and Wishart, 1989.

Chapman, Don, *Oxford Playhouse High and Low Drama in a University City*, Hatfield: University of Hertfordshire Press/The Society for Theatre Research, 2008.

Chothia, Jean, *English Drama of the Early Modern Period, 1890–1940*, London: Longman, 1996.

—, 'The New Woman and Theatre in 1894', in Hubert Hermans, Wessel Krul and Hans van Maanen (eds), *1894: European Theatre in Turmoil*, Amsterdam: Rodopi, 1996, pp. 27–40.

—, 'Sean O'Casey's Powerful Fireworks', in Mary Luckhurst (ed.), *A Companion to Modern British and Irish Drama 1880–2005*, Oxford: Blackwell, 2006, pp. 125–37.

Clarke, Peter, *Hope and Glory: Britain 1900–2000*, 2nd edition, Harmondsworth: Penguin, 2004.

Cochrane, Claire, *Shakespeare and the Birmingham Repertory Theatre 1913–1929*, London: Society for Theatre Research, 1993.

—, 'The Pervasiveness of the Commonplace: The Historian and Amateur Theatre', *Theatre Research International*, Vol. 26, No. 3 (2001), pp. 233–42.

—, *Twentieth-Century British Theatre: Industry, Art and Empire*, Cambridge: Cambridge University Press, 2011.

Cockin, Katherine, 'Women's Suffrage Drama', in Maroula Joannou and June Purvis (eds), *The Women's Suffrage Movement: New Feminist Perspectives,* Manchester: Manchester University Press, 1998.

—, *Edith Craig (1869–1947): Dramatic Lives*, London: Cassell, 1998.

Collins, L. J., *Theatre at War, 1914–18*, Basingstoke: Palgrave Macmillan, 1999.

Colls, Robert, *The Identity of England*, Oxford: Oxford University Press, 2002.

Colls, Robert and Philip Dodd (eds), *Englishness: Politics and Culture 1880–1920*, Beckenham, Kent: Croom Helm, 1987.

Coward, Noël, *Present Indicative*, London: Methuen, 1986.

—, *Future Indefinite*, London: Methuen Drama, 2004.

Croall, Jonathan, *John Gielgud: Matinee Idol to Movie Star*, London: Bloomsbury, 2011.

Crome, Len, *Unbroken: Resistance and Survival in the Concentration Camps*, London: Lawrence & Wishart, 1988.

Davies, Andrew, *Other Theatres: The Development of Alternative and Experimental Theatre in Britain*, Basingstoke: Macmillan, 1987.

—, 'The War Years', in Michael Balfour (ed.), *Theatre and War 1933–1945: Performance in Extremis*, New York: Berghahn Books, 2001, pp. 54–64.

Davies, Cecil, *The Adelphi Players: The Theatre of Persons*, London: Routledge, 2014.

Davies, Hazel Walford, 'Case Study: Refashioning a Myth, Performances of the Tale of *Blodeuwedd*', in Baz Kershaw (ed.), *The Cambridge History of British Theatre. Volume 3 Since 1895*, Cambridge: Cambridge University Press, 2004, pp. 273–87.

Davis, Jim, 'The East End', in Michael R. Booth and Joel H. Kaplan (eds), *The Edwardian Theatre: Essays on Performance and the Stage*, Cambridge: Cambridge University Press, 1996, pp. 201–19.

Davis, Laura and Jeanette McVickers (eds), *Virginia Woolf and Her Influences: Selected Papers from the Seventh Annual Conference on Virginia Woolf*, New York: Pace University Press, 1998.

Davis, Tracy C., 'Ibsen's Victorian Audience', *Essays in Theatre*, Vol. 4, No. 1 (November 1985), pp. 21–38.

—, 'Edwardian Management and the Structures of Industrial Capitalism', in Kerry Powell (ed.), *The Cambridge Companion to Victorian and Edwardian Theatre*. Cambridge: Cambridge University Press, 2004, pp. 111–29.

Day, Barry (ed.), *The Essential Noel Coward Compendium: The Very Best of his Work, Life and Times*, London: Methuen Drama, 2009.

Day, Gary, 'Introduction', in Gary Day (ed.), *Literature and Culture in Modern Britain, Volume Two: 1930–1955*, London: Longman, 1997, pp. 1–27.

— (ed.), *Literature and Culture in Modern Britain, Volume Two: 1930–1955*, London: Longman, 1997.

Day, Helen, 'Female Daredevils', in Viv Gardner and Susan Rutherford (eds), *The New Woman and Her Sisters: Feminism and Theatre 1850–1914*, Hemel Hempstead: Harvester Wheatsheaf, 1992, pp. 137–57.

Deeney, John, 'When Men Were Men and Women Were Women', in Clive Barker and Maggie B. Gale (eds), *British Theatre between the Wars, 1918–1939*, Cambridge: Cambridge University Press, 2000, pp. 63–87.

De Jongh, Nicholas, *Not in Front of the Audience: Homosexuality on Stage*, London: Routledge, 1992.

—, *Politics, Prudery and Perversions: The Censoring of the English Stage 1901–1968*, London: Methuen, 2000.

Dellamora, Richard (ed.), *Victorian Sexual Dissidence*, Chicago: University of Chicago Press, 1999.

Dellar, Pamela and Gillian Holtby (compilers), and Barbara Robinson (ed.), *The Swelling Scene: The Development of Amateur Drama in Hull from 1900*, Beverly, Hull: Highgate Publications, 1996.

Devine, Kathleen (ed.), *Modern Irish Writers and the Wars*, Gerrards Cross: Colin Smythe, 1999.

D'Monté, Rebecca, 'Feminizing the Nation and the Country House: Women Dramatists 1938–1940', in David James and Philip Tew (eds), *New Versions of Pastoral: Post-Romantic, Modern, and Contemporary Responses to the Tradition*, New Jersey: Fairleigh Dickinson University Press, 2009, pp. 139–55.

—, 'Moving Back to "Home" and "Nation": Women Dramatists, 1938–1945', in Teresa Gómez-Reus and Terry Gifford (eds), *Women in Transit Through Literary Liminal Spaces*, Basingstoke: Palgrave Macmillan, 2013, pp. 139–50.

—, 'Drama, 1920–1945', in Maroula Joannou (ed.), *The History of British Women's Writing, 1920–1945*, Basingstoke: Palgrave Macmillan, 2013, pp. 182–98.

Doane, Mary Ann, *Femmes Fatales: Feminism, Film Theory, Psychoanalysis*. London: Routledge, 1991.

Dobson, Michael, *Shakespeare and Amateur Performance: A Cultural History*, Cambridge: Cambridge University Press, 2011.

Duff, Charles, *The Lost Summer: The Heyday of the West End Theatre*, London: Nick Hern, 1995.

Dunn, Kate, *Exit Through the Fireplace: The Great Days of Rep*, London: John Murray, 1998.

Dymkowski, Christine, 'Case Study: *Diana of Dobson's*, 1908', in Baz Kershaw (ed.), *The Cambridge History of British Theatre. Volume 3 Since 1895*, Cambridge: Cambridge University Press, 2004, pp. 110–26.

Earl, John and Michael Sell (eds), *The Theatres Trust. Guide to British Theatres 1750–1950: A Gazetteer*, London: A & C Black, 2000.

Ellmann, Richard, *Oscar Wilde*, New York: Vintage, 1988.

Eltis, Sos, 'The Fallen Woman on Stage: Maidens, Magdalens, and the Emancipated Female', in Kerry Powell (ed.), *The Cambridge Companion to Victorian and Edwardian Theatre*, Cambridge: Cambridge University Press, 2004, pp. 222–36.

—, 'Private Lives and Public Spaces: Reputation, Celebrity and the Late Victorian Actress', in Mary Luckhurst and Jane Moody (eds), *Theatre and Celebrity in Britain, 1660–2000*, London: Palgrave Macmillan, 2005, pp. 169–88.

Esslin, Martin, *Theatre of the Absurd*, 3rd edition, London: Penguin, 1968.

Evans, Gwenan and others, *A Few Drops of Water: The Story of the Questors Theatre 1929–1989*, London: Mattock Press, 1989.

Eyre, Richard and Nicholas Wright, *Changing Stages: A View of British Theatre in the 20th Century*, London: Bloomsbury, 2000.

Farfan, Penny, *Women, Modernism and Performance*, Cambridge: Cambridge University Press, 2004.

—, 'Noel Coward and Sexual Modernism: *Private Lives* as Queer Comedy', *Modern Drama*, Vol. 48, No. 4 (Winter 2005), pp. 677–88.

—, 'Women's Modernism and Performance', in Maren Tova Linett (ed.), *The Cambridge Companion to Modern Women Writers*, Cambridge: Cambridge University Press, 2010, pp. 47–61.

Farnell, Gary, 'The New Woman (Which Is Not One) in Githa Sowerby's *Rutherford and Son*', *Women's Writing*, Vol. 21, No. 4 (2014), pp. 509–522.

Fawkes, Richard, *Fighting for a Laugh: Entertaining the British and American Armed Forces 1939–1946*, London: Macdonald and Jane's, 1978.

Field, Frank, *British and French Writers of the First World War: Comparative Studies in Cultural History*, Cambridge: Cambridge University Press, 1991.

Finney, Gail, *Women in Modern Drama: Freud, Feminism, and European Theater at the Turn of the Century*, Ithaca, NY: Cornell University Press, 1989.

Firchow, Peter Edgerly, *W.H. Auden: Contexts for Poetry*, Delaware: University of Delaware Press, 2002.

Fitzsimmons, Linda, 'Typewriters Enchained: The Work of Elizabeth Baker', in Viv Gardner and Susan Rutherford (eds), *The New Woman and Her Sisters: Feminism and the Theatre 1850–1914*, London: Harvester Wheatsheaf, 1992, pp. 189–201.

Foulkes, Richard, *Repertory at The Royal: Sixty-Five Years of Theatre in Northampton 1927–92*, Northampton: The Northampton Repertory Players, 1992.

Freeman, Mark, 'Splendid Display; Pompous Spectacle: Historical Pageants in Twentieth-Century Britain', *Social History*, Vol. 38, No. 4 (2013), pp. 423–55.

Frith, Simon, 'The Pleasures of the Hearth: The Making of BBC Light Entertainment', in *Formations of Pleasure*, London: Routledge and Kegan Paul, 1983, pp. 101–23.

Fuller, J. G., *Troop Morale and Popular Culture in the British and Dominion Armies 1914–1918*, Oxford: Clarendon Press, 2006.

Fussell, Paul, *The Great War and Modern Memory*, Oxford: Oxford University Press, 2000.

Gale, Maggie B., 'Women Playwrights on the London Stage: 1918–1968', *Europa*, Vol. 1, No. 4 (1995), pp. 77–84.

—, *West End Women: Women and the London Stage 1918–1962*, London: Routledge, 1996.

—, *J. B. Priestley*, London: Routledge, 2008.

Bibliography

Gale, Maggie B. and John Stokes (eds), *The Cambridge Companion to the Actress*, Cambridge: Cambridge University Press, 2007.

Gardner, Viv, 'Introduction', in Viv Gardner and Susan Rutherford (eds), *The New Woman and Her Sisters: Feminism and the Theatre 1850–1914*, London: Harvester Wheatsheaf, 1992, pp. 1–14.

Gardner, Viv, 'Provincial Stages, 1900–1934: Touring and Early Repertory Theatre', in Baz Kershaw (ed.), *The Cambridge History of British Theatre. Volume 3 Since 1895*, Cambridge: Cambridge University Press, 2004, pp. 60–85.

Gardner, Viv and Susan Rutherford (eds), *The New Woman and Her Sisters: Feminism and the Theatre 1850–1914*, London: Harvester Wheatsheaf, 1992.

Gielgud, John, with Richard Mangan (ed.), *Sir John Gielgud: A Life in Letters*, New York: Arcade, 2011.

Girouard, Mark, *Life in the English Country House: A Social and Architectural History*, London: Penguin, 1980.

Gómez-Reus, Teresa and Terry Gifford (eds), *Women in Transit Through Literary Liminal Spaces*, Basingstoke: Palgrave Macmillan, 2013.

Goodman, Lizbeth, *Contemporary Feminist Theatres: Each to Her Own*, London: Routledge, 1993.

Goorney, Howard, *The Theatre Workshop Story*, London: Eyre Methuen, 1981.

Goorney, Howard and Ewan MacColl (eds), *Agit-Prop to Theatre Workshop: Political Playscripts 1930–50*, Manchester: Manchester University Press, 1986.

Grove, Robin, 'Auden and Eliot: Theatres of the Thirties', in Mary Luckhurst (ed.), *A Companion to Modern British and Irish Drama 1880–2005*, Oxford: Blackwell, 2006, pp. 138–50.

Gualtieri, Elena, '*Three Guineas* and the Photograph: The Art of Propaganda', in Maroula Joannou (ed.), *Women Writers of the 1930s: Gender, Politics and History*, Edinburgh: Edinburgh University Press, 1998, pp. 165–78.

Gullace, Nicoletta F., *"The Blood of Our Sons": Men, Women, and the Renegotiation of the British Citizenship during the Great War*, Basingstoke: Palgrave Macmillan, 2002.

Hall, Peter, *Making an Exhibition of Myself*, London: Sinclair-Stevenson, 1993.

Halpern, Richard, *Shakespeare Among the Moderns*, Ithaca, NY: Cornell University Press, 1997.

Hand, Richard J. and Michael Wilson (eds), *London's Grand Guignol and the Theatre of Horror*, Exeter: University of Exeter Press, 2007.

Hanson, Neil (ed.), with Tom Priestley, *Priestley's Wars*, Ilkley, Yorkshire: Great Northern Books, 2008.

Harben, Niloufer, *Twentieth-Century English History Plays: From Shaw to Bond*, Basingstoke: Macmillan, 1988.

Hartley, Jenny, 'Clothes and Uniform in the Theatre of Fascism: Clemence Dane and Virginia Woolf', in Angela K. Smith (ed.), *Gender and Warfare in the Twentieth Century: Textual Representations*, Manchester: Manchester University Press, 2004, pp. 96–110.

Harvie, Jen, *Staging the UK*, Manchester: Manchester University Press, 2005.

Haste, Cate, *Keep the Home Fires Burning*, London: Viking, 1977.

Hawkins, Alun, 'The Discovery of Rural England', in Robert Colls and Philip Dodd (eds), *Englishness: Politics and Culture 1880–1920*, Beckenham, Kent: Croom Helm, 1987, pp. 62–88.

Hayes, Nick and Jeff Hill (eds), *Millions Like Us? British Culture in the Second World War*, Liverpool: Liverpool University Press, 1999.

Hermans, Hubert, Wessel Krul and Hans van Maanen (eds), *1894: European Theatre in Turmoil*, Amsterdam: Rodopi, 1996.

Hinton, James, *The Mass Observers: A History, 1937–1949*, Oxford: Oxford University Press, 2013.

Hoare, Philip, *Noël Coward: A Biography*, New York: Simon & Schuster, 1995.

—, *Oscar Wilde's Last Stand: Decadence, Conspiracy, and the Most Outrageous Trial of the Century*, New York: Arcade, 1997.

Holder, Heidi J., 'The East-End Theatre', in Kerry Powell (ed.), *The Cambridge Companion to Victorian and Edwardian Theatre*, Cambridge: Cambridge University Press, 2004, pp. 257–76.

Holdsworth, Nadine, 'Case Study: Ena Lamont Stewart's *Men Should Weep*, 1947', in Baz Kershaw (ed.), *The Cambridge History of British Theatre. Volume 3 Since 1895*, Cambridge: Cambridge University Press, 2004, pp. 228–41.

—, *Joan Littlewood's Theatre*, Cambridge: Cambridge University Press, 2011.

Holledge, Julie, *Innocent Flowers: Women in the Edwardian Theatre*, London: Virago, 1981.

Hopkins, Chris, *English Fiction in the 1930s: Language, Genre, History*, London: Continuum, 2006.

Howard, Tony and John Stokes (eds), *Acts of War: The Representation of Military Conflict on the British Stage and Television Since 1945*, Cambridge: Scolar Press, 1996.

Hubble, Nick, *Mass Observation and Everyday Life: Culture, History, Theory*, Basingstoke: Palgrave Macmillan, 2010.

Hunt, Hugh, Kenneth Richards and John Russell Taylor (eds), *The Revels History of Drama in English: Volume VII 1880 to the Present Day*, London: Methuen, 1978.

Hynes, Samuel, *The Edwardian Turn of Mind*, Princeton, NJ: Princeton University Press, 1968.

—, *A War Imagined: The First World War and English Culture*, London: Bodley Head, 1990.

Ibell, Paul, *Theatreland: A Journey through the Heart of London's Theatre*, London: Continuum, 2009.

Ingelbien, Raphaël, 'Symbolism at the Periphery: Yeats, Maeterlinck, and Cultural Nationalism', *Comparative Literature Studies*, Vol. 42, No. 3 (2005) pp. 183–204.

Innes, Christopher, *Edward Gordon Craig*, Cambridge: Cambridge University Press, 1983.

—, *Modern British Drama: 1890–1990*, Cambridge: Cambridge University Press, 1992.

—, 'Modernism in Drama', *The Cambridge Companion to Modernism*, Michael Levenson (ed.), Cambridge: Cambridge University Press, 1999, pp. 130–56.

—, 'Defining Irishness: Bernard Shaw and the Irish Connection on the English Stage', in Julia M. Wright (ed.), *A Companion to Irish Literature*, Vol. 2, Oxford: Wiley Blackwell, 2010, pp. 35–49.

James, David and Philip Tew (eds), *New Versions of Pastoral: Post-Romantic, Modern, and Contemporary Responses to the Tradition*, New Jersey: Fairleigh Dickinson University Press, 2009.

Jarrett-Macauley, Delia, *The Life of Una Marson 1905–1965*, Manchester: Manchester University Press, 1998.

Joannou, Maroula (ed.), *Women Writers of the 1930s: Gender, Politics and History*. Edinburgh: Edinburgh University Press, 1998.

—, '"Hilda, Harnessed to a Purpose": Elizabeth Robins, Ibsen, and the Vote', *Comparative Drama*, Vol. 44, No. 2 (2010), pp. 179–200.

— (ed.), *The History of British Women's Writing, 1920–1945*, Basingstoke: Palgrave Macmillan, 2013.

Joannou, Maroula and June Purvis (eds), *The Women's Suffrage Movement: New Feminist Perspectives*, Manchester: Manchester University Press, 1998.

Kahn, Coppèlia. 'Remembering Shakespeare Imperially: The 1916 Tercentenary', *Shakespeare Quarterly*, Vol. 52, No. 4 (2001), pp. 456–78.

Kaplan, Joel H. and Sheila Stowell, *Theatre and Fashion: Oscar Wilde to the Suffragettes*, Cambridge: Cambridge University Press, 1995.

Kearney, Colbert, 'The Voice of the Man in *The Plough and the Stars*', in C. C. Barfoot and Rias van den Doel (eds), *Ritual Remembering: History, Myth and Politics in Anglo-Irish Drama*, Amsterdam: Rodopi, 1995, pp. 97–104.

Keegan, John, *The First World War*, London: Pimlico, 1999.

Kelly, Katherine E. (ed.), *Modern Drama by Women 1880s–1930s: An International Anthology*, London: Routledge, 1996.

—, 'Pandemic and Performance: Ibsen and the Outbreak of Modernism', *South Central Review*, Vol. 25, No. 1 (Spring 2008), pp. 12–35.

Kelsall, Malcolm, 'Manderley Revisited: *Rebecca* and the English Country House', in *Proceedings of the Bristol Academy 83* (1993), pp. 303–15.

Kennedy, Dennis, *Granville Barker and the Dream of Theatre*, Cambridge: Cambridge University Press, 1985.

—, 'British Theatre, 1895–1946', in Baz Kershaw (ed.), *The Cambridge History of British Theatre. Volume 3 Since 1895*, Cambridge: Cambridge University Press, 2004, pp. 3–33.

Kent, Brad, 'Shaw's Everyday Emergency: Commodification in and of *John Bull's Other Island*', *SHAW*, Vol. 26 (2006), pp. 162–79.

Kershaw, Baz, 'Curiosity or Contempt: On Spectacle, the Human and Activism', *Theatre Journal*, Vol. 55, No. 4 (2003), pp. 591–611.

— (ed.), *The Cambridge History of British Theatre. Volume 3 Since 1895*, Cambridge: Cambridge University Press, 2004.

Koritz, Amy, 'Dancing the Orient for England: Maud Allan's "The Vision of Salome"', *Theatre Journal* Vol. 46, No. 1 (March 1994).

Kosok, Heinz, *The Theatre of War: The First World War in British and Irish Drama*, Basingstoke: Palgrave Macmillan, 2007.

Lacey, Stephen, *British Realist Theatre: The New Wave in Its Context 1956–1965*, London: Routledge, 1995.

—, 'When Was the Golden Age? Narratives of Loss and Decline: John Osborne, Arnold Wesker and Rodney Ackland', in Mary Luckhurst (ed.), *A Companion to Modern British and Irish Drama 1880–2005*, Oxford: Blackwell, 2006, pp. 164–74.

Lahr, John, *Coward the Playwright*, London: Methuen, 1982.

Leask, Margaret, *Lena Ashwell: Actress, Patriot, Pioneer*, Herfordshire: University of Hertfordshire Press and The Society for Theatre Research, 2012.

Ledger, Sally, 'New Woman Drama', in Mary Luckhurst (ed.), *A Companion to Modern British and Irish Drama 1880–2005*, Oxford: Blackwell, 2006, pp. 48–60.

Lennard, John, 'Staging "the Holocaust" in England', in Mary Luckhurst (ed.), *A Companion to Modern British and Irish Drama 1880–2005*, Oxford: Blackwell, 2006, pp. 316–28.

Luckhurst, Mary, 'Drama and World War 1', in Mary Luckhurst (ed.), *A Companion to Modern British and Irish Drama 1880–2005*, Oxford: Blackwell, 2006, pp. 301–15.

— (ed.), *A Companion to Modern British and Irish Drama 1880–2005*, Oxford: Blackwell, 2006.

Luckhurst, Mary and Jane Moody (eds), *Theatre and Celebrity in Britain, 1660–2000*, London: Palgrave Macmillan, 2005.

MacColl, Ewan, 'Introduction: The Evolution of a Revolutionary Theatre Style', in Howard Goorney and Ewan MacColl (eds), *Agit-Prop to Theatre Workshop: Political Playscripts 1930–50*, Manchester: Manchester University Press, 1986, pp. ix–lvii.

MacKenzie, John, *Propaganda and Empire: The Manipulation of British Public Opinion, 1880–1960*, Manchester: Manchester University Press, 1984.

McArthur, Euan, *Scotland, CEMA and the Arts Council, 1919–1967*, Aldershot: Ashgate, 2013.

McAteer, Michael, *Yeats and European Drama*, Cambridge: Cambridge University Press, 2010.

McCann, Graham, *Bounder! The Biography of Terry-Thomas*, London: Aurum, 2008.

McConachie, Bruce, 'The *Playboy* Riots: Nationalism in the Irish Theatre', in Phillip B. Zarrilli, Bruce McConachie, Gary Jay Williams and Carol Fisher Sorgenfrei (eds), *Theatre Histories: An Introduction*, 2nd edition, London: Routledge, 2010, pp. 292–8.

—, 'Theatres of the Avant-Garde, 1880–1940', in Phillip B. Zarrilli, Bruce McConachie, Gary Jay Williams and Carol Fisher Sorgenfrei (eds), *Theatre Histories: An Introduction*, 2nd edition, London: Routledge, 2010, pp. 354–87.

—, 'Theatre and Performance in Modern Media Cultures, 1850–1970', in Phillip B. Zarrilli, Bruce McConachie, Gary Jay Williams and Carol Fisher Sorgenfrei (eds), *Theatre Histories: An Introduction*, 2nd edition, London: Routledge, 2010, pp. 299–326.

McCullough, Christopher, 'Harley Granville Barker: A Very English *avant-garde*', *Studies in Theatre and Performance*, Vol. 27, No. 3 (2007), pp. 223–35.

Bibliography

McDonald, Jan, 'New Women in the New Drama', *New Theatre Quarterly*, Vol. 6, No. 21 (February 1990), pp. 31–42.

—, 'Towards National Identities: Theatre in Scotland', in Baz Kershaw (ed.), *The Cambridge History of British Theatre, Volume 3: Since 1895*, Cambridge: Cambridge University Press, 2004, pp. 195–227.

McLaine, Ian, *Ministry of Morale: Home Front Morale and the Ministry of Information in World War II*, London: George Allen & Unwin, 1979.

McLoughlin, Kate, 'War and Words', in Kate McLoughlin (ed.), *The Cambridge Companion to War Writing*, Cambridge: Cambridge University Press, 2009, pp. 15–24.

— (ed.), *The Cambridge Companion to War Writing*, Cambridge: Cambridge University Press, 2009.

Makaryk, Irena R. and Marissa McHugh (eds), *Shakespeare and the Second World War: Memory, Culture, Identity*, Toronto: University of Toronto Press, 2012.

Maloney, Paul, '"Wha's Like Us?" Ethnic Representation in Music Hall and Popular Theatre and the Remaking of Urban Scottish Society', in Ian Brown (ed.), *From Tartan to Tartanry: Scottish Culture, History and Myth*, Edinburgh: Edinburgh University Press, 2010, pp. 129–50.

Mao, Douglas and Rebecca L. Walkowitz, 'The New Modernist Studies', *PMLA*, Vol. 123, No. 3 (2008).

— 'Introduction: Modernisms Bad and New', in Douglas Mao and Rebecca L. Walkowitz (eds), *Bad Modernisms*, Durham: Duke University Press, 2006.

Mayer, David, 'Introduction', in David Mayer (ed.), *Playing Out the Empire: 'Ben-Hur' and Other Toga Plays and Films, 1883–1908 – A Critical Anthology*, Clarendon: Oxford, 1994, pp. 1–22.

— (ed.), *Playing Out the Empire: 'Ben-Hur' and Other Toga Plays and Films, 1883–1908—A Critical Anthology*, Clarendon: Oxford, 1994.

—, 'Encountering Melodrama', in Kerry Powell (ed.), *The Cambridge Companion to Victorian and Edwardian Theatre*, Cambridge: Cambridge University Press, 2004, pp. 145–63.

—, 'The Actress as Photographic Icon: From Early Photography to Early Film', in Maggie B. Gale and John Stokes (eds), *The Cambridge Companion to the Actress*. Cambridge: Cambridge University Press, 2007, pp. 74–94.

Mazer, Cary M., *Shakespeare Refashioned: Elizabethan Plays on Edwardian Stages*, Ann Arbor: UMI Research Press 1981.

—, 'Granville Barker and the Court Dramatists', in Mary Luckhurst (ed.), *A Companion to Modern British and Irish Drama 1880–2005*, Oxford: Blackwell, 2006, pp. 75–86.

Medd, Jodie, '"The Cult of the Clitoris": Anatomy of a National Scandal', *Modernism/Modernity*, Vol. 9, No. 1 (2002), pp. 21–49.

Melman, Billie, *Women and the Popular Imagination in the Twenties: Flappers and Nymphs*, Basingstoke: Macmillan, 1988.

Merkin, Ros, 'The Religion of Socialism or a Pleasant Sunday Afternoon?: The ILP Arts Guild', in Clive Barker and Maggie B. Gale (eds), *British Theatre between the Wars, 1918–1939*, Cambridge: Cambridge University Press, 2000, pp. 162–89.

—, *Liverpool Playhouse: A Theatre & Its City*, Liverpool: Liverpool University Press, 2011.

Merriman, Andy, *Greasepaint and Cordite: How ENSA Entertained the Troops during World War II*, London: Aurum Press, 2013.

Monk, Claire and Amy Sargeant (eds), *British Historical Cinema: The History, Heritage and Costume Film*, London: Routledge, 2002.

Morrison, Victor, 'Domestic and Imperial Politics in Britain and Ireland: The Testimony of Irish Theatre', in Mary Luckhurst (ed.), *A Companion to Modern British and Irish Drama 1880–2005*, Oxford: Blackwell, 2006, pp. 7–12.

Mullin, Michael, 'Augures and Understood Relations: Theodore Komisarjevsky's *Macbeth*', *Educational Theatre Journal*, Vol. 26, No. 1 (1974), pp. 20–30.

Newey, Katherine, 'Ibsen in the English Theatre in the *Fin de Siècle*', in Mary Luckhurst (ed.), *A Companion to Modern British and Irish Drama 1880–2005*. Oxford: Blackwell, 2006, pp. 35–47.

Nicholson, Steve, 'Theatre Pageants in the Second World War', *Theatre Research International*, Vol. 18, No. 3 (1993), pp. 186–96.

—, *British Theatre and the Red Peril: The Portrayal of Communism 1917–1945*, Exeter: Exeter University Press, 1999.

—, 'A Critical Year in Perspective: 1926', in Baz Kershaw (ed.), *The Cambridge History of British Theatre. Volume 3 Since 1895*. Cambridge: Cambridge University Press, 2004, pp. 127–42.

—, *The Censorship of British Drama 1900–1968, Volume Two 1933–1952*, Exeter: University of Exeter Press, 2005.

—, '1930s Drama', in Tony Sharpe (ed.), *W. H. Auden in Context*, Cambridge: Cambridge University Press, 2013, pp. 217–27.

Parrinder, Patrick, *Nation and Novel: The English Novel from Its Origins to the Present Day*, Oxford: Oxford University Press, 2008.

Payne, Ben Iden, *A Life in a Wooden O: Memoirs of the Theatre*, New Haven, CT: Yale University Press, 1977.

Peacock, D. Keith, *Thatcher's Theatre: British Theatre and Drama in the Eighties*, London: Greenwood Press, 1999.

Plain, Gill, 'The Shape of Things to Come: The Remarkable Modernity of Vernon Lee's *Satan the Waster* (1915–1920)', in Claire Tylee (ed.), *Women, the First World War and the Dramatic Imagination. International Essays (1914–1999)*, New York: Edwin Mellen Press, 2000.

Platt, Len, *Musical Comedy on the West End Stage, 1890–1939*, Basingstoke: Palgrave Macmillan, 2004.

Powell, Kerry, *Women and Victorian Theatre*, Cambridge: Cambridge University Press, 1997.

— (ed.), *The Cambridge Companion to Victorian and Edwardian Theatre*, Cambridge: Cambridge University Press, 2004.

Prins, Yopie, 'Greek Maenads, Victorian Spinsters', in Richard Dellamora (ed.), *Victorian Sexual Dissidence*, Chicago: University of Chicago Press, 1999.

Bibliography

Raby, Peter, 'Theatre of the 1980s: Breaking Down the Barriers', Kerry Powell (ed.), *The Cambridge Companion to Victorian and Edwardian Theatre*, Cambridge: Cambridge University Press, 2004, pp. 183–206.

Rajabi, Helen Maryam, 'The Idea of Race in Interwar Britain: Religion, Entertainment and Childhood Experiences', unpublished thesis, University of Manchester, 2013.

Raitt, Suzanne and Trudi Tate (eds), *Women's Fiction and the Great War*, Oxford: Clarendon Press, 1997.

Richards, Jeffrey, *The Ancient World on the Victorian and Edwardian Stage*, Basingstoke: Palgrave Macmillan, 2009.

Robert, Krisztina, 'Constructions of "Home", "Front", and Women's Military Employment in First-World-War Britain: A Spatial Interpretation', *History and Theory*, Vol. 52, No. 3 (2013), pp. 319–43.

Rose, Jacqueline, *The Case of Peter Pan: Or the Impossibility of Children's Fiction*, Philadelphia: University of Pennsylvania Press, 1992.

Rosenthal, Daniel, *The National Theatre Story*, London: Oberon, 2013.

Roshwalt, Aviel and Richard Stites (eds), *European Culture in the Great War: The Arts, Entertainment and Propaganda, 1914–1918*, Cambridge: Cambridge University Press, 2002.

Rowell, George and Anthony Jackson, *The Repertory Movement: A History of Regional Theatre in Britain*, Cambridge: Cambridge University Press, 1984.

—, *The Old Vic Theatre: A History*, Cambridge: Cambridge University Press, 1993.

Russell, Dave, 'The Making of the Edwardian Music Hall', in Michael R. Booth and Joel H. Kaplan (eds), *The Edwardian Theatre: Essays on Performance and the Stage*, Cambridge: Cambridge University Press, 1996, pp. 61–85.

Said, Edward, *Orientalism*, New York: Vintage, 1979.

Samuel, Raphael, 'Workers' Theatre 1926–36', in David Bradby, Louis James and Bernard Sharratt (eds), *Performance and Politics in Popular Drama: Aspects of Popular Entertainment in Theatre, Film and Television 1800–1976*, Cambridge: Cambridge University Press, 1981, pp. 213–30.

—, 'Theatre and Socialism in Britain (1880–1935), in Raphael Samuel, Ewan MacColl and Stuart Cosgrove (eds), *Theatres of the Left, 1880–1935: Workers' Theatre Movements in Britain and America*, London: Routledge and Kegan Paul, 1985, pp. 3–76.

—, Ewan MacColl and Stuart Cosgrove (eds), *Theatres of the Left, 1880–1935: Workers' Theatre Movements in Britain and American*, London: Routledge & Kegan Paul, 1985.

Schafer, Elizabeth, *Ms-Directing Shakespeare Women Direct Shakespeare*, London: The Women's Press, 1998.

—, *Lilian Baylis: A Biography*, Hertfordshire: University of Hertfordshire Press, 2006.

Schrank, Bernice, 'The Politics of O'Casey's War Plays: Pacifism and Progress in *The Silver Tassie* and *Oak Leaves and Lavender*', in C. C. Barfoot and Rias van den Doel (eds), *Ritual Remembering: History, Myth and Politics in Anglo-Irish Drama*. Amsterdam: Rodopi, 1995, pp. 75–83.

Scullion, Adrienne, 'Scottish Theatre and the Impact of Radio', *Theatre Research International*, Vol. 17, No. 2 (1992), pp. 117–31.

Sedgwick, Eve Kosofsky, 'Foreword: T times', *Tendencies*, Durham, NC: Duke University Press, 1993.

Senelick, Laurence, 'Politics as Entertainment: Victorian Music-Hall Songs', *Victorian Studies*, Vol. 19 (1975–6), pp. 149–80 (p. 156).

—, *The Chekhov Theatre. A Century of the Plays in Performance*, Cambridge: Cambridge University Press, 1999.

—, *Lovesick: Modernist Plays of Same-Sex Love, 1894–1925*, London: Routledge, 1999.

Shafer, Stephen C., *British Popular Films 1929–1939: The Cinema of Reassurance*, London: Routledge, 1997.

Sharpe, Tony (ed.), *W. H. Auden in Context*, Cambridge: Cambridge University Press, 2013.

Shepherd, Simon, *The Cambridge Introduction to Modern British Theatre*, Cambridge: Cambridge University Press, 2009.

—, *Direction*, Basingstoke: Palgrave Macmillan, 2012.

Sherry, Vincent (ed.), *The Cambridge Companion to the Literature of the Great War*, Cambridge: Cambridge University, 2005.

Showalter, Elaine, *Sexual Anarchy: Gender and Culture at the Fin de Siècle*, New York: Viking, 1990.

—, Elaine Showalter, 'It's still Salome', *Times Literary Supplement*, 2 September 1994, p. 13.

Sinfield, Alan, *Literature, Politics and Culture in Postwar Britain*, London: Continuum, 1997.

—, *Out on Stage: Lesbian and Gay Theatre in the Twentieth Century*, New Haven, CT: Yale University Press, 1999.

—, 'Noël Coward and Effeminacy', in Joel Kaplan and Sheila Stowell (eds), *Look Back in Pleasure: Noël Coward Reconsidered*, London: Methuen, 2000, pp. 33–43 (pp. 39–40).

Smith, Angela K. (ed.), *Gender and Warfare in the Twentieth Century: Textual Representations*, Manchester: Manchester University Press, 2004.

Smith, Leslie, *Modern British Farce: A Selective Study of British Farce from Pinero to the Present Day*, Basingstoke: Palgrave Macmillan, 1989.

Stokes, John, 'Body Parts: The Success of the Theatre in the Inter-War Years', Clive Barker and Maggie B. Gale (eds), *British Theatre between the Wars, 1918–1939*, Cambridge: Cambridge University Press, 2000, pp. 38–62.

Stowell, Sheila, 'Drama as a Trade: Cicely Hamilton's *Diana of Dobson's*', Viv Gardner and Susan Rutherford (eds), *The New Woman and Her Sisters: Feminism and the Theatre 1850–1914*, London: Harvester Wheatsheaf, 1992, pp. 177–88.

—, *A Stage of Their Own: Feminist Playwrights of the Suffrage Era*, Ann Arbor: University of Michigan Press, 1992.

Strobl, Gerwin, *The Swastika and the Stage: German Theatre and Society, 1933–1945*, Cambridge: Cambridge University Press, 2007.

Styan, J. L., 'Elizabethan Open Staging: William Poel to Tyrone Guthrie', *Modern Language Quarterly*, Vol. 37, No. 3 (1976), pp. 211–20.

Sutherland, Lucie, 'The Actress and the Profession: Training in England in the Twentieth Century', in Maggie B. Gale and John Stokes (eds), *The Cambridge Companion to the Actress*, Cambridge: Cambridge University Press, 2007, pp. 95–115.

Tanitch, Robert, *London Stage in the 20th Century*, London: Haus Publishing, 2007.

Tate, Trudi, 'The World War: British Writing', in Kate McLoughlin (ed.), *The Cambridge Companion to War Writing*, Cambridge: Cambridge University Press, 2009, pp. 160–74.

Taylor, Philip M., *The Projection of Britain: British Overseas Publicity and Propaganda, 1919–1939*, Cambridge: Cambridge University Press, 1981.

Thomas, David, David Carlton and Anne Etienne, *Theatre Censorship: From Walpole to Wilson*, Oxford: Oxford University Press, 2007.

Thirsk, Joan, 'Obituary: Ruth Spalding', *The Independent*, 26 May 2009.

Tickner, Lisa, *The Spectacle of Women: Imagery of the Suffrage Campaign 1907–14*, Chicago: University of Chicago Press, 1988.

Tilghman, Carolyn, 'Staging Suffrage: Women, Politics, and the Edwardian Theater', *Comparative Drama*, Vol. 45, No. 11 (2011), pp. 339–60.

Todman, Dan, *The Great War: Myth and Memory*, London: Hambledon and London, 2005.

Townsend, Joanna, 'Aftermath: Rodney Ackland's *The Pink Room*', in Tony Howard and John Stokes (eds), *Acts of War: The Representation of Military Conflict on the British Stage and Television Since 1945*, Cambridge: Scolar Press, 1996, pp. 61–81.

Trotter, Mary, 'Gregory, Yeats and Ireland's Abbey Theatre', in Mary Luckhurst (ed.), *A Companion to Modern British and Irish Drama 1880–2005*, Oxford: Blackwell, 2006, pp. 87–98.

Trout, Steven, *Robert Graves: Goodbye to All That and Other Great War Writings*, Manchester: Carcanet Press, 2007.

Turnbull, Olivia, *Bringing Down the House: The Crisis in Britain's Regional Theatres*, Bristol: Intellect, 2008.

Tylee, Claire, *The Great War and Women's Consciousness: Images of Militarism and Womanhood in Women's Writing, 1914–64*, Basingstoke: Macmillan, 1990.

— (ed.), *Women, the First World War and the Dramatic Imagination: International Essays (1914–1999)*, Lewiston: The Edwin Mellen Press, 2000.

Tylee, Claire, Elaine Turner and Agnes Cardinal (eds), *War Plays by Women: An International Anthology*, East Sussex: Psychology Press, 1990.

Tynan, Kenneth, *A View of the English Stage 1944–65*, London: Methuen, 1984.

Tyson, Brian, *The Story of Shaw's Saint Joan*, Montreal: McGill-Queen's Press, 1982.

Walkowitz, Judith R., 'The "Vision of Salome": Cosmopolitanism and Erotic Dancing in Central London, 1908–1918', *The American Historical Review*, Vol. 108, No. 2 (April 2003), pp. 350–1.

Wallis, Mick, 'Delving the Levels of Memory and Dressing up in the Past', in Clive Barker and Maggie B. Gale (eds), *British Theatre between the Wars 1918-1939*, Cambridge: Cambridge University Press, 2000, pp. 190–214.

—, 'Drama in the Villages: Three Pioneers', in Paul Brassley, Jeremy Burchardt and Lynne Thompson (eds), *The English Countryside 1918-39: Regeneration or Decline?*, Woodbridge, Suffolk: The Boydell Press, 2006, pp. 102–15.

Wansell, Geoffrey, *Terence Rattigan*, London: Fourth Estate, 1995.

Warden, Claire, *British Avant-Garde Theatre*, Basingstoke: Palgrave Macmillan, 2012.

—, '*Hassan*: Iraq on the British stage', *Theatre Notebook*, Vol. 66, No. 3 (December 2012), pp. 160–80.

—, '"We Are Here to Salute the Red Army": Basil Dean and His Russian Adventures', *Theatre Survey*, Vol. 54, No. 3 (2013), pp. 347–66.

Wardle Irving, *The Theatres of George Devine*, London: Jonathan Cape, 1978.

Waterman, Ray, 'Proltet: The Yiddish-Speaking Group of the Workers' Theatre Movement', *History Workshop*, No. 5 (Spring 1978), pp. 174–8.

Waters, Maureen, 'Lady Gregory's "Grania": A Feminist Voice', *Irish University Review*, Vol. 25, No. 1 (1995), pp. 11–24.

Watson, Don, 'The ABCA Play Unit and the Far East, 1945–1946', *Labour History Review*, Vol. 60, No. 3 (1995), pp. 39–42.

Webb, Paul, *Ivor Novello: Portrait of a Star*, London: Haus Books, 1999.

Weeks, Jeffrey, *Coming Out: Homosexual Politics in Britain, from the Nineteenth Century to the Present*, London: Quartet, 1977.

Weingärtner, Jörn, *The Arts as a Weapon of War: Britain and the Shaping of National Morale in the Second World War*, London: Tauris Academic Studies, 2006.

Welch, Robert, *The Abbey Theatre, 1899-1999: Form and Pressure*, Oxford: Oxford University Press, 2003.

Wharton, Gary, *Suburban London Cinemas*, Stroud, Gloucestershire: Sutton Publishing, 2008.

Wheatley, Alison E., 'Laughing Anne: An Almost Unbearable Spectacle', *Conradiana*, Vol. 34, Nos 1–2 (2002), pp. 63–76.

Whitebrook, Peter, *William Archer A Biography*, London: Methuen, 1993.

Williams, Gordon, *British Theatre in the Great War: A Revaluation*, London: Continuum, 2003.

Winter, Jay, 'Popular Culture in Wartime Britain', Aviel Roshwalt and Richard Stites (eds), *European Culture in the Great War: The Arts, Entertainment and Propaganda, 1914-1918*, Cambridge: Cambridge University Press, 2002, pp. 330–48.

Wohl, Robert, *The Generation of 1914*. London: Weidenfeld, 1980.

Woolf, Michael, 'In Minor Key: Theatre 1930–55', in Gary Day (ed.), *Literature and Culture in Modern Britain, Volume Two: 1930-1955*, London: Longman, 1997, pp. 86–106.

Worthen, John, *T. S. Eliot: A Short Biography*, London: Haus Publishing, 2009.

Wright, Julia M. (ed.), *A Companion to Irish Literature*, Vol. 2, Oxford: Wiley Blackwell, 2010.

Bibliography

Wyllie, Andrew, *Sex on Stage: Gender and Sexuality in Post-War British Theatre*, Bristol: Intellect, 2009.

Yoshino, Ayako, *Pageant Fever: Local History and Consumerism in Edwardian England*, Tokyo: Waseda University Publications Department, 2011.

Zarrilli, Phillip B., Bruce McConachie, Gary Jay Williams and Carol Fisher Sorgenfrei (eds), *Theatre Histories: An Introduction*, 2nd edition. London: Routledge, 2010.

Internet sources

Barlow, Adrian, "'The Word Is Said": Rereading the Poetry of John Drinkwater', www.johndrinkwater.org/jdpages/…/Thewordissaid-Drinkwaterlecture.pdf.

Billington, Michael, 'The Marrying of Ann Leete'. *Guardian*, 7 September 2004. http://www.guardian.co.uk/music/2004/sep/07/popandrock

Embassy Theatre, review of Theatre Workshop's *Uranium 235* (1952), http://www.vam.ac.uk/users/node/8814

Fink, Howard, 'Beyond Naturalism: Tyrone Guthrie's Radio Theatre and the Stage Production of Shakespeare', *Theatre Research in Canada* (1981), http://journals.hil.unb.ca/index.php/TRIC/article/view/7519/8578

Harker, Ben, 'Mediating the 1930s: Documentary and Politics in Theatre Union's *Last Edition* (1940)', http://usir.salford.ac.uk/12133/3/Chapter_2_-_Ben_Harker.pdf.

New York Times, http://query.nytimes.com/mem/archive-free/pdf?res=F70616FE3D5E12738DDDAD0894DA415B828CF1D3

Sydney Morning Herald, 30 July 1937, http://trove.nla.gov.au/ndp/del/article/17395554

Theatre Archive Project, Frith Banbury – Interview Transcript, 14 March 2005, http://sounds.bl.uk/related-content/TRANSCRIPTS/024T-1CDR0032282X-0100A0.pdf

Trove, http://trove.nla.gov.au/ndp/del/article/17395554

University of Westminster, 'Screen Plays: Theatre Plays on British Television', http://screenplaystv.wordpress.com/about/

Warden, Claire, 'Ewan MacColl, "The Brilliant Young Scots Dramatist": Regional Mythmaking and Theatre Workshop', *International Journal of Scottish Theatre and Screen*, Vol. 4, No. 1 (2011), http://journals.qmu.ac.uk/index.php/IJOSTS/article/view/11

NOTES ON CONTRIBUTORS

Claire Cochrane is Professor of Theatre Studies at the University of Worcester, UK. She is the author of two books on the Birmingham Repertory Theatre: *Shakespeare and the Birmingham Repertory Theatre 1913–1929* (1993) and *Birmingham Rep: A City's Theatre 1962–2002* (2003). Her most recent book *Twentieth Century British Theatre Industry, Art and Empire* was published in 2011. She has also published widely on Shakespeare in performance, amateur theatre and developments in Black British and British Asian Theatre.

Penny Farfan is Professor of Drama at the University of Calgary, Canada. She is the author of *Women, Modernism, and Performance* as well as many articles and book chapters on modernism and performance and on contemporary women playwrights. She is also the editor (with Lesley Ferris) of *Contemporary Women Playwrights: Into the Twenty-First Century* and a past editor of *Theatre Journal*.

Steve Nicholson is Chair of Twentieth Century and Contemporary Theatre in the School of English at the University of Sheffield, UK. His research has centred primarily on British political theatre and playwrights in the twentieth century, and the interplay between politics, morality and aesthetics. His books include *British Theatre and the Red Peril: The Portrayal of Communism 1917–1945*, a four-volume series on *The Censorship of British Drama, 1900–1968* and *Modern British Playwriting: The 1960s*.

INDEX

Index

Avant-Garde Theatre 4, 19–20, 30, 31, 33, 35, 63, 104, 203, 205, 207, 209, 218
Aveling, Edward 17

Babes in the Wood 182, 234
Bagnold, Enid 117, 197
  Chalk Garden, The 4, 197, 295
  Diary without Dates, A 117
Bailey, Peter 23
Bairnsfather, Bruce 64–5
  Better 'Ole, The 65
Baker, Elizabeth 34
  Chains 41
Baker, Reginald 111
Baker's Daughter, The 135
Baldwin, Stanley 95, 141
Balfour, Arthur 32
Balfour, Michael 190
Ballet Rambert 99, 159
Ballets Russe 20, 105, 113, 206
Banbury, Frith 134, 158, 235
Barke, James 176, 191
  Night of the Big Blitz, The 176, 191
  When the Boys Come Home 191
Barker, Clive 85, 112, 125
Barker, Harley Granville 14, 15, 16, 33, 35, 47, 72, 75, 90, 144, 200, 202, 203, 204, 205
  Madras House, The 40–1, 43
  Marrying of Ann Leete, The 44
  Voysey Inheritance, The 35, 40, 203
  Waste 33, 35, 44
Barrie, J. M. 15, 75–6, 126, 127, 190, 193, 206
  Admirable Crichton, The 15, 38
  Adored One, The 43
  Dear Brutus 38, 126
  Kiss for Cinderella, A 75–6
  Little White Bird, The 21
  Mary Rose 126
  Peter Pan; or, The Boy Who Wouldn't Grow Up 15, 22, 126
  Quality Street 126
  Well-Remembered Voice, The 127
Battle of Britain, the 157

Bax, Clifford 33, 146
  Rose without a Thorn, The 146
Baxendale, John 193
Baxter, Beverley 1, 152
Baylis, Lilian 14, 90, 143, 161
BBC Drama Repertory
  Company *see* radio
Beardsley, Aubrey 218
Beauty and the Beast (1914) 66
Beauty Baths (1915) 69
Beckett, Samuel 31, 32, 102, 122, 147, 178, 198
  Endgame 31
  Happy Days 31
  Not I 31
  Waiting for Godot 178
Bedroom and Bath 85
Beerbohm, Max 217
Behn, Aphra 46
Belasco, David 26
Bell, Florence,
  Alan's Wife 17
Ben Hur, film (1907) 25
Ben Hur, play (1902) 15
Bengal Entertainment Services
  Association (BESA) 156
Bennett, Arnold 34
Benson, Frank 8, 48, 50, 204
  Shakespeare's War Cry 89
Bensusan, Inez 46
Beresford, J. D. *see also* Richmond, Kenneth
  Howard and Son 70
Bergner, Elisabeth 189
Berkeley, Reginald 146
  Lady with the Lamp, The 146
Berkoff, Steven 219
Besier, Rudolf *see also* Spottiswoode, Sybil
  Kultur at Home 73–4
Bidder, George 72
Billingham, Peter 100, 159–60, 164
Billington, Michael 44, 180
Bing Boys are Here, The (1916) 63
Bing Boys on Broadway, The (1918) 63
Bing Girls are There, The (1917) 63

320

Index

Index

Index